Introduction to Communication Research

Introduction to Communication Research

John C. Reinard
California State University, Fullerton

WCB Brown &
Benchmark
PUBLISHERS

Madison, Wisconsin • Dubuque, Iowa

Book Team

Executive Editor *Stan Stoga*
Developmental Editor *Mary E. Rossa*
Production Editor *Connie Balius-Haakinson*
Visuals/Design Developmental Consultant *Marilyn A. Phelps*
Visuals/Design Freelance Specialist *Mary L. Christianson*
Marketing Manager *Pamela S. Cooper*
Advertising Coordinator *Susan J. Butler*

WCB Brown & Benchmark

A Division of Wm. C. Brown Communications, Inc.

Executive Vice President/General Manager *Thomas E. Doran*
Vice President/Editor in Chief *Edgar J. Laube*
Vice President/Sales and Marketing *Eric Ziegler*
Director of Production *Vickie Putman Caughron*
Director of Custom and Electronic Publishing *Chris Rogers*

Wm. C. Brown Communications, Inc.

President and Chief Executive Officer *G. Franklin Lewis*
Corporate Senior Vice President and Chief Financial Officer *Robert Chesterman*
Corporate Senior Vice President and President of Manufacturing *Roger Meyer*

Cover and interior designs by Fulton Design

Copyedited by Bonnie Gruen

Credits: pp. 111, 114, 120, 134: Used through courtesy of Ava C. English;
p. 115: Used through courtesy of Walter Glanze Word Books.

A Times Mirror Company

Library of Congress Catalog Card Number: 93–73712

ISBN 0–697–06458–1

Printed in the United States of America by Wm. C. Brown Communications, Inc.,
2460 Kerper Boulevard, Dubuque, IA 52001

10 9 8 7 6 5 4 3 2 1

For my mother, Billie Erich

CONTENTS

PREFACE

Research is not library work.

Nor is it statistics.

Nor is it field observation.

Research is an argument. In particular, communication research is a process by which we answer questions and try to draw conclusions from information gathered about message-related behavior. The tools of scholarship (libraries, statistics, and field work) are ways we attempt to find high-quality evidence. Thus, this book attempts to train students to gather research evidence, to develop research arguments, and to think critically about them. In short, this book is designed to teach students how to "do scholarship." It teaches students how steps in scholarship are essential parts in making cases and offering research conclusions.

This book represents the product of many years of experimentation with instruction of the introductory research methods. In fact, for years "underground" copies of the materials in this book and related resources were used to teach highly successful classes at nearly a dozen Western universities. Such experiences led to refinements that are reflected in this book and instructor's manual. Experience has shown these materials to be suitable for substantive courses taught at the sophomore and junior levels. The point of view of this book—though compatible with all instructors with whom the author has come into contact—is focused on meeting student needs, not to impress professors.

This book is written for—and to—students who are taking their first course in research methods. Its chief objective is to equip students to be critical users of the broad realm of communication research. By the end of the course, students should know how to do a few things. First, they should know how to present and evaluate a research argument. They should know how to construct an argument from literature, not just know what a literature review looks like on the surface. Since most of the classes that follow the research methods course require students to do research-based writing, they need to know how to complete the process of drawing conclusions and making arguments from the literature. Second, the students must know how to deal with the brass tacks of research: they must know how to isolate a problem statement; they must know how to distinguish independent and dependent variables; they must know how to criticize and evaluate definitions; they must know what theories are and why they are important; they must learn how to use the library; they must know the methods of sound research and standards for evaluating and proposing worthwhile studies; they must know how to compose scholarship; they must understand how to collect data and execute a logical design; they must understand the rudiments of data analysis. This list is not a random collection, but an explicit set of learning criteria for courses in which this book is most appropriate.

This book emphasizes understanding of concepts blended with a clear set of survival skills needed by students. Traditionally, writers of research methods textbooks have faced a dilemma of sorts. On one hand, to deal with research, all the possible methods often have been reviewed. The students sometimes have formed the impression that research methods are so overwhelming that the subject is beyond their understanding. On the other hand, those books that have attempted to be very selective in their coverage have left out reference materials students needed when reviewing research in the library or when undertaking proposals for future research projects. This textbook includes key survival information followed by "Special Discussions," which are clearly identified as enrichment information. By focusing on the needs that students have indicated in past classes, this book has been designed to develop basic skills of scholarship while also surveying major approaches. It is a serious attempt to present a student-adapted set of broadly-based and comprehensive materials for the unique needs of the undergraduate research methods course.

Four qualities distinguish this undertaking from others in the field.

- It introduces students to the diversity and methods (both introductory qualitative and quantitative) of research in the field. The material, though challenging in its breadth, is dedicated to the sophomore and junior level students' needs to deal with research in the field.
- It very deliberately takes a critical thinking approach to introducing strategies of qualitative and quantitative research in communication. Students learn how research arguments are made and how to evaluate them.

- It is designed to prepare students to do rudimentary research and to criticize scholarship.
- Since communication research courses serve students from several communication areas—including speech communication, journalism, telecommunications, public relations, and speech and hearing science—examples from all these areas are deliberately included in discussions of content.

This textbook is divided into four sections that correspond to the major units successfully taught in introductory communication research methods courses. The first section deals with an "Introduction to the Field" of communication as a research area. Students are guided through two chapters that introduce communication research as a distinct form and that review the issues involved in composing the communication research problem, using hypotheses, and isolating types of variables.

The second part of the textbook, "Understanding Rudiments of Research Reasoning," establishes a point of view for the book and addresses the hands-on skills that undergraduate students need almost immediately. The section is composed of four chapters. The first deals with "Using Communication Research Sources" and focuses on library research skills and strategies. The second discusses the composition of communication research including the anatomy of research articles and the mechanics of writing different forms of scholarly and classroom reports. The third emphasizes the critical thinking skills that are taught in the introductory research methods course. The nature of the research argument is described, evaluation of evidence used by researchers to make their claims is explained, and standards to critique these efforts are mentioned. The location of research arguments is reviewed and the major forms of reasoning used to draw research conclusions are addressed. Finally the unique flaws in research reasoning are mentioned. This chapter brings home the theme that research is an exercise in critical thinking. The fourth chapter concerns conceptualizations in communication research including use of theory and definitions.

The third section of the book emphasizes the "Design of Research" of both qualitative and quantitative studies (though most space is spent on quantitative methods since neophyte students usually are least conversant with these tools).The primary task in this section lies in presenting essential materials that students need to know without ignoring other unique applications that have invigorated the field. Six chapters are dedicated to these research building blocks. The first two deal with conducting textual analyses of messages and undertaking participant observation studies. The third and fourth chapters discuss designing descriptive empirical research (including questionnaire and interview studies) and conducting experimental studies. The remaining two chapters involve sampling and measurement in communication research. In each case, examples across the broad realm of communication studies are covered.

The fourth part of the book concerns "Statistical Analysis of Data." The individual chapters involve traditional topics of such an introductory treatment. The first chapter addresses beginning descriptive and correlational statistics. The second chapter introduces the logic of statistical hypothesis testing and applies it to the case of comparisons between two means. The final chapter extends significance testing to cases that go beyond two means, including analysis of variance and chi square test applications. This final chapter includes "survival guide" introductions to advanced statistics that students may read but should not be expected to use in the introductory course.

To assist students, the textbook format is designed to promote efficient study and review. Several features should make this work convenient for students. Each chapter

- starts with an outline of all major topics
- begins with an orienting paragraph to describe the thrust of the chapter
- ends with a list of key terms to review when studying the chapter

- includes margin notes to point out important concepts covered in the text
- presents special boxed discussions at different locations in the text to identify additional valuable enrichment materials
- highlights key terms in boldface the first time they appear
- relies on tables when they may reduce otherwise extended text discussions
- concludes with a chapter summary/study guide that students will find very helpful when reviewing for examinations

Many people helped me develop this work. My sincere thanks must go to my own teachers of research methods. These teachers included not only those who provided instruction in empirical methods, but those who directed my studies in rhetorical theory, argumentation, and qualitative methods. The students in my introductory research methods courses over more than the last decade deserve thanks since this book reflects the product of experimention to find ways to teach this course most effectively. I wish to thank Stan Stoga of Brown & Benchmark for advancing this project and providing me with the gift of his candid insights and thoughtful encouragement. My special thanks also is extended to Mary Rossa of Brown & Benchmark who shepherded me through the extended final phase of the work and helped me adapt this manuscript to its current size and approach. I am very grateful to the scholars and teachers who reviewed drafts of this work and provided invaluable advice and support for the direction of this project: John D. Bee, University of Akron; Judith Dallinger, Western Illinois State; Lyle Flint, Ball State University; William J. Schenck-Hamlin, Kansas State University, and Judy R. Sims, University of Wisconsin, Eau Claire. I appreciate the encouragement of my colleagues at California State University, Fullerton, who both welcomed this work's completion for use in our own classes and urged me on. Finally I wish to thank my family. Without their willingness to permit my dedication of many hours, it would not have been possible to complete this volume.

Introduction to the Field

The Role of Research in Communication

Communication Problem Statements and Hypotheses

CHAPTER 1

The Role of Research in Communication

The purpose of all higher education is to make men aware of what was and what is; to incite them to probe into what may be. It seeks to teach them to understand, to evaluate, to communicate.

–Otto Kleppner

BEFORE WE GET STARTED . . .

Welcome to communication research! Though you may be skeptical, ''doing'' communication scholarship is an exciting and very satisfying personal experience. Rather than just accepting what others tell you, you will learn how we draw conclusions in our field. You will see how research should look so that you can evaluate work that often gets passed off to us. Along the way, you will learn how to improve your thinking, your scholarly writing, and your ability to evaluate research arguments. Getting there can be challenging, but it is well worth the trip. This book does not assume that you have any background in research methods—just an interest. To get started, you need to know why you are here and what communication research is. This chapter is designed to get you moving in the right direction.

WHAT IS RESEARCH IN COMMUNICATION?

A field defines itself by its research. Research determines what content is taught in courses, the social contributions the field makes, and the sort of publicity an area gets.

Research

Research is the systematic effort to secure answers to questions. These questions are not mundane ones, such as, Have you seen my keys? or Want to see a movie? Instead, research questions deal with issues requiring reference to data[1] and information, such as: Did Patrick Henry deliver the "Give Me Liberty or Give Me Death!" speech?[2] Do women self-disclose private information more often than men do?[3] and Do people who arrive "fashionably late" to parties receive higher credibility ratings than people who arrive on time?[4] Research is not an "ivory tower" pursuit by a few elect scholars. It is a very practical effort to get answers for questions. Research usually requires examining past inquiry into the issue. We often rely on reports found in libraries to learn about related work and to avoid repeating past mistakes. Regardless of sources of information, all research involves gathering information that goes beyond our personal feelings or hunches. We search for some light on the facts of matters when we do research.

> **research defined**

Sometimes people distinguish between two types of research. We conduct **basic research** to learn about relationships among variables, regardless of any immediate commercial product or service. Most of the things we call "pure" scientific research fall into this category. Though researchers hope to make useful contributions, no economic payoffs are imminent. We conduct **applied research** to develop a product or solve an immediately practical problem. When communication researchers survey employee attitudes as part of a consulting contract, the work is considered applied research. Even so, trying to separate basic and applied research causes problems. Regardless of whether pure or applied research is involved, the methods of inquiry *are identical*. Furthermore, last year's basic research may be today's source of new products. Work that was originally initiated to find out how to store information in digital form is now the basis for patents on satellite transmission of television signals. Though the terms have their place, for our purposes, it is enough to know that good research can be basic or applied.

> **basic research distinguished**
>
> **from applied research**

Communication Research

Regrettably, many people have difficulty separating communication research from work in psychology, sociology, or literature. They figure that since "meanings are in people" (Berlo, 1960, p. 175), any study of people is communication research. Straightening out this exaggerated view has taken some serious thinking. In 1968 a group of communication scholars met in New Orleans under a grant from the National Science Foundation to wrestle with the basic issues of distinguishing communication research and instruction. They concluded that "research in speech-communication focuses on the ways in which messages link participants during interactions" (Kibler & Barker, 1969, p. 33). The scope of our research area was clear. Other fields might study personality traits, trends in society, or the beauty of poetry. But communication research is a specialty that studies message-related behavior.

> **communication research defined in New Orleans conference**

SPECIAL DISCUSSION 1–1
Behavior of Researchers

It is possible to overstate the matter, but there is a set of norms—almost a culture—that distinguishes people who do research. In his book, *Foundations of Behavioral Research* (1986, p. 9), Fred Kerlinger described these characteristics.

Universalism: Scientific laws are the same everywhere. A scientific law states a relation between phenomena that is invariable under the same conditions.

Organized skepticism: Researchers are responsible for verifying the results on which they base their work. [Researchers do not accept claims blindly. They question research claims and offer criticism for each other.]

Communality: Researchers are willing to share knowledge freely and contribute to public knowledge. [Researchers are expected to put some evidence on the line. Failure to share research fully with others violates this norm.]

Disinterestedness: Researchers must ban ulterior motives and be relatively free from bias. Any known or possible biases must not be admitted. ["Disinterested" does not mean "uninterested." Disinterested only means that one can be impartial because one does not have a personal or financial stake in the outcome. Certainly, researchers do not study matters without passion. They care. But they must be willing to let their conclusions be influenced by the data and by the data only. If a researcher receives a grant from sponsors who specify the results they wish the researcher to find, the researcher loses the "disinterest" that separates research from ordinary pandering.]

---

communication
studies
message-related
behavior as a
specialty

message defined

verbal cues
distinguished

nonverbal cues
defined

Communication might be defined as "the process by which participants transact and assign meaning to messages" (Reinard, 1991, p. 4). You may have been asked by a relative or an acquaintance what your major is. When you answered, "communication," you may have received a puzzled expression in response. Unless you explain things, they may have thought that you were learning to install telephones. Thus, you may share with them that you are training to be a "message specialist" or "message scientist." You can also explain that your concentration in communication prepares you in a specific area of communication. To be clear, you need to explain that a **message** is the set of verbal and nonverbal cues communicators exchange. **Verbal cues** are the words people use in communication. Sometimes people confuse "verbal" cues with "spoken" cues (as in the phrase "verbal agreement"). Yet, spoken cues are called "oral cues" (from the "orifice" or mouth). **Nonverbal cues** are communication elements beyond the words themselves. Variations in voice, facial expression, gesture, movement, touch, timing, physical closeness, media treatments, and format are all nonverbal cues. Taken together, these verbal and nonverbal cues provide plenty for us to study.

THE CHALLENGES OF COMMUNICATION RESEARCH

Communication covers a very broad set of topics, and no single research method is embraced by the field. To study communication—even its specialties of journalism and speech and hearing science—we must have very broad knowledge. This breadth both challenges students and invites them to enter the field and make contributions.

The Challenge of Breadth

The number of communication applications can seem enormous, but there really is a rational order to it. James H. McBath and Robert C. Jeffrey (1978), were asked to identify the professional areas in communication on behalf of the Speech Communication Association and the National Center For Educational Statistics, which were trying to organize information about careers in many fields. The list of communication specialties now used by the NCES is shown in table 1.1. The left column shows the official taxonomy.[5] In the column to the right you will see some of the sorts of research claims that are made in each of these areas. As you can tell, each area is broad enough to permit inquiry into many interesting issues.

The Multiple Methods Challenge

In studying literature, qualitative methods most often are used. In history, the historical method is employed. In psychology, the experiment holds a prominent position. Yet, communication researchers use all methods to answer questions. Thus, modern students are exposed to many methods. Though single studies may use multiple methods, for the most part, a piece of research tends to rely on qualitative *or* quantitative methods.[6]

communication uses both qualitative and quantitative tools

Qualitative Methods

Qualitative methods of study use descriptions of observations expressed in predominantly non-numerical terms. Sometimes qualitative methods make passing reference to statistics (as when TV critics refer to Nielsen ratings of various programs), but statistics are largely secondary to the attempt to answer research questions. Table 1.2 lists some chief types of qualitative methods.

qualitative methods defined and isolated

There is more to qualitative methods than the type of data alone—though the type of data plays a very big part.[7] Most qualitative research in our field tends to *describe* or *interpret* communication exchanges. These studies try to describe the human condition by using general views of social action. They may critique communication by relying on standards of excellence derived from a body of existing theory. Researchers who use qualitative methods try to interpret the meanings to be found in communication exchanges. They often look at individual examples of communication research, rather than trying to find patterns that run across individuals. Our language is very broad, but the differences in emphasis will become pronounced as we continue.

qualitative research emphasizes description or interpretation of communication events

TABLE 1.1 Broad Areas of General Communication

Communication Taxonomy (McBath & Jeffrey, 1978)	Description (Crawford, 1980, with permission)
1. The Broad Areas of Mass Media Communication:	
Advertising	The study of mass media methods of influence to promote a product, service, or cause
Communication Technology	The study of the mechanisms and technologies of mass media
Communication Policy	The study of public policy and regulation of mass media communication and freedom of speech
Film as Communication	The role of popular and technical cinema in society
Journalism	The study of the methods of reporting and organizing news for presentation in print media
Public Relations	The study of methods of managing publicity and press relations for an organization, person, or cause
Radio	The study of the methods and uses of radio communication
Television	The study of the methods and uses of televised communication
2. Specific Areas of Speech Communication Research:	
Code Systems	The study of the uses of verbal and nonverbal symbols and signs in human communication
Intercultural Communication	The study of communication among individuals of different cultural backgrounds
Interpersonal Communication	The study of communication interactions occurring in person-to-person and small group situations
Conflict Management	The study of the role of communication in the creation and control of conflict
Organizational Communication	The study of interrelated behaviors, technologies, and systems functioning within an organization
Oral Interpretation	The study of literature through performance involving the development of skilled verbal and nonverbal expression based on critical analysis of written texts (aesthetics of literature in performance, criticism of literature in performance, group performance, oral tradition)
Pragmatic Communication	The study and practice of communication, the object of which is to influence or facilitate decision making
Argumentation	The study of reason giving behavior
Debate	The study of decision making in which adversaries present arguments for decision by a third party
Discussion and Conference	The study of methods of decision making in which participants strive by consensus to discuss and explore an issue
Parliamentary Procedure	The study of the means used to handle deliberation in large, legislative bodies through the use of formal rules and procedures to regulate debate and discussion
Persuasion	The study of the methods used to influence the choices made by others

TABLE 1.1 —*Continued*

Communication Taxonomy (McBath & Jeffrey, 1978)	Description (Crawford, 1980, with permission)
Public Address	The study of speakers and speeches, including the historical and social context of platforms, campaigns, and movements
Rhetorical and Communication Theory	The study of the principles that account for human communicative experiences and behavior
Speech Communication Education	The study of communication in pedagogical contexts (communication development, oral communication skills, instructional communication)
Speech and Hearing Science	The study of the physiology and acoustical aspects of speech and hearing (biological aspects of speech and hearing, phonological aspects of speech and hearing, physiological aspects of speech and hearing)

TABLE 1.2 Types of Qualitative Studies

Description	Examples
Historical-critical methods: research designed to describe a period, person, or phenomenon for the purpose of interpreting or evaluating communication and its effects.	*Historical studies:* • Studying whether Lincoln's Gettysburg Address really met with negative reaction at the time it was delivered[8] • Studying the true impact on Americans of Orson Welles's 1938 "War of the Worlds" broadcast • Studying dominant methods of treating stuttering during the last two hundred years *Criticism:* • Evaluating use of argument by Ronald Reagan in his presidential debates • Evaluating whether newspaper reports of the news gave politically balanced reports of the U. S. entry into the Iraq-Kuwait crisis • Evaluating the ethical use of surgery in the treatment of speech-handicapped patients in the nineteenth century
Qualitative observational studies: methods designed to use predominately attribute-type data to interpret contemporaneous communication interactions. *Case studies and interpretive studies:* intensive inquiries about single events, people, or social units (interpretive studies attempt to look for themes or stories that are helpful to 'interpret' or understand the case).	*Case studies:* • Investigating the practice of a successful speech therapist to pick up some pointers • Studying the communication inside a newspaper that is in the process of being sold

TABLE 1.2 *—Continued*

Description	Examples
Participant observation studies: inquiries in which the researcher takes the role of an active agent in the situation under study (sometimes may be used to gather quantitative data).	• Studying the process of news writing for a television station by joining the writing staff to report events from the inside • Investigating the development of public strategy for a political campaign by joining a campaign as an active worker who makes observations from within the organization
Ethnomethodology: originally developed by anthropologists to study societies of humans, an approach (rather than a rigorous method) in which researchers find an ethnic group, live within it, and attempt to develop insight into the culture; emphasis is on ordinary behavior that participants take for granted to find hidden meanings and unwritten rules people use to make sense of their world.	• Investigating how people react to television by living with an isolated group of people without television and watching their reactions in the days and weeks that follow introduction of televisions • Inquiring into the specialized language of street gang members by moving around with a gang during an extended time period
Discourse/conversational analysis: a method of examining utterances people exchange for the purpose of discovering the rules and strategies people use to structure, sequence, and take turns in speaking to learn how people manage their interactions with others.	• Studying the structure of interpersonal arguments between husbands and wives • Examining judge and attorney communication by looking at the structure of the abbreviated exchanges • Inquiring into children's speech development by identifying language competency levels among six-year-old and eight-year-old school children
Creative studies: use of the method of performance or demonstration to explore an aesthetic or creative experience.	• Examining the problems of communicating Renaissance poetry to modern audiences by undertaking special performances in oral interpretation to contemporary student audiences • Examining whether a public relations campaign using multimedia news releases is perceived as a suitable way to transmit information by designing such a campaign directly

Quantitative Methods

quantitative methods isolated

Some research data are in numbers. In fact, **quantitative research methods** are inquiries in which observations are expressed predominantly in numerical terms. As table 1.3 shows, quantitative research has two major branches: surveys (of all varieties) and experiments.

quantitative research tends to be explanatory, often involving prediction, frequently by using causal models

Why would researchers in their right minds want to represent the world of communication as a bunch of numbers? Surely there must be something going on other than a preference some people have for numbers. Though the type of data distinguish these methods from qualitative tools, the research issues probed also tend to be different. Quantitative research tends to be *explanatory,* especially when experiments are involved, or it attempts to use precise statistical models to

TABLE 1.3 Quantitative Methods

Description	Examples
Survey methods: techniques that involve carefully recorded observations that provide quantitative descriptions of relationships among variables.	
Descriptive or observational surveys: direct observations of behavior by use of some measurement (the researcher does not manipulate or change any variables).	• Discovering what sorts of things small group communicators say that predict their becoming group leaders • Identifying the relationship between the number of newspapers a person reads on a regular basis and the amount of fear of society rated on a measure of state anxiety
Content analysis: "a systematic, quantitative study of verbally communicated material (articles, speeches, films) by determining the frequency of specific ideas concepts, or terms." (*Longman Dictionary of Psychology and Psychiatry,* 1984. P. 176; Used through courtesy of Walter Glanze Word Books.) *Opinion Surveys:* assessments of reports from individuals about topics of interest.	• Studying the amount of violence on children's television programs • Inquiring into the amount of newspaper space dedicated to stories about the women's movement • Analyzing the types of speech defects shown by children in samples of spontaneous speech • Analyzing opinion surveys regarding which candidate people think won a political debate • Examining whether the public believes that speech correction therapy should receive increased funding in the public schools • Assessing surveys of the favorite television programs people watch
Experimental methods: studying the effect of variables in situations where all other influences are held constant. Variables are manipulated or introduced by experimenters to see what effect they may have.	• Studying the impact of the use of evidence by exposing one group to a speech with evidence and another group to a speech without evidence • Studying of the effect of color in advertising by exposing one group to an ad with color printing and another group to an ad without color printing

achieve comprehensive understandings of human communication (as in survey studies and polls of public opinion). These methods often try to explain communication behavior by looking at processes that allow researchers to *predict* future behavior, frequently using models of causal processes. Thus, quantitative research usually attempts to answer questions about *many* people. Hence, any statistical tools are means to ends—not ends in themselves. If researchers wish to have precise explanations that characterize processes, or if they wish to develop methods to study or measure communication behavior, quantitative research methods are invited. Of course, the research question guides selection of methods, not the other way around. It is improper to decide that you want to be either a quantitative or qualitative researcher. You have to choose methods to suit research questions.

The Focus of this Book

All research methods require the same basic skills of framing a question, searching the library, and reasoning to conclusions from data. Thus, this book will discuss these common tasks. The first section introduces the field as a research area, methods for isolating the research problem (a surprisingly difficult task, as it turns out!), and hypotheses. The second section, "Understanding Rudiments of Research Reasoning," deals with locating information in the library, writing the research argument, evaluating research evidence, and using theory and definitions. As you can see, the first two sections of the book consider topics all researchers must know, regardless of the particular methods they select to analyze data.

The third section examines the "Design of Research," including participant observation methods and documentary studies that sometimes are considered qualitative methods: content and interaction analyses. Empirical methods are dominant in the last part of the book since they reflect the sorts of things that reasonably can be learned in a one-term course on research methods and they fit the major interests of current communication students. The use of other qualitative methods, such as conversation analysis, rhetorical analysis, and ethnography are defined but not covered in depth. Completing such research requires detailed understanding of sets of underlying theoretic orientations. Hence, after taking advanced coursework in linguistics you may demonstrate skills by completing a conversational analysis. After taking advanced coursework in rhetorical theory you can count on completing rhetorical criticisms. After completing work in social interactionism, you may be expected to complete an ethnographic study (though rarely at the undergraduate level). Each method presumes advanced study that you must complete elsewhere. This choice is not a judgment about the value of one method over another (no single method is best for all research questions), but reflects a practical choice to make your learning reasonable. The final section of this book addresses "Statistical Analysis of Data" and introduces the fundamentals of these methods.

The common theme throughout this book is that research is an argument in which scholars (including you) are supposed to employ their best thinking and available evidence. Both the merit of the data and worth of research reasoning must be evaluated. Therefore, research requires us to train our minds and our abilities to express ourselves—as well as to be familiar with tools for inquiry.

The Scholarly Rigor Challenge

Research must meet standards of excellence. In particular, we must conduct our research with the recognition of five key challenges.[9]

scholarly rigor:
1. systematic

1. *Research is systematic.* Productive research follows steps that carry out some sort of design. Researchers ask questions and implicitly agree in advance to search for answers by examining pertinent information. Unexpected results often emerge. The effect is called **serendipity** and refers to researchers' finding something of value while looking for something else. It seems that systematic researchers stand the best chance of grasping the importance of unexpected findings.

serendipity
identified

2. *Research is data driven.* Issues that ask us to investigate things that cannot be tested in this life (e.g., does God exist?) are not matters that we can settle by our research methods. As such, researchers are supposed to be willing to change their minds in light of new data. If data cannot be collected, or if we are unwilling to alter our opinions, the issue is not suitable for research. **2. data driven**

3. *Research is a sound argument.* Though students sometimes are surprised to learn it, research actually is a process of advancing arguments. **Arguments** in this context are claims advanced on the basis of reasoning from evidence. Flippant or sloppy thinking is not valued. Sound reasoning is vital for effective research. Thus, logic and the methods to evaluate arguments are valuable tools in judging research. **3. sound argument**

4. *Research is capable of replication.* By attempting to replicate or reproduce the research of scholars, we can tell if research findings are generally true or accidental. If research methods are so vaguely described that it is impossible to repeat the procedures in a study, the worth of the entire research project is questioned. Regardless of whether replications actually are completed, the *ability* to replicate studies is essential for any piece of sound research. **4. capable of replication**

5. *Research is partial.* There is always more that could be added about a topic. Research findings are partial because we may discover new relationships involving other variables that make us modify or qualify the conclusions we have found. Thus, researchers do not claim to have discovered "The Truth" for all time. Instead, they advance tentative—but meaningful—insights for communication phenomena. **5. partial**

The Personal Challenge

Research can be demanding and may involve personal challenges that are taxing or even uncomfortable. As you beginning looking at research methods, it might help to know that students who do well in research methods classes tend to consider these personal issues.

1. *Ability to think in an orderly way.* Though learning research methods will help you improve your critical thinking abilities, orderly thinking is a key to success. In research one quickly finds that half-considered ideas are exposed as weak. One must train one's mind to separate the relevant from the irrelevant, the observable from the unobservable, and the complete from the incomplete. **1. orderly thinking**

2. *Ability to write clearly.* Research involves communicating the effort to others. To succeed, you must write crisply and clearly. Writing research and scholarship is not the same as writing a typical essay, short story, or letter. Research writing is very precise, structured, and to the point. Effective writing does not mean writing beautiful prose, but using crystal clear language, grammar, and support. While we are on the subject, let's get something else straight: first drafts are not acceptable in research. Everybody's first draft of a paper is lousy. Despite what you may have been told in high school, you must revise, edit, and polish research to put it in proper form. You may be familiar with the writing of William Faulkner. After having been awarded the Nobel Prize for literature, a reporter asked him what it felt like to have been recognized as one **2. data driven**

of the world's greatest writers. He responded, "I am not one of the world's greatest writers, but I am among the world's top two or three greatest *re*writers." Faulkner had to revise his work, and so do the rest of us. Taking a course in research should help you improve your writing abilities.

3. set aside prejudices

3. *Ability to set aside personal prejudices in light of data.* In research and scholarship, we must be willing to let the data decide our conclusions, even if we do not like them very much. When Galileo first observed moons around planets other than earth, many Church fathers refused to look through his telescope since Church doctrine had decided that such things were impossible and no data were allowed to contradict it. Galileo was persecuted in southern Europe for letting data—not prejudice—guide his conclusions. Though the world now respects Galileo's position, many people are unwilling to let the data decide matters. They have a difficult time studying research methods since research methods place priority on the data, not only prior beliefs.

4. organized and follow instructions

4. *Ability to stay organized and follow instructions.* Research requires following careful research protocols and methods. Thus, it is important for scholars—even those studying research methods for the first time—to follow directions and stay organized. Students must fight the urge to leave out a step, take a shortcut, or ignore instructions. There is much that is creative in research, but one must harness that creativity by being organized and following instructions in detail. Researchers know that details matter.

5. reason to study research method

5. *Why study communication research methods?* There are many reasons you may wish to study communication research techniques. Among the most common reasons students complete research methods courses are

- to learn to think rigorously and critically, especially about research evidence that is advanced for acceptance in a variety of popular and scholarly applications
- to learn how to find answers to questions about communication
- to acquire survival skills to help read and use the field's literature
- to learn how to sort through research for an answer

Any of these reasons justifies looking into research methods. Your personal goals for approaching this subject can be a great resource for you.

The Ethical Challenge

Research is not amoral. Conducting research is bound up in the ethical standards our society has accepted. Research is judged not only by the rigor of procedures and the results obtained, but by the ethics of the researchers.

ethical codes of conducts

Formal codes of conduct have been developed by many organizations to guide practitioners and researchers. The most well known of these guides is the Code of Conduct for the American Psychological Association. Others exist in our field as well.

The American Association for Public Opinion Research has developed a Code of Conduct for researchers primarily in public survey research. Regulations of the United States Office of Education, the Department of Health and Human Services, and some federal laws have protected the rights of individuals who are subjects of research. Clear breaches of ethical standards are treated harshly in the field. Violations can—and have—resulted in termination of employment and virtual expulsion from the field. Ignorance of such codes is not considered an excuse since reasonable adults are expected to think about the likely consequences of their conduct before they act.[10]

Confidentiality is protected by such codes. This requirement means that all information gathered from individual subjects is secret. Of course, sometimes participants in a study are willing to be identified by name, or to have specific details about themselves revealed. In such cases, the researchers must get their "informed consent" (in writing) to report such information. Confidentiality also implies that a person has a right to privacy. If people believe that questions asked of them are too personal or that researchers are violating their rights to privacy, the individual has a right to refuse to cooperate without punishment. Similarly, if people have moral or ethical reasons that would prevent them from participating in a study, they have a perfect right to refuse. You may have taken a class in which part of your grade required participation in research. If you had declined to participate in a project, another project (such as a library report) that would be ethically acceptable to you would have been available to you as an alternative. To protect privacy, researchers usually try to avoid gathering unnecessary personal information, keep composite information only (destroying original questionnaires or data sheets), and get informed consent.

confidentiality requirement

Professional responsibility means that researchers follow accepted rules of conduct with thoroughness and attention to concerns of subjects. Researchers must communicate their concern for privacy to people involved in their studies and must tell them about the procedures involved. Though researchers need not tell subjects the hypotheses they are testing until after the project is complete, they are obliged to explain the study at the end of the inquiry. The professional researcher cares for the rights of study participants.

professional responsibility

The Structure of the Field Challenge

People in speech communication, speech and hearing science, journalism, and telecommunications work in a field that is structured across many departmental lines. Similarly, communication research has been promoted by many organizations whose members often cross the barriers created by organizational frameworks at different schools. It is helpful to know what the major organizations in our field do to showcase our research.

Speech Communication Association

Founded in November of 1914, the Speech Communication Association is the field's oldest organization actively promoting research. Originally called the National Association of Academic Teachers of Public Speaking, it changed its name

organizations that structure the field

Special Discussion 1–2
Classical Roots of the Communication Field

Communication is one of the world's oldest academic studies. The first book on communication was written by Ptah Hotep, a teacher of the sons of Egyptian Pharoahs, sometime around 2675 B.C.E. The book was called *Precepts* and served as a textbook on communication for many centuries. Yet, widespread communication studies did not really begin until around 500 B.C.E, when the city-state of Athens instituted a democratic system and people found that they had to speak for themselves to exercise their rights. Athenian freemen were expected to participate in the popular assembly (if they gave consistently bad advice they could be banished outright) and on juries (often including 200 or more people). People needed communication skills and they were eager to find teachers to help them. The first groundswell of teachers to make their way to Athens were called sophists. Today that term signifies a person who uses clever but fallacious arguments. In ancient times, however, sophists were teachers who traveled around instructing people wherever there was a market. These teachers gave very practical instruction that was useful to common folk who direly needed to improve their communication skills. A Sicilian named Corax, generally believed to be the earliest of these teachers, "invented" the study of communication (called rhetoric) sometime around 470 B.C.E. At the very least, he wrote the first detailed work on the art of effective public speaking, *Rhetorike Techne,* which included details on organization and uses of arguments from probability. Other sophists included Protagoras (called the father of debate), Theodorus of Byzantium (who studied figures of speech such as puns), and Prodicus of Ceos (an early expert in the study of words or 'philology').

Surely the greatest contributor to communication studies in the classical age was Aristotle (384–322 B.C.E.). He made the first attempt to develop a complete rhetoric that was philosophically compelling. In his book *Rhetoric,* he defined our study as "the faculty of discovering in the particular case what are the available means of persuasion." Thus, rhetoric was not a *practice* but a *field of study*—an advance that still gives us intellectual integrity as a distinct field. Though Aristotle did not write about all the canons of rhetoric, he became associated strongly with them because he discussed many of them in detail. These canons were five major categories that may be studied to help understand communication: *invention* (types and sources of ideas); *arrangement* (organization of ideas); *style* (use of words); *delivery* (use of voice and gesture); and *memory* (ability to recall passages and examples for utterance). When universities were founded during the middle ages, three primary subjects were studied, logic, rhetoric, and grammar. Remnants of this tradition can be still seen today: the speech communication student wears a silver tassel at graduation ceremonies to symbolize study of "oratory" in the silver age.

> **Special Discussion 1–2**
> **(Continued)**
>
> The study of speech and hearing science also has its roots in ancient times. Plutarch, the Greek biographer, recounted that Demosthenes had a monotonous voice and stammered when he spoke. Under the guidance of an actor named Satyrus (the oldest known speech therapist?) he improved his diction through a number of drills including speaking with pebbles in his mouth. Though the deaf were routinely put to death in ancient Rome and Greece, during the middle ages, speech and hearing science was pursued as a sacred duty. In the seventh century, when Bishop St. John of Beverly was successful in teaching a deaf-mute to speak, the Roman Catholic Church promptly declared it a miracle. Later developing a code of charitable deeds, the Church promoted compassion for handicapped people in general, but it also unknowingly declared speech and hearing science not a profession but an act of charity.

to the Speech Association of America, which remained the name until 1970 when the organization adopted its current title. In addition to promoting research and employment networking at its annual convention, the Speech Communication Association publishes several journals that report research:

- *Quarterly Journal of Speech* (founded in 1915). The oldest journal in the field; now deals with general speech communication focusing heavily on communication and rhetorical theory and criticism.
- *Communication Monographs* (founded 1934). Originally designed to publish lengthy research pieces (initially called *Speech Monographs*— and hence, libraries still list it with a call number that includes the letter *S*); now dedicated to communication theory with emphasis on quantitative studies.
- *Communication Education* (founded 1952—formerly *Speech Teacher*). In the 1980s, this journal was divided into two publications: *Communication Education* and *Speech Communication Teacher*.
- *Text and Performance Quarterly* (founded 1981). Dedicated to oral interpretation of literature and aesthetics in communication.
- *Critical Studies in Mass Communication* (founded 1984). Study and analysis of mass media communication.
- *Journal of Applied Communication Research* (founded 1973, SCA sponsorship begun 1991). Research on applied topics designed to solve field problems.

Two additional yearbooks are also published by SCA, the *International and Intercultural Communication Annual* and the *Free Speech Yearbook*.

International Communication Association

Founded in 1949 as the National Society for the Study of Communication, the name was changed to the International Communication Association in the mid-1960s. This organization encourages participation from all branches of communication (except for Speech and Hearing Science), drawing especially strong links between those studying mass communication and those studying interpersonal communication. Every three years the annual convention is held outside the United States. Its major journals are the following:

- *Journal of Communication* (founded 1951). Designed to promote the broad study of communication; from 1974 through 1991 ICA turned over editorship to the Annenberg School of Communication at the University of Pennsylvania; oriented primarily toward studies of mass media, television, and popular culture.
- *Human Communication Research* (founded 1974). A premier outlet for research in communication theory with emphasis on quantitative studies.
- *Communication Theory* (founded 1991). Dedicated to essays on theoretic and metatheoretic developments in communication.

At the time of the writing of this book, ICA is preparing to inaugurate a new journal, *Political Communication*. ICA also sponsors the *Communication Yearbook* containing commissioned essays and top papers from its annual convention.

American Speech-Language-Hearing Association

Though once part of the Speech Communication Association, the American Academy of Speech Correction was founded in 1926. The organization changed its name four times after 1926, settling on the American Speech-Language-Hearing Association in 1979. ASHA is best known for its certification programs for practitioners of speech correction and speech and hearing science. It also promotes research and scholarship by its publications:

- *Journal of Speech and Hearing Disorders* (founded 1936). Called the *Journal of Speech Disorders* until 1948, this journal features research and theoretic essays across the realm of speech and hearing science.
- *Journal of Speech and Hearing Research* (founded 1958). Dedicated to research, measurement issues, research methods, and applied work in speech and hearing science.
- *ASHA* (founded 1959). Focuses on professional speech and hearing research issues and the administration of the organization.
- *Language, Speech and Hearing Services in Schools* (founded 1970). Attention paid to issues of interest to speech and hearing specialists with emphasis on speech-handicapped children.
- *American Journal of Speech-Language Pathology* (founded 1991). Focuses on clinical practice issues for therapists and clinicians.

From time to time, the association also has published a *Monograph* series and *ASHA Reports* containing proceedings from annual meetings.

Association for Education in Journalism and Mass Communication

The largest national professional organization in mass communication is the Association for Education in Journalism and Mass Communication. Founded as the American Association of Teachers of Journalism in November 1912, it adopted its current name in 1982. In addition to hosting annual meetings that showcase research, the organization sponsors the following journals:

- *Journalism Quarterly* (founded 1924). Originally called *Journalism Bulletin,* it features predominately nonquantitative studies of journalism.
- *Journalism Educator* (founded 1945). Focuses on educational issues and essays related to instruction.
- *Journalism Monographs* (founded 1966). Includes extended studies in mass communication issues and theory.
- *Mass Communication Review* (founded 1973). Studies the influence of mass communication on society.
- *Newspaper Research Journal* (founded 1979). Includes commentary and research related to print communication.
- *Public Relations Research Annual* (founded 1989). Includes reviews of special research topics in public relations.

Interest groups also publish materials that do not yet have the full status of journals including *The Journalist,* the *International Communication Bulletin,* and *Media Law Notes.*

Broadcast Education Association

Called the Association of Professional Broadcast Education for many years, this organization focuses its attention exclusively on electronic media and its effects. This group publishes the following journals:

- *Journal of Broadcasting and Electronic Media* (founded in 1956). Originally called the *Journal of Broadcasting,* this journal features essays and research on broadcasting with emphasis on showcasing quantitative research and applied commentaries.
- *Feedback* (founded 1959). Includes essays and news on the broadcast education field.

Of course, research in mass media is promoted by other organizations as well. The American Association for Public Opinion Research launched *Public Opinion Quarterly* in 1937 to share work in public opinion research and survey methods. The breadth of the field was enhanced by adding the *Public Relations Review* in 1975 to complement the *Public Relations Quarterly* (founded 1937).

American Forensic Association

Founded in 1949 by a group of debate coaches and teachers of competitive forensics, the organization was dedicated to issues surrounding competitive forensics. Through 1963, AFA published the *Register,* a quarterly newsletter that included some research. The *Journal of the American Forensic Association* was begun in 1964 and is now called *Argumentation and Advocacy,* reflecting the change in content beyond the traditional arenas of competitive forensics. The organization sponsors national forensic events and promotes research through a program of competitively awarded grants.

Special Interest Organizations

Many organizations focus on specialized concerns. Some have their own publications and conferences, whereas others meet along with other professional organizations. Though a complete listing would be inappropriate here, some of the most prominent of such groups are listed below:

- Intercultural Communication: Society for Intercultural Education Training and Research.
- Women and Communication: The Organization for Research on Women and Communication (publishes journal); Women in Communication, Inc.
- Forensics: National Forensic Association; Cross Examination Debate Association; Delta Sigma Rho-Tau Kappa Alpha, Pi Kappa Delta, Phi Rho Phi (honor societies). (All publish their own journals.)
- General Communication: Association of Communication Administrators (publishes own journal); International Society for the History of Rhetoric; Commission on American Parliamentary Practice; Religious Speech Communication Association.
- Journalism and Telecommunications: Alpha Epsilon Rho, Sigma Delta Chi (honor societies); Public Relations Society of America; National Association of Broadcasters; American Newspaper Publishers Association.

Regional Organizations

Every region has at least one organization representing the interests of that area and publishing at least one journal. Your study of research methods will be helped greatly by familiarity with the organization that is dominant in your area. Your instructor can give you information about joining your regional organization. All these organizations have student membership rates and agreements with other regional organizations to give complimentary copies of their publications to sustaining members of the other regional associations.

SUMMARY

Research is the systematic effort to secure answers to questions. Research questions deal with issues requiring reference to data and information. Research regularly invites examining past inquiry into the issue. Basic research is conducted to learn about relationships among variables, regardless of any immediate commercial product or service. Applied research is conducted to develop a product or solve an immediate practical problem. Yet, regardless of whether pure or applied research is involved, the methods of inquiry are identical. In 1968 the New Orleans conference concluded that "research in speech-communication focuses on the ways in which messages link participants during interactions." Thus, communication research is a specialty that studies message-related behavior. Communication might be defined as "the process by which participants transact and assign meaning to messages." A message is the set of verbal and nonverbal cues communicators exchange. Verbal cues are the words people use in communication (as opposed to oral cues, which are spoken). Nonverbal cues are communication elements beyond the words themselves.

There are many challenges in communication studies. First, the challenge of breadth involves the large number of communication applications. Second, the multiple methods challenge means that communication researchers use both qualitative and quantitative methods. Qualitative methods of study use descriptions of observations expressed in predominantly non-numerical terms. Most qualitative research in our field tends to *describe* or *interpret* communication exchanges. Quantitative research methods are inquiries in which observations are expressed predominantly in numerical terms. Quantitative research tends to be *explanatory*, especially when experiments are involved, or it attempts to use precise statistical models to achieve comprehensive understanding of human communication (as in survey studies and polls of public opinion). These methods often try to explain communication behavior by looking at processes that allow researchers to *predict* future behavior, frequently using models of causal processes. Thus, quantitative research usually attempts to answer questions about *many* people. The third challenge, the scholarly rigor challenge, means that research involves recognition of five key conditions: research is systematic, though unexpected results often emerge (the effect is called serendipity and refers to researchers' finding something of value while looking for something else); research is data driven; research is a sound argument (arguments in this context are claims advanced on the basis of reasoning from evidence); research is capable of replication; research is partial. The fourth and personal challenge means that successful students of research tend to consider the following issues: the personal ability to think in an orderly way; the ability to write clearly; the ability to set aside personal prejudices in light of data; the ability to be organized and follow instructions; the recognition of the reason to study communication research methods (to learn to think rigorously and critically; to learn how to find answers to questions about communication; to acquire survival skills to help read and use the field's literature; to learn how to sort through research for an answer). Fifth, the ethical challenge means that researchers must abide by formal codes of conduct (including guaranteeing confidentiality, which requires that all information gathered from individual subjects is secret), and must act with professional responsibility (by following accepted rules of conduct with thoroughness and attention to concerns of subjects). Sixth, the structure of the field challenge involves recognizing that communication research is promoted by many organizations whose members often cross the barriers created by organizational frameworks at different schools.

TERMS FOR REVIEW

research
basic research
applied research
communication
message
verbal cues
nonverbal cues
qualitative methods
historical-critical methods
qualitative observational studies
case studies and interpretive studies
participant observation studies
ethnomethodology

discourse/conversational analysis
creative studies
quantitative methods
survey methods
descriptive or observational surveys
content analysis
opinion surveys
experiment
serendipity
arguments
confidentiality
professional responsibility

NOTES

[1]Let's get something straight at the outset. The word ''data'' is a plural word. Thus, we have to say, ''data *are*'' and ''data *were*,'' NOT ''data *is*'' and ''data *was*.'' A single piece of data is called a datum, but people do not use that word very often. Instead they refer to a datum as ''a piece of data,'' a usage that sounds natural to most people.

[2]He didn't.

[3]They do.

[4]We don't know.

[5]Well, almost. A couple of areas have been added here, including conflict management, journalism, radio and television, and public relations. In the original effort, mass communication careers already were distinguished from other careers in communication.

[6]Reasonable people may differ on the classification of some of these types of studies, but the perspective advanced here represents a mainstream view with which you are most likely to find others in agreemet.

[7]The language and content of the distinction drawn between qualitative and quantitative research emphases is drawn from the contribution of an anonymous reviewer of the first version of the manuscript for this book.

[8]It was received very positively. The story of the audience not responding positively to the Gettysburg address is another Lincoln myth, similar to the myth of the speech having been written on the back of an envelope at the last minute.

[9]This discussion benefits from Tuckman (1978, pp. 10–12).

[10]The Archbishop of York challenged British scientists to consider the ethical consequences of their research by urging them to ask, ''What applications will be made of my research?'' before they undertake research.

CHAPTER 2

Communication Problem Statements and Hypotheses

The one real object of education is to leave a man in the condition of continually asking questions.

–Bishop Creighton

BEFORE WE GET STARTED . . .

Students who learn about research methods for the first time tend to think that the hardest part of inquiry is carrying out a study. In fact, the hardest part is finding the right question to ask and the right hypothesis to advance. Accordingly, this chapter will discuss the roles of problem statements and hypotheses and provide steps to guide you in developing your own.

QUALITIES OF PROBLEM STATEMENTS

Problems we investigate are the questions for which we expect to find answers through research. Hence, selecting and wording problem statements are vital parts of the research craft. Inexperienced researchers sometimes do not recognize how important problem statements are—until they have gotten in over their heads. Problem statements must be specified in advance of completing studies for two reasons. First, they set limits on relevant information. They allow researchers to know what information to

problems isolated

problem statements:
1. set limits on relevant information
2. structure inquiry

examine and what information to set aside. Second, clear purposes structure inquiry. Problem statements invite certain methods and techniques. If the problem statements suggest an experiment, the inquiry will be structured to provide careful control and clear manipulation of variables. The question we ask guides us to the methods that are relevant to its proper answer. Of course, problem statements may be revised—usually involving language or adding qualifiers—after some inquiry into the topic. Yet, a working problem statement should be constructed to get the process rolling.

Useful Problem Statements

It is important to pose problem statements that are possible to answer. Thus, there are two prerequisites for useful problem statements.

Problem Statements Must Be within the Researcher's Capabilities

questions must be within the researcher's competence

Let's be honest about it: many questions you care about cannot be answered by you now—or ever. Some questions cannot be answered unless you have the money or special skills that are not yet yours. You may be interested in learning if the disintegration of the Soviet Union led to an increase in the number of "underground press" publications in the independent states. But if you do not speak Russian, you probably cannot complete such a study. Furthermore, you may not have a way to get access to formal collections of "underground" publications. Fundamentally, you must choose problem statements that are "do-able" given your resources and abilities.

Problem Statements Must Be Narrow but Not Trivial

some questions are too broad to answer

Perhaps the biggest difficulty with problem statements is that some are either too broad to answer or so limited as to be insignificant. Students often are assigned the task of composing problem statements to investigate at a later time. Without thinking, some students propose such problems as: the causes of stuttering; the rise of public relations as a profession; ways to increase communication among spouses; the speaking habits of American preachers. Writing a term paper or research article to answer these questions is unrealistic. Similarly, a subject can be narrowed down to the point where its answer is trivial. Under the appropriate heading, "Brilliant Deductions," comedian Jay Leno (1991, pp. 1–7) reported on newspaper accounts of studies that seemed to ask trivial questions:

some questions are so narrow as to be trivial

> With investigative techniques that rival Sherlock Holmes's, today's scientists are peeling back the layers of knowledge—arriving at undreamed-of discoveries. Take the following headlines for example . . .
> Smaller families require less food [Leno's comment: So that would mean bigger families require more food? I'm confused.]
> Farmers buy most farmland [Leno's comment: Gee, I wonder what they do with it?]
> Ability to swim may save children from drowning [Leno's comment: I guess we'll just have to use bigger weights.]
> Sewers are not good playgrounds [Leno's comment: Sounds like just another overprotective mom.]
> Americans are unlikely to give up eating during recession [Leno's comment: "We thought about it, but then we got hungry" department.]

> Jail crowding caused by increase in criminals, new study concludes [Leno's comment: "Let's not jump to any conclusions."]

Some communication problem statements are so insulated that researchers may forget the importance of studying meaningful message-related behavior. For instance, one student attended presentations made by applicants for a university job:

> As one successful candidate described her research into male reactions at baby showers, . . . [the student] says she couldn't help but think, "What the hell does this have to do with anything?" (Kiefer, 1992, p. 10)

Good research questions must avoid the extremes of breadth and triviality.

Criteria for Sound Problem Statements
Proper phrasing of problems is required to make them useful. We will consider some criteria for worthwhile research problems.

1. *Problem statements must be stated unambiguously, usually as questions.* **unambiguous** These problem statements have been found in published research articles: **statements, usually in question form**

> Does the Intercultural Communication Workshop significantly improve the American participants' intercultural communication competence? (Hammer, 1984, p. 253)
> What differences in motivation for attendance are there between [*sic*] infrequent, occasional, and frequent movie-goers? (Austin, 1986, pp. 117–188)

Sometimes problems have "subproblems" that narrow down the issues into increasingly compact units. In some articles, the research problem is phrased as a purpose statement. In other research pieces, the problem statement emerges near the end of the literature review as a summary claim to be tested. They don't have to be followed by question marks to be problem statements.

2. *Except for simple descriptive studies, problem statements must include at* **include two** *least two variables.* Researchers try to relate one variable to another. The **variables** term "variable" has a very special meaning in research. A **variable** is a symbol **variable defined** to which numbers may be assigned. This statement sounds as though it is restricted to quantitative studies, but it is not. The following question has clear variables in it: Has the number of threat appeals declined in American preaching from 1900 to 1990? We might survey manuscripts of preachers of each time period to count the number of such appeals at each time frame. The use of threat appeals is a variable. It is capable of taking on two numbers—either preachers use them in sermons or they do not (100 percent or 0 percent use). Of course, the number of such threats is an obvious variable. The time frame, 1900 to 1990, also is a variable. The opposite of a variable is a "constant." A **constant** is a **constant defined** symbol to which only one number may be assigned. Many research questions ask about relationships between some variables while holding others constant. Look at this problem statement: Among upper-division college students, what is the relationship between communication apprehension and grades in public speaking? The grade level of the college students is held constant, since it is restricted only to upper-division college students. You might sometimes

hear researchers talk about the need to have control in their studies. What they mean is that they want to take variables that can be nuisances and make constants out of them.

Some problem statements involve such low-level questions that only one variable is involved, such as

- what proportion of daily newspapers do people read?
- which medium of advertising is most popular among small businesses?
- how many women chair communication departments in America?

Though in the early stages of research such questions may be useful to characterize a process or field, they elicit rather low levels of information.

problems must be testable

3. *Problem statements must be testable.* A testable problem must be capable of yielding more than one answer. Yet sometimes researchers ask questions that have only one answer. Look at these examples from the work of pupils and some established scholars:

Example	**Deficiency**
How can politicians sell themselves to the public?	The example asks about a logical possibility—what *can* politicians do? Future options are nearly endless and there is no way to find an appeal that is *not possible* in the future.
Is there a pattern to the ways people watch television?	The example is answerable only by saying "yes." Anything forms a pattern, even if the regularity is random. The question answers itself by its own construction.
Do charismatic leaders increase group productivity?	This example cannot be answered because the notions of "charismatic leaders" and "productivity" are so broad that they cannot be pinned down. The problem is not in testable language.

problems make no value judgments

4. *Problem statements must not advance value judgments.* Research can reveal whether computerized therapy reduces stuttering in children. But it cannot tell if computerized therapy *should* be used for stutterers. That choice requires moving beyond research and evaluating pragmatic choices. Research questions, therefore, may not substitute value judgments for appeals to facts, as in the following attempts: Is public speaking training *better* at reducing communication apprehension than counseling therapy? *Should* trials be videotaped? Is it a *bad idea* for newspapers to use unnamed sources for news reports?

must be grammatical

5. *Problem statements must be clear grammatical statements.* In the fever of enthusiasm, some scholars may compose incomplete or ungrammatical problem statements that are inevitably unclear. By expressing problem statements with

great clarity, it is possible to promote thoughtful research that gets the job done efficiently. The following format can be used to construct worthwhile problem statements. The format involves filling in blanks in the following question:

format for phrasing problem questions

What is the relationship between ___ and ___?

By substituting variables of interest, many research questions can be composed. Of course, as with most advice, this format is just a starting point since statements may require great modification to put them in their final form. Some problems involve more than two variables. Even so, all problems ask about relationships between variables, and useful problems may be found in clear formal statements. Pupils sometimes advance first drafts of problem statements that are sentence fragments (little more than topic titles). Yet, useful problems can be developed by thoughtful revisions as in these examples:

First Draft Example	**Revised Example**
(from a student of mass communication) "The image of girls in children's programming"	"What is the relationship between the frequency of girls as characters in children's programming and their portrayal in submissive or dominant roles?"
(from a student of interpersonal communication) "Self-disclosure and relationship development"	"What is the relationship between the amount of self-disclosure among romantic partners and their level of communication satisfaction?"
(from a student of speech and hearing science) "Adult aphasia and therapy"	"What is the relationship between the use of group or individual therapy for adult aphasic patients and their use of correct initiation and response to questions?"

Using nonstandard grammar can also cause misunderstandings. A student turned in this problem statement: "Does humor make a speech more persuasive?" In standard English one cannot say "more" without following it with a "than." Anything less than this form is a sentence fragment. "More" than what? one might ask. More than nothing? More than it once was? More than messages using other types of appeals? Indeed all comparative forms (such as higher, lower, less, and fewer) require "than" to complete the sentence. It is wise to use standard grammar if problem statements are to be capable of standing on their own and guiding research.

Sometimes overwritten problem statements that include motives and explanation create difficulty. This submission is an example of such an overwritten statement: "In an effort to avoid potential charges of sexual harassment, do male managers avoid socially oriented interpersonal communication episodes with female employees?" The introductory phrase was not a meaningful part of the problem statement, but an *interpretation*

SPECIAL DISCUSSION 2–1
What Problem Statements Are Not

Though we may find some useful standards for research questions, it is also a good idea to know what *are not* useful research questions. These pseudo-problem statements may trick us into spending time on them when, in fact, they may not be worth our time.

1. Questions asking for obvious yes or no answers (after Leedy, 1989, p. 49). It is not worthwhile to ask, "Do communication classes affect the skills of students?" Any stimulus has some kind of effect— even if it is an insignificant one. The answer may be trivial, such as "Yes, the classes affect students very little."
2. Questions asking about applying a statistical tool (after Leedy, 1989, p. 48). These questions confuse the method of answering the question with the research questions themselves. Problem statements should ask for relationships, not statistical methods.
3. Questions proposing personal learning goals (after Leedy, 1989, p. 47–48). In fact, personal references have no role in productive problem statements. The following example is inappropriate: "The purpose of this study is to learn ways advertisers sell products." Problem statements do not "learn" anything. The problem statements should get to the point and ask about relationships.
4. Questions that already have been competently studied (after Auer, 1959, p. 64). If the question already has been answered effectively, there is little reason to repeat the research.
5. Questions that cannot really be solved (after Auer, 1959, pp. 66–67). Whether because of the lack of resource materials or because the question deals with broad, unresolvable, philosophical issues, such questions are not suitable for research.

---

of results. Eventually the question became: "Do male managers in complex organizations report fewer socially oriented interpersonal communication episodes with female employees than with male employees?"

problem statements are used in both qualitative and quantitative research

Now that we have noticed that problem statements play a vital role in research, it is obvious that each area in our field makes great use of them. Table 2.1 shows examples of the sorts of research questions we might probe. Both qualitative and quantitative research efforts require full problem statements to guide efforts. It is not surprising that questions such as those listed might be asked regardless of research. You should look at the list of sample questions to see if any stimulate your interest or give you some ideas of directions you may wish to take on your own.

USING HYPOTHESES

hypothesis defined

Whereas problem statements *ask* about relationships that might be found, hypotheses give direct declarative *answers* to the problem. A **hypothesis** is "an expectation about events based on generalizations of the assumed relationship between variables" (Tuckman, 1978, p. 27). Here is an analogy that might explain how research is completed (after Auer, 1959, p. 72–73). Suppose you were

TABLE 2.1 Examples of Problems in Communication Research

Qualitative Research Examples	Quantitative Research Examples
Speech Communication	
In what ways have studies of the use of facial expressions changed since 1600 through 1990?	What is the relationship between the use of facial displays of interest and interpersonal attraction?
What methods of speech preparation were used in the Lincoln-Douglas debates?	What is the impact of heckling a speaker on audience arousal of sympathy for the speaker?
What communication training areas were most prominent among the founders of the American Society for Training and Development?	Do managers who use responsive listening behaviors with subordinates report greater communication satisfaction than other managers?
Speech and Hearing Science	
What were the major sources of influence on the development of the modern phonetic alphabet?	What is the relationship between the use of visualization therapy and traditional drills on reduction of stuttering in adults?
What events led to the founding of the American Speech-Language-Hearing Association's certification process for educational institutions?	Do speech-handicapped school children report lower self-esteem than other children?
What trends in the role for speech therapists in the treatment of brain injured patients have taken place from 1925 through 1990?	What is the relationship between timing of therapy for aphasic patients and their levels of phonological skill following therapy?
Mass Communication	
What changes in public funding have contributed significantly to the rise of the educational use of television?	What is the relationship between the use of satellite television in developing nations and changes in literacy rates?
What major justifications have been used by the Federal Communications Commission to deny renewal of licenses for radio and television stations?	What is the relationship between the amount of television watched by adults and the level of anxiety about personal safety?
What is the relationship between the establishment of ethics codes for public relations professionals and the rise of public relations as an academic discipline?	Do saturation advertising campaigns on television significantly increase product name recognition more than saturation campaigns using newspaper advertising?
Special Application Areas	
What phases were important to the development of communication education in the Western region of the United States from 1880 through 1940?	What is the relationship between the use of videotaping of speeches in the public speaking class and perceptions of speaker improvement?
What was the role of oral interpretation of literature in the practice of elocution of Dr. Rush?	What is the relationship between the size of oral interpretation programs in U.S. universities and the number of ethnic minority students involved in the activity?
What conditions in education led to the development and spread of tournament debating in America?	What is the relationship between the sex composition of debate teams and their win/loss records?

a detective solving a murder mystery. Before you answered the question, "Who killed John Doe?" with a formal hypothesis, you might explore several tentative **working hypotheses:** Professor Plum did it in the ballroom with the candlestick; Mrs. White did it with the revolver in the kitchen; Miss Scarlett did it with the rope in the library. Each working hypothesis could by tested against available information. Then you could eliminate each working hypothesis until one reasonable explanation emerged. You might finally conclude that Mr. Green did it in the bedroom with the knife. This hypothesis could be used as a formal criminal charge against the defendant, Mr. Green.

hypotheses are more than "educated guesses"

You may have heard that a hypothesis is an "educated guess." Unfortunately, most people using that definition place emphasis on the word "guess" rather than the word "educated." In fact, a hypothesis takes a general expectation—perhaps from a fully developed theory—and predicts what would be expected in the research project's new application. Furthermore, a hypothesis must have some kind of a rationale provided for it. There is a lot more education than guesswork involved in hypotheses.

hypotheses often are working tools of theory

Some claim that hypotheses are the working tools of theory.[1] They recognize that theorists apply their theories by developing hypotheses based on them (Giere, 1979, pp. 69–70). Though many hypotheses are based directly on applications of formal theories, some are not. Sometimes informal thinking is used to develop initial hypotheses.

Using Hypotheses to Test Explanations

Although a formal presentation of the logic to using hypotheses to test theoretic explanations is beyond the scope of this book, the rudiments of it can usefully be shared. Hypotheses allow us to contrast one theory against another by reasoning with tools of formal logic. A theory is an explanation of how concepts or constructs are related to each other. A hypothesis relates the theory to specific observations of variables. In logic, the structure that permits one to examine the soundness of "if . . . then" statements is called the "conditional syllogism." A

hypotheses are used to examine theories in conditional syllogisms

conditional syllogism is a formal logical system in which the major premise makes an "if-then" statement. In fact, when applied to the logic of hypothesis testing, the major premise of a conditional syllogism states that if a theory is true, then a hypothesis derived from it will be supported by data. Using these terms, the conditional syllogism takes one of two valid forms:

Major Premise:	If the theory is true, then the hypothesis will be supported by data.	MP: If the theory is true, then the hypothesis will be supported by data.
minor premise:	The theory is true.	mp: The hypothesis is not supported by data.
Conclusion:	(Therefore) the hypothesis is supported by data.	C: (Therefore) the theory is not true.

Researchers test hypotheses by gathering data to see if either of these two valid forms appears.[2] Though both are valid, the first one is fairly rare in practice. Researchers with supported hypotheses probably want to know if the underlying theories are tenable, not the other way around. The second example is very interesting since it helps researchers test whether a theory is untenable. In this way, hypotheses let researchers get evidence that may falsify theories if they are untrue. Thus, hypotheses can help test theories by determining when they need to be rejected in light of the facts. Logically, it does not work the other way around. We do not use hypotheses to prove a theory is true—we use hypotheses to find out if the theory has or has not survived one additional test.

Reasoning from hypotheses involves comparing different theoretic expectations and eliminating options. Arthur Stinchcombe (1968, p. 22) explained:

> The basic logical process of science is the elimination of alternative theories (both those we know and those we do not) by investigating as many of the empirical consequences of each theory as is practical, always trying for the greatest possible variety in the implications tested.

Since hypotheses allow us to eliminate alternative explanations, Stinchcombe suggested the desirability of attempting to pit the predictions of one theory against another in "crucial experiments." Though there is some difficulty in doing so, the idea that we make progress by attempting to eliminate unacceptable theories by testing hypotheses remains central in our studies.

hypotheses used to eliminate alternative theories

Requirements of Hypotheses

To have worthwhile research hypotheses, scholars must meet several categories of obligations, including the following:

requirements for hypotheses:

1. *Hypotheses must state relationships between variables.* Hypotheses make statements or predictions. They are not simple statements of definitions. It is not a hypothesis to state: "Intercultural communicators speak with different cultural influences." Similarly, the statement "Intercultural communicators speak differently" is not a hypothesis. "Speak differently" is not a variable. What does it mean? Speaking rapidly? Speaking with an accent? Speaking with great reserve? We do not know.

1. state relationship between variables

2. *Hypotheses must be consistent with what is known in the literature.* Often, as we have seen, hypotheses are derived directly from theories. Hypotheses should be rooted in past knowledge, rather than ignorant of it. If past research has shown that the amount of television violence has been increasing, it would not be consistent to advance a hypothesis predicting that the amount of violence in prime-time television has been decreasing.

2. consistent with literature

3. *Hypotheses must be testable.* Though powerful, research methods cannot deal with matters beyond observations that can be made in this life. Consider this "wannabe" hypothesis: "Public speaking instruction improves self-confidence better than oral interpretation instruction." This hypothesis asks the researcher to make a personal value judgment. One could advance a testable hypothesis by stating the issue as: "Public speaking instruction increases self-confidence more than oral interpretation instruction." Research questions must deal with matters that can be resolved by examining information. Of

3. testable

—hypotheses can deal with attitudes or values

TABLE 2.2 Hypothesis Phrasing Difficulties	
Submitted Hypotheses	**Comment**
Stuttering rate and age of onset.	This hypothesis is not even a sentence!
A journalism student earns more money after graduation than their peers.	This statement is an insult to grammar. "A journalism student" is predicted to differ from "*their* peers." Singular and plural pronouns must agree for correct grammatical construction.
People who own computers have less communication satisfaction with their wives.	The construction has two flaws. (1) Language is vague, though some specific meaning must be intended. People who own computers could be male or female, single or married. But this writer has assumed that people who own computers are husbands. (2) The sentence is a fragment. In English, one cannot use the word "less" without the word "than" appearing in the sentence somewhere else. As stated, the sentence leaves us hanging. It states that computer owners have "less communication satisfaction with their wives" than what? than whom? We do not know because the sentence is not complete.
Communication teachers who grade on the curve increase difficulties for students.	The hypothesis is ambiguous. "Difficulties" could mean almost anything. Specific observable difficulties must be identified instead of the current vagueness.
Communicators in Latino families differ from communicators in Anglo families.	The ambiguity of this hypothesis makes it unacceptable and untestable. "Differ" is not a variable. Thus, this hypothesis does not have two variables put into relationship. Furthermore, the form of the difference is hopelessly vague.
Because women have been stereotyped, they are not credible television news broadcasters.	This double-barreled statement does not ask about a relationship, but asks us to *explain* a relationship when it is found to exist. It would not test the hypothesis if one found that women newscasters in the major television markets were *not* perceived as lowly credible sources. Neither would it test the hypothesis if women newscasters *were* perceived as lowly credible sources (only the reasons are asked).

course, hypotheses can deal with evaluations people make. Researchers frequently study attitudes and values. But in these cases, the hypotheses still are matters that can be tested by gathering specific information.

4. clear, grammatical, and unambiguous declarative sentences

4. *Hypotheses must be clear, grammatical, and unambiguous, usually in the form of a declarative sentence.* Since a hypothesis answers a research question, we expect it to be a crisp declarative statement. Declarative statements are sentences that make claims, rather than ask questions. Even so, you might be surprised at the number of beginning research students who compose hypotheses that are not full declarative sentences. Table 2.2 provides a sample of such "wannabe" hypotheses submitted to the author by students. In addition to the examples, you can see a brief statement of the flaw in the hypothesis.

SPECIAL DISCUSSION 2–2
How to Generate Ideas for Hypotheses

When a student is learning the methods of research it is easy to wonder how to select an issue for a hypothesis. The same basic question interested Graham Wallas (1926). He examined the habits of well-known scientists to see if he could find some clues. His work led him to conclude that there are four stages that researchers follow to develop their basic ideas.

Stage 1: Preparation. Established researchers begin by reading as much as they can about the subject. Often they find that the same problem has been approached from very different perspectives (the researchers read them all). Somewhere along the line, one idea begins to stand out as more interesting than the others.

Stage 2: Incubation. Researchers almost uniformly let the idea sink in. They "sleep on it" and find that—without thinking about it—one idea winds up surging forward almost without an intentional effort.

Stage 3: Illumination. Surely the most mysterious part of the process, this stage involves the emergence of an idea into one's consciousness. Sometimes researchers talk about moments of "insight" or sudden awareness. Regardless of the label, a new solution emerges with some very new and creative ways of looking at things.

Stage 4: Verification. Solid researchers follow the insightful idea by testing it against information. Often, a "great idea" will be revealed as a half-baked notion. Just as frequently, however, the researcher will find ways to modify, correct, or improve the ideas or hypotheses.

Constructing Sound Hypotheses

Two formats can help you compose and develop worthy hypotheses. The first predicts that a difference will be observed and has the following form: **format to compose hypotheses**

> Subjects {or people} who are
> high in {or low in, characterized as, exposed to, etc.}
> *(insert favorite input variable of interest)*
> will have higher {or more, or greater, or less}
> *(insert favorite output variable of interest)*
> than others {or others who are high in, or low in, or not characterized as, not exposed to, etc.}
> *(insert favorite input variable of interest).*

format for hypotheses predicting differences

This format is found in such hypotheses as the following:

> Subjects who are high in self-esteem will have higher attitude change in response to a persuasive message than others who are low in self-esteem.

A second way to phrase hypotheses involves statements of simple relationships. A common pattern for these hypotheses is   **format for hypotheses predicting relationships**

> There will be a direct {or positive, or negative, or inverse, or curvilinear} relationship

between *(insert favorite first variable of interest)*
    and *(insert favorite second variable of interest).*
or
As *(insert favorite first variable of interest)*
    increases {or decreases, etc.},
        the *(insert favorite second variable of interest)*
            decreases {or increases, etc.}.
Such a hypothesis could be phrased as follows:

> As the amount of eye contact used by speakers increases, the credibility ratings of the speakers increases.[3]

Though you probably will need to revise your final wording somewhat, these patterns are simple ways for you to begin constructing your own hypotheses.

Types of Hypotheses in Quantitative Studies

distinguishing the material hypothesis

In quantitative research, we often subdivide hypotheses into two forms: material hypotheses and null hypotheses. Sometimes called the research hypothesis or just "the hypothesis," the material hypothesis states what the researcher wishes to support by gathering data. There are two forms of research hypotheses to consider. **Nondirectional** material hypotheses state that simply there will be some kind of relationship between variables (they are sometimes called "two-tailed" hypotheses because of the way statistics are used to test them). Suppose, for example, that we wished to compare the amount of television watched by children from Protestant and Catholic homes. A nondirectional hypothesis would predict the existence of a difference, but would not specify which children were above the average of television viewing. This nondirectional hypothesis can be abbreviated by using the Greek letter mu (μ) to represent the population average of each group. We could use μ_1 to represent the average amount of TV viewing by children in Protestant homes, μ_2 for the average TV viewing by children in Catholic homes. The nondirectional research hypothesis would appear as

nondirectional hypotheses identified

notation for nondirectional hypotheses

$$H_1: \mu_1 \neq \mu_2.$$

directional hypotheses distinguished

Directional material hypotheses state the form of the differences. Suppose a researcher suspected that Protestant children watch more television than Catholic children. The directional hypothesis would appear as

$$H_1: \mu_1 > \mu_2.$$

The symbol > means "greater than" and the symbol < means "less than."[4] This hypothesis predicts the direction of the differences.

null hypothesis distinguished

As the name suggests—null, nil, *nada*—a **null hypothesis** states that there is no relationship between variables. Using the same abbreviations as previously employed, the null hypothesis would be represented as

$$H_0: \mu_1 = \mu_2.$$

What good is such a hypothesis for researchers? Null hypotheses are used in quantitative research as statistical hypotheses. Researchers try to find data that reject null hypotheses. In a nutshell, here is the logic behind it. Testing our material hypothesis requires that we present a case for it. But any data we find could be dismissed by our opponents as atypical. So, we reason the other way around. We pretend—just for the sake of argument—that the null hypothesis is true. Then we ask if data we have gathered are so inconsistent with the world of the null hypotheses that it is improbable that the data could be found if the null hypothesis were true. Quantitative researchers set exact odds that they are willing to take for such matters, but we don't have to get into that now. The form for the argument goes like this:

null hypotheses used as a statistical hypothesis

one argues for material hypotheses by rejecting null hypotheses

MP: If p, then q	MP: If the null hypothesis is true, then data we collect will not show significant differences between groups compared.
mp: not q	mp: the data we collect show significant differences between groups compared.
C: (Therefore) not p	C: (Therefore) the null hypothesis is not true.

rejecting the null supports the research hypothesis

Then, by a process of elimination we can conclude that the research hypothesis is tenable.

This language may seem a bit strange because of all the negative terms we have to use. But the situation is much like the presumption of innocence we have in our court system (Erickson & Nosanchuck, 1977, pp. 145–149). We start with a null hypothesis that the defendant is not guilty. Then the prosecution tries to show that facts make it unlikely that the defendant has acted like someone who is not guilty. People are not found innocent—there is no way to get positive evidence to show that evil acts *have not* occurred. Instead, a defendant is found either ''guilty'' or ''not guilty'' of the specific charges. As you can see, we use null hypotheses all the time. Technically, we are not allowed to say that a null hypothesis is ''accepted.'' You can think it, but don't say it or write it. We cannot logically accept a statement without evidence, but the null hypothesis claims that there is no evidence of anything to begin with. So, if we do not reject the null hypothesis, we can only say that we ''failed to reject the null hypothesis.'' Similarly, we never can claim to ''prove'' or ''confirm'' a research hypothesis. Another future study might destroy our research hypotheses. The strongest statements we are allowed to make are that research hypotheses are ''supported'' or ''found tenable.'' The hypothesis actually only survived one more test—so these claims are fairly strong ones to make. If you read an article where the researcher oversteps these bounds, you know that the article has at least one flaw and may contain other mistakes as well.

null hypotheses like the presumption of innocence in criminal trials

cannot ''accept'' a null, but can ''fail to reject''

IDENTIFYING VARIABLES IN HYPOTHESES AND PROBLEMS

Hypotheses put variables into relationship with each other. They identify the roles of variables and their functions in research.

Isolating Variables in Hypotheses

When looking at hypotheses, it is important to identify the chief variables involved. Yet, students sometimes confuse the number of *variables* in the hypothesis with the *levels* of a variable. For instance, how many variables are there in this hypothesis?

> H_1: People with high self-esteem read newspapers more often than people with low self-esteem.

If you think that there are two variables, self-esteem and amount of newspaper reading, you are correct. Some look at this example and see three variables: high self-esteem, low self-esteem, and amount of newspaper reading. But, high and low self-esteem are merely *levels* or degrees of the same variable, self-esteem. It is important not to confuse levels of a variable with a completely new variable.

How many variables are in this hypothesis?

> H_1: Women are persuasive sources.

Assuming that persuasiveness is measured on a standard attitude scale, there is no second variable in the hypothesis. Sampling only "women" holds *constant* the potential variable of sex. We suspect that the author really wanted to know if women and men differed in their persuasiveness. But the author didn't say so. It is as important to spot the difference between a constant (a control) and a true variable in a hypothesis as it is to resist confusing levels of variables for variables themselves.

Hypotheses use variables to make predictions. Some variables are used to start predictions and others are predicted effects. Examining hypotheses lets us identify the role of variables. There are two major variable types, independent and dependent.

Independent Variables

independent variable

Independent variables predict outcomes (dependent variables) posited in hypotheses. These variables are easy to remember. The *in*dependent variables are the same as *in*put variables. These independent variables are starting points for making predictions.

moderator variables identified

Sometimes researchers refer to **moderator variables.** Moderators are variables that mediate the independent variable's prediction of the dependent variable. In reality, moderator variables are just independent variables that help predict the effects of chief independent variables. For instance, look at the following hypothesis:

> Female communication students who study research methods pursue graduate studies more than male communication students who study research methods and female communication students who do not study research methods.

The independent variable in this study is whether one takes research methods courses. A moderator variable has been added: student sex. Moderator variables permit subtle relationships to be explored.

TABLE 2.3 Hypotheses and Variable Identification	
Hypothesis	**Variable Identification**
H: Anglo speakers will stand a further distance away from receivers than will Asian speakers.	independent variable: national background of speaker dependent variable: distance from receivers
H: Stuttering children will report higher levels of anxiety than nonstuttering children.	independent variable: stuttering level of children dependent variable: anxiety
H: The voting behavior of lowly educated people exposed to negative political campaign advertisements will be affected more than will the voting behavior of highly educated people exposed to positive political campaign advertisements.	independent variables: (1) type of political campaign advertisement; and (2) level of voter intelligence (NOTE: depending on the rationale, level of voting behavior could be identified as a moderator variable) dependent variable: voting behavior
H: Regardless of level of ego-involvement, newspaper readers with sophisticated listening skills will have greater critical thinking ability than newspaper readers with unsophisticated listening skills.	independent variable: sophistication level of listening skills dependent variable: critical thinking ability (ego-involvement is a constant, not a variable)
H: National politicians will use more metaphorical language and more examples of ambiguity than will local politicians.	independent variable: type of politician (national or local) dependent variables: amount of metaphorical language and number of examples of ambiguity
H: Students who are high in communication apprehension will show greatest improvement in communication competence when presented with teachers using nondirective styles in comparison with highly communication apprehensive students exposed to teachers using directive styles.	independent variable: type of style used by teachers dependent variable: communication competence (high communication apprehension is a constant, not a variable)
H: Computer literate people will initiate fewer conversations than will computer illiterate people.	independent variable: level of computer literacy dependent variable: amount of initiation of conversations

Dependent Variables

Dependent variables are variables whose values or activities are presumed to be conditioned upon the independent variable in the hypothesis. The dependent variable is the consequence, the *predicted* variable, and/or the *output* variable. If the hypothesis is true, changes seen will be in the dependent variable. Thus, in our research hypothesis, the dependent variable is the degree to which students pursue graduate studies.

dependent variables

It is important to identify independent (input) and dependent (output) variables by looking at a hypothesis. Yet, many students may have some initial difficulty with this skill. It is useful to have some examples to work with as we develop our skills. Table 2.3 shows some hypotheses along with identification of independent and dependent variables. You should cover up the right side of the table to see if you can identify the independent and dependent variables accurately. After time you will find it easy to identify these two forms of variables.

SUMMARY

Problems we investigate are the questions for which we expect to find answers through research. Problem statements must be specified in advance of completing studies for two reasons. First, problem statements set limits on relevant information. Second, clear purposes structure inquiry. Problem statements invite certain methods and techniques. Useful problem statements must satisfy two prerequisites: (1) problem statements must be within the researcher's capabilities; (2) problem statements must be narrow but not trivial. There are five requirements for phrasing worthwhile problem statements: First, they must be stated unambiguously, usually as questions. Second, except for simple descriptive studies, problem statements must include at least two variables. A variable is a symbol to which numbers may be assigned. The opposite of a variable is a "constant." A constant is a symbol to which only one number may be assigned. To control variables, researchers take variables that can be nuisances and make constants out of them. Third, problem statements must be testable. Fourth, problem statements must not advance value judgments. Fifth, problem statements must be clear grammatical statements.

A hypothesis is "an expectation about events based on generalizations of the assumed relationship between variables." Though sometimes called an "educated guess," a hypothesis takes a general expectation—perhaps from a fully developed theory—and predicts what would be expected in the research project's new application. Furthermore, a hypothesis must have a rationale for it. Hypotheses are the working tools of theory. They allow us to contrast one theory against another by reasoning with tools of formal logic. A conditional syllogism is a formal logical system in which the major premise makes an "if-then" statement. When applied to the logic of hypothesis testing, a conditional syllogism's major premise states that if a theory is true, then a hypothesis derived from it will be supported by data. Researchers test hypotheses by gathering data to see if valid forms of the conditional syllogism appear. Hypotheses may compare different theoretic expectations to eliminate options. Pitting one theory's prediction against another is called conducting "crucial experiments."

Worthwhile research hypotheses must: 1. state relationships between variables; 2. be consistent with what is known in the literature; 3. be testable; 4. be clear, grammatical, and unambiguous, usually in the form of a declarative sentence. There are two generic ways to phrase hypotheses. The first predicts that a difference will be observed. The second involves statements of simple relationships. In quantitative research, we often subdivide hypotheses into two forms. First, the material hypothesis states what the researcher wishes to support by gathering data. There are two forms of material hypotheses to consider: (a) nondirectional material hypotheses state that simply there will be *some kind* of relationship between variables (they sometimes are called "two-tailed" hypotheses because of the way statistics are used to test them); (b) directional material hypotheses state the form of the differences. Second, the null hypothesis states that there is no relationship between variables. The null hypothesis is used in quantitative research as a statistical hypothesis that a researcher tries to get data to reject. Quantitative researchers start by assuming the truth of the null hypothesis (just for the sake of argument) and then ask if data are inconsistent with the world of the null hypotheses. If it is improbable that the data could be found if the null hypothesis were true, researchers conclude that it is unreasonable to continue presuming that the null hypothesis is true.

Hypotheses put variables into relationship with each other and identify their roles and functions in research. There are two major forms of variables. Independent variables predict the outcome (dependent variable) posited in the hypothesis. Moderator variables are types of independent variables that mediate the chief independent variable's prediction of the dependent variable. Dependent variables are variables whose values or activities are presumed to be conditioned on the independent variable in the hypothesis.

TERMS FOR REVIEW

problems
variable
constant
hypothesis
working hypothesis
conditional syllogism

nondirectional hypothesis
directional material hypothesis
null hypothesis
independent variable
dependent variable
moderator variable

NOTES

[1]There is some controversy regarding whether all hypotheses are applications of theories. Ray and Ravizza (1988) state that hypotheses are "developed in relation to an explicit or implicit theory" (p. 370). Similarly, the authors of the *Longman Dictionary of Psychology* (1984) explicitly state that all hypotheses are "based on theory" (p. 361, used through courtesy of Walter Glanze Word Books). Yet, others hold that hypotheses sometimes are derived from very casual speculation (Mason & Bramble, 1989, p. 72). We find this second view to be typical of the facts and endorse it here.

[2]The first example is a valid form called *modus ponens,* which is the method of affirming (from the Latin *ponere* which means "to affirm"). The second is. called *modus tollens,* which is the method of denial (from the Latin *tollere* which means "to deny").

[3]One also could phrase this statement in a slightly more technical form such as, "There is a direct relationship between the amount of eye contact used by speakers and credibility ratings."

[4]In English grammar, of course, one can say "less than" only when the things identified *cannot* be counted. If things can be put in numerical terms, one grammatically is required to say "fewer than." Thus, the signs at the supermarket *should* say "Use the Express Lane if you have 10 or *fewer* items"—but they don't. Yet, we still say "less than" when translating the term <, recognizing that it is not English.

Understanding Rudiments of Research Reasoning

CHAPTER 3

Using Communication Research Sources

In the last analysis, research per se *constitutes a method for the discovery of truth which is really a method of critical thinking.*

–Clifford Woody

BEFORE WE GET STARTED . . .

Why? What? When? How? Where? This chapter addresses these questions to prepare you for effective research. To do any kind of research, you must spend some time in the library. This chapter will teach you how to make fast work of library inquiry. It will provide practical help on how to use—not simply examine, but *use*—research sources to build research arguments. Hence, you will learn to structure your initial forays through the library, and you will learn the survival skills you actually should apply in your work.

APPROACHING RESEARCH MATERIALS

Research involves sifting materials to make cases. This section will answer some questions about these research dimensions: why? what? when?

The Why: Research Uses Past Work to Develop Arguments

Looking at past work helps us build research arguments. In this sense, an **argument** is a process of advancing conclusions based on reasons and evidence. Research argues to conclusions from the raw materials of information. In turn, the reasons may be tested with established standards of sound argument. Past inquiry guides us in several ways.

argument defined

- *Past Research Gives Premises for Argument.* A **premise** is a statement in a logical argument that is the foundation for others drawn from it. Therefore, you can use past research as a premise for new research arguments. The reasoning does not prove the conclusion is true, of course, but you can justify advancing some possible directions for future research.

1. finding premises for arguments

- *Past Research Gives Evidence for Argument.* Many issues—even in a field as wide open for research as communication—have been investigated successfully in the past. We may look both at the results and at the theories that have guided research. Past research also helps us learn when a theory's limits have been found. Such information and commentary can be recorded for later use in our own arguments.

2. finding evidence for arguments

- *Past Research Helps Balance Reliance on Authority and Empirical Data.* When reviewing literature you will encounter many different opinions. When an authority's interpretations stay close to the facts, you may feel justifiably comfortable accepting them. But when authorities ignore the facts or refuse to stick to them, their comments may be suspect. Since research is an argument, the papers you write are also arguments. Some inexperienced researchers try to ignore past work and use entirely new methods and ideas. Keith Stanovich calls this misguided approach the **Einstein syndrome** (1986, ch. 8) since researchers who suffer from it fail to connect their ''sudden breakthroughs'' with lessons from others. By discarding previous lessons as irrelevant (hardly ever a justifiable claim), they fail to learn from the successes of others. So, it is useful to spend time looking at ways writers and scholars have conceptualized, justified, studied, and interpreted a research area.

3. balancing scholarly opinions against data

''Einstein syndrome'' defined

The What: Purposeful Library Research—Information to Get

Though you must take the time getting to know the specialized language of a subject, your library research will be most productive if you know what you want to find. Don't interview experts or go to the library unless you have first decided what you are looking for. Don't worry about closing your mind to new information. You will find unexpected material along the way, and you will want to take advantage of it. But do not go the library just looking for ''background.'' What is background anyway? How do you know when you have enough background? Experienced researchers know that background materials flow naturally from a search for specifics. Regardless of your problem statement, some of the most obvious things to seek at the library are

research should be conducted with a goal or purpose

topics to look for in library research

- definitions of key concepts and variables
- ways concepts and variables have been measured and studied
- summary statements that people (especially textbook writers) seem to make about the subject

- classic research studies on a subject (the studies that all the textbooks seem to reference)
- research that shows what methods to use
- research that shows what mistakes to avoid

Sometimes you may find surprisingly little on your subject. That absence is very useful information. It suggests that the subject cries out for investigation. It also may indicate that most people have found the subject trivial (so what? most people may not have thought about the subject the way you have). Get used to finding that past research has not answered your particular research question. Many parts of the field are new, and you may find valuable things to investigate for yourself.

Where do you find information to answer these questions? Table 3.1 lists sources that can help answer many questions (along with a rating of the usefulness of each source). Sometimes you do not find what you wish in these sources. For instance, you usually expect textbook writers to define their terms, but there are exceptions. Wayne C. Booth wrote an entire book called *The Rhetoric of Fiction* (1964) without ever defining the term "rhetoric." Research articles rarely state definitions. Instead, they may refer to sources with acceptable definitions. Thus, you should consider the resources indicated in table 3.1 when you explore the library. Aside from looking at textbooks and articles (for which guidance will be given later in this chapter), there are three other types of resources you should examine:

encyclopedias

- *Encyclopedias.* You may find useful context, reviews of general issues, and definitions from encyclopedias. In mass communication, for instance, encyclopedias can be useful sources *early* in the library search effort, since many provide annual updates that describe new technologies and changes in communication law. You may also wish to check specialized encyclopedias available for each field.

dictionaries

- *Specialized Dictionaries.* Dictionaries of usage (such as Webster's) are poor sources for technical definitions because they usually are not written by people in the field you are investigating. On the other hand, dictionaries of psychology, communication, mass media, and speech and hearing science attempt to provide correct technical definitions.

handbooks and annual reviews

- *Handbooks and Annual Reviews.* Though you may think of a handbook as the same thing as an employee manual, the term has been enlisted by scholars to refer to books containing summaries of literature and brief reviews of common topics. Most handbooks offer both summaries and criticisms of controversial issues.

As you read, you will see references to other sources that you can track down later. Students sometimes read a literature review from a book and accept it as sufficient. Unfortunately, such literature reviews tend to be dated by over a year by the time the book is published. Furthermore, some authors may summarize literature inaccurately or with a biased point of view. By checking original sources, you can find

TABLE 3.1 A Smart Guide to Sources Useful for Obtaining Information in Library Searches

Ratings of Sources*

Matters to Investigate	Categories of Sources			
	Textbooks	Handbooks	Specialized Encyclopedias, Dictionaries	Articles
Definitions of key concepts and variables	A	B	A	C
Ways concepts and variables have been measured and studied	C	B	D	A
Summary statements about the subject	A	A	F	C
Classic research studies in the field	A	A	F	B
Research that shows what methods to use	C	B	F	A
Research that shows what mistakes to avoid	C	B	F	A

*These subjective ratings indicate   A: excellent source
B: often useful source
C: occasionally useful source
D: rarely useful
F: forget it

Source	Sources for Information Comment

Encyclopedias

International encyclopedia of communications. (1989). New York: Oxford University Press. (4 vols.)	Precis of over 500 topics of interest to communication
Hudson, R. V. (1967). *Mass media: A chronological encyclopedia of television, motion pictures, magazines, newspapers, and books in the United States.* New York: Garland.	Covers mass media history from 1638 through 1985 in the United States
Sills, D. L. (Ed.). (1968). *International encyclopedia of the social sciences.* New York: Macmillan. (18 vols.)	Dated, but useful background with emphasis on classic work in the social sciences

Dictionaries

Devito, J. A. (1986). *The communication handbook: A dictionary.* New York: Harper & Row.	Definitions of terms and essays on broad communication topics
Longman dictionary of psychology and psychiatry. (1984). New York: Longman.	Definitions of over 21,000 terms; one of the largest of such dictionaries
English, H. B., & English, A. C. (1958). *A comprehensive dictionary of psychological and psychoanalytical terms.* New York: McKay.	An oldie but goodie; contains clear explanations and criticisms of different schools of thought

TABLE 3.1—*Continued*

	Sources for Information
Source	**Comment**

Dictionaries—Continued

Diamant, L. (Ed.). (1989). *The broadcast communications dictionary,* 3rd ed., rev. & exp. New York: Greenwood Press.
Listings limited to broadcast terms definitions on mass media operations and technology

Longman dictionary of mass media and communications. (1982). New York: Longman.
Definitions of terms used across mass media specialties

Robbins, S. D. (1961). *A dictionary of speech pathology and therapy,* 2nd ed. Framingham, MA: SCI-ART Publishers.
Emphasis on terms that describe therapies and types of speech disorders

Nicolosi, L., Harryman, E., & Kresheck, J. (1978). *Terminology of communication disorders: Speech, language, and hearing.* Baltimore: The Williams and Wilkins Company, 1978.
Terms emphasizing speech, hearing, and language diagnostic items for the therapist and clinician

Morris, D. W. H. (1988). *A dictionary of speech therapy.* London, UK: Taylor and Francis.
Terms related to treatment and measurement in speech correction

Urdang, L. (Ed.). (1988). *The dictionary of advertising.* Lincolnwood, IL: NTC Business Books.
Emphasis on layout, public relations, art design, and advertising jargon

Weiner, R. (1990). *Webster's new world dictionary of media and communications.* New York: Webster's New World.
Coverage of technical terms in journalism and telecommunications

Ellmore, R. T. (1991). *NTC's mass media dictionary.* Lincolnwood, IL: National Textbook.
Terms in journalism and telecommunications

Handbooks

Berger, C. R., & Chaffee, S. H. (Eds.). (1987). *Handbook of communication science.* Newbury Park, CA: Sage.
Twenty-eight chapters with essays covering major aspects of social science communication research

Arnold, C. C., & Bowers, J. W. (Eds.). (1984). *Handbook of rhetorical and communication theory.* Boston: Allyn and Bacon.
Fourteen topics covered of interest to general communication theory and rhetorical studies

Tardy, C. H. (Ed.). (1988). *A handbook for the study of human communication: Methods and instruments for observing, measuring and assessing communication processes.* Norwood, NJ: Ablex Publishing Corp.
Fifteen measurement tools in communication described and their validity discussed

Communication yearbook, (1977–). Newbury Park, CA: Sage.
Essays and top papers of each division of the International Communication Association

Mass communication review yearbook (1980 through 1987). Newbury Park, CA: Sage.
Studies on mass communication and applied areas (no longer published)

Gerbner, G., & Siefert, M. (Eds.). (1984). *World communications: A handbook.* New York: Longman.
Reviews of communication technology globally, emphasizing international development

World media handbook. (1990). New York: United Nations.
Listings of mass media publications and associations for each nation with emphasis on those hosting UN centers

TABLE 3.1—*Continued*

Source	Sources for Information Comment

Handbooks—Continued

Rosen, P. T. (Ed.). (1988). *International handbook of broadcasting systems.* New York: Greenwood Press.	Descriptions of global systems of radio and TV broadcasting
Travis, L. (Ed.). (1971). *The handbook of speech pathology and audiology.* New York: Appleton-Century-Crofts.	A classic work detailing contributions in speech and hearing science
Lindzey, G., & Aronson, E. (Eds.). (1985). *The handbook of social psychology,* 3rd ed. New York: Random House. (2 vols.)	Syntheses of theory and research on areas in social psychology, often communication related
Nimmo, D. D., & Sanders, K. R. (Eds.). (1981). *Handbook of political communication.* Beverly Hills: Sage.	First handbook on subject with primary emphasis on U.S. politics
Swanson, D. L., & Nimmo, D. (Eds.). (1990). *New directions on political communication.* Newbury Park, CA: Sage.	Companion to 1981 handbook; includes bibliography of post-1981 materials
Jablin, F. M., Putnam, L. L., Karlene, H. R., & Porter, L. W. (Eds.). (1987) *Handbook of organizational communication: An interdisciplinary perspective.* Newbury Park, CA: Sage.	Chapters on organizational communication contexts, structures, issues, and processes across academic fields
Goldhaber, G., & Barnett, G. A. (Eds.). (1988). *Handbook of organizational communication.* Norwood, NJ: Ablex Publishing Corp.	Reviews of methods and application areas in organizational communication
Knapp, M. L., & Miller, G. R. (Eds.). (1985). *Handbook of interpersonal communication.* Newbury Park, CA: Sage.	Emphasis on reviews of interpersonal communication since the 1960s
Asante, M. K., & Gudykunst, W. B. (Eds.). (1989). *Handbook of international and intercultural communication.* Newbury Park, CA: Sage.	Essays on intercultural and international communication issues
International and intercultural communication annual. (1974–). Newbury Park, CA: Sage.	Articles, research summary essays, and book reviews
Free speech yearbook. (1960–). Carbondale: Southern Illinois University Press.	Reviews of free press/free speech issues and case studies
Public relations research annual. (1989–). Hillsdale, NJ: Lawrence Erlbaum.	Original research in public relations and publicity
Isaac, S., & Michael, W. B. (Eds.). (1981). *Handbook in research and evaluation,* 2nd ed. San Diego: EdITS.	Designs and critical standards for evaluating research

out what the research really discovered. Furthermore, by browsing through journals published shortly after the original articles, you can tell if serious objections and reactions were raised to them.

The When: Guiding Yourself with the Research Outline

use of a planning outline

Sometimes new students hear horror stories from other students about long hours spent in the library. The stories tell more about the inefficiency of the students than of the use of resource materials. The easiest way to use time effectively is to create a research planning outline—a very efficient way to help you complete your research. Because we recommend this method so strongly, we will tell you how to use a research planning outline and later we will show you an actual search completed with one. Box 3.1 shows a research planning outline for a paper on the credibility of newspaper sources. Here's how to put one together:

- Divide a large piece of paper into three columns (you may wish to turn a sheet of paper sideways to have enough room).
- Title the first column ''Paper Outline,'' title the second column ''Research Items,'' and title the third column ''Sources to Check.''
- In the column labeled ''Paper Outline'' put together a very rough outline of the paper or assignment you plan to write. You cannot know every detail of the paper, of course, but you know that *any* paper must define terms and summarize research issues somewhere along the way. Make sure to leave plenty of space so you can add new items if necessary.
- In the column labeled ''Research Items'' list the information you need to have to write each section of the paper.
- In the third column labeled ''Sources to Check'' list library sources to review. The sources identified in table 3.1 can be useful resources to examine early in your work. The last part of this chapter on key library tools introduces some major sources that you can review to complete the third column.

At the library, start at the top of your outline and work your way through. Instead of spending hours looking for random information, you can find materials in an orderly fashion without getting sidetracked into interesting but pointless areas. It may seem obvious that you should plan your time efficiently by making some notes, but the next time you visit a library watch the other students. You won't see many people who have organized their time. Some of them may look very frustrated. They will spend more time than you in the library—but they will have less to show for it. Plan your time, and you will have all you need.

Setting limits on the scope of your research is critical before you look for resources. If you have an exhaustive literature review for which a month's preparation time is provided, you may set limits very broadly. If you have only a week to complete a review of chief definitions, you may need to limit your examination to key books, specialized dictionaries, ''think piece'' articles, and articles that have summarized related research.

■

BOX 3.1

PAPER OUTLINE:	RESEARCH ITEMS:	SOURCES TO CHECK:
Credibility of Newspaper Sources		
I. Definitions		
A. Source credibility →	Definition of source credibility →	Handbooks of Communication, Mass Communication
	(check other terms: ethos, prestige) →	Books: persuasion Dictionaries: *Longman of Psych* and *Mass Communication*
B. Kinds of Source → Credibility	Dimensions of Credibility (Check measurement methods) →	Articles: Abstracts: *Psychological Abstracts, Journalism Abstracts, Index to Journals in Communication Studies through 1990*
II. Credibility Research in Newspapers		
A. Impact of → Newspaper Credibility	Studies of credibility by → readers (not TV or radio studies)	Unpublished work, *Resources in Education*
B. Levels of → Credibility of Different Newspapers	Surveys of credibility → ratings of readership pool	Unpublished work, *Resources in Education*

■

THE HOW: MANAGING RESEARCH MATERIALS

Learning from experience is an effective way to develop research skills, but it is very inefficient. Thus, it would be a good idea to develop some survival skills to *prepare* for your first literature searches.

Techniques for Bibliographic Research

Work in the library is dominated by assembling bibliographic materials of one sort or another. You must remain flexible to find and record information as it comes your way.

Mastering the Library

Each library has some unique qualities. Thus, it is a good idea to tour your local library and find out its approaches. You will find that the person at the reference desk is ready and willing to help you. Do not ask the librarian how to read an index or

learning local library qualities

SPECIAL DISCUSSION 3–1
Ten Commandments of Library Use

Librarians can be very helpful, but many students do not know how to work with them. "The most common complaint heard among reference librarians about their work is that few people know how to ask reference questions" (Katz, 1982, p. 16). Two librarians (Gardner & Zelevansky, 1975) suggested these ten commandments:

    I. Thou shalt be prepared with a valid, logical and/or reasonable query and not an inchoate question, without form and void.

    II. Thou shalt request all information in the beginning.

    III. Thou shalt be honest and true with thy librarian in revelation of what thou seekest, much as thou wouldst not hold back symptoms from thy physician.

    IV. Thou shalt exhibit the patience of Job in waiting at the librarian's desk (or at the other end of the telephone) so that when the answer to thy query is divined, the search shall not have been in vain.

    V. Thou shalt express thine appreciation of labor well done by thy librarian through written testimony to his/her supervisor.

    VI. Thou shalt indeed not designate the "Source," but rather utter clearly that which is sought.

    VII. Thou shalt not require thy librarian to be accountable for that which is not yet published.

    VIII. Thou shalt not require thy librarian to interpret data in chapter and verse.

    IX. Thou shalt not scorn a wise referral, for surely any sage counsel cannot lead thee far astray and may indeed bear fruit.

    X. Thou shalt not steal.

Reprinted from *Special Libraries*, v. 66, no. 7 (July 1975), p. 326. © by Special Libraries Association.

---

how to do a project you have been assigned. This book and your instructor are supposed to teach you that. Remember, you will want the library people to help you if you run into a special problem—don't burn them out with questions you can get answered in class or by reading this book. You soon will grow comfortable with the layout of things and will be able to make library searches with ease.

Tactical Skills in Bibliographic Research

To do effective bibliographic research you need to learn some basic skills:

importance of brevity

- Take notes in brief form. Your working notes or cards (containing quotations and summary information) should be selective and to the point. Long quotations or lists of statistics often can be summarized since you rarely will report such specifics in your projects.

- Practice good note-taking skills. Since examining information requires you to summarize materials, it is vital to take notes accurately. Most people either take too many notes or too few. You should get the main ideas first. Then, you may add appropriate details or explanations.

  importance of good note-taking skills

- Follow proper reference form. In different branches of communication, the proper citations follow the *MLA Handbook for Writers of Research Papers* (3d Ed.), or the *Publication Manual of the American Psychological Association* (3d Ed.). By the late 1980s nearly all communication journals accepted the latter proper quotation and reference form style sheet (hence, this book uses it). All materials should be quoted fully and in context. You may wish to photocopy key pages just to be safe. If other sources are referenced in quoted material, you must obtain full citations for them. Though you should avoid editing others' words, if a portion of a quotation must be omitted, ellipses (. . .) should be put in its place. If words or phrases must be added to make a statement clear, the additions should be placed within brackets [ ]. If you notice a grammatical or spelling error, leave the words as in the original statement and follow the offending passage with the word *sic* within brackets (*sic* means "thus" or "so" in Latin).

  proper quotaton and reference form

- *Avoiding inadvertent plagiarism.* **Plagiarism** is "the act of using another person's ideas or expressions in your writing without acknowledging the source" (Gibaldi & Achtert, 1988, p. 20). Most students realize that it is plagiarism to copy others' words without giving credit. But it also is plagiarism to express another person's *ideas* without giving credit. Penalties for using uncredited sources are severe and may include academic punishment, failing grades, or expulsion. There is an obvious way to avoid plagiarism: document everything except your unique interpretations and comments regarding research literature. If you make a statement you think is common knowledge, think again. What is "common knowledge" may be a matter of opinion. So, it makes sense to back up what you say with source materials—otherwise, omit the uncredited material.

  plagiarism defined

Library Research Strategies

Getting started in the library can be invigorating. Plunge in with your research issues list, note cards, and plenty of writing materials. But plunge in with a strategy to guide you. Look at your research outline sheet. Then go wherever you need to trace down that information. Two major library research strategies can help give you a starting place.

selecting a library search strategy

General to Specific

Starting with general sources and then finding leads to specific sources is useful when you do not have an extensive background on the subject. At the beginning of your research career, that condition will occur most often. Furthermore, if the topic is fairly broad, you may wish to start with the general to specific method, just to make sure that you do not omit important theoretical foundations of the work. If you do not know enough to be sure about which strategy to use, this one is for you.

general to specific strategy

SPECIAL DISCUSSION 3–2
Bibliographic Research Records: Elements of a Bibliographic Card

It is helpful to record key information on note cards. Box 3.2 shows such a card. In fact, you should have some blank 4×6 cards before you enter the library (you could use larger cards, of course, but don't use 3 × 5 cards—they are just too small to use flexibly). As you go through resource materials, keep track of your work by completing full bibliographic cards. If you have a laptop computer, you may have software to record note cards on disk for electronic sorting later. Regardless of the tools you use, the following are some things that should be on all bibliographic cards:

BOX 3.2

Organization Support Required to Stop Sex Harassment

Bingham, Shereen G. "Communication Strategies for Managing Sexual Harassment in Organizations: Understanding Message Options and their Effects." *Journal of Applied Communication Research,* 19 (1991): 88–115.

"Successful management of sexual harassment by individuals is likely to be enhanced when appropriate and easily accessed support from the organization is in place." (p. 110.)

Study was a literature review of sex harassment and compliance gaining communication strategies that might halt it.

- Title. A newspaper-type headline title that summarizes information on the card and helps with filing material. Record only one thought on each card—to continue material, simply start another card.
- Citation. Use full citations in proper bibliographic form. Don't abbreviate this part since it will prove very time-consuming later (you may have multiple works from the same authors, or from authors who share the same last name, which you will have to sort out later).
- Quotation or Abstract: The Two Types of Bibliographic Cards. If you use direct quotations, place them within quotation marks. If materials refer to other sources, include the original citations on your note card (you will want to check on exact wording by going to the original source later). Using abstracts (summaries in your own words) of methods, findings, and conclusions will help you keep track of all sources you examine so that you do not visit the same sources repeatedly. Additionally, using cards allows you to compare recent work on a subject with previous thinking.

SPECIAL DISCUSSION 3–2
(Continued)

- Commentary. Add brief comments of your own about the work (placed within brackets to emphasize that they are not claims of the author of the original work). Such comments are also called **annotations** and offer additional explanations, evaluations, or criticisms to help understand the material.

After collecting information on cards, you may sort them by key topics. You can start with the general questions listed in this chapter:

- definitions of key concepts and variables
- ways concepts and variables have been measured and studied
- general summary statements about the subject
- the classic research studies in the field
- problems that researchers have struggled to solve
- research that shows what methods to use
- research that shows what mistakes to avoid

If you notice a void in any category, let that category be the object of a brief, intensive visit to the library. You can insert dividers between sections (do not buy dividers that have printed letters on them—you are filing information by topics, not by the alphabet). If you do an exhaustive literature search you might want to compile a master "key" of any subdivisions. Of course, you should review your bibliography cards frequently to keep current on the status of your inquiry. Curiously, students who "do not have time" to put together bibliography cards nearly always need *more* time to complete projects than students who use this valuable tool.

Start your research with general textbooks, handbooks, yearbooks, and specialized encyclopedias. Sometimes students do not know what textbooks to grab. There is a simple method. Look at your problem and ask yourself the title of the class in which people usually study such a subject. Textbook publishers prefer using textbook titles that reflect names of courses for which they are intended. Write down keywords from the course title. Then, look up the books whose titles include those keywords. **Keywords** are terms under which information about the topic may be found. Hence, if you are interested in looking at communication styles of leaders in business, you may rightly think that this topic usually is covered in courses on organizational communication, business and professional communication, and management communication. Look up a few books to find their location in the library. Then, browse through them (starting at the index sections) to select the most useful sources.

keywords defined

Though general sources may not answer your research questions directly, start with them, and copy down relevant statements. Most important, write down references the authors used in *their* general surveys. After looking at a handful of textbooks, you probably will have enough specific references to know where to go for further detailed information. Try to choose sources that have the most promising sounding titles. It is fairly easy to tell whether an article is worth reading since most scholarly articles have boring yet descriptive titles. Though there are exceptions, standard phrases used in titles (or subtitles) can tell you a lot about the article. For instance, the following phrases often reveal what to expect:

- ''A Case Study of . . .'' (translation: a situation examined in detail)
- ''An Experimental Study of . . .'' (translation: a quantitative study—in the field or laboratory—in which variables were manipulated under controlled settings)
- ''A Survey of . . .'' (translation: a quantitative study in which an area is characterized without any manipulation of variables)
- ''Theories of . . .'' (translation: a review and critique of theories or orientations)
- ''Measurement of . . .'' (translation: a review/critique; or suggestions for a new method to measure a construct)
- ''On the Meaning of . . .'' (translation: a review/critique of major approaches to define a concept)
- ''A Content Analysis of . . .'' (translation: a quantitative analysis of some examples of communication)
- ''A (Burkean, Aristotelian, Fantasy Theme, etc.) Analysis of . . .'' (translation: a rhetorical critique of a piece of communication, movement, or source of communication)
- *Foundations of* . . . (translation: usually books covering the broad domain of a subject)
- *Handbook of* . . . (translation: a book containing essays and brief guides to literature and methods in an area of study)
- *A Theory of* . . . (translation: a book or an article advancing a theory or fundamental orientation)

Most historical studies do not identify the method of inquiry. Instead, the titles just announce the object of the historical inquiry. Look at references you find in your searches to tell what articles may be most relevant. Do not just read citations. Consider what they are about.

Specific to General

Sometimes you may read an article or essay that peaks your interest. Perhaps you have asked your instructors about a specific topic. You may have received a reference to help you get started. You can begin with these specific sources and write down the citations to related research and theory identified in them. Then you may repeat the process with the new sources. Soon, information ''snowballs'' as one reference leads to others.

You will find that different articles often reference the same ''classic'' research or theories. You will want to take the time to note such patterns across studies. You can also extend the search by using other abstracts and citation indices. This search method is effective when you have a specific starting piece or author name and are interested primarily in unearthing other general findings. Furthermore, the method can be helpful when you are uncertain about the most common key words used to index the research.

THE WHERE: KEY LIBRARY TOOLS

Entire books have been written about library resources (e.g., Rubin, Rubin & Piele, 1990; Beasley, 1988; Paradis, 1966) and you probably already know how to find general materials. But the best training to find scholarly research materials is brief guidance, followed by library experience. Rather than cover such matters exhaustively, we will guide you to *some* of the most helpful tools for communication studies. Library tools really boil down to two forms, hierarchical systems and key word systems.

Hierarchical Systems for Books and Collections

Hierarchical systems of filing tell you where common material is found—in the same location in the library. Such things as card catalogs and special collections files are examples of these hierarchical guides. These guides help you find books, handbooks, and other collections. **hierarchical systems**

You may remember large wooden card files listing the books possessed by libraries. They are only a memory now. By 1989 two-thirds of college libraries had replaced the card files with some form of computerized catalog (H. Smith, 1991, p. 61). Of the many computerized library systems, the Online Public Access Catalog (O.P.A.C.) has been adopted in most libraries. Listings are available on book titles, names of authors, or subjects. A typical listing for such a search item appears in figure 3.1. You may wish to read all the listings in a given subject heading to select the most recent books available, just to make sure that you do not miss recent contributions. You will also want to notice any **subject tracings** or keywords that indicate other subject headings under which the book is listed. You can use these headings if you reach a dead end with your current keywords. **systems of book catalogs**

subject tracings identified

To identify the call numbers of the works relevant to your topic, you will use one of two major systems currently in use. The Dewey Decimal System was invented by Melvil Dewey in 1873 to help organize the library at Amherst College when he was an undergraduate student there (see Paradis, 1966, p. 4; Best, 1981, pp. 313–315). The method became dominant in public libraries, and many college libraries use it today. Yet, it became difficult to add new specialized topics gracefully. Over time, many libraries adopted the Library of Congress method, which was first developed by Herbert Putnam pursuant to an 1880 act of Congress. The Library of Congress classification is used in research libraries and government depositories (libraries that regularly receive copies of federal government documents). (See table 3.2.) **the Dewey Decimal System**

the Library of Congress method

Services are available that index critiques of new books. For trade publications—books that are likely to be sold at the major commercial bookstores—some guides may be worth checking, depending on your topic. *Book Review Digest* presents summaries and critiques, and the *Book Review Index* lists the places where book reviews have been published. For speech and hearing scientists, the *Technical Book Review Index* can be particularly valuable. For rhetorical studies and film and **indices and guides to books**

FIGURE 3.1
Sample Catalog
Listing

	TITLE	Handbook of communication science / editors, Charles R. Berger & Steven H. Chaffee.
1——	IMPRINT	Beverly Hills: Sage Publications, c1987.
2——	DESCRIPT	946 p.
3——	SUBJECT	Communication.
	ALT AUTHOR	Berger, Charles R.
		Chaffee, Steven H.
4——	NOTE	Includes bibliographies and indexes.
5——	ISBN	0803921993 :

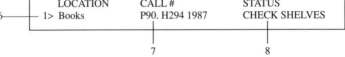

	LOCATION	CALL #	STATUS
6——— 1>	Books	P90. H294 1987	CHECK SHELVES
	7		8

NOTES: This item was taken from the OPAC listing at the California State University, Fullerton Main Library.

1. The imprint contains information necessary for a citation including the city of publication, the publisher, and the date (the listing is in error; the city of publication was Newbury Park, CA at the time this book was published, as the book's title page clearly stated).*
2. The book is described as 946 pages long including indices and author biographies.
3. Since the subject matter was communication, you may use this keyword to browse other related topics.
4. Features of the book to help readers use it.
5. ISBN (International Standard Book Number) serial number assigned by book numbering agencies such as R. R. Bowker Co. in the United States.
6. Location of each copy of the book in the library. Copy number one is listed among the other ordinary books of the library.
7. The call number is the code number for the book and, in this case, follows the Library of Congress classification system.
8. The book is located on the shelves and is not checked out, nor in the reference room, overdue, on hold, or the like.

*There is a lesson for us in this example. When doing original library work, it is important to look at the books directly to check the details, rather than assuming (sometimes in error) that the catalog listing is correct.

mass media criticism, the *Index to Book Reviews in the Humanities* provides a guide to 685 related publications. In mass communication, the guides tend to be narrow and fairly dated. Among the most popular has been *Basic Books in the Mass Media,* edited by Eleanor Blum and covering selected books through the late 1970s.

Keyword–Based Systems

use of index and abstract sources

Keyword–based systems, such as *Psychological Abstracts* and *Communication Abstracts,* send you to different locations in the library to find articles and papers. The major guides to these materials are known as indices and abstracts. There are two major categories of such keyword guides to books and articles—computerized systems and hardcopy systems—which simply list the same materials in different form.

TABLE 3.2 Dewey Decimal System and Library of Congress Classifications with Emphasis on Categories for the Communication Field

Dewey Decimal System		Library of Congress	
000	General Works:	A	General Works
		B	Philosophy, Psychology, Religion
	070 Journalism	B	Philosophy (General)
		BC	Logic
100	Philosophy and Related Fields	BF	Psychology (for social psychology, see HM) including communication theory
	120 Epistemology, Causation, Humankind	BH	Aesthetics
		BJ	Ethics
	140 Specific Philosophic Systems	C	History
	150 Psychology	D	World History
	160 Logic	E, F	American History
	170 Ethics	G	Geography, Anthropology
		H	Social Science
200	Religion	H	Social Science (General)
		HA	Statistics
300	Social Sciences	HE	Transportation and Communication (telecommunication 7601–8688; radio and television 8689–8700)
	310 Statistics		
	340 Law	HF	Commerce (business administration and personnel management 5001–5549; advertising 5801–6191)
	350 Public Administration		
	370 Education		

Computer Searches and CD-ROM Sources

The computer age has come to most libraries. Some of the early awkwardness in the computer systems has been overcome, and you will find electronic searches fairly simple tasks.

Databases. Communication databases have made quick work of literature searches. Two forms of computerized materials are available, although additional forms are in the offing at the time this book is written. For students, the cheapest and easiest systems use **CD-ROM** form, translated as "Compact Disc—Read Only Memory." These CDs are the same sorts of discs that are found in music stores and in stereo sets. But instead of containing music in digital form, they contain databases that can be searched rapidly. They are called "Read Only Memory" because you cannot record onto them, you can only read from them. The CD-ROM systems run on personal computers in the library or on networks linked to terminals ordinarily used to find books in the library. After finding references, you can decide which citations, summaries, or texts you wish to have printed or stored on discs.

CD-ROM records described

CD-ROMs contain indices and directories of sources. Thus, you may treat them as highly efficient substitutes for hauling around many volumes of abstracts and indices. Once you use these systems, you will wonder why anyone would ever

TABLE 3.2—*Continued*

Dewey Decimal System	Library of Congress
400 Language	HM Sociology (social psychology, 251–291)
	HQ Social groups (family and marriage 503–1064)
410 Linguistics	HS Societies
420 English Languages	HT Communities, Classes, Races
500 Pure Sciences	K Law
	L Education
600 Technology (Applied Sciences)	M Music
610 Medical Sciences (including	N Fine Arts
speech and hearing disorders	P Language and Literature
616.85)	P Philology and Linguistics (general)
	PE English
620 Engineering	PN Literature (drama 1600–3299; oratory, speech
650 Management and Auxiliary	communication, debating, recitations 4001–4355; journalism,
Services	communication law, practical journalism, amateur
	journalism, by region or country 4699–5650)
700 Arts and Recreation	Q Science
800 Literature	R Medicine
900 History	RC Internal Medicine (stuttering, speech correction, and
	therapies 423–430)
	RF Otorhinolaryngology
	S Agriculture
	T Technology
	U Military Science
	V Naval Science
	Z Library Science—Bibliography

use any other methods. There are limits, of course. First, for materials before 1980, you may have to use hard copy versions. Second, many libraries are still developing adequate subscriptions to CD-ROM services and some subjects may not yet be supported locally. *Dialog* has become the most popular system and includes nearly all communication journals and unpublished papers (the latter listed with ERIC, Education Resources Information Clearinghouse). The on-line help and master keyword lists help you find sources rapidly.

use of on-line databases
On-line database systems connect the researcher with a central computer and can be used to search for books, articles, and reports on key topics. The on-line search usually results in listing large numbers of entries in bibliographic format. Since on-line searches have been around for some time, there are many of them. Some require that you work through your local library, but others require only that you have a computer that can be connected to a telephone line. Table 3.3 lists some of the major database search systems. You should keep in mind, however, that unlike CD-ROM systems, which are

TABLE 3.3 Computer Search Systems

Forms of Materials	Names of System	Content and Commentary	Useful For
Full Text Listings			
	NEXIS	Information from newspaper sources	Mass media, public relations, and historical background
	VU/TEXT	Information primarily from newspapers emphasizing business issues; also has ABI/INFORM materials	Organizational communication, public relations, and mass media
	LEXIS	Legal research	Communication and the law, mass communication law
	Magazine ASAP	Information from popular magazines indexed in *Magazine Index*	Mass communication and historical background
	Trade and Industry ASA	Information from *Trade and Industry Index*	Organizational communication and public relations
	Mead Data Central	Business-related information public relations	Organizational communication
Other Computerized Systems of Existing Hardcopy Index Services			
	BRS/AfterDark	Highly popular private service; provides non-daytime access to multiple indices, including PsychINFO, ERIC, ABI/INFORM, and many others useful in communication	Social sciences, popular subjects, and access to major databases
	Linguistics and Language Behavior Abstracts	Same as *Linguistics and Language Behavior Abstracts*	Speech and hearing science
	CIS/Index	Same as CIS/Index	Rhetoric and public address, mass communication
	Dissertation Abstracts Online	Same as *Dissertation Abstracts*	All fields
	ERIC	Same as *Resources in Education* and *Current Index to Journals in Education*	Most social science subfields in education and communication
	Legal Resource Index	*Legal Resource Index*	Communication and the law, mass communication law
	National Newspaper Index	*National Newspaper Index*	Mass media, historical background
	PsychINFO	*Psychological Abstracts*	Social sciences
	Social Sciences Index	*Social Science Index*	Social sciences

TABLE 3.3—*Continued*

Forms of Materials	Names of System	Content and Commentary	Useful For
Other Systems			
	SciSearch	*Science Citation Index*	Speech and hearing science
	Social SciSearch	*Social Sciences Citation Index*	Social sciences
	Sociological Abstracts	*Sociological Abstracts*	Social sciences, communication theory, mass communication
	Dialog	World's largest information retrieval system developed by Lockheed Corporation—this one is the great grandaddy of all the others (*Dialog* also operates *Knowledge Index*)	Full listing of materials in all fields
	ABI/INFORM	Articles and abstracts in business and management	Organizational communication and public relations
	Management Contents	Abtracts of periodicals	Organizational communication materials in business and public relations
	InfoTrac	Broad databases including book reviews and articles	Communication theory, mass communication, rhetoric, and organizational communication
	Bibliographic Retrieval Services	Wide range of reference databases	Social sciences, mass communication, organizational communication
	System Development Corporation	Review of a large number of sources in the broad sciences	Social and natural sciences
	CompuServe Information Service	News retrieval from newspapers and wire services, financial information, and corporate profiles	Mass communication, historical background and organizational communication
	Knowledge Index	Evening and weekend access to databases on almost every subject including over four million books, articles, convention papers, government documents, and technical reports	Full range of natural and social sciences as well as popular periodicals
	Dow Jones News/Retrieval Service	Information from the *Wall Street Journal, Barron's,* and the *Dow Jones News Wire* beginning in 1979	Organizational communication and financial background
	The Source	Specialized electronic bulletin boards on over 75 topics, UPI News Service, stocks, bonds, travel services	Organizational communication and public relations

John C. Reinard, *Foundations of Argument: Effective Communications for Critical Thinking.* Dubuque, IA: Wm. C. Brown Communications, Inc. Reprinted with permission.

free to library users, firms charge for on-line services, usually by the number of entries the search produces. Thus, you must plan these searches carefully.

Using Keywords   The following steps can make learning to use key words fairly simple.

1. Select keywords from the problem statement. Pause before you look at electronic indices to jot down the keywords that describe topics you are investigating. Some common sense is required. If you are looking for information about the impact of televising a speech on the speaker's credibility, you may list such words as ''television,'' ''speeches,'' and ''credibility.'' *Dialog* includes automatic prompts so that you can use the precise vocabulary of the system. In on-line searches, using very broad terms might produce long lists of irrelevant materials—a waste of time for you and potentially costly as well.

    1. find keywords

2. Develop alternative lists of descriptor terms. Unless you have a lot of experience researching a topic, your initial keywords may not be the same ones used by the index service staffs. You may need to think creatively. For instance, for many years the *Education Index* listed studies of ''communication apprehension'' under the subject heading ''bashfulness.'' You need to prepare synonyms in case the first keywords do not work for you. Fortunately, many indexing services have guides to help you in selecting keywords, and CD-ROM systems have automatic prompts.

    2. finding alternative keywords

3. Combine keywords. In an on-line search you need to see if keywords (tested individually by you to make sure that they are meaningful in the system) can be combined. That is, instead of asking for one topic at a time, you might combine keywords. For instance, you might use the three keywords ''television,'' ''speeches,'' and ''source credibility'' (the latter actually is two keywords, but it serves as one for us). The computer system would start by looking for all the listings on ''television.'' Then, the system would subdivide the list to identify citations that also have the keyword ''speeches.'' Finally, it would make a pass for listings that also contained the term ''credibility.'' Eventually, the system would produce a very focused list.

    3. combining keywords

4. Undertake on-line activity. During the search, the computer will prompt you with questions and will respond to your input. Since the systems listed in table 3.3 are a bit different from each other, we will not take the time to explain the rules for one or two favorite systems. But you will find that the prompting systems are very extensive and are easy to use. You may wish to change databases and search different materials. Though it is admittedly a bother, it is vital to record (preferably on your research outline) things you have searched and keywords you have used. Without such a record, you may find yourself examining the same materials more than once.

    4. undertaking on-line activity

In many cases you may wish to have the list of abstracts, citations, and references printed out or ''downloaded'' to a disk of your own. Make sure that facilities are set up for you when you request these services. It is frustrating to ''log off'' and then find that no hardcopy system was attached. Take the time to consult with your local librarian so you understand in advance the options that are available to you.

Indices and Abstracts

use of index and abstract sources

Though computerized systems have collected indices and abstracts, you may have to rely on hard copy volumes to find some sources. An index lists locations of resource materials and articles. On the other hand, an abstract also provides a brief summary of the work. Since indices and abstracts are often found in companion reference works, we can describe them together here. Regrettably, no single hard-copy index covers the breadth of our field. So, you may wish to check different sources to find citations to the most valuable articles. Certainly, among the first you may wish to reference is the *Index to Journals in Communication Studies Through 1990,* edited by Ronald J. Matlon and Sylvia P. Ortiz (1992). The current edition covers major communication journals, excluding only those in speech and hearing science, public relations, and management communication. Table 3.4 lists major indices and abstracts along with brief descriptions. Since these sources are organized differently from each other, you will need to spend a moment or two (it doesn't take long) to find out how each guide is arranged. Once you are comfortable with the major guides for your area, you will be surprised how easy it is to find information.

Sometimes you may want to look at popular press treatments, such as when you need to find reactions to speakers or communication trends. The indices to nonscholarly literature have been omitted from the tables in this chapter. Surely the most popular of these sources is the *Reader's Guide to Periodical Literature,* an index that includes more than 130 general public interest magazines. For magazines published a very long time ago, you can check *Poole's Index to Periodical Literature, 1802–1906* and the *Nineteenth Century Reader's Guide to Periodical Literature 1890–1899.* For popular sources outside the United States, you might want to review the *Canadian Index* or the *Subject Index to Periodicals* (for British periodicals). Major newspapers also index their publications. Similar guides can be found to government documents, regulations, and reports. Your local librarian can direct you to them.

guides to special resources

Suppose you wonder if there is any commentary or criticism of a scholarly work. The *Social Science Citation Index* and the *Science Citation Index* list the articles that have cited a particular reference. Sometimes the references are in passing, but sometimes the citations indicate extended critiques.

Special bibliographies can also help you find useful materials on many topics. Some of the most useful include the following:

Bibliographic Index. Lists publications containing at least fifty references on a subject (useful for finding reviews of literature).

Mass Media Bibliography: An Annotated, Selected List of Books and Journals for Reference and Research (edited by Eleanor Blum and F. Wilhoit, 2d ed., Urbana: University of Illinois Press, 1990). Includes over two thousand entries in applied areas of mass communication and broadcasting.

Global Guide to Media and Communications (edited by John A. Lent, Munchen, Germany: Saur, (1987). Bibliography of books, dissertations, articles, and monographs on mass media of specific countries or regions.

TABLE 3.4 Indices and Abstracts to Scholarship in Communication for Major Divisions of the Field

Source	Description	Useful For
Education Index	Journal articles, book reviews, and chapters in yearbooks	Communication theory, mass, rhetoric, and public address communication education
Social Science and Humanities Index (from 1974 divided into separate publications):	Publications within and outside the United States	
Humanities Index	Periodicals; reviews of books	Rhetoric, mass communication theory, journalism
Social Science Index	Periodicals in broad range of social science	Mass communication, communication theory, intercultural communication
Topicator	Unique titles in advertising, communication, and marketing	Mass communication, advertising
C.R.I.S.	Combined retrospective index set to journals in sociology 1895–1974	Communication theory, mass organizational communication, group processes
Canadian Education Index	Periodicals, books, pamphlets published in Canada	Speech and hearing science, communication education
Index to Doctoral Dissertations International (also found with Dissertation Abstracts; Comprehensive Dissertation Index 1861–1972)	All doctoral dissertations in the United States and Canada	All fields
Master's Abstracts	Master's theses across fields submitted by cooperating institutions (not as comprehensive as dissertation holdings)	All fields
Business Periodicals Index	120 periodicals in business related issues	Organizational communication
Index Medicus	Monthly reviews of medical journals	Speech and hearing science
Rehabilitation Literature	Material on physically handicapped people	Speech and hearing science
Resources in Education (formerly Research in Education)	Otherwise unpublished convention papers and reports; copies available on microfiche	All subject matters, but dominant in social sciences
Deafness, Speech and Hearing Abstracts	Listings and abstracts from 250 journals	Speech and hearing science

TABLE 3.4—*Continued*

Source	Description	Useful For
Psychological Abstracts	Summaries of research in psychology	Mass communication, communication theory, group processes, organizational communication
Sociological Abstracts	Summaries of research from over 1000 international journals	Mass communication, communication theory
Linguistics and Language Behavior Abstracts	International journals related to linguistics	Language, speech and hearing science
Journalism Abstracts	Dissertations and theses on journalism submitted by cooperating institutions	Mass communication, journalism
Communication Abstracts	21 communication subfields indexed and summarized	All aspects of communication except speech and hearing science
Current Contents: Social and Behavioral Sciences (previously Current Contents: Behavioral, Social & Educational Sciences)	Reproduces tables of contents of 1300 journals; articles from multi-authored books (other Current Contents available for other fields)	Communication theory, mass communication, organizational communication
International Indexes to Film & Television Periodicals	International listings of articles on television	Mass communication
Journal of Broadcasting: Author and Topic Index to Volume 1 through 25	Index of single journal from 1956 through 1981	Mass communication
Journalism Quarterly Cumulative Index	Index of single journals from 1924 through 1983	Journalism
Child Development Abstracts and Bibliography	Child development issues from 1927	Speech and hearing science
Index to Journals in Communication Studies through 1990	15 journals in communication, speech, rhetoric, and mass communication	Major areas of the field except speech and hearing science
Exceptional Child Education Resources	Journals in special education	Speech and hearing science

SPECIAL DISCUSSION 3–3
Using Legal Resource Materials

Materials in the law often must be examined to study mass communication law, legal communication, and freedom of speech. Though you may not be at a school with extensive collections in the law, you still are not far from a county law library, which you can use. It is helpful to understand legal citations. For instance, a law in the *United States Code,* may be cited as 12 U.S.C. § 724. The citation is read, "Title 12 of the *United States Code,* Section 724." The *U.S. Code Annotated* summarizes major laws, and the *U.S. Code Service* lists related court decisions, legislative history, and provides additional references in each category

Supreme Court decisions are identified as in *Roe v. Wade,* 410 U.S. 113 (1973). The case title lists the plaintiff and the defendant. The number following the title is the volume number of *U.S. Reports* in which the decision is located. The page number on which the decision begins is listed next. The date is placed in parentheses after the rest of the citation. The *Supreme Court Reporter* indexes cases with abstracts of legal issues raised in the case. *Lawyer's Edition of the U.S. Supreme Court Reports* provides a legal analysis and includes statements from the briefs and arguments actually made by the lawyers. As general collections, West's Digests are popular. They include the *General Digest* that summarizes cases and the *Federal Practice Digest* organized by topic areas.

Many guides can help you to find articles in the law. The *Index to Legal Periodicals* is the major guide to U.S. law journals, just as the *Index to Foreign Legal Periodicals and Collections of Essays* is the counterpart for law journals in foreign countries. The *Law Review Digest* provides bimonthly summaries of law journal articles, and the *Index to Periodical Articles Related to Law* covers sources other than law journals.

Journalism: A Guide to the Reference Literature (edited by Jo A. Cates, Englewood, CO: Libraries Unlimited, 1990). Selective bibliography of articles on broadcast and print journalism).

USING THE LIBRARY

Practical library searching involves confronting challenges. We should look at ways to manage our search to solve problems.

Conducting the Library Session

If you are armed with your library research planning outline, you can be highly efficient. Box 3.3 shows a diary of an actual search using the library search outline found in box 3.1. Based on initial thinking, the student was able to list some potential sources to examine. As you can see, the library session can be quite efficient when you use such a research planning outline. Without such a method, you are just treading water in the library. By the way, this search provided the student with all

■ _____

BOX 3.3

Diary of a Library Search Using the Research Outline Method

Using a research outline is recommended for library research. Now you will see how this method was used in an actual library search. This box shows a diary of the work during an actual library search in which the research outline found in box 3.1 was applied.

10:10 A.M. Entered library. Went to on-line system to find call numbers for Handbooks of *Communication* (P 90.H293), *Mass Communication* (not in library), *Mass Communication Review Yearbook* (P 87.M28 1987), books on persuasion (e.g., *Persuasion* by R. Bostrom: BF 637.P4 B6 1983), Longman Dictionaries of *Psychology* (BF 31.L66 1984—in reference room), and *Mass Media* (P 87.5 .L66 1982—reference room).

10:20 A.M. Went to stacks section P 90.H293. Found *Handbook of Communication* edited by Poole et al. in 1973 (OK for definitions). Looked up source credibility in index and on page 230 found definition of credibility as "believability" in chapter written by McGuire. Bibliography card prepared. Looked in *Mass Communication Review Yearbooks*—no discussions of definitions indicated in index. Quickly browsed shelf. Looked at *Handbook of Communication Science* (P 90.H294.1987) edited by Berger and Chaffee—checked index; no definition discussed but criticisms of factor analysis studies noted on pages 464–465 in chapter written by Gerald Miller. Made bibliographic note. Checked nearby series called *Progress in Communication Sciences*—no discussion of source credibility. Saw general communication books and looked in their indices. Mortensen's *Communication* (P 90. M65) had definition of credibility as "image of a source in any communication situation [p. 147]." Made bibliography card.

10:50 A.M. Went to stacks for persuasion books. Found Bostrom book. Whole chapter on credibility—covers kinds of source credibility and dimensions in simple language; decided to check it out. Other books defined credibility in same way as previously found definitions.

11:15 A.M. Went to reference room to find *Longman Dictionary of Psychology* (nothing) and *Longman Dictionary of Mass Communication* (nothing).

11:25 A.M. Went to reference area to find indices to articles. CD-ROM for *Dialog* available including all materials for *Psychological Abstracts, Journalism Abstracts,* and *Resources in Education* (among others). Used menu on computer to find all works on "source credibility"—118 listed. Used menu to request "source credibility" and "mass communication"—none listed. Went back to search for source credibility. Requested screen listing of bibliographic references. Entries listed one at a time by pressing "Page Down" key on keyboard. Read titles of entries looking for keywords. Found studies of credibility by newspaper readers, surveys of newspaper credibility (sometimes comparisons to TV credibility), and surveys of credibility ratings. Prepared bibliography cards on eight sources (two were unpublished sources listed in *Resources in Education*—library has these on microfiche next to the microfilm for newspapers—all numbers for the item

BOX 3.3

(Continued)

written down.) Found new conceptual articles (e.g., McCroskey and Young) and studies in newspaper credibility. Prepared bibliography cards on each source. Requested that the abstracts for these sources be listed on the screen to be sure the sources were the best to use). Given the number of abstracts, chose not to print out full text.

11:55 A.M. Went to lunch

12:45 P.M. Went to microfiche area to get two unpublished sources. Skimmed papers on microfiche reader. Made one bibliographic note on each article.

1:25 P.M. Went to journal holdings and found remaining articles. Photocopied McCroskey and Young article and 1987 article by Gaziano and McGrath in *Journalism Quarterly.* Made bibliographic cards on other sources.

1:55 P.M. Left.

Though the student may find that citations in the copied articles require returning to the library, the research effort is pretty much done at this point—all in fewer than three hours. This search did not require a return visit to the library until the next class assignment. If a library search outline plan had not been followed, who knows how long this student would have stayed in the library?

the information needed to construct a meaningful critical explication of a research area—and the paper got an "A."

Troubleshooting in the Library

For all the fascination libraries have for us—the collected wisdom of ages is just waiting for us—inexperienced people can become frustrated. We will consider some typical student complaints, along with some suggested solutions.

When the Source is Unavailable

Sometimes a key source is not available at your library (it happened in our example in box 3.3). The sources may have been checked out, the library may not own the resource, or the materials may have been lost or vandalized. There are two ways around this problem. You can use interlibrary loan programs. Every library has such a cooperative venture. At the interlibrary loan desk you can request other libraries to lend you the missing work. If an article is involved, other libraries often will send you a photocopy. Interlibrary loans are not as slow as often believed, but if you require instant information, you may need to seek another option. Another way around this problem involves reading other articles that offer some descriptions about the key source. By triangulating information from different sources, you may get an idea of what was done in the original piece. This method is dangerous, however, since

when sources are unavailable:

interlibrary loan

triangulating reports of research

writers are selective in describing others' work, and because secondary summaries may contain flaws. Furthermore, the method of triangulation is very, very time-consuming for the amount of benefit it produces.

When There is ''No Information on My Topic''

A word to the wise: do not say to your instructor, ''There is no information on my topic.'' Your instructor knows that somewhere, someone has said something *relevant* to your topic. Your *specific* research question may not have been answered yet (much to your credit, since you are an original thinker), but there is always something out there related to your topic. To find materials you should try the ''known to unknown'' search pattern. With this strategy, you take your research issue, such as the impact of teleconferencing on interpersonal attraction of group members, and then look at research into each concept separately. You might investigate the things that affect interpersonal attraction generally. Such material is *known*. But you may observe that there is little information about attraction in teleconferencing settings. This material remains *unknown*. One might decide from what is known generally to develop arguments about possible relationships that might exist between teleconferencing methods and attraction. By looking at the issue broadly, it is possible to unearth much valuable information.

use the known to unknown search strategy

When the Journals Are Missing

missing journals: using microforms and checking on changed journal names

Sometimes journals may not be on the shelves. Before panicking, find out if the library has microform copies. Sometimes journals are available but the names have been changed. For instance, if you chase down a citation (from another source) to a journal called *Communication Studies* for 1983, you may grow nervous when the listing of publications shows that the library has this journal only from 1989 forward. In reality, this journal was called the *Central States Speech Journal* until volume 40 in 1989, though the call number remained the same. Titles change often enough that you should not give up at first. Yet, if you find that journals truly are not available, you will need to contact interlibrary loan services for help.

When the Material Is Technical and Complex

dealing with very technical material: use specialized dictionaries

Research articles sometimes seem complicated and bewilderingly technical. Rather than get bogged down, you may wish to rely on some of the specialized dictionaries listed in table 3.1. Sometimes books and critiques are available to help you put some perspective on the matter. Most journal essays and articles place abstracts at the beginning of articles. These guides are good starting points to technical and complex materials. Begin by asking ''What was the purpose of the research?'' By doing so, you often can grasp extended background discussions. Then ask ''What method or reasoning was used to draw conclusions?'' Sometimes you may wish to outline these methods (briefly) in your own notes. Finally ask, ''What did the work find and conclude?'' Many times the conclusion is an afterthought, but sometimes it is the lion's share of the materials.

ask key questions

SUMMARY

Research uses past work to develop arguments. Argument is a process of advancing conclusions based on reasons and evidence. Past research guides us by (1) providing premises for argument (a premise is a statement in a logical argument that is the foundation for others drawn from it); (2) giving evidence for argument claims; (3) balancing reliance on authority and empirical data. The "Einstein syndrome" occurs when misguided researchers fail to connect what has been learned from a new "sudden breakthrough" and, thus, do not learn from the successes of others.

Some of the most obvious things to seek in library encounters are definitions of key concepts and variables; ways concepts and variables have been measured and studied; summary statements that people make about a subject; classic research studies on a subject (the studies that all the textbooks seem to reference); research that shows what methods to use; research that shows what mistakes to avoid. Aside from looking at textbooks and articles, you should examine encyclopedias, specialized dictionaries, and handbooks and annual reviews.

You should use a research outline. To manage research materials, you should observe sound bibliographic techniques. First, you must master the library by learning its unique qualities. Second, you should practice tactical skills in bibliographic research, including taking notes in brief form; practicing good note-taking skills; following proper reference form; avoiding inadvertent plagiarism ("the act of using another person's ideas or expressions in your writing without acknowledging the source").

There are two major library research strategies. The general to specific approach starts with general sources to find leads to specific sources.

Scholarly article titles reveal whether an article is worth reading since they have descriptive titles that often use standard phrases. Second, the specific to general method begins with specific sources to obtain citations to related research and theory.

Hierarchical systems reveal where common material is found—in the same location in the library. Keyword based systems send you to different locations in the library to find articles and papers. CD-ROMs contain indices and directories of sources. On-line database systems are used to search for books, articles, and reports. Steps in the process of an on-line search include selecting keywords from the problem statement (keywords are terms under which information about the topic may be found); developing alternative lists of descriptor terms; combining keywords; and undertaking on-line activity. An index lists locations of resource materials and articles, whereas an abstract also provides a brief summary. Since no single hardcopy index covers the entire wealth of our field, you may wish to check different sources to find citations to the most valuable articles.

Using the library includes managing the actual conduct of the library session. Troubleshooting the library is necessary to avoid difficulties: (1) when a source is unavailable you may use interlibrary loans or (less advised) triangulate information from secondary descriptions; (2) when there seems to be no information on your topic, you should use the "known to unknown" search pattern; (3) when the journals are missing, you should check microform copies, check for name changes, or contact interlibrary loan services; (4) when the material is technical and complex, you may rely on resource tools, interpretations from books, and critiques and abstracts.

TERMS FOR REVIEW

premise
argument
Einstein syndrome
plagiarism

annotations
keywords
subject tracings
CD-ROM

CHAPTER 4

Composing Communication Research

God is love but get it in writing.

–Gypsy Rose Lee

BEFORE WE GET STARTED . . .

Research is not like other writing. Researchers select words carefully and waste no time explaining things that can be looked up elsewhere. Students new to the craft may be surprised that research writing is so terse. To be a successful scholar, you need to know how research is mapped out and composed.

CONSTRUCTION OF THE ARTICLES YOU WILL READ AND REVIEW

You may have wondered why research articles look the way they do. This section will help you understand how articles are designed so that you can use them comfortably. As an aid you will find pages from a brief article that show how each part is handled.

construction of research articles

Title

Let's be blunt about it. Research articles have boring titles. They could have catchy, poetic titles, but indexing services might misplace them if their titles did not reveal the content. Such titles as ''The Effects of Source Credibility of Women on Attitude Change'' may not have verve and punch, but you know what is studied.

specific titles aid accurate indexing

Abstract

Many journals include abstracts. The abstract is a courtesy summary for the reader, not part of the article itself. It can help you decide whether to read the entire article. For your own term papers, an abstract is not necessary, but it is required for work that is published or presented at professional meetings.

abstract is courtesy summary to the reader

Introduction and Context of the Problem

In introductions to articles and research papers the author must explain why the topic is relevant to the field and indicate the article's approach. Authors mention the field's name frequently in their introductions to let both editors and readers know that the article is central to the field, rather than peripheral to it. Studying the relationship between age and self-esteem may be interesting, but it is not a communication question since no message-related behavior is involved.

introduction:
1. shows why the topic is relevant to the field

Some articles cannot be understood without some background. Thus, authors may extend introductory remarks to place the topic into perspective. Though the lines of reasoning may differ, the context of the research often is explained by a combination of three methods: quoting authoritative sources; referring to past research; and arguing directly for the need for this work. As part of the context, scholars are expected to advance clear definitions for concepts of interest, and articles attempt to argue that this research is needed—or at least invited. Authors tend to use three major reasons to justify their research:

2. context of problem

Filling a Gap in Knowledge

One or more variables of interest may have been examined separately, but there may be a void in the area that the researchers want to probe. Finding a gap in knowledge is a good foundation for arguing that new research would be wise. Thus, scholars review literature to find ''holes'' that invite new work.

justifying new research:
1. showing a gap in knowledge

Solving Practical Problems

Sometimes there is an immediate need to help overcome a tangible problem. In such efforts, literature from popular sources such as controversial books, newspaper articles, and magazines may be referenced. Research foundations or government agencies may identify practical issues that they want addressed. Sometimes practical problems involve measurement difficulties. For many years it was difficult to

2. solving practical problems

study communication apprehension (of which stagefright is only one particular form) since valid measures were unavailable. James McCroskey (1978) used this problem to justify studies to validate a new measure, called the Personal Report of Communication Apprehension.

Extending and Improving on Past Research

3. extending and improving on past research

Research articles frequently end with suggestions for future inquiry. Though most follow-up work tends to be completed by the same researcher who made the initial suggestions, the recommendations are clear calls for additional research. Sometimes inquiry is invited because past methods were flawed and improvements are needed.

Statement of the Problem

importance of stating the problem

Among the most important parts of research articles is the statement of the problem. Some researchers state it in the introduction. Some state it near the end of a brief literature review. Some research skips it altogether, a choice that usually is a hallmark of unfocused study.[1] The problem statement tends to be placed early in research articles because it helps readers understand the new research contribution and the author's goals. Sometimes problem statements are hidden as "purpose statements." Thus, when you read, "The purpose of this research was to discover the extent of the use of 'devil terms' in the speeches of Sen. Joseph McCarthy," you should recognize that it is equivalent to a problem statement that asks, "What was the extent of the use of 'devil terms' in the speeches of Sen. Joseph McCarthy?" When reading articles you should look for these problem statements—wherever they are hiding—and include them in your notes.

problems often appear as purpose statements

Review of Literature

review of literature elements

Though not always formally labelled, every research article contains a literature review. The review of literature extends the context of the problem by providing additional discussion, definitions, and notes on methods. Three basic questions should be answered in this section:

- What do we already know or do?
- How does the new research question relate to what we already know or do?
- Why select this particular method of investigation?

The literature review usually is (informally) divided into sections that serve as the researcher's justification for undertaking the study, which for quantitative articles and papers, often follow this order:

- Conceptual definition of the variable or issue of interest (if there are controversies about legitimate conceptual definitions, this section discusses them and explains the author's decisions about the matter);
- Problems with identifying, observing, or measuring variables or issues (often summarized by the term "operational definitions," this discussion concerns strengths and weaknesses of ways researchers actually try to conduct studies on a variable or issue);

- Explanation of the importance or usefulness of the variable or issue (by citing past research that used the variable or issue successfully or by pointing to its practical importance);
- Underlying theories that explain the important roles or functions of the variable or issue (any limitations on the usefulness of specific theories are placed here);
- The invitation to current or future research (gaps in knowledge, solving practical problems, extending past research).

After the review of the first chief variable or issue is covered, the method is repeated with a second, and so forth, through the entire list.

For qualitative articles and papers, the review of literature usually includes the following topics, though rarely with explicit subdivisions:

- Definitions of any key concepts presumed in the article (for example, redemptive rhetoric, conversational analysis, and so on), including controversies about proper conceptual definitions and the author's decisions about them;
- Explanation of underlying theoretic foundations that underlie the methods used to approach communication (such as social interactionism, the interpretive approach, the "great man" theory of history, and so on) and any adaptations the author believes should be made in applying these systems;
- Identification and justification for examining the communication domain chosen including discussion of the potential value of such a study and any other invitations to current or future research in the area;
- Background for the communication form to be studied, including historical or social information.

Researchers often end literature reviews with statements of the status of the subject. Lists of chief conclusions and priorities for future inquiry often appear. Such summaries can be very helpful when researchers have reviewed a fairly large body of research and thinking related to a subject. (See box 4.1.)

Rationale for Hypotheses

Immediately before a statement of any hypotheses, you should expect to find a paragraph or two in which a rationale for hypotheses is provided. If our thinking about the related literature is correct, then the hypotheses are what we expect to see. If an article does not include hypotheses (such as in box 4.1), it should have very specific problem statements. Some authors fail to give a specific rationale for hypotheses. But experienced researchers usually take time to show links between the literature review and hypotheses.[2] Bruce Tuckman explained (1978, p. 315):

isolated

> Hypotheses may be justified on two grounds—logical or empirical. Logical justification requires the development of arguments based on concepts or theories related to the hypotheses, while empirical justification requires reference to other research. It is necessary to provide justification for each hypothesis to insure the reader of its reasonableness and soundness. (Justification is especially critical in the proposal.)

justifications of hypotheses

BOX 4.1
Differences in Impact Between Local and National Televised Political Candidates' Debates

THE WESTERN JOURNAL OF SPEECH COMMUNICATION 46 (Summer of 1982), 291–298

Differences in Impact Between Local and ——— Title with key
National Televised Political Candidates' Debates† words

ALLEN LICHTENSTEIN* ——— Author

Televised debates between Presidential candidates have become an integral part of the American political scene. In 1960, 1976 and 1980 the major candidates for President appeared before television cameras for the "Great Debates." Those who participated did so because of their belief in the importance of the debates for winning the election.[1] With the major emphasis on winning and losing, however, the debates took on the appearance of and generated the media coverage of the "Super Bowl" of politics. According to Sears and Chaffee, "Instead of their overt content, news reports of the debates were preoccupied with 'who won' and generally with the competitive, horse-race aspect."[2]

Interest in the Presidential debates has been very high. In 1960, ——— Context of
90% of American households watched at least some of the Problem and
Nixon/Kennedy debates, and for the Ford/Carter debates in 1976, Review
the figure was 83% for American adults.[3] Reviews of research stud- (combined)
ies of the 1960 debates by Katz and Feldman and of the 1976 debates by Sears and Chaffee suggest that a substantial proportion of voters formed opinions and made decisions about the election prior to viewing the debates.[4] The debates did not, therefore, generally alter or form preferences but, rather, reinforced existing predispositions and made voters more sure of their choice: "Debates would be expected mainly to reinforce both the standing party allegiances

---

*Mr Lichtenstein is Assistant Professor of Speech Communication at the University of New Mexico, Albuquerque 87131.

[1] Herbert E. Alexander and Joel Margolis, "The Making of the Debates," in *The Presidential Debates: Media, Electoral, and Policy Perspectives,* ed., George F. Bishop, Robert G. Meadow and Marilyn Jackson-Beeck (New York: Praeger Publishers, 1978), p. 29. Sidney Kraus, "Presidential Debates: Political Option or Public Decrees?" in *The Great Debates: Carter vs Ford, 1976,* ed., Sidney Kraus (Bloomington: Indiana University Press, 1979), p.3.

[2] David O. Sears and Steven H. Chaffee, "Uses and Effects of the 1976 Debates: An Overview of Empirical Studies," in *The Great Debates: Carter vs. Ford, 1976,* p. 229.

[3] *With the Whole Nation Watching: Report of the Twentieth Century Fund Task Force on Television Presidential Debates* (Lexington, Massachusetts: Lexington Press, 1979), p. 42.

[4] Elihu Katz and Jacob J. Feldman, "The Debates in Light of Research," in *The Great Debates, Carter vs. Ford, 1976,* p. 211: Sears and Chaffee, p. 253. Churchill L. Roberts "From Primary to Presidency: A Panel Study of Images and Issues in the 1976 Election," *Western Journal of Speech Communication,* 45 (1981), 1.

**BOX 4.1
(Continued)**

and the candidate preferences built up over many prior months of campaigning, primary elections and conventions."[5] These findings are consistent with other research about the impact of television on attitudes. Television is apparently far more effective in strengthening attitudes than in altering them.[6]

The lack of research on televised debates, other than those concerned with Presidential elections, increases the probability that findings may be improperly generalized. Such generalizations do not take into account important differences in televised debates between candidates for local offices and the "Great Debates" for the office of President. For example, few local campaigns can attract the publicity and public interest of the race for the Presidency. Because of this, local candidates may be less known to the public and their positions on various issues less clear. Then, too, Presidential candidates affect local races on the same ballot (the coattail effect), but the opposite would be a rare occurrence. Finally, there appears to be less interpersonal communication concerning local races. According to Rothschild:

> Kline (1972) was one of the first to report on key differences in communications effects as a function of the level of the election race. He presented a review and re-analysis of data from several national and local election field studies which generally examined the agenda setting function of the media. Kline concluded that there are two types of elections. Presidential elections affect people of varying involvement levels in similar ways, and voting tends to be quite stable. Party elections (i.e., below the presidential level) are quite unstable situations for the low-involvement voter. Here peo-
Gap in —————— ple rely on simple presentations and deviate from party
knowledge identification as a result. Because they did not have enough
identified information to make a rational decision, people relied on their simple recall of images, consequently, in Kline's scenario, the predominant image received the vote. This finding is important in demonstrating that, while the limited effects model holds in the high level election, the media can have considerable power in the low level race.[7]

---

[5]Sears and Chaffee, p.253.

[6]Joseph T. Klapper in *The Effects of Mass Communication* (New York: Free Press, 1960), p. 11, argues that "Research has pretty well established that such [persuasive] mass communication is more likely to reinforce existing opinions than to change them, and more likely to produce modifications than conversions."

[7]Michael L. Rothschild, "On the Use of Multiple Methods and Multiple Situations in Political Communications Research," in *Political Communication: Issues and Strategies for Research,* ed., Steven H. Chaffee (Beverly Hills, California: Sage Publications, 1975), p. 247.

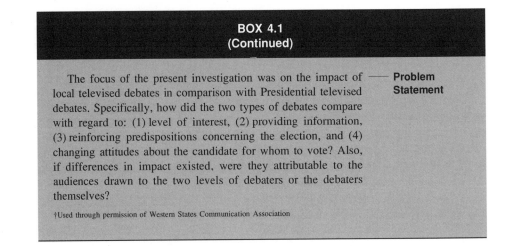

BOX 4.1
(Continued)

The focus of the present investigation was on the impact of —— **Problem Statement**
local televised debates in comparison with Presidential televised
debates. Specifically, how did the two types of debates compare
with regard to: (1) level of interest, (2) providing information,
(3) reinforcing predispositions concerning the election, and (4)
changing attitudes about the candidate for whom to vote? Also,
if differences in impact existed, were they attributable to the
audiences drawn to the two levels of debaters or the debaters
themselves?

†Used through permission of Western States Communication Association

The hypotheses are often set off in reduced type with symbols such as H_1, H_2, H_3 to indicate different hypotheses. If a hypothesis is not clearly identified, the article just plain doesn't have one.

Method

methods described in enough detail for replication

The method section of a study describes what the researchers did in enough detail so that others could repeat or replicate it. For qualitative studies—such as evaluating the speeches of Susan B. Anthony or engaging in extended naturalistic studies of police—the method section tends to be *very* brief. Often, no formal section labelled "Method" appears, though many historical-critical studies include justifications for critical standards or analysis tools. For quantitative studies, the methods should be explained in detail, complete with subheadings discussed below.

Data or Documentary Sample

content analyses samples of documents samples in empirical studies

Regardless of the type of research, some actual documents or sample data are used. Researchers explain the characteristics of such materials, where they come from, and how they were selected. For content analysis of mass media communication, the materials in the sample are documents, including oral and video records. The authenticity and accuracy of the records and any ommisions of materials must be explained. For empirical or experimental work, samples of people (often called "subjects") typically are gathered. In addition to reporting the number of subjects, sample characteristics (such as age and sex), and sources (for example, college students, adults in field settings, volunteers), any methods for random sampling should be detailed (since this method requires extra steps).

Operational Definitions of Variables

operational definitions distinguished

Conceptual definitions—such as those found in specialized dictionaries—give you an idea of the meaning of a term. An **operational definition,** on the other hand, is nothing like a dictionary definition. It isolates a concept by specifying the steps

---

SPECIAL DISCUSSION 4–1
Anatomy of Articles That Present New Theories

Some articles present research, and some present theories and conceptual discussions. Just as articles that present research have a fairly well-known organizational pattern in common, articles that advance new theories also have some common features.

The first part of a theory article begins with the review of the context of the problem. Theories of attitude change review work on predicting attitude change, argumentation theories review different ways to describe arguments, and theories on the effects of violence on television review the status of theory on violence. The conclusion of the context of the problem is a statement of the desirability of isolating a different theoretic perspective. Sometimes articles attempt to "trash" past efforts, but this strategy is not highly regarded by scholars. Showing a meaningful new contribution is enough of a justification for the new orientation.

The second major section of the theory article is expected to define all terms clearly and concisely. The discussion of definitions is detailed and filled with justifications, since definitions are based on key assumptions, and new theories are expected to state them explicitly.

The third section includes statements of key propositions (in predictive theories) and implications of definitions (in the case of definitional theories). These statements include defining the roles of key concepts.

Fourth, the theory article is expected to present information on the usefulness of applying the theory. Any advantages in interpreting research and explaining phenomena should be reviewed. In addition, any limitations are advanced. Finally, the implications for future work with the theory are listed and explained as part of a call for future research.

---

researchers follow to make observations of the variables. These descriptions include (1) manipulations or tasks completed to make observations; (2) special measures used for key variables; or (3) methods for assignment of subjects to different conditions based on some common characteristics. Articles should provide information on the accuracy and reliability of their operational techniques. Reports of reliability for measurements have been routinely demanded in most professional journals since the early 1980s. Thus, justifications—not just descriptions—for the choices made to make observations are a major part of the discussion of measures used.

Procedures

Researchers describe how the study was completed—step by step. The best studies are written so clearly that you could understand what it was like to be a subject in the study. Information on instructions, debriefing, and protection of subjects should be shared.

procedures identified

Methods for Analysis of Data

in quantitive
studies, data
analysis refers to
statistics

Though qualitative studies rely on theoretic orientations to interpret data, empirical and experimental studies employ statistical tools to examine hypotheses. Specific names, such as "*t* tests" or "analysis of variance" are mentioned with little explanation, since they are recognized by scholars who have taken a course such as the one you probably are completing now. If statistics are not so widely understood, the author may explain them in detail. Box 4.2 shows this section from a research article.

Results

results section does
not interpret
findings

The results section of an article does not explain the meaning of study findings—that is reserved for the discussion section. The results are simply that—presentations of findings—without comment on their substantive importance. The results section often includes tables and sometimes graphs to report analyses. Since the results section is technical, researchers are expected to provide enough detail to help readers understand what was found. This section tends to be brief.

Discussion

discussion interprets
results

Though short articles may combine the results and discussion sections (as in our example), most authors write a separate discussion section. The discussion section is the researcher's chance to argue about the meaning of results. Though researchers are given freedom to draw conclusions, the rules of sound reasoning must be obeyed, and the arguments must appeal to research evidence (and not go far beyond it). Structurally, the discussion section usually interprets hypothesized and unexpected results, the significance of the study, study limitations (problems that may be overcome in future research), and implications for future inquiry. Since the literature review raised invitations to new research, the discussion of results should respond to *each* issue raised early in the paper. Otherwise, the research would not have been a fitting response to research invitations. Box 4.3 shows how such a commentary is included in the discussion.

Conclusion

conclusion is a
summary

The conclusion usually consists of one or two paragraphs in which the researcher summarizes what was done in the study. The conclusion is not a stirring call to future inquiry—it simply summarizes what was accomplished.

References

references using the
APA format

The final part of a research article is the list of references. To understand the *detail* of citation methods, it is a good idea to review the *APA Publication Manual* directly. In addition, you will find practical advice on ways to improve your own writing and preparation of a professional-looking research paper.

BOX 4.2

METHOD

Method

During the Fall of 1980, public television station KNME-TV in Albuquerque, New Mexico aired "The Candidates," a series of debates between candidates seeking election to a variety of local offices. These were shown during the same general time period that the Reagan/Anderson and Reagan/Carter debates appeared on the major networks. Like the Presidential debates, "The Candidates" was sponsored by the League of Women Voters.

Materials

One major difference between the Presidential debates and "The Candidates" was in the number of races covered. There is only one national election, the race for President. In contrast, on the local level were a multitude of offices whose candidates all competed for limited publicity. Thus, while "The Candidates" differed from the Presidential debates insofar as the number of races covered, this situation reflects actual differences in the different level election as described by Kline.

Sample

In order to make a comparative analysis of audience perception and impact of the local and Presidential debates, a telephone survey was undertaken. Interviews were conducted with 234 randomly

Measures

selected persons from the KNME mailing list.[8] The interview, which took approximately seven minutes, consisted of 25 questions concerning "The Candidates," the Presidential debates, and, if the respondent saw both, a comparison of the two. The interviews were conducted in early January 1981 by trained volunteers.[9]

Results obtained from such a sample cannot be generalized to the general public or any other population. It is not the purpose of this study to do so. However, results showing substantial differences in audience perception and impact between Presidential and local candidate TV debates, for even one group, would be important. These results could lend support to the idea of the inability to make generalizations concerning televised political candidate debates from Presidential debate research alone. They would suggest further that the impact of any televised candidate debate is strongly influenced by the particular situation and context in which the debate is held.

---

[8]Two hundred thirty-four respondents completed the interview of the initial 300 contacted, resulting in a completion rate of 78%.

[9]The training included instructions and practiced interviews. In addition, randomly selected interviews were monitored during the study to insure the accuracy and the neutrality of the procedure. The survey was conducted in January to allow enough time to elapse after the election so that the respondents' answers would reflect their reactions to the debates themselves rather than the candidates.

**BOX 4.2
(Continued)**

RESULTS AND CONCLUSIONS

Table 1 Viewing of "The Candidates" and the Presidential Debates

Saw "The Candidates"	
one	8%
two	17%
three or more	14%
total (saw at least one)	39%
Saw The Presidential Debates	
Reagan/Anderson only	4%
Reagan/Carter only	27%
both	49%
total (saw at least one)	80%

Although there was considerable interest in the local debate series, the Presidential debates were far more popular (see table 1). This finding is not surprising given the publicity and news coverage for the Presidential debate series. Also, the national debates were aired over commercial networks, and "The Candidates" appeared on a local public television station. Even if the races were perceived as being of equal importance, the publicity and coverage difference would account for a considerable portion of the difference in viewership.[10]

The local and national races were not viewed as equally important by the public; the Presidential election was thought to be more important. The overwhelming difference is not surprising and supports Kline's conclusions.[11] Interestingly, however, 76 percent of the respondents watched the Reagan/Carter debate, and only 54 percent saw the Reagan/Anderson one. This result may be due to the greater support and interest that Jimmy Carter generated, but these figures and this explanation cast doubt on the notion that viewers tuned in the debates to learn more about the unknown candidate. If that were the case, Anderson would be expected to draw a larger audience.

Analysis of results by percentages

[10]According to the February 1981 Nielsen NS1 report, the weekly cumulative DMA audience for KNME is 54%. This compares with 93% for KGGM, the CBS affiliate; 92% for KVAT, the ABC affiliate; and 90% for KOB, the NBC affiliate.

[11]Rothschild, p. 247.

BOX 4.2
(Continued)

Expectedly, both Presidential debates drew substantially more viewers than the entire series of local candidate debates. However, 80 percent of the people who tuned in one local debate came back to see at least one more. This may indicate that "The Candidates" was considered useful to the people who saw it, a conclusion supported by the results displayed in table 2.

The local debates were perceived as considerably more informative and influential to the viewers than the Presidential debates. Influence, however, probably took several different forms. An undecided voter could have made up his or her mind, a "leaner" would have made a definite decision, and an already decided voter could have switched or become undecided. Local debate viewers reported being more influenced in general, changing their minds more, and being made more sure of their choices.

BOX 4.3

results and
discussion

TABLE 2 IMPACT OF "THE CANDIDATES" AND THE PRESIDENTIAL DEBATES

	Local Debate Viewers (%)	Presidential Debate Viewers (%)
Decided voting choice before seeing debates	40	70
Learned more about candidates from seeing debates	80	55
Voting decision influenced by debates	57	29
Voting preference changed because of debates	20	9
More sure of choice because of debates	79	63
	(90)	(187)

BOX 4.3
(Continued)

Two possible explanations exist for the differing impact of the televised debates for different level elections. The first explanation is that different types of people are drawn to the different level debates. According to this explanation, people who watch local debates tend to be more interested in politics, more open minded, and in general, engage in more information seeking behavior.[12] Their tuning into the local debates is an example of information seeking. Thus, the greater impact of the local debates can be attributed to the specific reasons that this select group of people watch them. The second explanation, following Kline's conclusions, is that the differing nature of the campaigns and the publicity surrounding them cause the differences in impact; the type of people drawn to the programs is not the crucial factor.

These alternative explanations can be tested by comparing the influence of the two types of debates on people who saw both. If the people-centered explanation is true, then there should be no difference in the impact of the local and the Presidential debates on viewers who saw both. If the local debate had greater impact on those people who saw both types (following the general pattern for their sample), the "nature of the audience" explanation would not be supported.

Results indicated that the kind of debate televised, and not audience characteristics, determined impact. . . . A nearly identical pattern appeared for these people who saw both levels of debate as for the entire sample. Although they were more decided about the Presidential debates before viewing, they learned more from the local candidates' debates, were influenced more, changed their minds more, and were made sure of their choices more often.

The impact on the Presidential debate viewers, for this sample, shows consistency with the 1960 and 1976 findings. Seventy percent of the people decided their choice for President before watching the debates, compared with only 40% for the local candidates. Because of the greater coverage and publicity of the Presidential race, voters tended to make decisions early, possibly by January prior to the election. Televised debates appear a more important information source for local elections which lack the coverage of the national races. Results support this view: 80% of the viewers said they learned more about the candidates from seeing the local debates, whereas only 55% of the Presidential debate viewers reported such learning. This is consistent with Kline's findings about the different roles of mass media in the different level elections.[13]

---

[12]Rothschild, p. 247.

[13]Maxwell E. McCombs and L. Edwards Mullins, in "Consequences of Education: Media Exposure, Political Interest and Information Seeking Orientation," *Mass Communications Review*, 1 (1973), 27–31, discuss the association of information-seeking behavior and education. Public television audiences tend to be skewed toward the higher educated. Jack Lyle, in *The People Look at Public Television* (Washington, D.C.: Corporation for Public Broadcasting, 1975), points out the upper SES and education skew for the public television audience.

**BOX 4.3
(Continued)**

Not only was "The Candidates" more informative, it was also more influential. Almost twice as many of the local debate viewers (57%) as the Presidential debate viewers (29%) felt their votes were influenced by the debates. For both groups of viewers, the major effect was to reinforce previously made decisions rather than change voting preferences. Although these results support conclusions of research of the 1960 and 1976 Presidential debates, both types of influence, change and reinforcement, were greater with the local televised debates. Twenty percent of "The Candidates" viewers changed their minds as opposed to only 9% for the Presidential debates. Seventy-nine percent were made more sure by the local debates, 63% by the national.

. . .

Respondents who saw both local and national debates were asked which they thought were more informative, interesting and influential. The results (see table 5) revealed a curious paradox: people who saw both were more influenced by the local debates . . . and perceived the local debates as more informative; however, they also saw the Presidential debates more interesting and influential.

TABLE 5 PERCEPTIONS OF THE DEBATES*

	Local Debates (%)	Presidential Debates (%)
More informative	40	31
More interesting	19	57
More influential	24	41
	(76)	(76)

*Questions were asked of persons who saw both local and Presidential debates.

The explanation for this paradox may very well lie in the discrepancy between an individual's own reactions and his or her perceptions of how other people react. The belief in the power of the Presidential debates is widely held. Findings of this study, consistent with the findings of research from the Presidential debates from 1960 and 1976, suggest limited informational and cognitive effects. Yet, this research is unfamiliar to the majority of the public. There persists the belief that the Presidential candidate debates are more important than the research would indicate.

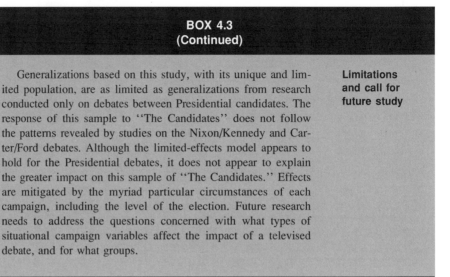

BOX 4.3
(Continued)

Generalizations based on this study, with its unique and limited population, are as limited as generalizations from research conducted only on debates between Presidential candidates. The response of this sample to "The Candidates" does not follow the patterns revealed by studies on the Nixon/Kennedy and Carter/Ford debates. Although the limited-effects model appears to hold for the Presidential debates, it does not appear to explain the greater impact on this sample of "The Candidates." Effects are mitigated by the myriad particular circumstances of each campaign, including the level of the election. Future research needs to address the questions concerned with what types of situational campaign variables affect the impact of a televised debate, and for what groups.

Limitations and call for future study

WRITING SCHOLARSHIP

demands of effective writing

There is no way around it. Research involves crisp and clear writing. You may expect to develop your own writing skills as a result of studying research methods. You might have to write only short papers in the class you are taking, but you certainly will be expected to *write well.* Though developing good writing skills is, and should be, a lifelong undertaking, you can take some immediate steps to improve your writing. This section provides some practical advice about planning and structuring your scholarly writing.

Using Proper Formats and Subdivisions

desirability of using subdivisions

The flow of a paper can get lost unless you use some helpful aids. The most obvious way to enhance understanding is to use headings to highlight your main points. Like it or not, your instructors often have to grade your papers while facing frequent interruptions. In all but your shortest projects, headings and subheadings can help keep main ideas in the instructor's mind despite distractions (we are talking about "defensive writing" here). You should start with a major heading for each main point on your outline and add subheadings as the discussion gets involved or lengthy.

Style

meaning of style

Style does not mean a special sense of fashion or personal flair. **Style** is the choice and use of words. Any other use of the term is a figure of speech. Many books that discuss good writing practice use the word "style" in their titles (such as *The Elements of Style,* by William Strunk and E. B. White, (1979). You can make rapid progress by reading about ways to make your writing clear and precise.

SPECIAL DISCUSSION 4–2
Outlines as "Recipes for Success"

It is nearly impossible to do good research without an outline. You may rarely have needed an outline to write papers in high school, but that situation is all over now. Make it your policy to begin each assignment by composing a rough outline before doing anything else—this step may serve as the basis of your library research outline. List the major topics you need to cover on a large sheet of paper. Leave space between headings and fill in details of substructure for each of your outline topics. Then check the logic of your outline. Are there any unsupported statements? Are there any sections where the reasoning is weak? You can usually spot these problems on your outline and correct them before investing much time in the project.

Students often resist working from outlines because they think that they can sit down and write a paper without one. In research work, however, they often find themselves face to face with four facts. First, without an outline describing each detail of the paper, they cannot take breaks for meals, phone calls, exercise, or emergencies. Second, without an outline it may be difficult to make changes. If a student finds that a project should be modified according to a professor's advice, it is easy to change an outline, but it is very painful to change complete pages and paragraphs that have already been written. Third, without working from a full outline, it is difficult to plan time to research the topic or to fill in previously undiscovered gaps. Fourth, without a complete outline, it may be difficult to get help from a professor in the early stages of a project. A professor asked for advice on completing a research paper can do little if there is no outline to review. There is no doubt about it. Working from an outline is not a luxury—it is the only way to go.

Clear writing is led by very organized thoughts. In addition to outlining, other methods can promote clear writing. Making active use of **internal organizers**—phrases that preview, summarize, and transition between main points—can underscore your content. It is helpful to preview all the subpoints before you cover any of them. A full summary of each subpoint provided at subsection endings emphasizes the order of ideas in the paper. Using summaries and previews increases the chances that your ideas will be understood. **internal organizers identified**

It is important to avoid ambiguity in scholarly writing. You should use terms that are direct and, whenever possible, you should rely on language that is understandable to the greatest number of intelligent people. Einstein expressed this concern best: "Ideas should be stated as simply as possible, but no simpler." You should not avoid topics that are technical—quite the contrary! But your writing should use only those specialized terms that are essential. Furthermore, you should define every major term you use. Clear writing often can be enhanced by employing paragraph structures that have obvious topic sentences. If you use active **ambiguity shunned in scholarly writing**

use summaries, previews, and topic sentences

summaries, previews, and internal organizers, avoid ambiguity, and rely on standard paragraph structures, your writing will be clear and understandable.

WRITING CLASSROOM REPORTS

need to revise written work

Communication students are often asked to write papers that refer to research. Though your instructors will give you specific details for each assignment, you should observe some general formats. This section will describe the obligations you should routinely expect to satisfy. It will cover three types of papers: the definitional criticism paper, the literature review (or explication) paper, and the research prospectus (or proposal).

As a general piece of advice, remember that scholarship is not written so much as it is rewritten. Yet, to revise your writing, you often need to get distance from your own work. For all your projects, you should complete a first draft as soon as you can and then set it aside for a day or so. When you begin revising, you will find plenty of things to improve. After time, you will learn to revise your work within a few hours of completing a first draft.

Strategies for a Definitional Criticism Paper

A definitional paper takes a concept of interest to you—such as propaganda, stuttering, or comparative advertising—and considers issues that involve the proper definition of the concept. You do not just choose your favorite definition. Instead, your paper should contrast different approaches to understand definitional questions.

Organizing a Definitional Criticism Paper

format and design of the definitional criticism paper

The definitional paper usually begins with an introduction that mentions the topic area and justifies it as a part of the study of communication. The introduction actively refers to the field and cites communication sources (and other related subjects) that have found the concept important enough to investigate. Any context needed to understand the topic is often included in the introduction, rather than as a completely separate discussion. Depending on the paper's length, the introduction ends by previewing the rest of the paper's main points.

contrasting different schools of thought

The bulk of a definitional paper compares and contrasts different schools of thought for the concept of interest. The writer does not try to explain how important the variable is in everyday life but considers the proper way to define the term. Schools of thought are distinguished by different details or key starting points. Each school of thought is usually introduced with a quotation expressing that point of view. Then comments are made to point out any weaknesses in the definition. Though chapter 6 will provide you with standards for definitions to satisfy, for now you should know that criticisms are made by applying specific criteria, not your personal feelings about the authors or their implied values. You should also examine problems that exist in finding useful operational definitions (measurement or methods to observe the concept in action) for your concept of interest.

evaluating definitions

After discussing each definitional school of thought and its limitations, you will need to offer some sort of conclusion. Is one definition clearly superior to the others? Are all the definitions acceptable but most applicable to different situations? Do you have an alternative definition that is superior to the others? If so, are you prepared to show how your new definition meets all the standards expected of a good definition? Any of these conclusions is acceptable, but you must choose an approach and defend it.

Isolating and Categorizing Schools of Thought

Students sometimes doubt their ability to identify different schools of thought. The task, however, is quite simple. You simply look for definitions of the concept and then categorize them. Most of the time definitions are found in specialized dictionaries and encyclopedias, or in books. Once you have found books that might contain such definitions, look for your term in the book indices. If it is there, jot down the definition on a bibliographic note card. Specialized dictionaries may provide more than one definition. Do not assume that the first definition is preferred. By protocol, dictionary authors list definitions in chronological order, though archaic definitions usually are placed at the end of the list. Make sure to identify any critiques of definitions, since you might want to use these comments to help complete your own paper.

> sources for definitional schools of thought

The easiest way to identify different schools of thought is to sort your bibliographic cards that contain definitions. Take the cards that seem to be saying the same thing and put them in one stack. Those definitions that add an element or that seem to move in a unique direction can be placed in a different stack. You soon will see that you have identified the major schools of thought on an issue. You may wish to reread definitions within each group to make sure that you have not missed meaningful distinctions. To write the paper, you will need to consider each school of thought. Sometimes students who are new to research ask instructors how many sources are to be included in such a paper. Though instructors sometimes set limits for novice researchers, the question really cannot be answered. To complete the work, all conflicting schools of thought must be included—involving only a few sources or, perhaps, dozens.

> methods to identify different schools of thought

Strategies for the Literature Review

Perhaps the most common papers you will write in your academic career will be literature reviews. These papers attempt to tell the reader what is known about a subject and the current status of the knowledge about the matter.

Organizing a Literature Review

The literature review generally has seven sections:

> review sections
> 1. justify subject as communication

1. An introduction that justifies the study of the topic in the field and previews the rest of the paper (it is typical to indicate how the topic is related to the field and to cite sources to support one's selection of the variables of interest);

2. context of the problem

2. The context of the problem (a section that is usually but not always included) that isolates the role of the concepts in communication studies by such methods as quoting authoritative sources, referring to past research that invites new work, or arguing directly for a need for this work;

3. background definitions of terms

3. The background definitions of terms (though not as extended as in a definitional paper), which assess *major* conceptual and operational definitions, including *problems* that researchers have faced when measuring or observing the concept or variable (general expository listings of operational definitions is not very interesting in a literature review paper—your attention should focus on operational problems that limit conclusions that researchers have drawn);

4. review of relevant theory

4. The relevant theory reviewed to explain how and why the variable or concept works in communication (theories should be stated in enough detail to show their ability to explain the role of your variable or concept in the communication process, but you need not complete full reviews of the theories);

5. survey of literature

5. The research survey, which usually is the longest part of the study. Based on limits set on your review scope, you may complete either an exhaustive or exemplary literature review:

exhaustive and exemplary literature reviews

Exhaustive literature reviews are research surveys that include all material related to the subject.

Exemplary literature reviews are surveys of only the most important contributions.

Published articles tend to use exemplary reviews because of space limits, and you probably will be asked to complete exemplary literature reviews in your classes (but don't let yourself off the hook—you must review research extensively before completing any sort of review);

6. research opportunities or heuristic merit described

6. A list of the opportunities for future research that suggest the **heuristic** merit of research (the term, heuristic, comes from the Greek word that means ''to invent;'' the heuristic merit of research, hence, is its ability to lead scholars to new inventions, ideas, explanations, or research avenues);

7. conclusion

7. A conclusion that summarizes the main points and states a bottom-line conclusion.

Selecting a Summary Organization

using a summary organization

The literature review is not a collection of mini-''book reports.'' Instead, it makes arguments for which the research studies serve as evidence. Studies are arranged to create a logical discussion of research findings. The most prominent summary patterns are found in table 4.1, though they are often combined in literature reviews.

chronological method most popular

You should select a literature summary pattern with care. If not much is known about a research subject, you may wish to rely on the known-to-unknown format. The most frequently used literature review strategy probably is the chronological method (remember: we are discussing *summary* patterns, not library *search* strategies). Even so, many students also find the topical or the known to unknown patterns very useful. The extensiveness of research and the question

TABLE 4.1 Review Summary Strategies

Summary Strategy	Description
Known to Unknown	Reviews literature by considering what (little) is known separately about each variable in the research review question and then announces what remains to be learned.
Deductive	Reviews literature by considering what is known in general categories, followed by increasingly specific categories that are related to the topic (e.g., starting with studies of communication climate, followed by related studies on communication climate in high-tech organizations, followed by perceptions of communication climate of women in high-tech organizations).
Problem-Solution	A problem and its cause are suggested, followed by a research suggestion that might solve the problem (e.g., the problem of identifying highly communication apprehensive students in the elementary schools has resulted in many children going without help in developing this social skill; thus, a research solution in the form of a quick rating scale to be completed by teachers following interviews with students is proposed as a solution).
Chronological	Studies are summarized in their order of publication from the oldest study through the most recent one.
Inductive	Study findings in a given area are summarized by producing general propositions (laws or rules) that are demonstrated by each subcollection of them (studies are grouped largely by their findings rather than their input variables).
Topical	Studies are summarized by reference to content categories into which the studies fall (e.g., studies related to effects of mass media sources, public figure sources communicating directly, and interpersonal sources on formation of voter opinion are covered in three different categories).

• Note: Experience suggests that you will find the patterns listed first as most useful for those situations in which there seems to be little research directly related to your specific research question.

investigated should guide selection of the method. You should remember that the review sticks to scholarly research completed on the subject. Personal applications are not relevant and should not be included.

You may be requested to write a general **explication** of a topic. The assign- **explication paper** ment requires you to complete a literature review that makes an issue clear and **indicated** comprehensive. Make sure to cover all points listed in this brief description of literature reviews to be certain that you have addressed all the important issues.

Research Prospectus

Of all the papers you may write, the research prospectus may be the most involving since it includes the components of definitional and literature review papers along with new suggestions for research. A **research prospectus** is a complete **research prospectus** proposal for a research activity to be completed at a future date. All the details **identified** are set out so that the study could be executed immediately after the proposal's acceptance.

Standard Steps

first five steps of
the research
prospectus
unchanged

The first five portions of a research prospectus are identical to those steps described for other papers. The remaining steps diverge.

1. An introduction specifying the relevance of the general subject matter to communication and overviewing the remaining parts of the paper begins the prospectus.
2. The context and the problem statement may be separated into different categories depending on the flow of the paper.
3. The significance of the problem area is frequently indicated before methods are described, though some prefer to make it part of the discussion section of the paper. This significance discussion shows why the area posed by the research question is meaningful and important, rather than peripheral and trivial.
4. A full statement of definition of terms is included. Concerns for both conceptual and operational definitions are a part of this discussion. The review is meant to justify later choices for identifying or measuring variables.
5. The review of the literature argues for variables chosen, sets up hypotheses, and presents evidence to support methods proposed.

unique steps:
rationale and
hypotheses

The following steps are unique to the prospectus:

6. The rationale and hypotheses are stated. These expectations are stated with a brief rationale for each. It is *not* a rationale to say, ''Based on the literature review, the following hypothesis was advanced. . . .''—explanations of the links are required.

methods described

7. The method to collect data is described. Quantitative researchers describe and justify proposed sample methods, measures, and materials for study, procedures, design, and additional control steps.

analysis methods

8. The proposed methods of analysis (including statistical tools) are explained and justified.

conclusions drawn
if hypotheses were
or were not
supported

9. A final section suggests conclusions that would be drawn if the hypotheses were supported and what would be concluded if the hypotheses were not supported. This section previews the discussion that would emerge if the study were completed. Some subdivide this section into discussions on study limitations, suggestions for future research, and potential importance of the research. Yet, these subdivisions are matters of preference by researchers.

additional elements

If a proposal is submitted to some group for evaluation, such as the submission of research for funding, a time table, budget, and proposed method of presenting and publishing results are also included along with the researcher's own professional credentials.

Common Mistakes

mistakes found in
writing the
prospectus

Research writing requires attention to detail. Naturally, students often make some mistakes in their initial efforts. Some of the most frequent errors (translation: your instructor has seen them and does not like them) are

- Selecting a problem that is too vast or too vague to investigate meaningfully (Borg, 1963, p. 38)
- Relying too heavily on secondary sources for literature reviews (Borg, 1963, p. 67)

- Concentrating research findings when reading research articles, thus overlooking valuable information on methods, measures, and so forth (Borg, 1963, p. 67)
- Failing to provide information on validity and reliability of research instruments to be used
- Reciting facts but not synthesizing or integrating them into meaningful generalizations (Borg, 1963, p. 233)
- Excessive use of secondary sources of information . . . frequently found in studies dealing with past events (Borg, 1963, p. 233)
- Analysis of data plan not specified in detail in advance
- Procedures not completely described
- Assuming the results of causal comparative or correlational research to be proof for a cause and effect relationship (Borg, 1963, p. 286)

SUMMARY

Research articles are organized in very specific ways. The titles of research articles are descriptive to aid in their indexing. The abstract summarizes an article as a courtesy for the reader. The introduction and context of the problem show why the general topic is relevant to the field. As part of the context discussion, scholars are expected to advance clear definitions and to argue that research is invited. The statement of the problem is included, though sometimes hidden as a "purpose statement." Though format differs from quantitative and qualitative studies, the review of literature extends the context of the problem by answering three basic questions: What do we already know or do? How does the new research question relate to what we already know or do? Why select this particular method of investigation? The rationale for hypotheses are provided immediately before a statement of any hypotheses. The method section of a study describes what the researchers did in enough detail so that others could repeat or replicate it. For qualitative studies, often no formal section labelled "Method" appears. For quantitative studies, the methods may be explained in detail under the headings of (1) data or documentary sample; (2) operational definitions of variables (conceptual definitions give you an idea of the meaning of a term; operational definitions isolate a concept by specifying the steps researchers follow to make observations of the variables); (3) procedures that describe how the study was completed; (4) methods for analysis of data (qualitative studies rely on theoretic orientations to interpret data, empirical and experimental studies employ statistical tools); (5) results, which simply present study findings; (6) discussion, which interprets results and other applications; (7) conclusion that summarizes what was accomplished; (8) references (which usually follow the APA format).

Scholarship must be written clearly. Using proper formats and subdivisions and paying attention to effective style (choice and use of words) can help you achieve clarity. In addition to outlining, you can make your writing clear by using internal organizers (phrases that preview, summarize, and transition between main points), avoiding ambiguity, and relying on standard paragraph structures. It is important to avoid ambiguity in scholarly writing by using terms that are direct and by employing language that is understandable to the greatest number of intelligent people. Furthermore, you should define every major term you use.

Writing classroom reports can involve three major forms. The definitional paper takes a concept of interest and considers issues that involve the proper definition of the concept. It involves following steps to isolate each key school of thought (usually through a process of sorting definitions into categories). The literature review paper attempts to tell the reader what is known about a subject and the current status of the knowledge about the matter. The literature review generally has seven sections: (1) introduction that justifies the study of the topic in the field; (2) context of the problem; (3) background definitions of terms; (4) review of relevant theory to explain the variable or concept; (5) survey of the research (completed either as an exhaustive literature review that includes all material related to the subject or as an exemplary literature review that surveys only the most important contributions); (6) list of opportunities for future research suggesting the heuristic merit of research (its ability to lead scholars to new inventions, ideas, explanations, or research avenues); and (7) summary of main points. In addition, the literature review follows clear strategies to summarize research. An explication assignment requires you to complete a literature review that makes an issue clear and comprehensive. The research prospectus is a complete proposal for a research activity to be completed at a future date. The first five steps of a research prospectus are identical to those described for other papers. The remaining steps include statement of the rationale and hypotheses; description of methods to collect data; justification of proposed methods of analysis; and conclusions that would be drawn if the hypotheses were supported or not supported. If a proposal is submitted to some group for evaluation, such as the submission of research for funding, a time table, budget, and proposed method of presenting and publishing results are also included along with the researcher's own professional credentials. In addition to effective writing of the prospectus, students need to avoid making critical errors in composing the prospectus.

TERMS FOR REVIEW

operational definition
style
internal organizers
exhaustive literature review

exemplary literature review
heuristic
explication
prospectus

NOTES

[1]You need to forget the notion that research must be good if it is published. Poor work can sometimes get published, and most published work gets into print despite weaknesses. Perfect research probably has not been completed in our field—although some has come very close. It is all right, therefore, to criticize portions of research articles for deficiencies that exist. You are not attacking the person writing the article when you do so, and you are not pretending to be superior to those authors when you evaluate research according to standards found in this book.

[2]Technically, failing to link the literature review to hypotheses makes the hypotheses *non sequitur* (''not in sequence''/''does not follow'') fallacies.

CHAPTER 5

The Communication Research Argument: Evidence and Reasoning

Science is simply common sense at its best—that is, rigidly accurate in observation, and merciless to fallacy in logic.

–Thomas Huxley

EVALUATING RESEARCH EVIDENCE AND INFORMATION
  Factual Information
  Opinions

EVALUATING RESEARCH ARGUMENTS
  Finding Research Arguments
  Patterns Of Argument In Each
    Section

BEFORE WE GET STARTED . . .

Most people think that research is a form of argument. But saying it and acting like it are two very different things. Students who are first exposed to research methods rarely understand that standard tests of good reasoning and logic apply directly to our field's inquiry. This chapter will show you where different kinds of arguments appear in research, what kind of evidence is used, and how to test arguments found in research studies. It will teach you how to separate worthy from unworthy research claims.

EVALUATING RESEARCH EVIDENCE AND INFORMATION

Scholars reason from evidence to advance their conclusions. But it is an oversimplification to say that research is just an exercise in persuasion. R. Michael Bokeno (1987) found that science requires arguments to be based on the methods of science without appealing to prejudices or biases of the masses. In fact, good research requires that one understand how to construct and evaluate sound arguments. It makes sense to look at evidence types and the sorts of reasoning patterns that researchers legitimately can make.

In research, **evidence** is information scholars use to support claims. Though you can group research evidence in many ways, you should consider two general categories: factual information including statistics; and opinions offered to interpret facts.

evidence defined

SPECIAL DISCUSSION 5–1
Urban Folklore and Fits of Fancy

We often hear reports that have the ring of truth even though they prove to be untrue. Some are simple rumors, but some are examples of "urban folklore." Two folklorists, Paul Dickson and Joseph C. Goulden (1983), have written extensively on the development of urban folklore. For instance, you may have heard the rumor that the city of New York hired big game hunters to shoot alligators living in the city's sewer system (apparently souvenirs from Florida flushed down toilets when they started to grow from baby alligator size). You may have heard the story about the person who visited several tanning booths in a single day and was hospitalized for third degree burns shortly thereafter. These stories are not true but they get repeated, often on national radio programs. Here is a list of damaging *untrue* stories that Dickson and Goulden warn us to reject (pp. 15–16):

- There is prune juice in Dr. Pepper.
- Proctor and Gamble uses a logo that promotes devil worship.
- Kentucky Fried Chicken served up a rat in a bucket of chicken purchased by a customer—this customer is now suing.
- Madelyn Murray O'Hair has filed a lawsuit to have "In God We Trust" taken off U.S. currency.
- A dead mouse was found in a Coke bottle—the person who found it sued for a million dollars and won.

During the 1991 Persian Gulf war, reports filtered out of Kuwait that Iraqi soldiers had entered hospitals, taken incubators for their own use, and left babies to suffer and die. A young woman (later identified as the Kuwaiti ambassador's daughter) tearfully testified before a committee of the House of Representatives about the events. When hospital employees finally were liberated by U.N. forces, the incubator story was exposed as a fraud.

Factual Information

Solid research appeals to facts, rather than to authority or personalities. Though different sorts of facts can be used to build research arguments, **factual evidence** consists of descriptions and characterizations of things. Sometimes these "things" are events of the past (as in historical research). Other times these "things" are new samples that we gather (as in experimental or descriptive research). The two major categories of factual information are reports and statistics.

factual evidence defined

Reports

reports defined

A **report** is an account of what took place either by a participant or by an outside observer. In qualitative as well as quantitative research, reports are actively used. Researchers can gather these reports themselves, or they can use reports that others previously have gathered. We need to understand the types of reports researchers use in their arguments and the ways that we should join with them to test such reports.

Reports may be subdivided into two groups. **Primary sources** provide information obtained from individuals who have firsthand experience with the events reported. On the other hand, **secondary sources** provide information obtained from individuals who do not have firsthand experience with the events. Diaries and news accounts written by eyewitnesses to speeches are examples of primary evidence. Most history books, however, are secondary sources since the authors usually were not eyewitnesses to all the events described. As you might suspect, we have greater confidence in research reports from primary sources than from secondary sources. There are exceptions of course, and researchers must always test the credibility of reports.

distinguishing primary and secondary sources

primary sources preferred

We ask questions that test the credibility of reports to determine whether evidence offers compelling support for a researcher's claims. If the evidence and reasoning are strong, then we may be eager to accept research claims. If the evidence is weak, there may be little reason to accept statements advanced by researchers. The major tests of reports are listed below.

tests of reporting evidence

1. Can the reports be corroborated? Reports sometimes are not consistent with other established facts. Yet, they are so often repeated that they take on lives of their own. For instance, apparently one-fourth of the population believes in astrology (Bastedo, 1981, p. 241). Students at the University of California at Berkeley have reported that astrological signs have been used to discriminate against them in employment, with Scorpio and Taurus applicants most often denied jobs (Bastedo, 1981, p. 242). The ''reports'' found in astrology books continue to announce that certain groups are successful and dominant in given fields. For instance, Aquarians are alleged to be scientific and somewhat unconventional, such as Edison, Galileo, and Copernicus, who were Aquarians. Politicians are claimed to be favored by other signs. Yet, John D. McGervey (1981) evaluated these reports by reference to *American Men of Science* (16,634 birthdates included) and *Who's Who in American Politics* (6,475 birthdates included), which listed prominent members of each professional area. There was no difference in (1) the signs of members of the two groups; and (2) the frequency of astrological signs in each profession. If anything, there was a tendency for members of each profession to be born in late summer (a pattern inconsistent with the view that scientists tend to be Aquarians). Starting with reports from fourteen popular books on astrology, Ralph Bastedo (1981) examined leadership ability, political stand, intelligence, astrological belief, and twenty-eight other variables claimed in astrological reports. *None* of the sets of astrological assertions was supported by data. More than a dozen studies have tested astrological reports and no corroboration for astrology can be found. So much credible research exposes astrological reports as untrue that it is remarkable that claims for astrology continue to be made. As a rule, if a report cannot be corroborated by other facts, it is not convincing.

2. Are primary sources used? Secondary sources often get stories wrong. You may have heard that in the 1960 presidential debates, polls supposedly

showed that people who watched television thought that Kennedy won and people who listened on the radio thought Nixon won. Yet, David Vancil and Sue Pendell (1987) found that although secondary sources often reported the myth, primary sources told a different story. In fact, credible polls that distinguished between TV viewers and radio listeners could not be found, though anecdotes about nonscientific samples were reported. You may hear this misinformation repeated—but always from secondary sources.

3. Is the reporter reliable? Researchers may have to rely on reporters who lack the special skills or education required to grasp what they witness. Sometimes reporters cannot report competently because of factors outside their control. For instance, historical researchers studying the debates in the British House of Commons often have been frustrated since reporters did not always take accurate shorthand notes of important debates. Indeed, G. Jack Gravlee (1981) found that in some of the most significant debates conducted in the House of Commons, incomplete notes taken by reporters without shorthand skills made it nearly impossible to be confident about the reports of actual speeches presented. In contemporary times, audio and video recordings have improved the situation.

Statistical Reports

To read communication research, you will have to deal with statistics. Political polls, surveys of speech therapy needs, and trends in the use of cable television involve statistics that are used by all sorts of researchers in communication (not just experimental researchers).

statistics defined

Statistics defined by common usage are just numbers. But a precise understanding of the meaning of statistics is essential for everyone, regardless of his or her avowed communication specialty. **Statistics** are quantitative reports based on observations in a sample. When researchers gather facts, they may wish to summarize them in numbers. If these numbers are based on samples, we call them statistics. If every single event in a population were included in the study (difficult to pull off, unless the population is very narrowly defined), then numbers that describe the population would be called **parameters**.[1] The numbers that people deal with can cause difficulty if researchers are not careful. Hence, it makes sense to ask a few simple questions to test their proper use. At a later point in this book, the forms of statistics will be discussed in increasing detail.

parameters distinguished

tests for statistical evidence used in research

Questions that test the credibility of statistics help researchers separate the worthy statistical information from the unworthy. Though these tests sometimes require introducing related statistical concepts, you will find that they are very simple notions in practice.

1. Are the statistics recent? Statistics are only as good as the time period they cover. In studies during the early 1970s statistics tended to show that men used very little touching when communicating with other men. By the later 1970s, that statistic was questioned by some surveys. Hence, in dealing with statistics, one must be careful to identify the most recent relevant statistics, not just those that are conveniently available.

2. Was the sampling properly completed? As the very name suggests, samples do not include every person or event in the population. Instead, events are left out when samples are drawn. But since screwy samples probably can be found to prove any fool thing, researchers are supposed to draw samples that represent the populations. The most famous example of a misleading sample is the *Literary Digest* presidential poll of 1936. The *Literary Digest* was a popular magazine that was as frequent in American homes as, say, the *Reader's Digest* is today. The magazine conducted the largest public opinion survey ever. It collected over two million responses. The *Literary Digest* predicted that Alf Landon of Kansas would win. In reality, Landon was crushed in a landslide election for Franklin Roosevelt. Obviously, there was something wrong with the sample (see Wheeler, 1977, p. 82–86). In the first place, magazine subscribers—not a representative group—were asked to mail postcards to the magazine to indicate their presidential preferences. In the second place, people who purchased new automobiles in the middle of the Great Depression—another unrepresentative group—were surveyed. In the third place, people with listed telephone numbers were contacted—but in the 1930s telephones were not the essential utility that they are today. In the fourth place, people were permitted to send in additional postcards during the survey. But the individual's previous "ballot" was not replaced with the new one. The new postcards were just added to the total. In the late part of the campaign, when even Republican voters turned against Landon, the survey method made the shift impossible to detect. The magazine went out of business early in 1937. These days, if people have heard of the *Literary Digest* at all, they know only the embarrassment the magazine brought on itself by its poor sampling. Research statistics must use sound sampling to be worthwhile.

3. Were the measures accurate? Statistics are only as good as the data they measure. For instance, Americans frequently are heard "talkin' baseball." Trying to list the all-time best pitchers can be difficult because we may disagree about which statistical measure of pitching is a valid one. One newspaper that was partial to the St. Louis Cardinals published its ranking of pitchers that, not unexpectedly, placed Cardinal Bob Gibson as best (Siler, 1975). The newspaper claimed that the pitcher with the greatest number of wins was the best. Of course, such a measure may not be valid since winning a game depends not on the pitcher alone, but on the successful batting and fielding of one's teammates. Arguably, it would improve validity to compare pitchers by looking at the earned run average. Furthermore, the "games won" measure also may be an inaccurate measure since the number of years a pitcher plays increases the potential number of games that can be won. The quality of conclusions depends on the accuracy of the measures.

4. Were the procedures and methods appropriate? Some public relations research has been criticized for using inappropriate procedures. For instance, in one mass media blitz, Coke and Pepsi compared taste tests ("Coke-Pepsi Slugfest," 1976). Coke drinkers were approached by the Pepsi people and asked to give their preferences between cola drinks from containers marked Q (Coke) or

FIGURE 5.1
Misleading Graph
Relating School
Spending to SAT
Scores
ETS Policy Notes,
Vol. 1, No. 1, July 1988.
Reproduced with
permission of the Policy
Information Center,
Educational Testing
Service.

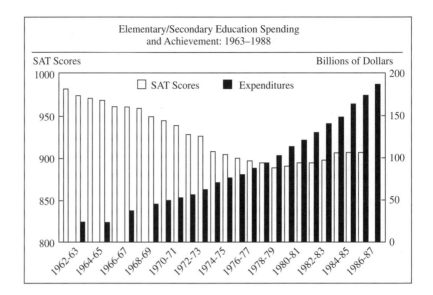

M (Pepsi). Pepsi "won." The procedures are doubtful since the labelling may have produced the reaction, not the quality of the drinks. Coca-Cola repeated the study placing Coke in *both* the M and Q containers. People still preferred the M container soda. Thus, the original Pepsi study should be treated suspiciously. Reasonable conclusions require using statistics from studies in which the procedures and methods are appropriate.

5. Were the statistics misleadingly presented? Sometimes statistics can be made to suggest things that they cannot really support. In 1988 an education policymaker produced a chart that apparently supported opposition to increased federal spending on U.S. education. The chart linked the amount of money spent on education to SAT scores, the latter of which had been declining. The chart (see figure 5.1) indicated that SAT scores declined as funding levels increased. But the chart was misleading. In the first place, SAT scores range from 400 to 1600, but the chart only showed the range from 800 to 1000. If appropriately drawn, the chart would have looked as figure 5.2 shows. In the second place, the money spent on education was a simple total of dollars, rather than dollars adjusted for inflation. If constant dollars had been used, the chart would have looked like figure 5.3, revealing a very modest increase in education investments over the years. In the third place, the SAT is not a measure of achievement, but a predictive tool. The chart originally presented was quite misleading.

Opinions

opinions defined

Though scholars work with the facts, they often use opinion statements as evidence in their research arguments. **Opinions** are interpretations of the meaning of collections of facts. Such opinions can be used to help researchers make sense of the facts that they have gathered.

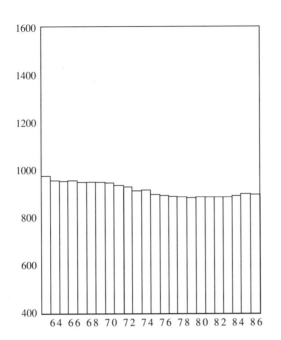

FIGURE 5.2
SAT Scores,
1963–1986
ETS Policy Notes,
Vol. 1, No. 1, July 1988.
Reproduced with
permission of the Policy
Information Center,
Educational Testing
Service.

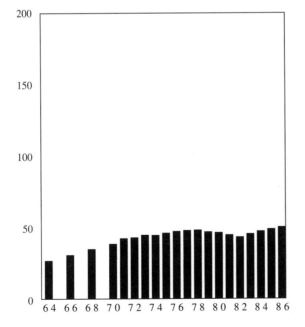

FIGURE 5.3
Elementary/Secondary
Education Spending
in Constant Dollars
(billions)
ETS Policy Notes,
Vol. 1, No. 1, July 1988.
Reproduced with
permission of the Policy
Information Center,
Educational Testing
Service.

Types of Opinion Information

**expert opinions
distinguished**

Researchers use opinions, regardless of whether they complete qualitative or quantitative research. Though opinions often come from laypeople, in research, we seek opinions only from people who are experts in the field of inquiry (sometimes called **expert opinions**). You may see quotations from experts who have summarized a body of literature or offered a judgment about the importance of an area of study. These statements are examples of expert opinion if they are derived from scholars who have special training and ability.

Testing the Credibility of Opinions

Researchers can ask key questions to determine when opinions deserve respect and when they should be discounted. This list of questions can be applied to opinion information regardless of the location of the opinion in a research article or paper.

1. *Is the opinion-maker competent?* Among other things, a trustworthy opinion is the result of competent examination of the facts by knowledgeable people. Often things that amaze laypeople disappear when examined by people with some competence on the issue. For instance, in the 1970s, an Israeli man named Uri Geller claimed to have supernatural powers. He claimed that his mind had the power to start watches, bend keys, guess the images others were thinking, and make things appear or disappear. He persuaded his manager, Yasha Katz, that he was a true psychic and for many years the manager expressed the opinion that Geller's activities were the result of actual psychic powers. Geller amazed many people including a host of celebrities and members of the public. When others trained in spotting magic tricks examined Geller's actions, each of his feats was revealed as a magic trick or sleight of hand (Randi, 1981; Marks & Kammann, 1981). Even manager Yasha Katz eventually admitted participating in Geller's magic tricks (in Randi, 1981, pp. 125–126). Thus, we probably should learn a lesson. Opinions from sources who have special competence deserve respect but opinions from the inexpert can be misleading.

2. *Is the opinion maker biased so much that the opinion is unreliable?* Everyone is entitled to his or her opinion (and most are *welcome* to them!). But a source who has very strong biases may not have reliable opinions. Consider these examples of clearly biased opinions found by comedian Jay Leno (1991) in United States newspapers:

> Headline: ''Attorneys don't want ban on lawyer-client sex''
> [Leno's comment: Now there's a shock.] (p. 10)
> Headline: ''MGM bounces checks, but says finances OK''
> [Leno's comment: Yeah, right, tell it to my landlord.] (p. 39)
> Headline: ''Ten Commandments declared obsolete by 'News King'
> Turner: TV Mogul Issues His Own 10 Rules''
> [Leno's comment: I guess if you've broken them all, they *are*
> obsolete.] (p. 16)

Obviously, such opinions are difficult to swallow given the source biases.

3. *Is the opinion consistent?* Naturally, opinions should be free of contradictions. In addition, if opinions are outside the mainstream of thought on a matter, one should be cautious about accepting them. Professor and former White House official Gary Sick published *October Surprise* (1991), in which he charged that the 1980 Ronald Reagan–George Bush campaign made secret arrangements with the government of Iran to delay the release of U.S. citizens held as hostages until after the election. Sick's opinion about alleged deceitfulness and potential criminal activity, however, was attacked by others for inconsistency of the opinion with judgments of contrary established facts (Emerson & Furman, 1991). Supporting the contrary opinions were denials by some key sources that they had made quoted statements to Sick, evidence that others on whom Sick relied were lying, and Secret Service records showing that key meetings between U.S. and Iranian officials could not have taken place as alleged.

Of course, sometimes inconsistent opinions are well founded and the "conventional wisdom" is unsound. Thus, researchers and readers of research should not discount inconsistent opinions when they offer superior reasoning and evidence to support their interpretations. For instance, for years communication scholars told people (and sometimes still do) that "brainstorming" was a more effective decision-making method than individual problem solving. Brainstorming involves gathering a group of people together to have a free-flowing oral sharing of ideas under strict time limits and set rules. In fact, the conventional wisdom was wrong. Fortunately, scholars who disagreed with accepted opinions possessed a lot of evidence to support their reasoning. Studies since 1964 have failed to support the superiority of making decisions by brainstorming. In fact, direct research indicates that brainstorming can lead people to generate fewer alternatives than when they are left alone (Lamm & Trommsdorf, 1971), and the method may be highly inefficient (Graham & Dillon, 1974). The body of research has impressively shown that the conventional wisdom has been horribly overstated (Jablin, Seibold, & Sorenson, 1977; Mongeau, 1993). Thus, when an inconsistent opinion is supported, we expect that very strong evidence and reasoning should exist for it.

EVALUATING RESEARCH ARGUMENTS

If researchers build arguments with evidence, they must use evidence in constructing arguments and lines of reasoning. These lines of reasoning are found in many different locations in research studies. You should know where to find them and how to evaluate them once you have identified them.

Finding Research Arguments

Research arguments are found in each major section of a research piece. These arguments function a bit differently in each section, but they are full arguments just the same. It helps to understand the sorts of arguments that people make in each section before considering ways to evaluate them.

The Review of Literature Argument

As you have learned, reviews of literature develop arguments that prove

four arguments developed in the literature review

- Why current study is invited (such as filling a gap in knowledge, solving a practical problem, or extending past research);
- What future methods should be used;
- What mistakes to avoid;
- Why a given research area is legitimate.

Literature review arguments set up the logical flow for the rest of the study. They also establish reasons for any hypotheses that are advanced. The research argument in the literature review tends to reason from specific *examples* of past research and from *applications of theories* related to the variables.

The Method of Study Argument

Though study methods may look like simple reports of tools that the researcher has selected, they are much more than descriptions. The researcher is expected to make a ''good faith'' effort to show that the methods are appropriate. Methods often involve explanations showing that

three arguments developed in study method

- Examples of communication behavior selected are relevant and representative;
- Methods of assessing and evaluating communication are sound responses to research questions;
- Tools of analysis are responsive to the data.

The explanations tend to be brief, but they should be appropriate to the problem questions that are asked. Researchers often use footnotes to indicate evidence and other related reasoning to support their choices. In addition, researchers frequently rely on *comparisons* of methods used in the current study with methods used in past efforts. These sorts of explanations are abbreviated arguments.

The Discussion Argument

The discussion of results of any study provides the researcher with a forum for making broad general interpretations. But there are limits to the sorts of conclusions that can be drawn. Researchers are expected to make statements about

four arguments developed in the discussion

- The answers to problem questions asked;
- The implications of the research findings;
- The theoretic importance of the research findings;
- The limitations of study findings and invitations to future inquiry.

tools of logic may be used to test these arguments

The methods and actual information examined in the study are the premises for these conclusions. Thus, the forms of reasoning used to draw conclusions can be judged by using the *tools of logic,* in which the relationships between argument premises and conclusions can be evaluated. Sometimes scholars draw conclusions that are irrelevant to research methods and findings. Sometimes the reasoning is logically flawed. Most of the time, of course, we hope that research conclusions are logically derived from the information in the study. Thus, researchers use formal lines of argument when asserting conclusions.

Patterns of Argument in Each Section

Different sections of research articles tend to feature some arguments more than others. It is helpful to know what major sorts of arguments are used in research and how to test them.

Inductive Reasoning to Conclusions

Inductive reasoning is "the process by which we conclude that what is true of certain individuals is true of a class, what is true of part is true of the whole class, or what is true at certain times will be true in similar circumstances at all times" (Mill in English & English, 1958, p. 259). Hence, we start with incomplete information on an issue and try to draw some (tentative) conclusions. This reasoning form typically appears at some locations more than others. It might help to mention some major species of inductive arguments. We will not attempt to do much more than introduce these forms.

margin note: **inductive reasoning defined**

The Ubiquitous Argument from Definition   is a method of reasoning in which people submit that things do or do not belong in a certain class (Reinard, 1991, p. 333; see also Ray & Zavos, 1966, pp. 89–93). Many times the arguments used in conclusions of articles are really just applications of definitions, though they may *sound* like explanations of facts. Researchers can get into very heated arguments about matters that cannot be settled by reference to facts because the dispute truly involves the proper meanings for words. Consider these statements that have stimulated researchers to engage in research and even to argue actively with each other:

margin note: **argument from definition defined**

- Arguments among people are transacted nonverbally (Willard, 1981; Burleson, 1980);
- All-news radio stations succeed because their programming is monotonous (Woal, 1987);
- The use of a logical positivist approach to conducting research is so concerned with abstraction and quantification of data that it fails to capture "the density of meaning present in the pre-structured social world [Delia & Grossberg, 1977, p. 37]" (see response from Miller & Berger, 1978, esp p. 47).

Though these statements may seem to be research matters that deal with the facts, they really are controversies about the proper meanings of words. No facts or data one could collect could prove or disprove the statements since the terms "argument," "monotonous," and "density of meaning," may be defined differently and are the true matters of dispute. In fact, the statements are assertions of definitions.

To test whether the argument from definition is acceptable, we ask the following questions:

margin note: **tests of arguments from definition**

1. Is there sound evidence for the appropriateness of "word meanings or usage" (Ray & Zavos, 1966, p. 93)?
2. If the reason for a conclusion is a definition, are conclusions properly limited to the meaning of terms in the research setting (after Ray & Zavos, 1966, p. 93)?
3. Is the definition truly equivalent to the term defined?

As you can tell, this method of arguing is one of the most frequent approaches taken by researchers. When reading research, therefore, we must be vigilant to see if an article deals with facts or with applications of special definitions.

argument from example and generalization defined

The Argument from Example and Generalization takes some particular cases and argues what is true of instances is generally true in the population of events. This method may be thought of as a form of pure inductive reasoning. As such, most conclusions in carefully controlled experiments are arguments by example and generalization. Even studies that analyze past speeches draw conclusions from specific communication instances. In fact, this method of reasoning is among the most popular forms of drawing conclusions in research.

tests of argument by example and generalization

Because we probably can find examples to prove almost anything, we need to examine such arguments very carefully. To test these arguments, we may ask:

1. Are the examples typical and representative?
2. Are enough examples cited?
3. Are the examples relevant to the conclusions drawn?

If the answer to any of these questions is unsatisfactory, the conclusions drawn from the reasoning can be limited accordingly.

analogy defined

The Argument from Analogy is often used in the sections of the study dedicated to the rationale and to the conclusion. Analogies compare "two things known to be alike in one or more features and . . . suggests that they will be alike in other features as well" (McDonald, 1980, p. 164). There are two forms of analogies: literal and figura-

literal and figurative analogies

tive. A **literal analogy** compares something to an event or object that really exists. A **figurative analogy** compares something to a hypothetical situation. Researchers argue from analogies when they claim that because past research has found a pattern of results, a new study might produce similar results despite some admitted differences from past inquiry. Researchers also use analogies when interpreting results, especially when they try to draw similarities between their research and theories that have been developed by others. Sometimes these claims are strained, and sometimes they are well founded. Denise Bostdorff (1991) examined the speaking of vice presidential candidates and found strong similarities between the speaking of 1984 candidate Geraldine Ferraro and Vice President Dan Quayle. Just as Ferraro took a role similar to the traditional female role in a comedic drama, so too, was Quayle viewed as taking this kind of role. Bostdorff flatly summarized, "The campaign of Dan Quayle paralleled, in many ways, that of Ferraro" (p. 1). Analogies frequently are used to draw conclusions advanced by scholars.

analogies used as more than illustrations

Some people think that analogies are best used as illustrations, rather than proof. But research arguments make such prominent use of analogies that you should not be surprised to see them used unashamedly. You may test whether the analogies are acceptable by asking some specific questions:

tests of analogies

1. Are the cases similar in many, rather than a few, essential respects?
2. Are there so many dissimilarities that the comparison is not reasonable?

3. Since literal analogies are preferred as proof, were literal analogies relied on instead of figurative analogies?

Analogies tend to occur most in conclusion discussions, but you should expect to find them in many locations in research pieces.

The Causal Argument reasons that "a given factor is responsible for producing certain other results" (Reinard, 1991, p. 197). Cause-and-effect reasoning appears in most historical and experimental studies, just as it should. Yet, causal arguments are often made in the conclusion and discussion sections of survey and descriptive studies—where they are usually *not* appropriate. Though experimental research uses methods to permit making cause and effect statements, descriptive research does not. Thus, we should read research that makes cause and effect conclusions with a jaundiced eye if only descriptive methods have been used.

causal arguments defined

Even studies that use appropriate methods to permit drawing cause-and-effect conclusions may present problems. To test whether cause and effect conclusions are used properly you should ask the following questions:

tests of causal arguments

1. Is there a direct and potent relationship between the cause and effect?
2. Can other causes actually explain the effects instead?
3. Can something else prevent the effect from occurring?
4. Is the cause capable of producing the effect all by itself (or must it be accompanied by other forces to produce the effect)?[2]

Deductive Reasoning and the Formal Tests Available. Though many research conclusions use inductive reasoning, not all do. A general principle is often applied to a related case. This method is called deductive since it starts with a general rule and then states that what is true of the larger class is true of specific events within it. You might have heard someone say that deductive reasoning is "reasoning from general to specific" and inductive reasoning is "reasoning from specific to general." But that claim is confusing and not very helpful. Some deductive arguments seem to move from one generalization to another generalization. Others seem to move from one set of specifics to other specifics. **Deductive reasoning** is simply a form of reasoning in which a valid conclusion necessarily follows from premises.

deduction defined

Deductive reasoning involves using syllogisms. A **syllogism** is a set of two premises that result in a conclusion. They are formal logical arguments and can be tested by rules developed by logicians. You do not have to study formal logic to appreciate how people use syllogisms in research. Articles with a strong theoretic rationale use deductive reasoning, as do articles appealing to some general principle to explain their research findings. Three major forms of syllogisms are used by researchers.

syllogism defined

The Categorical Syllogism starts with a categorical statement (an "allness" statement about things). Surely the most well-known categorical syllogism was expressed by Aristotle, the person who invented formal logic:[3]

categorical syllogism identified

SPECIAL DISCUSSION 5–2
The Special Fallacies of Research

Though fallacies of research reasoning are simply extensions of ordinary fallacies in any reasoning, there also are some additional fallacies that are unique to research (after Giere 1979, ch. 8).

The Delphi Fallacy involves the use of vague predictions as research claims. The fallacy takes its name from the Oracle of Delphi who gave predictions in such vague language that they were certain to come true. Once King Croesus asked the Oracle if he would be successful if he waged war on Persia. The Oracle responded, "If you wage war on Persia a mighty empire will be destroyed." So, Croesus waged war and an empire was destroyed—his own. The problem with vague predictions is that since they cannot be shown to be untrue, they are not really testable. Thus, vague predictions have no place in science.

The Jeanne Dixon Fallacy involves making multiple predictions and claiming partial support. "Psychic" Jeanne Dixon became famous when she claimed to predict the assassination of President Kennedy (she only predicted that Kennedy would die in office). Publishing hundreds of predictions each year, she publicizes those that are correct. But if you make enough predictions, some are likely to come true by dumb luck. This research fallacy occurs when scholars advance a host of hypotheses to support a theory, find most of them disproved, but claim "partial support" on the basis of the remaining hypotheses. Many know the power of this fallacy:

> There is a story, perhaps apocryphal, about a group of confidence men. . . . They contacted a lot of people (for purposes of example, say 1,000,000), told them that they had developed a new economic model that accurately predicts stock-market fluctuations, and mentioned one or two stocks which would shortly go up. . . . In fact, they had . . . made about fifty different predictions to fifty groups of 20,000. In some cases, the stock mentioned did go up. . . . After three or four series of predictions a few thousand people had had outstanding financial advice and many were lured to sign up and pay handsomely for future advice. (Alcock 1981, p. 96)

The Patchwork Quilt Fallacy involves making no predictions, but offering explanations after the fact. The fallacy gets its name from a quilt composed of random pieces of cloth, forming a pattern. Yet, in research, we expect justifications for selecting evidence. Erich Von Daniken wrote a book titled *Chariots of the Gods?* in which he noted similarities in architecture and recurrent legends that existed between the new and old worlds. He argued that these facts resulted from the earth being visited by beings from other worlds. When dissimilarities existed, he simply ignored them. Thus, we actually have no way to test whether Von Daniken is correct or incorrect. Moreover, pieces in his patchwork quilt were not justified as uniquely relevant to his explanation.

> ### SPECIAL DISCUSSION 5–2
> ### (Continued)
>
> *The Ad-Hoc Rescue* involves claiming support for a theory despite failed predictions. A large religious group that sells newsletters and calls on people door-to-door has predicted the end of the world for six different dates in this century. Each time the world did not end, they added additional explanations, including computation errors and imprecise biblical predictions. In the last few years they began denying ever making any predictions at all, though a written record shows to the contrary. Religious beliefs are personal matters, of course. But in research, the *ad hoc* rescue occurs when a theory that is claimed to predict matters fails and is followed by an effort to rescue it with random excuses. In scholarship, the false prophesy of a failed theory is enough to make people reject the entire research argument.

Major Premise: All men are mortal.
Minor Premise: Socrates is a man.
Conclusion: (Therefore) Socrates is mortal.

The terms all have names to help in applying rules. The biggest term of all, "things that are mortal," is called the major term. The smallest or most specific term, "Socrates," is called the minor term. The remaining term between the major and minor terms, "men," is called (appropriately) the middle term. Violations of proper structure make the reasoning "invalid" because the conclusion cannot follow logically from the premises.   **terms in the categorical syllogism**

    This method is a chief tool in the literature review and the discussion section argument. For instance, one article found that television is used by Korean immigrants to become socialized into the U.S. political system (Chaffee, Nass & Yang, 1990), concluding: **uses of the categorical syllogism**

> When a lack of both English language skills and U.S. political understanding pose a significant constraint on reading, television news can fill the gap [to secure political understanding]. For at least a short time, television becomes the principal agent of political socialization for many immigrants. . . . [T]elevision . . . links home political understanding with host political knowledge for those who have little choice. (284)

With some transposing, we may cast the argument in this form:

> MP: People who have a significant constraint on reading English use television to secure political understanding.
> mp: For at least a short time, immigrants have a significant constraint on reading English.
> C: For immigrants, television becomes the principal agent to secure political socialization.[4]

If the premises are true and the reasoning is valid, the conclusions are guaranteed to be true. Table 5.1 shows the major tests used to assess the validity of syllogisms. Obviously, we expect good research reasoning to pass these formal tests. You may use them to evaluate the merit of the reasoning researchers use in literature review arguments and conclusions.

TABLE 5.1 Rules for Syllogisms

Rules	Example of Forbidden Reasoning
The Categorical Syllogism	
1. The syllogism must have a middle term that is distributed (used in an "allness" statement) at least once.	MP: Some speakers are persuasive. mp: Harold Stassen is a speaker. C:　Therefore, Harold Stassen is persuasive.
2. No term may be distributed in the conclusion if it is not distributed in a premise.	MP: Communists want to help the poor. mp: John Anderson wants to help the poor. C:　Therefore, John Anderson is a communist. (This flaw is called an illicit conversion.)
3. A negative conclusion can occur only when one of the premises is negative.	MP: No communists like economic recessions. mp: Harold Stassen is not a communist.
4. Both premises cannot be negative.	C:　Therefore, (?)
5. If a conclusion describes a particular, one premise must be particular.	MP: All household pets are domestic animals. mp: No unicorns are domestic animals. C:　Therefore, some unicorns are not household pets. (This example implies that unicorns actually exist without showing the particular in a premise [Copi, 1968, p. 174].)
The Conditional Syllogism	
1. The minor premise must not deny the antecedent.	MP: If speakers are men, they will be credible. mp: Speakers are not men. C:　Therefore, (?)
2. The minor premise must not affirm the consequent.	MP: If speakers are men, they will be credible. mp: Speakers are credible. C:　Therefore, (?)
The Disjunctive Syllogism	
1. The major premise must include all alternatives.	MP: Either you can work full time or go to college. mp: You will work part time and go to college. C:　Therefore, (?)
2. The major premise must deny or affirm a term in the major premise.	MP: Either you can work full time or go to college. mp: You will neither work full time nor go to college. C:　Therefore, (?)
3. The alternatives must be mutually exclusive of each other.	MP: Either you can work full time or go to college. mp: You will work full time and go to college, too. C:　Therefore, (?)

The Disjunctive Syllogism   makes an "either-or" statement. These syllogisms are found in research arguments in which scholars try to compare the predictions of conflicting theories or expectations. For instance, there is a body of research on the impact of violent programming on television viewers. Two conflicting theories have been developed. One theory called *arousal* predicts that watching violence on TV leads people (especially children) to be aroused or stimulated to other acts of violence. A second theory called *catharsis* holds that watching TV violence reduced people's tendencies to engage in violence. A raft of studies contrasted these two views (see Huesmann, 1982). The rationale for the studies focused on an obvious disjunctive syllogism:

disjunctive
syllogism defined

MP: Either the arousal theory is supported by research or the catharsis theory is
    supported by research.
mp: [for example] The catharsis theory is not supported by the research.
C: (Therefore) The arousal theory is supported by research.

By the way, this syllogism has been the basis for major literature reviews (e.g., Milavsky, Kessler, Stipp & Rubens, 1982), revealing that it is both materially true and structurally valid. You will find similar arguments at different locations in research. It is very helpful to use the tests found in table 5.1 to evaluate the merit of such arguments.

The Conditional Syllogism   makes an "if-then" statement. When people speak of the logic of hypothesis testing, they are not kidding. The conditional syllogism is the method that is used in the hypothesis, methods, and discussion of results sections of research articles. All hypotheses boil down to "if-then" statements, such as "If stutterers are given delayed speech feedback, then the amount of stuttering will decrease." The major premise of a conditional syllogism is simply a hypothesis. The minor premise of one of these syllogisms must either affirm the "if" part of the hypothesis or deny the "then" part of the hypothesis. The methods section of a research article is designed to describe the materials and procedures that are used to complete the minor premise. The conclusion is simply a statement of the results that must occur if the hypothesis points to a valid conclusion. The material for the conclusion describes the eventual findings related to the hypothesis. If the hypothesis, the methods, and the results all match up, then a logical argument for the hypothesis can be made. If there is an error, then the hypothesis cannot be supported.

conditional
syllogism defined
used in the logic of
hypothesis testing

The form of the conditional syllogism is as follows:

MP: If stutterers are given delayed speech feedback, then the amount of stuttering
    will decrease.
mp: Stutterers in a study are given delayed speech feedback.
C: (Therefore) the amount of stuttering will decrease.

Each section of the research article serves as support for the premises and conclusions. If the truth of the premises and conclusions is accompanied by valid reasoning, then the hypothesis is supported. The rules for the valid use of the conditional syllogism are found in table 5.1.

SUMMARY

Scholars reason from evidence to advance their conclusions. Two categories of research evidence are used: factual information, including statistics, and opinions offered to interpret facts. Factual information consists of descriptions and characterizations of things. The two forms of factual information are reports and statistics. A report is an account of what took place whether by a participant or by an outside observer. Primary sources of reports provide information obtained from individuals who have firsthand experience with the events reported, whereas secondary sources are from individuals who do not have firsthand experience. To test the credibility of reports, you should ask (1) Can the reports be corroborated? (2) Are primary sources used? (3) Is the reporter reliable? Statistics are quantitative reports based on observations in a sample. If every single event in a population were included in the study, then the numbers that describe the population would be called parameters. To test the credibility of statistics you should ask (1) Are the statistics recent? (2) Was the sampling properly completed? (3) Were the measures accurate? (4) Were the procedures and methods appropriate? (5) Were the statistics misleadingly presented?

Opinions are interpretations of facts. Expert opinions come from people who are experts in the field of inquiry. To test the credibility of opinions, you may ask (1) Is the opinion-maker competent? (2) Is the opinion-maker biased so much that the opinion is unreliable? (3) Is the opinion consistent?

Research arguments are found in each major section of a research piece. Reviews of literature develop arguments that prove why current study is invited, what future methods should be used, what mistakes to avoid, and why a given research area is legitimate. The method of study argument involves the researcher's "good faith" effort to show that the methods are appropriate. The discussion argument provides the researcher with a forum to reason about the answers to problem questions, implications of the research findings, theoretic importance of the research findings, limitations on study findings, and invitations to future inquiry. Different sections of research articles feature different arguments. Inductive reasoning (the process by which we conclude that what is true of certain individuals is true of a class, what is true of part is true of the whole class, or what is true at certain times will be true in similar circumstances at all times) is found in reasoning to conclusions. There are several sorts of inductive arguments including: (1) the ubiquitous argument from definition (in which people submit that things do or do not belong in a certain class); (2) the argument from example and generalization (which takes some particular cases and argues what is true of instances is generally true in the population of events); (3) the argument from analogy, which is often used in the sections of the study dedicated to the rationale and to the conclusion, and compares "two things known to be alike in one or more features and ... suggests that they will be alike in other features as well" (a literal analogy compares something to an event or object that really exists whereas a figurative analogy compares something to a hypothetical situation); (4) the causal argument (which reasons that a given factor is responsible for producing certain other results).

Deductive reasoning involves inference in which a valid conclusion necessarily follows from premises. It includes some use of a syllogism (a set of two premises that result in a conclusion). The categorical syllogism starts with a categorical statement and is a chief tool in the literature review and the discussion section arguments. The disjunctive syllogism has an "either-or" statement in the major premise and is found in research arguments that try to compare the predictions of conflicting theories or expectations. The conditional syllogism has an "if-then" statement in the major premise and is used in the hypothesis, methods, and discussion of results sections of research articles. The major premise of a conditional syllogism is simply a hypothesis.

TERMS FOR REVIEW

evidence
factual evidence
reports
primary sources
secondary sources
statistics
parameters
opinions
expert opinions
inductive reasoning
argument from definition

argument from example and generalization
argument from analogy
literal analogy
figurative analogy
causal argument
deductive reasoning
syllogism
categorical syllogism
disjunctive syllogism
conditional syllogism

NOTES

[1]Don't confuse the word "parameter" with a boundary or limit on some subject. The word for a boundary is "perimeter"—close in spelling, but miles away in meaning. A parameter, speaking in metaphorical terms, can refer to the defining characteristics of a population of events. But the parameters we most often look at are averages and amounts of variability. A boundary could be one of many parameters researchers look at (not very often though), but most parameters are not boundaries. Got it? Don't say parameter when you mean boundary or perimeter. They do not mean the same thing at all.

[2]This distinction between types of causes involves what are called necessary and sufficient causes or conditions. A *necessary condition* is one of several contributors required to produce the effect. A *sufficient condition* is capable of producing the effect all by itself. People often say that a cause is "necessary but not sufficient" when they mean that more than one contributor to the effect must exist to produce the effect.

[3]Think about it. *Some*body had to invent logic. Aristotle did so about 2300 years ago.

[4]You may have noticed that the syllogism took some twisting to make it fit. If it weren't twisted, the syllogism would not be valid, as in: MP: Television links home political understanding with host political knowledge for those who have little choice; mp: For at least a short time, television becomes the principal agent of political socialization for many immigrants; C: (therefore) When a lack of both English language skills and U.S. political understanding pose a significant constraint on reading, television news can fill the gap [to secure political understanding]. In this argument the middle term is used in the conclusion without having been distributed in the major premise; it also uses the reworded conclusion as the major premise.

CHAPTER 6

Conceptualizations in Communication Research

There is nothing so practical as a good theory.

–Kurt Lewin

BEFORE WE GET STARTED . . .

Research is guided by the conceptualizations scholars use. Theories play a central role in scholarship and give us ways to organize bodies of knowledge. Indeed, a purpose of research is to develop theoretic explanations for things. Yet, using concepts requires defining them so that they can be studied. Thus, this chapter explains what theories are, the forms of coherent definitions, and standards you can use to evaluate them.

DEVELOPING THEORETIC CONCEPTUALIZATIONS IN COMMUNICATION

importance of theory

Research attempts to find relationships and explain them. Theories help us understand these relationships. Whether or not we are aware of it, most significant claims we make rely on theory-oriented statements. Moreover, formal and informal theories are sources of research hypotheses. In fact, theory construction is a purpose of all research, scholarship, and science. Some have made this goal central to research. Look at these typical statements about theory in research:

- Research is guided by theory and contributes to theory (Tucker, Weaver & Berryman-Fink, 1981, p. 14).
- The basic aim of science is theory (Kerlinger, 1986, p. 8).
- We found the fundamental aim of science to be the development of explanatory conceptualizations, called *theories* (Mason & Bramble, 1989, p. 29).
- A researcher's aim . . . is *to generate theoretical explanations for observed patterns of human communication* (M. J. Smith, 1988, p. 10).

In general, research is a means to an end, not an end in itself. The goal of research is to develop theories and explanations. Thus, we should consider whether communication is scientific enough to have true theories, the anatomy of theories, and the roles communication theories have for us.

Is Communication "Scientific" Enough to Have Theories?

To decide whether communication can be approached as a science (or social science), it makes sense first to define "science" and remove some myths about it.

Prerequisites for Science

Science is as much a frame of mind as it is anything else. Stuart Chase (1954, p. 110) described science as "a label for our attempts to find out how the universe works by means of careful observation rather than armchair speculation." Though this description is accurate, there are several competing views of science that you may have heard. Horace and Ava English in their *Comprehensive Dictionary of Psychological and Psychoanalytical Terms* (1958) reviewed the major approaches along with a comment about each one's usefulness, starting with:[1]

> **science as an attitude**

> **meanings of science:**

1. The study of natural phenomena by the methods of the physical and biological sciences (p. 479)

> **1. science as something done in science departments**

The first view claims that science is what people in the natural sciences do. Yet, the definition excludes things properly included as sciences. English and English explained:

> This usage, while common, arbitrarily excludes most investigations and systematizations of knowledge in the psychological and social disciplines. Such a division is not warranted either by historical development or by the contemporary state of affairs, and it gives to science in English a narrower connotation than that of related expression in other European languages (pp. 479–480).

"Science" comes from the Latin word *scientia,* which means "knowledge." Thus, it would seem that systematic ways to obtain knowledge about the facts might bear some relationship to science. Yet, the first definition excludes them.

A second definition of science holds that it is

2. Organized and systematic knowledge (p. 480)

> **2. science as any organized knowledge**

Scholarship and research are not the only ways to answer questions and draw conclusions. In fact, reasonable actions are sometimes based on nonresearch methods. The most well-known nonscholarly methods include the following (after Peirce, 1955, esp ch. 2):

- The method of tenacity, in which we claim to know something because we have always known it (the method of tenacity may be correct most of the time, but it is misguided when facts change and decisions need to be revised).
- The method of authority, in which a claim is accepted because authority figures have accepted it (though this method leads people to correct conclusions most of the time, under some conditions, it may be flawed).
- The a priori (Latin for "from the earlier part") *method,* which claims knowledge before having any experience with it (thus, we believe a priori that "all men are created equal" without needing to gather data on the matter—this method usually leads to timeless conclusions that are beyond research).
- The method of trial and error, which claims knowledge by making repeated trials to eliminate unacceptable answers (eventually, persistent failures disprove so many alternatives that an answer will emerge—though trial and error provides very sure knowledge, "learning through experience" is a very slow and inefficient way to develop claims about things we know).

Research, on the other hand, makes claims by using the tools of scholarship and science, which involve two processes: making observations of things and using the tools of reasoning to evaluate different explanations of observations. Research method may be used in two ways to help draw conclusions:

- Developing claims from reviews of literature, using documents such as past studies to help compose problem statements. Such a literature review permits research conclusions to be drawn from research documents previously unrelated to each other. A variation in the research literature review argument is **meta-analysis,** which combines quantitative results from many studies to reveal the overall sizes of effects that exist among variables.
- Using the scientific approach to guide development of claims involving application of the scientific method. Though the scientific method has been described by different scholars as including various numbers of steps, at minimum, it involves collecting data and establishing "a functional relationship among these data" (Bachrach, 1981, p. 4). Some others list as many as seven steps (Jones, 1973). The steps are not necessarily followed in order. In fact, most researchers find that they cycle back from one step to another. The important thing is that the scientific method forces scholars to stay close to the facts of a matter. We will suggest four steps to the scientific method:[2]

    1. Observing facts either casually or formally leading to developing a fundamental research question.
    2. Developing a working hypothesis or theoretical solution to guide the research (though researchers may revise their ideas and develop formal explanations).
    3. Testing expectations against information.
    4. Establishing a conclusion or functional relationship based on deciding whether the working hypothesis or theoretic solution is supported.

In fact, any time researchers check expectations against information, they are applying the scientific method. Indeed, both quantitative and qualitative research can be completed using the scientific method.

Yet, many projects that *never* reference data to check expectations (part of the scientific method) would be included in this definition's view. English and English criticized this definition as follows:

> This usage, though occasionally useful, is as much too broad as the first is too narrow (p. 480).

A third view holds that science is the use of particular methods to develop knowledge (across subject fields).

3. A particular body of knowledge—e.g., physics, physiology, psychology—distinguished by the special set of operations employed in gathering empirical facts and by a distinctive set of constructs employed in interpreting the data (p. 480).

3. science as the application of the scientific method

This definition tells us that a field becomes a science when it uses the scientific method. After time, as well, each field begins to concentrate on some key concepts of its own to study. In our field, we have focused on such concepts as communication apprehension, speech and hearing disorders, and broadcast of messages through television and radio. Using the scientific method makes a field a science even before a great deal of information exists on it. For instance, we could ask when chemistry became a science instead of a magician's bag of illusions. Chemistry certainly is a science now. Yet, how many chemistry studies had to be completed before we recognized chemistry as a science worthy of the name? The question sounds a bit silly. The reason is that chemistry—as with all fields that qualify as sciences—became a science when the scientific method was used in research. The method to gather information defines a field as a science, not simply the results of applying the method. Thus, we can define **science** as a way of testing statements by systematic application of the scientific method.[3]

science defined

Is Communication a Science?

Since science has been defined as the use of the scientific method to gather information, we might ask if communication can be considered a science. It all depends on the method a researcher chooses to use. If a communication scholar relies on nonresearch methods of knowing about communication—tenacity, authority, *a priori* belief, and trial and error—then the scholar is not "doing science." If communication scholars rely on the method of aesthetics or art to explore communication (as is often done in oral interpretation of literature studies), then the inquiries would not be defined as "science." On the other hand, if the scholar uses the research methods to know things about communication, then communication is a science. All communication research states problems, sets criteria for permissible interpretation, and makes careful observations of communication transactions. Thus, using research methods in communication makes communication a scientific study area.

communication is a science if the scientific method is used

To say that communication is a science if the methods of science are used to study it, however, should not be misinterpreted. We are only talking about the *study* of communication, not the practice of communication by artists and practitioners. The study of communication is a science if one chooses to use the

though study of communication may be a science its practice is an art

> ## SPECIAL DISCUSSION 6–2
> ## Models, Laws, Rules, and Metatheories
>
> Theory construction has developed a language of its own. Though the terms defined below are often mixed together, they are really different things.
>
> - Model　Though a model (such as a communication model) often is just a picture used to explain a concept, it is actually an expression that not only states relationships but displays them. All mathematic statements (for example, $E=mc^2$) and physical prototypes are models since they display relationships.
> - Law　"A verbal statement, supported by such ample evidence as not to be open to doubt unless much further evidence is obtained, of the way events of a certain class consistently and uniformly occur" (English & English, 1958, p. 288).[4] Of course, all laws have limits (for example, the laws of falling bodies don't apply to objects outside a vacuum), and communication laws often hit their boundaries very rapidly.
> - Rule　"A theory that explains a pattern of effects by referring to human intentions, reasons, or goals" (M. J. Smith, 1988, p. 354). Rules express patterns of expected activity, though changing intentions, reasons, or goals may make people occasionally appear inconsistent (people break rules on occasion, but the rules are a regularity nonetheless).
> - Metatheories　Ways we think about theories are called "metatheories" to indicate notions "beyond the theories" themselves. Metatheories influence issues to explore, definitions, and designs in research. Some prominent metatheories include positivist/atomist views, phenomenology, general systems theory, and constructivism.

scientific method to inquire into it. The *practice* of communication remains an art to be performed and refined.

Anatomy of Theories

misinterpreting theory

We had better get rid of a common misconception. Theories are not just wild ideas people have. When somebody tells us that he or she "has a theory" about something, it usually is just a bold, unsupported claim. True theories must meet certain obligations and standards to earn the label. Theories allow us to organize and—if we do it right—understand communication phenomena. Kenneth Hoover (1979, p. 37) explained this role for theory:

> Science rests its claim to authority upon its firm basis in something called "reality." We occasionally described science as, simply, reality testing. Since everybody thinks they [*sic*] know what reality is, science acquires a fundamental appeal. Yet the necessary partner of realism in science is that wholly imaginary phenomenon, *theory*. Without the many roles that theory plays, there would be no science (and, some would argue, there would be no understandable "reality" either).

It would help if we understood what a theory truly is and what its elements are.

Definition of a Theory

A **theory** is "a body of interrelated principles that explain or predict" (*Longman Dictionary of Psychology,* 1984, p. 744).[5] Obviously, theories are not just wild ideas that people have. Instead, a theory is a logical system that organizes and explains the facts. Though theories are often modified as they develop and reflect research, they still are composed of elements that have a fairly fixed form. Theories help answer research questions. Furthermore, their development and modification are objectives of research.

theory defined

Components of Theory

It would be wise to understand elements that must be present for a true theory to exist. All theories must have three characteristics: an abstract calculus, theoretic constructs, and rules of correspondence (after Deutsch & Krauss, 1965, ch. 1).

elements of a theory

An **abstract calculus** is simply the logical structure of relationships. The word "calculus" refers to any deductive system. So, what is a deductive system? A deductive system is a logical method in which conclusions are drawn from premises. The logical form called the "conditional syllogism" is often used by researchers, for example:

1. abstract calculus defined

> Major premise: If p, then q
> Minor premise: p
> Conclusion: (therefore,) q

The relationships in the theory are its abstract calculus. This example states that as one event occurs another event should also occur. The exact form of the relationships defines the nature of the theory. For instance, suppose we had a theory with a principle stating that as a speaker's physical attractiveness increases, the speaker's persuasiveness also increases. The theory has a major premise such as:

> Major premise: If a speaker's physical attractiveness increases, then the speaker's persuasiveness will increase.

To test the soundness of the theory, we could gather data and see if we could complete the rest of the argument. We might plan an experiment that had a persuasive message given by an attractive source (and for control purposes, an unattractive source as well). If the theory has any merit, the results of the experiment should be reflected in facts that are consistent with the logical conclusion that must follow from the premises. For instance,

> Major premise: If a speaker's physical attractiveness increases, then the speaker's persuasiveness will increase.
> Minor premise: (An experiment is completed in which) a speaker's physical attractiveness increases.
> Conclusion: (therefore, the experimental results must show that) the speaker's persuasiveness increases.

If the facts do not support the conclusion that must follow logically, then no valid argument can be made for the theory.

The abstract calculus is just the relationship expressed in the statement, if p, then q. The statement that as one increases, the other does too is the statement of relationship, regardless of the terms involved in the relationship. But, to have a theory, we do need some specific terms. These terms are the second element in any theory.

2. constructs defined

Theoretic constructs are the terms that we substitute into the abstract calculus of a theory. In specific terms, **constructs** are "generalizations about observables according to some common property" (Deutsch & Krauss 1965, p. 5). Constructs are general terms that group many instances of activity together into meaningful units. But constructs are the generalizations, not the events themselves. For instance, self-esteem is a construct. So is source credibility. So is newspaper sensationalism. But nobody has ever seen your self-esteem. Nobody has ever seen your source credibility. Nobody can see your newspaper's sensationalism. These terms are used to describe a collection of variables that have been found. Though nobody has seen your self-esteem, there are behaviors—variables—that people have seen about you. People could say that you have been observed: (1) stating that you trust your own opinions; (2) setting high goals for yourself; and (3) stating that you believe that you are competent in many ways. But people don't talk that way. Instead, these variables in your activity may be summarized by the useful general term, "self-esteem." So, constructs are summary descriptions about collections of specific variables.

In the theory we have been considering, two constructs have been identified: physical attractiveness and persuasiveness. These key terms cannot be seen. Instead, collections of variables share attractiveness in common (such as measurable evaluations of personal appearance, style of dress, and ratings of personal beauty) and collections of variables share persuasiveness as a common feature (such as variables of measurable attitude change, reported behavioral intentions to perform future activities, and changes in reported value systems). These key terms—constructs—are the matters related by the abstract calculus of a theory.

hypothetical constructs defined

Even though constructs are general terms, it is possible to get full definitions for them. You may sometimes hear of **hypothetical constructs** or concepts. These are constructs for which we cannot make observations directly. Such things as "cognitive consistency," "motivational inertia," and "individual needs" are examples of matters that have been axioms employed in some very interesting theories. They cannot be seen, but they can often be useful as starting assumptions to get us thinking in interesting directions.

3. rules of correspondence defined

Rules of correspondence show how well the theory's constructs and abstract calculus can be applied to actual experience. They are used to apply theories. We occasionally hear people say that something "looks good in theory" but won't work in practice. But if a theory won't work in practice, it's a bad theory. It is a contradiction in terms to say that a theory won't work in practice. All theories must have sound rules of correspondence.

all elements required for theory to exist

The three components of a theory are like a three-legged stool. If any one of the legs is knocked away, the entire structure falls. Similarly, if any element of theory is missing, one does not have a theory that can stand. In the theory on source physical attractiveness we have been examining, rules of correspondence are fairly strong. Among methods to study physical attractiveness, some research has shown people pictures of speakers who varied in physical attractiveness (for review see Berscheid, 1985). Persuasion has been studied in a host of ways, ranging from measures of attitude change to reviews of historical trends. Of course, in some cases, one must wait for rules of correspondence to catch up to the theory.

Requirements of Theory

Some strange things masquerade as theories. It is important to recognize them so that you are not mislead. Fortunately, two requirements help separate true theories from counterfeits.

1. The requirement of falsification holds that any theory must deal with statements that could be falsified by data and information if the theories were untrue.[6] In the Middle Ages through the Renaissance, it was believed that fire was caused by something called "phlogiston." This substance had to be present to cause a fire, but it was completely combusted (leaving no trace) by fire. So, if you rubbed two sticks together and got a fire, you knew phlogiston had been present, even though you could not prove it now. If you could not start a fire by rubbing sticks together, then there simply was no phlogiston in the sticks (you could look and you wouldn't find any). The problem, of course is that the theory of combustion was incapable of falsification. Today we know that phlogiston does not exist, but in those days there was no acceptable evidence that one could produce that could disprove the phlogiston theory. Phlogiston, then, was not a true theory. Today, similar problems abound and articles of faith sometimes are advanced as scientific theory. We must recognize the difference if we are to avoid wasting our time.

   theories must be capable of being falsified if they are incorrect

2. The requirement of tentativeness demands that scholars recognize that a theory's answers are provisional. Theories can only describe part of the reality that exists. Other theories may emerge at a later time that provide improved explanations. We do not mean that existing theories are proven wrong by new ones. Instead, relationships are redefined by new theories. Sometimes existing theories are shown to be special cases of the new theory's applications. Using theories means that a researcher's explanations are not the only ones that will be found. Thus, conclusions should be developed with a certain amount of tentativeness.

   theories are only tentative explanations

Functions of Theory

Theories can operate for four different but interrelated purposes. These purposes are a sort of hierarchy of theory, and they all play an important role in scholarship.

1. **Description** is the lowest level of theorizing, in which behavior is characterized into different forms. For instance, there has been continuous interest in identifying what are called "compliance gaining message strategies." Much of the original theorizing by Marwell and Schmitt (1967) attempted simply to identify the sorts of methods that people are using to influence others. In recent times, Scott Jacobs and Sally Jackson (1979a,b) have dedicated

   1. description

much of their time describing patterns of conversations in actual and potential exchanges people can have. They have found that interpersonal conflicts include the additional categories of hints, prompts, and projections from other people. Such work can challenge ways people think about basic concepts.

2. explanation defined

2. **Explanation** involves taking an event and treating it as an instance of a larger system of things (after Homans, 1961, p. 10). In general, we attempt to explain things that have occurred. Logical explanations occur when a behavior is shown to be a logical application of theory. The Uses and Gratifications theory, for instance, has been used to explain the reasons people regularly watch TV quiz programs (McQuail, Blumler & Brown, 1972).

3. prediction

3. **Prediction** describes what can be expected in the future. Prediction sometimes is considered a separate step for theories, but as one writer put it

> Predicting events that will occur in the future and explaining events that have occurred in the past are, except for a difference in temporal perspective, essentially the same activity as long as scientific statements are abstract (Reynolds, 1971, p. 5).

prediction may be one means for explanation

In fact, predicting is one useful way to explain things. Attempts to predict future events are prominent in many theories in communication. For instance, Berger and Calabrese (1975) developed a theory of initial interactions people have with each other. The theory submits that we communicate in ways that help us reduce our uncertainty when we meet new people. One specific prediction in this theory has received a lot of attention: "High levels of uncertainty cause increases in information seeking behavior" (p. 103). This statement has guided researchers' expectations for future studies. Moreover, it allows people a way to predict what might happen when they meet new people.

4. control identified

4. **Control** is the power to direct things. Some theories provide information to influence our own personal environment. Thus, control really is the degree to which we can find useful additional applications for the explanations of a theory. Certainly if people know what is expected to occur in the future, they can use that information to affect their environment.

Applications of Theory

Researchers use theories in ways that reflect their preferences. Developing theories involves setting priorities and making some choices.

Data First versus Theory First Inquiry

**data first inquiry identified
theory first inquiry identified**

In general, there are two approaches to theory and inquiry. Sometimes called the "inductive approach" to research, the first method involves gathering information and then developing theoretic explanations. Rather than becoming locked into a formal theory, one gathers information on an open canvas of observation. Researchers doing exploratory work often employ this approach. In addition, scholars who study samples of naturally occurring conversations tend to use this approach (they often try to gather samples of conversation to develop theories rather than to test existing theories). The second approach is just the opposite: one develops

TABLE 6.1 Theory First versus Data First Research		
	Theory First	**Data First**
Advantages	1. "Theories may develop from any source and are not limited to phenomena that can be observed with current measuring instruments" (M. J. Smith, 1988, p. 13).	1. One does not enter research with biases.
	2. One may be free to take advantage of serendipity since unexpected findings are readily identified.	2. One may be free to follow unexpected directions.
	3. Promotes efficient research since key variables of interest are identified early.	3. One stays close to data and avoids tendencies toward reification (the fallacy of thinking that abstract concepts are concrete things).
Disadvantages	1. Researchers may force theoretic explanations on information even if it is inappropriate to do so.	1. "Explanations are limited to phenomena that can be observed with current measuring instruments" (M. J. Smith, 1988, p. 13).
	2. Theories may become articles of faith to their followers, even after the theories have outlived their usefulness.	2. Does not test alternative theoretic explanations, but develops suggestions for theory.
	3. Theories are difficult to construct and require exhaustive thinking beyond the energies of most scholars.	3. Promotes inefficient research since key variables of interest are not identified early.

theoretic thinking and then gathers data to apply and test it. Table 6.1 shows the advantages and disadvantages typically claimed for each approach. As you can see, some of the advantages argued for the data-to-theory method involve the flexibility of the approach. Similarly, most of the advantages of the theory-to-data method deal with the rigor and logic it provides.

There is hot controversy among scholars about the desirability of each approach. For all the division drawn between them, however, they share some elements in common. When first developing theories, researchers make informal notes about activities they find interesting. Such unstructured data collection leads to thinking that may evolve into tentative theories for testing. Thus, to develop theories, some sort of data collection (though we may not want to call it formal research) enriches the effort. Similarly, it is hard to imagine how researchers could select variables to study unless they had some hunches that stimulated them to look at some activities instead of others. Arthur Bachrach described how these undeveloped (and unstated) theoretic orientations appear: "I think all investigators make these on-the-spot hypotheses. Some call them hunches: I choose to call them hypothesitos, which is semi-Spanish for "little hypotheses" (1981, p. 70). Thus, it really may be impossible to have "theory free" research. There is always some idea behind selecting concepts and variables for study. But some researchers prefer

both approaches share much in common

data first researchers use theories or little hypotheses to select variables for study

not to work from fully developed theoretic statements at the beginning of their inquiries. Theory development *both* follows and precedes researchers' observations. Thus, it is clear that theory and observation go hand-in-hand in the research craft.

Normative, Ethical, and Rhetorical Theories

Predictive theories are not the only sorts of theories we have in communication. We often hear about such things as "rhetorical theory," "information theory," or "argumentation theory." Such theories are known as normative or ethical theories. In communication studies, you are likely to see references to both predictive and normative theories. Furthermore, these two categories have promoted very different sorts of research efforts.

normative and prescriptive theories identified:

Normative and prescriptive theories are those whose principles involve defining the qualities that make communication meaningful or desirable. The area of normative theory comes from work in what sometimes is called "normative science," which is "a discipline that systematically studies man's attempts to determine what is correct, valuable, good, or beautiful" (English & English, 1958, p. 349).[7]

1. ethical and rhetorical theories identified

Ethical theory and rhetorical studies have gone hand in hand. In specific terms, **ethical and rhetorical theories** consist of principles that describe good and effective communication respectively. The theories developed by Aristotle, Cicero, Campbell, Whately, and Perelman are examples of rhetorical theories. Though these theories contain some statements that make predictions (such as Aristotle's proposition that "*ethos* is the most potent of all means to persuasion"), most statements are meant to organize principles of communication that describe appropriate and effective communication. Rather than predict relationships alone, these theories try to define how communication may be suitable and worthy. Ethical theories posit standards of what are considered to be good actions of people. As applied to communication, ethical theories are used to explain whether communicators (called rhetors) used suitable and worthy methods to influence others.

DEVELOPING DEFINITIONS FOR CONCEPTS

Theories provide relationships among concepts, but if a concept cannot be defined, it cannot be studied. Thus, early in the research process terms must be defined to identify variables clearly. Careful definitions determine whether research can be understandable and coherent.

definitions as premises for research

Not only do definitions give us a shorthand for research, they can be taken as premises for research. They can also suggest ways to complete studies and suggest the sorts of information that might be collected. Thus, the research definitions a researcher selects can be premises for later decisions. For instance, the concept of source credibility has been the object of several definitions. One view defined credibility as "image of a source in any communication situation" (Mortensen, 1972, p. 147). Adopting this definition, a host of researchers identified handfuls of credibility factors, ranging from source competence to source tallness (the latter was found in a clever study by McCroskey and Young [1981]). On the other hand, an alternative definition of source credibility explained it as "the attitude toward a source of communication held at a given time by a receiver" (McCroskey, 1972, p. 63). When researchers have adopted this definition, only the attitude factors of source credibility (character and competence) have been studied. In very real ways, a scholar's definitions are premises for subsequent research selections.

You probably have thought that definitions were things found in *Webster's* or *Random House* dictionaries. But these dictionaries were developed to provide accounts of the ways people have used words, not technical meanings for terms. In scholarship, we mean something very precise when we use the term "definition." Scholars consider **definitions** to be statements asserting that one term may be substituted for another. One way or another, definitions tell us what concepts and variables really mean by isolating their essential qualities. These definition statements are not shown to be "true" in a strict sense because they are not tested against data. But we test the degree to which definitions are truly useful, reasonable, and applicable in research. To grasp the use of definitions, it is helpful to look at two forms: conceptual and operational definitions.

[margin: definition defined]

Using Conceptual Definitions

A **conceptual (or constitutive) definition** relies on other concepts to describe a term. Most of the time what we call "dictionary definitions" are conceptual definitions. For instance, "salience" may be defined as the "prominence" of something. This type of definition gives us a feeling for a term by relating it to other terms.

[margin: conceptual definitions]

Levels of Conceptual Definition: Daily, Poetic, and Scholarly

People define things in three general levels: daily, poetic, scholarly.[8] Much of the difficulty people have in understanding research is the result of confusing these three types of definitions. Thus, we should distinguish among them.

Daily definitions are statements generally adopted by members of a society. Consider a term used extensively in intercultural communication studies: "culture." A daily definition of this word might be the customs, arts, and crafts of people in a society. This definition is almost general knowledge and can be useful when we talk to each other. Yet, for research purposes, it may not be detailed enough to serve as a premise for study.

[margin: daily definitions distinguished]

Poetic definitions are statements that involve figurative interpretations of objects. We sometimes hear of "poetic license" or exaggerations. These exaggerations are examples of poetic definitions. A poetic definition of "culture" might be "the civilizing tradition that elevates and invigorates society." This definition cannot be taken literally because it makes a poetic judgment of the term. We understand that poetic definitions are not to be taken as highly specific statements. Yet, we sometimes confuse poetic definitions with other sorts of definitions.

[margin: poetic definitions distinguished]

Scholarly definitions are highly specific statements that have technical meanings for a group of scholars. The scholarly definition of culture is "the peculiar and distinctive 'way of life' of a group or class, the meanings, values, and ideas embodied in institutions, in social relations, in systems of belief, in mores and customs, in the uses of objects and material life" (Hall & Jefferson, 1975, p. 10). This definition certainly is technical. But it is useful to researchers, because it identifies elements to be examined (and perhaps measured) when studying culture.

[margin: scholarly definitions distinguished]

The Problem of Clarity

One difficulty scholars have in being clear involves some sorry compromises researchers often make. Interchanging definitions, using circular definitions, and assuming "mutual understanding," are prominent among them.

Inappropriateness of Interchanging Definitions.

It is dangerous to use daily, poetic, and scholarly definitions interchangeably. Yet, many times researchers do just that. Psychologist Arthur Bachrach (1981, p. 81) explained:

interchanging
nonscholarly
definitions with
scholarly definitions
is a difficulty

> A major error is the transference of a daily definition (or, less likely, a poetic one) to scientific usage.... It might also be observed at this point that the transfer of scientific communication to the daily or poetic realm would be equally inappropriate.

In research we must rely on scientific definitions, rather than daily definitions. To summarize research accurately, we must know when scholarly definitions are used and when research is based on very different definitional premises.

The Problem of Circularity.

circular definitions
are to be avoided

Circularity occurs when definitions repeat things. One must attempt to avoid circularity that often comes with daily definitions. Rather than explain concepts, many daily definitions refer us to other concepts which, after definition, send us back to the term we started with. For instance, returning to a previous example, a daily definition of "culture" might be the "society" of a group of people. So, what is the society of a group of people? Answer: it's their culture. You have probably seen the Olympic flag in which five circles intersect. Circular definitions are Olympic flag statements. One term moves us to another term, which then cycles back to give us the first term again. We must be careful about permitting daily definitions to be used where scholarly definitions are required. It is not acceptable to say that speeches are dull since they are boring, that speakers are credible since they are respected, or that audiences are attentive since they are alert. These statements merely state equivalently that speeches are boring since they are dull, that speakers are respected since they are credible, and that audiences are alert since they are attentive. Each statement uses Olympic flag circular definitions that refer back to the original terms. Technically,

circular definitions
are illogical

circular definitions are flawed because they are illogical. They commit the fallacy of begging the question in which the conclusion of an argument is used as a premise for the argument. Thus, using circular definitions is unreasonable for researchers. Useful definitions must not be circular.

Assuming Mutual Understanding.

relying on
assumption of
common
understanding is a
difficulty

Researchers who mistakenly assume that "everybody knows" what they mean, even though there is no useful scholarly definition, often cause confusion. Former U.S. Supreme Court Justice Felix Frankfurter asserted that although he could not define obscenity, "I know it when I see it." Such assumption of common understanding is dangerous in research. If we cannot define what we mean, we probably cannot make important statements about it. Furthermore, as philosopher Willard Quine (1946) commented: "The less a science has advanced the more its terminology tends to rest upon an uncritical assumption of mutual understanding'' (p. 84). Using daily definitions often boils down to our assuming that ''everyone knows'' what we mean, even though scholarly definitions are not available. The problem, of course, is everybody does not really know what we mean precisely. If communication is to be recognized as a mature area of inquiry, it is vital that the assumption of common understanding *not* be made in research.

Sources of Conceptual Definitions

To find definitions you will need to go to the library and find how scholars have defined terms. You can find definitions in many different places. Sometimes research articles have titles indicating that they contain definitional discussions. For instance, Gilda Parrella (1971) discussed the rather gnarled concept of ''empathy'' in an article titled ''Projection and Adoption: Toward a Clarification of the Concept of Empathy.'' Similarly phrased titles can reveal when articles deal with conceptual and definitional issues. Yet, most articles do not get into detailed discussions of definitions. The following are three additional locations where you can find useful definitional treatments:

- Handbooks and collected essays. Many conceptual essays regularly appear in handbooks and annual reviews.
- Textbooks. Many textbooks you have used in your classes take the time to define their terms and explain their choices by reviewing competing definitions (if you have sold your books, shame on you!—you will need to visit the library to renew acquaintances with them).
- Specialized dictionaries. The quickest way to find definitions is by searching specialized dictionaries, such as *Longman Dictionary of Psychology and Psychiatry: A Walter D. Glanze Book; The Communication Handbook: A Dictionary,* by Joseph A. Devito; *The Broadcast Communications Dictionary,* edited by L. Diamant; and *A Dictionary of Speech Pathology and Therapy,* by Samuel D. Robbins. Some of these dictionaries provide only one definition for each concept, reflecting the ''best'' choice in the opinion of the editors. Thus, you will need to examine several sources.

guidelines for evaluating constitutive definitions

Criticism of Conceptual Definitions

In research literature you will find more than one meaning for the central core of a concept. These meanings may have very different implications for ways you may study the concept. So, it is important to evaluate the meaning of these definitions in some detail. Sound conceptual definitions are found by sifting through competing alternatives. This sifting requires relying on standards to judge whether definitions are useful and reasonable. Below are five of the most useful of these guidelines (after Auer 1959, p. 70):

1. Conceptual definitions must include all situations or individuals properly included in the term defined. Conceptual definitions cannot leave out examples of the concept that might be found. The term ''persuasion'' sometimes is defined as

an intentional use of messages to change attitudes and behaviors. Some criticize this definition since it seems to exclude examples of accidental or unintentional persuasion. Since they view accidental persuasion as a part of persuasion, they think that the suggested definition is unreasonable.

2. Conceptual definitions must exclude situations or individuals that are not properly included in the term defined. Definitions must have limits. After all, if something is defined as everything, it is uniquely nothing. Some definitions are so broad that the constructs are left terribly confused. For instance, Paul Cozby defined "self- disclosure" as "any information about himself which Person A communicates verbally to a Person B" (1973, p. 73). This definition makes nearly anything a person says to another "self-disclosure," including public speeches, sales persuasion, and insincere exchanges. But the literature of the field usually describes self-disclosure as a "risky" process in which one person "reveals" potentially damaging information that the other person would not know otherwise. Since too much is included in Cozby's definition, it has doubtful value.

3. Conceptual definitions must not use the term defined. It is not very helpful to define a "fear appeal" as "an appeal that arouses fear." The term is used to define itself. This sort of definition creates logical difficulties. Consider the paradox created by using the term defined as part of the definition. In developing his theory of types, Bertrand Russell showed the following square (Bachrach, 1981, p. 83):

Every statement
in this square
is false.

The situation is a paradox. If the statement in the square is true, then it has declared itself to be false. If the statement in the square is false, then it must be true. It turns into an intellectual mess. When a term defined is included in the definition, the potential for this sort of pointless paradox is great.

4. Conceptual definitions must be more precise than the term defined. Definitions should use specific terms. Accepting definitions that are broader (and more vague) than the original term defeats the entire process of trying to define terms precisely. One textbook defined "power" as "a quality inherent in the relations between two or more people" (Myers & Myers, 1982, p. 196). The new terms were even broader than power. Eventually, the authors proposed a list of requirements for power. As it was, the definition was difficult to use since it was not more precise than the term defined.

5. Conceptual definitions must exclude loaded language. Definitions should avoid making value judgments. The extra emotional language means the definition

is not strictly equivalent to the term defined. Definitions should stick to specifics. For example, "democratic group leadership" could be defined as "exercise of direction that respects the individual while promoting the greatest good for the greatest number." We can hope so, of course, but this definition does not actually *characterize* democratic leadership. Definitions must avoid loaded language to be reasonable.

Using Operational Definitions

An **operational definition** describes what is to be observed by specifying what researchers must do to make observations. Operational definitions do not, however, give you a "feeling" for the concept. Instead, they tell you the steps that you must follow to make an observation. They usually take the form of descriptions of research methods or specific examples of observations. An operational definition is like a recipe. The recipe tells you steps to follow in preparing food, but it does not tell you conceptually how the dish tastes. Similarly, a restaurant guide could describe the appearance and taste of meals, but operational definitions might indicate the steps taken by the chef to create the dish.

operational definitions distinguished

Researchers know the importance of having both conceptual and operational definitions. They make it possible to shuttle back and forth between two worlds: the conceptual and the empirical. As you might imagine, there probably is only a small number of reasonable constitutive definitions for a concept. But there can be many potential operational definitions from which the researcher may select. For instance, one might define communication competence as: "the ability to interact well with others" (Spitzberg, 1988, p. 68) or "the extent to which judgments about the observed communicator match conceptions of the 'ideal' " (Pavitt, 1990, p. 9). These definitions describe communicator competence by relating it to other concepts. Operational definitions, on the other hand, identify observations by describing the methods to make an observation. For instance, one could state that communicator competence is operationally defined as one's score on Wiemann's communicative competence scale (1977), or any other measure of competence that is widely available. Thus, the use of constitutive and operational definitions go hand-in-hand in isolating research for further study.

though only few reasonable conceptual definitions, there may be many potential operational definitions

An Attempt at Precision of Definition

After one has reasonable conceptual definitions, researchers who want to get specific must use operational definitions. Although operational definitions sometimes are used in the absence of conceptual definitions, doing so is a mistake. When used in combination with conceptual definitions, however, operational definitions help us get as specific as possible with our definitions. The more specific we can be, the more precise our research evidence will be. Operational definitions take conceptual definitions and describe the methods that would be used to make direct observations of instances and examples. In research dealing with the effects of the speaker's use of notes on attitude change, operational definitions of "attitude change" would include descriptions of scales to be used. Since operational definitions are attempts to get specific, the desire for precision requires their use.

operational definitions promote precision

TABLE 6.2 Operational Definitions and Problem Restatements

Problem: Does the Intercultural Communication Workshop significantly improve the American participants' intercultural communication competence? (Hammer, 1984, p. 253)

Variables	Operational Definitions
Intercultural Communication Workshop	The Intercultural Communication Workshop taught at the University of Minnesota
Intercultural Communication Competence	Scores on a set of scales used by observers to rate behaviors of workshop participants as they described their reactions to potential situations involving people of different cultures.

Restatement: Does the Intercultural Communication Workshop taught at the University of Minnesota significantly increase the scores on a set of scales used by observers to rate behaviors of American participants as they described their reactions to potential situations involving people of different cultures?

Problem: What differences in motivation for attendance are there between infrequent, occasional, and frequent movie-goers? (Austin, 1986, pp. 117–88)

Variables	Operational Definitions
Motivation for attendance	Scores on a seventy-item measure of motivation for attendance
Types of movie-goers (infrequent, occasional, and frequent)	Scores on a checklist indicating the frequency of subject movie-going

Restatement: What differences in scores on a seventy-item measure of motivation for attendance are there between subjects' scores on a checklist indicating the frequency of subject movie-going?

definitions for terms in the problem statement

After identifying the problem statement, it should be possible to restate it with operational definitions substituted for the variable names. For instance, look at the problem statements found in table 6.2 and the translations into operational terms. In each case operational definitions were used for each variable. Restated, each variable may be described as shown in table 6.2. By doing so, the link between the general understanding provided by conceptual definitions and those provided by the operational definitions can be seen.

Operational definitions are not entire definitions by themselves. Thus, researchers must cover *both* conceptual and operational matters. Researchers should use operationalizations that are consistent with their conceptual definitions. But without stating conceptual definitions first, it may be very, very difficult to tell if operational definitions make sense. If the researcher provides references to sources where conceptual definitions may be found, there may be little harm since you can look at the original if you wish. But operational definitions should be fitting exemplifications of the concept or variable defined.

Forms of Operational Definitions

Operational definitions can be of three forms, and these types can be used in combination in a single study.

1. **Manipulated independent variables** sometimes are called "stimulus variables" because researchers introduce and control them in experiments. In a classic study, for instance, a researcher wanted to see the effects of source credibility on student audiences at Northwestern University (Haiman, 1949). The independent variable, source credibility, was manipulated by having speeches advocating national health insurance introduced as having come from different sources: Thomas Parran, then Surgeon General of the United States; a Northwestern University sophomore; and Eugene Dennis, then Secretary of the American Communist Party. This manipulation of the independent variable was effective in showing that credible speakers are most persuasive.

   manipulated independent variables identified

2. **Measured/assigned variables** are not introduced or controlled by the researcher, but are carefully observed and/or measured. Often these variables are characteristics that can be identified, though it would be impossible (or unthinkable) to manipulate them. If one wanted to learn whether women were more persuasible than men, it would be impossible to manipulate the sex of the receiver, but one could identify men and women and *assign* their persuasibility ratings to distinct categories for analysis. If one wants to know whether highly dogmatic people talk more in small group discussions than lowly dogmatic people, researchers might *measure* the degree of dogmatism using established scales.

   assigned or measured independent variables identified

3. **Direct classification** of variables operationally defines concepts by simple identification or classification of observable characteristics of information. The direct assignment operational definition describes what information must be observed for the presence of a variable to be claimed. For instance, Stephanie Greco Larson (1991) explored whether the portrayal of sexual violence on television soap operas, specifically *All My Children,* sent a message that "when women say 'no' they really mean 'yes' [which] contradicts overt attempts to demonstrate the seriousness of sexual aggression" (p. 156). To operationalize sexual violence, Larson used the method of direct assignment to identify whether kisses between romantic partners were forced or not forced. "A forced kiss was any kiss accompanied by a physical struggle which demonstrated resistance, even if this resistance was [*sic*] temporary" (p. 157). The method of direct assignment was used by identifying information that would have to exist for the variable to be operating.[9]

   direct classification identified

Standards for Operational Definitions

standards for evaluating operational definitions

Operational definitions are examined in detail when measurements are involved. Direct tests of the consistency and accuracy of measures are parts of the process of describing measurement tools. Yet, operational definitions are expected to meet some minimum standards. Herbert Feigl (1945) established a set of criteria for sound operational definitions that gives useful guidance.

1. *Empirically based and definite.* The word "empirical" means observable (though many people think that it refers to scientific information). For operational definitions to make sense, they must be specific, and they must be related to something that can be identified through observation.

2. *Logically consistent.* If operational definitions are inconsistent with conceptual definitions, then the operationalizations may be irrelevant to the concept under investigation. The operational definition must have clear relationships with conceptual definitions.

intersubjectivity defined

3. *Intersubjective.* **Intersubjectivity** is the degree to which different researchers with essentially different beliefs draw essentially the same interpretations of the meaning of observations. Certainly people have different views, but they also share some common interpretations. This area of shared agreement on meaning is what we mean by intersubjectivity. A useful operational definition should be one that different scholars could identify as related to the concept at hand. Hence, the use of the same sort of operational definitions across studies is one (though fallible) index of the degree of intersubjectivity for the operational definition.

4. *Technically possible.* A good operational definition should be capable of being put into direct application in research. If an operational definition requires technologies that are not yet available or that are not morally or tactically possible, the operationalization's usefulness is cast into doubt.

5. *Repeatable.* Operational definitions must be capable of repeated use by different researchers. Sometimes therapists claim that they can tell operationally whether a patient is responding positively to therapy by looking at the patient's general demeanor. If the therapist is asked how he or she is able to draw conclusions from that vague operationalization, the therapist may respond that it is based on his or her own experience. Such a defense of an operational definition—even if true—means that a scholar is using a vague method that probably cannot be employed by others. If others cannot duplicate a scholar's methods, the operationalizations fail to meet the standard of repeatability.

6. *Suggestive of constructs.* Operational definitions are examples of constitutive definitions put into direct observation and experience. But they can also point researchers toward new concepts as well. To advance theory, operational definitions can stimulate attention to other concepts. Thus, the ability of operational definitions to suggest other constructs can be helpful in advancing comprehensive theory building by scholars.

SUMMARY

Theory construction is a purpose of all research, scholarship, and science. A science is a particular body of knowledge—for example, physics, physiology, psychology—distinguished by the special set of operations employed in gathering empirical facts and by a distinctive set of constructs employed in interpreting the data. Thus, we can define science as a way of testing statements by systematic application of the scientific method. Since all communication research states problems, sets criteria for permissible interpretation, and makes careful observations of communication transactions, using these methods makes the study of communication a scientific study area, though the practice of communication may remain an art.

A theory is a body of interrelated principles that explain or predict. It has three components: (1) an abstract calculus, which is the logical structure of relationships; (2) theoretic constructs or generalizations about observables according to some common property ("hypothetical constructs" or concepts referring to constructs for which we cannot make observations directly); (3) rules of correspondence that show how well the theory's constructs and abstract calculus can be applied to actual experience. Two requirements help separate true theories from counterfeits: (1) the requirement of falsification holds that any theory must deal with statements that could be falsified by data and information if the theory were untrue; (2) the requirement of tentativeness demands that scholars recognize that a theory's answers are provisional. Theories have four interrelated functions: (1) description in which behavior is characterized into different forms; (2) explanation that takes an event and treats it as an instance of a larger system of things; (3) prediction that describes what can be expected in the future (prediction also is a way to explain things); (4) control, which is the power to direct things.

There are two approaches to theory and inquiry. Sometimes called the "inductive approach" to research, the "data first" method involves gathering information and then developing theoretic explanations. The second approach, "theory first," develops theoretic thinking and then gathers data to apply and test it. In actual practice, theory development *both* follows and precedes researchers' observations since theory and observation go hand in hand. Normative and prescriptive theories are those whose principles involve defining the qualities that make communication meaningful or desirable. The area of normative theory comes from work in what sometimes is called "normative science," which is a discipline that systematically studies people's attempts to determine what is correct, valuable, good, or beautiful. Ethical and rhetorical theories consist of principles that describe good and effective communication respectively.

If a concept cannot be defined, it cannot be studied. Not only do definitions give us a shorthand for research, they may be taken as premises for research, may suggest ways to complete studies, and may invite some sorts of information for collection. Definitions are statements asserting that one term may be substituted for another. There are two forms of definitions: conceptual and operational definitions. A conceptual (or constitutive) definition relies on other concepts to describe a term. There are three general levels people use to define things: daily definitions (statements generally adopted by members of a society); poetic definitions (statements that involve figurative interpretations of objects); and scholarly definitions (highly specific statements that have technical meanings for a group of scholars). Researchers often make some sorry compromises: interchanging daily, poetic, and scholarly definitions; using circular definitions; and assuming "mutual understanding." Conceptual definitions can be found in many different places including some articles, handbooks and collected essays, textbooks, and specialized dictionaries. To criticize conceptual definitions you can apply the following guidelines: (1) conceptual definitions must include all situations or individuals properly included in the term defined; (2) conceptual definitions must exclude situations or individuals that are not properly included in the term defined; (3) conceptual definitions must not use the term defined; (4) conceptual definitions must be more precise than the term defined; and (5) conceptual definitions must exclude loaded language.

An operational definition describes what is to be observed by specifying what researchers must do to make observations. Using both conceptual and operational definitions makes it possible to shuttle back and forth between two worlds, the conceptual and the empirical. Though there is probably only a small number of reasonable conceptual definitions for a concept, there can be many potential operational definitions from which the researcher may select. Operational definitions are not entire definitions by themselves. Thus, researchers must cover *both*

conceptual and operational matters, because without stating conceptual definitions first, it may be very difficult to tell if operational definitions make sense. Operational definitions can be of three forms: (1) manipulated independent variables (sometimes called "stimulus variables" because researchers introduce and control them in experiments); (2) measured/assigned variables (not introduced or controlled by the researcher, but carefully observed and/or measured); (3) direct classification variables (operationally defining concepts by simple identification or classification of observable characteristics of information). Operational definitions are required to be: (1) empirically based and definite; (2) logically consistent; (3) intersubjective (the degree to which different researchers with essentially different beliefs draw essentially the same interpretations of the meaning of observations); (4) technically possible; (5) repeatable; (6) suggestive of constructs.

TERMS FOR REVIEW

meta-analysis
science
theory
abstract calculus
constructs
hypothetical constructs
rules of correspondence
description
prediction
normative and prescriptive theories
ethical and rhetorical theories
explanation

control
definitions
conceptual definitions
daily definitions
poetic definitions
scholarly definitions
operational definitions
manipulated independent variables
measured or assigned variables
direct classification
intersubjectivity

NOTES

[1]Used through courtesy of Ava C. English.

[2]This listing is based on that provided by Auer (1959, p. 25) which, in turn, was based on the writing of John Dewey (1910).

[3]This statement is not a circular definition. The term, "scientific method," has been defined here by the distinctive steps of the approach. There has been no reference back to science in the definition of "scientific method." It also should be noticed that the definition does not use the term defined since the term "scientific method" is a single term that cannot be broken down into smaller units of "scientific" and "method" without also dissolving the meaning it has been given here.

[4]Used through courtesy of Ava C. English.

[5]Used through courtesy of Walter Glanze Word Books.

[6]This view is developed in detail by Sir Karl Popper in the volumes *Conjectures and Refutations* (1968a), *The Logic of Scientific Discovery* (1968b), and *Objective Knowledge* (1972).

[7]Used through courtesy of Ava C. English.

[8]This section of our discussion benefits from the writing and headings developed by Arthur J. Bachrach (1981, 80–84). Though Bachrach calls the third type of definition "the scientific definition," we have decided to call it a scholarly definition, reflecting the broad scope of research method they play.

[9]Larson found support for her expectation. It seems that the soap opera rewarded "persistent men" and sent mixed messages about sexual violence generally.

Design of Research

Conducting Textual Analyses

Participant Observation and Naturalistic Research

Descriptive Empirical Research

Experimental Research

11

Sampling

12

Measurement in Communication Research

CHAPTER 7

Conducting Textual Analyses

The interest in life does not lie in what people do, nor even in their relations to each other, but largely the power to communicate with a third party. . . .

–Virginia Woolf

**ANALYSIS OF MESSAGE
QUALITIES**
QUALITATIVE ANALYSIS
    Neo-Aristotelian Criticism
    Burke's Dramatistic Criticism
    Method

The Never-Ending Development of
    Critical Methods
QUANTITATIVE ANALYSIS
    Content Analysis
    Interaction and Relational Analyses

BEFORE WE GET STARTED . . .

Many studies examine the content and flow of messages directly. These methods for analyzing message qualities, are popular in communication studies. This chapter introduces three major forms of these studies to you: qualitative work in the form of critical assessment, quantitative work using content analysis, and interaction analyses.

ANALYSIS OF MESSAGE QUALITIES

**nomothetic and
idiographic research
distinguished**

Much communication research analyzes message structures. Researchers use this approach when they want to focus on message qualities that are unique, rather than generic. They distinguish between nomothetic and idiographic research. *Nomothetic research* finds general laws that apply to many instances. *Idiographic research* develops a full understanding of "a particular event or individual" [English & English, 1958, p. 347]."[1] Though analyzing message qualities is often suited to nomothetic research, the methods discussed in this chapter also can be appropriately used for intensive idiographic studies of a single communication event, such as a presidential debate or a discussion between a particular pair of communicators. We will consider the three general categories of communication analysis: critical views; formal content analysis of messages, especially of public and mass media communication; and interactional and relational analyses of conversations.

QUALITATIVE ANALYSIS

Rhetorical criticism is a dominant area in communication studies. By criticizing speeches, written messages, and movements, researchers discover new insights or theories. The term **rhetorical criticism** means the use of standards of excellence to interpret and evaluate communication (in turn, **rhetoric** is the study of the available means of persuasion). By studying texts of speeches and other examples of messages, one can understand social and historical movements, discover useful techniques, and form explanations for effective communication practices.

rhetorical criticism and rhetoric defined

In full **criticism,** however, standards of excellence are announced (which, in turn, can be argued as relevant or irrelevant) for application. To the extent that a message meets the standards, it is evaluated positively. The further away from the standard the message is, the harsher the negative evaluation. Sometimes we use the term **impressionistic criticism** to refer to the statements of opinion (or personal impression) made by reviewers. Yet, scholarly criticism is not a matter of personal opinion—it is a direct application of standards. We can evaluate a critic's argument since the standards are known in advance and we can double-check descriptions of data.

criticism identified

impressionistic criticism identified

In essence, therefore, all criticism involves three steps. First, standards of excellence are presented. Second, the data (messages) are described and applied against the standards. Third, the degree to which the data meet or fall short of the standards is described. Thus, researchers make critical statements that point out how far an actual message is from the ideal. To determine what is good or bad, right or wrong, sound or unsound in communication, scholars rely on systems of categories that list matters to examine.

the three steps of criticism

Neo-Aristotelian Criticism

When Aristotle developed his discussion of rhetorical communication about 2300 years ago, he employed categories that came to be known as the canons of rhetoric. Over time, when people used the canons to organize their criticism, their work was called neo-Aristotelian criticism ("neo" means "new"). Hence, neo-Aristotelian criticism is a new use of Aristotelian standards. Aristotle was not the only major writer who used the canons of rhetoric. Among others, Cicero and Quintilian also used them. Yet, they offered very different advice. Technically, we should reserve the term "neo-Aristotelian criticism" for situations in which Aristotle's standards are used, "neo-Ciceronian" when Cicero's standards are referenced, and "neo-Quintilianic" when Quintilian's standards are employed. When selecting a standard, critics are expected to identify sources used to develop criteria for evaluation. Thus, critics must prepare by reading a lot.

canons not unique to Aristotle

critics using the canons must find a standard

When applying the canons of rhetoric, critics must use these major topics:

invention defined:
- **Invention** refers to the types and sources of ideas. Invention of ideas is derived from all forms of appeals used by a communicator. Most neo-Aristotelian critics subdivide invention into three categories of appeals.[2] The first

ethos
category, ethos, is sometimes called "ethical appeal." **Ethos** is the speaker's credibility and includes the methods the speaker uses to build and use credibility in a speech. The second category, pathos, is also known as "pathetic

pathos
appeals." **Pathos** is the use of emotional or motivational appeals by a speaker. Both the sources of the appeal and the emotions of the audience are

logos
considered by the critic. The third category is **logos,** which most critics treat as logical appeals, including the evidence and reasoning used by a speaker, though *logos* is a Greek word that can't be directly translated into English (in context, this term means the rational idea behind things *and* the symbolic expression of those ideas through words).

arrangement defined
- **Arrangement** is the organization of ideas in a message. In this category, critics assess the structure of the introduction, body, conclusion, previews, transitions, and organizing patterns.

style defined
- **Style** is the choice and use of words (although we sometimes see commercials claiming that using a particular brand of cologne will give a person "style," this meaning is not the classical sense of the term). The critic looks at the suitable vocabulary of the speaker, the tone of the words used, and the clarity of expression.

delivery defined
- **Delivery** is the use of nonverbal cues used by communicators when presenting messages. Major nonverbal categories of voice, movement, and eye contact are examined to find clues to effective communication.

memory defined
At one time a fifth canon, memory, was included in a list of "Five Canons of Rhetoric." **Memory** was the speaker's ability to recall passages and examples for utterance. Though communicators often train their memories to avoid using notes, memory is rarely examined by critics today. Hence, memory is sometimes called the "lost canon" (Hoogestraat, 1960).

Neo-Aristotelian critics constantly ask whether the speaker made good choices of persuasive appeals from the means that were available to him or her.

applications and
limits
The method often can be extended to more than one speech involved in a movement or a campaign. The neo-Aristotelian method has been employed successfully in much research, including now-classic studies of Lincoln's speaking at Cooper Union (Mohrmann & Leff, 1974), the analysis of Richard Nixon's November 3, 1969, address defending his Vietnam policy (Hill, 1972), and the speeches of Woodrow Wilson (Craig, 1952). The method may be difficult to apply to messages relying chiefly on extralogical strategies. The strategy of a speaker who chants at an audience is difficult to capture within the categories of this approach. Despite its limits, however, this method is a useful way to organize criticism of messages.

Burke's Dramatistic Criticism Method

elements of the
Burkean approach
Many critics have benefited from the thinking of Kenneth Burke (1945, 1950), a poet, essayist, and critic. Burke's communication notions start with the idea that

---

SPECIAL DISCUSSION 7–1
Fantasy Theme Analysis

Fantasy theme analysis is a method of analyzing collections of communication to determine underlying "world views" that people hold, judging by the messages that they use (Cragan & Shields, 1981). This approach assumes that groups of people form images or "rhetorical visions" of the way the world is organized. Though the term "fantasy" is used in these discussions, it does not necessarily refer to something that is fanciful but untrue (some "fantasies" have a factual basis). The method does not attempt to judge the quality of messages, although most scholars comment on quality in passing. Thus, fantasy theme analysis draws conclusions that are more sociological than most other communication studies do. It uses communication to find clues about the ways people think about the world.

The process of fantasy theme analysis involves three steps. Though they are not always distinct, they tend to be typical in nearly all such inquiries.

- First, researchers collect samples of all sorts of communication from groups of people who speak out on an issue.
- Second, researchers sift the messages to find recurring phrases, themes, or strategies. They look for expressions that communicators use. They look for common themes that are used in different messages.
- Third, researchers attempt to label the fundamental fantasy themes that indicate the "rhetorical visions" held by the collective mind of the group of people who use them. The researchers ask how people must view the world given the common patterns they use.

Fantasy theme analyses have been completed on many different areas ranging from the rise of the interdenominational Christian Church (Disciples of Christ) (Hensley, 1975) to the relationship styles of characters in romance novels (Hubbard, 1985).

---

people are essentially the same, with the same drives and motives. But they have grown apart from each other by society's artificial boundaries. Thus, the job of communication is to help bring people together. The key concept in this system is identification. **Identification** unites people by the use of shared ideas, images, and attitudes. If you identify with another person, you accept that person's words because they almost seem to be your own thoughts. Thus, Burke explained, "Wherever there is persuasion, there is rhetoric. And wherever there is 'meaning' there is 'persuasion' " (1950, p. 172).

> concept of
> identification defined

You have heard Shakespeare's words that "All the world's a stage and all of us merely actors. . . ." Taking that notion very seriously, Burke called his system the dramatistic pentad and asked critics to look at communication as they

> the dramatistic
> pentad:

would examine a play. He viewed communication as including five categories (that's where the word "pentad" comes in):

1. act defined

1. The **act** is the symbolic action (the speech, for instance) actually exchanged. The message document is examined. The critic is expected to provide evidence of its textual authenticity and complete accuracy.

2. scene defined

2. The **scene** is the setting in which the act takes place. The setting includes the entire situation in which the message is exchanged. Primary and secondary audiences, their expectations, and the effects of the message are all assessed. But the general condition of society also is a matter that influences the ability of the speech to create a sense of identification.

3. agent defined

3. **Agent** refers to the actor or rhetor who performs the act. The history of the individual is researched to determine why he or she said the sorts of things that were contained in the message. Thus, this category requires critics to complete biographical criticism and determine authorship for the act. The first three elements of the pentad are matters that critics might be concerned about regardless of the critical method they use. The remaining elements are unique to the Burkean system.

4. agency defined

4. **Agency** consists of the symbolic and linguistic strategies used to secure identification. Sometimes these linguistic strategies are arguments. Sometimes they are appeals to common interest. Sometimes they are subtle uses of language such as irony or satire. The critic explains the strategies used to achieve identification by communicators. Speakers usually rely on a small number of such strategies (or "agencies") in a single message. For instance, in 1965 at a rally in Montgomery, Alabama, a young man named Stokely Carmichael (now Kwame Toure) grabbed a microphone and began to shout "black power!" over and over. Soon some members of the audience began to join in. Before long, the entire crowd was chanting in unison, "Black power, black power, black power." After the chanting, Carmichael was cheered loudly and his calls for action were received enthusiastically by the crowd. This strategy of chanting was not an argument, but the language created a sense of oneness between the audience and the speaker. The Burkean concept of agency requires critics to identify this strategy and explain how it helped the speaker and audience achieve identification with each other.

5. purpose defined

5. **Purpose** of the message is the intention of the rhetor. A message's impact can be evaluated by determining whether the speaker's intentions are satisfied. But the intention of a speaker is also checked to see if the purposes are clear, relevant, and socially responsible.

Taken together, the dramatistic pentad provides a way to organize communication and to explain how people influence each other.

The flexibility of Burke's approach is attractive to many scholars, because they are not obligated to use traditional methods that focus on formal arguments and systems of appeals. The method has been used to analyze scores of key messages ranging from the defense strategy of Clarence Darrow in the *New York v. Gitlow* case (Sanbonmatsu, 1971) to the rhetoric of the frontier women's suffrage movement in the United States (Burkholder, 1989). People who use the Burkean system focus heavily on the language used by communicators. Though this attention can lead to valuable insights, the method has its limitations. First, the way messages are judged is largely based on their effects: if identification is promoted, the messages are effective. There is no artistic standard beyond the "bottom line." Second, the method occasionally may be difficult to replicate since it is not really a fixed system. Burke's added interest in developing notions of redemptive rhetoric and his suggestion that there might be a sixth element to the pentad called "attitude" indicates that the system is so fluid that it may prove for serious scholars to pin it down. Even so, the Burkean approach has aroused a great deal of respect and use among critics in communication.

The Never-Ending Development of Critical Methods

Scholars are always developing additional methods and models. The way scholars actually do criticism is not restricted to the two formal systems described here. A few examples might give you an idea.

the constant development of new methods

Starting in the late 1970s some critics started examining communication by using the "mythic perspective." Though most people define myth as an untrue story, those who use the mythic perspective do not view it that way. They prefer to define myths as something like "a story about a particular incident which is put forward as containing or suggesting some general truth" (Sykes, 1970, p. 17). These stories are the legends and folklore that we take as part of a culture. Critics try to identify the underlying stories to which speakers appeal. Then they explain how some appeals are more influential than others. Applications have been made to the broad news coverage of the Patty Hearst kidnapping of the mid-1970s (Mechling, 1979), mass media treatment of the "New Frontier" rhetoric of President John Kennedy (Rushing, 1986), and the structure of Hitler's *Mein Kampf* (McGuire, 1977). Though there is controversy about whether myths should be restricted to stories that are believed to be true, the use of myth has become a popular way to look at some communication.

mythic perspectives

Comparisons of speeches with religious models, such as the Sermon on the Mount, have been popular in the literature of speech criticism. For instance, Malinda Snow (1975) examined Martin Luther King's letter from the Birmingham Jail and found that its structure was consistent with the most complex epistles of St. Paul. Since these religious images are prominent in western cultures, it is not surprising that such comparisons can be made.

comparisons with religious models

One of the most influential alternative views was developed by Walter R. Fisher in his "narrative paradigm," which analyzes messages by looking at them as stories. In his book, *Human Communication as Narration: Toward a Philosophy of Reason, Value, and Action* (1987), Fisher explained that people have a natural need to tell stories to each other. Through explaining stories, people develop understandings of each other. Fisher suggested some standards by which critics can evaluate the stories people use. First, Fisher believes that good stories, like good reasons, have strong probability. Second, Fisher asks critics to evaluate the "narrative fidelity" of messages. Narrative fidelity is the consistency of new

narrative paradigm

accounts with other stories people have heard. Since most communication makes use of story telling, the method has created considerable interest.

creative analogies

Sometimes a creative analogy can be used to explain communication that defies traditional understanding. For instance, Larry S. Richardson (1970), a musician and communication scholar, examined the unusual speaking of Stokely Carmichael by comparing it with the interaction between an audience and a jazz musician who is improvising on a theme. Carmichael's deliberate repetition and frequent movement from one idea to the next without transition was explained by the same sort of dynamic that leads a jazz musician to repeat a successful "hot lick" and to shift quickly to another motif when the audience begins to lose interest. By looking for creative analogies, critics can explore interesting new ways to investigate communication.

Creative methods of criticism do more than evaluate messages. They also help develop new theories. Furthermore, applying new approaches may reveal insights that can help people improve their own communication effectiveness.

QUANTITATIVE ANALYSIS

Texts and messages are often examined with quantitative methods. Though there are many quantitative tools, we will consider the two most prominent options: content analysis and interaction and relational analysis.

Content Analysis

content analysis defined

Content analysis is a systematic method of analyzing the content and treatment of communication, which usually results in the development of objective and quantitative information (see Kerlinger, 1986, p. 477). For instance, if you wanted to find the number of references to sex in primetime television programs, you might identify categories of sexual content as (a) noncriminal sex acts, (b) criminal sex acts, and (c) sexual language and innuendo, and then count the number of references during a sample of television programming (see Sapolsky & Tabarlet, 1991).

Using Content Analysis

uses of content analysis

Content analysis is a very flexible method that has been widely applied to texts by linguists, journalists, communication scholars, as well as professionals in psychology and sociology. Content analyses are useful for monitoring the content of mass media communication. The information can be highly revealing, as were the famous studies showing an increase in violence in children's cartoons at a time when violence in other television programs did not increase (Gerbner, 1971), the emphasis on the "cult of femininity" (not feminism) in women's magazines (Ferguson, 1983), and the generally evil portrayal of businesspeople in television entertainment programs (Therberge, 1981; cf. Thomas & LeShay, 1992). Content analyses can be useful when characterizing communication and making intriguing comparisons.

Though once used almost exclusively by scholars in mass media studies, content analysis methods are now used in many other settings. In studies of organizational communication, comments by employees may be assessed with content analysis methods. Speech therapists sometimes content-analyze the conversation of aphasic clients to find clues about the type of injury the patient has. An interesting twist has been the use of content analysis of newspapers to gauge trends in society (Naisbitt & Auberdene, 1982).

Performing Content Analysis

Some fairly standard elements should be included in any sound content analysis. Though many content analyses can be completed by a computer, others involve work done by hand. We will consider the basic steps along with an example.

Defining and Limiting the Communication Population.

The communication domain must be isolated so that it is consistent with the problem question raised by the researcher. Furthermore, the population to be sampled should be defined narrowly enough to permit gathering manageable types of information. For studies on the rise of the number of sexual references in rock music lyrics, it is important to decide which types of rock are to be included (rap, heavy metal, light rock) and which sources are to be used to select such lyrical material (lists from *Billboard* and local top 40 lists have notoriously different listings). Suppose the problem statement asked about the relationship between the sex of a person in a television ad and that person's portrayed occupation (Dominick & Rauch, 1972). A sensible communication population would be the commercials aired on the three major TV networks during prime time. Other time periods might not feature a mix of people in commercials and, hence, might not be helpful in answering the research question. Similarly, radio ads might not provide enough information about occupations of participants to permit a reasonable study.

content analysis steps: 1. define communication population to be studied

Selecting Coding Units and Classification Systems.

Coding units are categories used to count the communication forms in the examples chosen. In the example of studying jobs of men and women in TV commercials, the researcher needs a comprehensive list of occupations. Fortunately a list is readily available from the U.S. Department of Labor's *Occupational Outlook*. This list is very detailed and some categories that never appear in TV commercials may be eliminated. The general groupings of occupations include: managerial and professional specialties; technical sales and administrative support; service occupations; precision production, craft, and repair; operators, fabricators, and laborers; farming, forestry and fishing. Regardless of the categories that one chooses, the classifications should

2. selecting coding units

- Be "exhaustive" and cover all the possibilities (to make sure, categories will sometimes include an "other" division, but the number of items that fall into that category should be fairly small)
- Be mutually exclusive (that is, an event should not fall into more than one category)
- Include a coding rule for placing objects in categories (criteria should be established in advance to decide what must occur for an item to be coded at all).

In formal content analysis, categories are established before collecting data.

Many different units of analysis might be coded, of course. In the above example, the unit of analysis included men or women who appeared on screen for at least three seconds and who had at least one line of dialog. There are other ways that information could be coded of course. If it had been appropriate the researchers could have coded the amount of time males or females were shown on the screen. They could have rated whether men or women were portrayed positively or negatively on a seven point scale ranging from -3 (very negative) to $+3$ (very positive). They could have rated the number of words spoken by each character. In short, researchers have great freedom in selecting many different things that can be enumerated or counted. When examining newspapers, the number of column inches dedicated to a topic is often identified. Sometimes researchers attempt to identify themes, which are recurring assertions made by communicators (after Budd, Thorp & Donohew, 1967, p. 34). For instance, Lee Brown (1961) used content analysis to study the use of anti-Roman Catholic themes developed to oppose the presidential candidacy of John F. Kennedy. He found eighteen major themes in anti-Kennedy campaign materials mailed to voters, including such outrageous assertions as the claim that Roman Catholics are assassins of presidents (supported by the observations that ''Lincoln, Garfield, and McKinley were assassinated by Roman Catholics''). Klauss Krippendorf (1980) observed that content analysts have examined five kinds of units to study: (1) a physical unit (such as number of articles, inches of space, or number of pages); (2) a syntactic unit (such as number of words, phrases, or sentences); (3) a referential unit (such as presence or absence of objects); (4) a propositional unit (such as statements or arguments); and (5) a thematic unit (such as repeating patterns of ideas or treatments). In the above example, the problem question could be answered best by simply tallying the number of times male and female characters in commercials were portrayed as having different occupations.

3. sampling messages

Sampling Messages. The sampling from the population of events must be large enough to permit meaningful conclusions to be drawn. Furthermore, the samples are completed so that the communication can be claimed as representative of the larger population. Content analysts usually take pains to explain how they gathered their samples and when the sampled communication actually occurred. In the above example, a sample was drawn for the same one week period across the three major networks. Sometimes it is not possible to obtain every event in a sampling frame. Researchers may select a reduced number of events. There are many ways to sample, and there is no one best method. But you can choose from several options (Budd, Thorp, & Donohew, 1967, pp. 21–23):

- Random—in which every instance in the population has an equal chance of being selected
- Stratification—in which strata are identified (such as geographic region, type of radio station format, type of ad) and a random sample within each strata is proportionately selected

- Interval—in which a sample is drawn by selecting instances of communication at specific units (such as coding every third commercial during prime time for a month)
- Cluster—in which groups of messages appear in a cluster that already exists (such as the cluster of articles that appears in a single newspaper)
- Multistage—in which instances are selected sequentially (such as selecting commercials from one month, selecting one week from that month, selecting three hours from the days of the week, and so on).

Researchers are expected to sample events so that the conclusions drawn can be representative of such communication. In the above example, a sample of commercials during one week of prime-time broadcasting on the three major TV networks was sampled, producing a total of 230 women and 155 men.

Coding Message Content.   Content must be coded to produce numbers that can be tallied and reported. Whether general themes or specific measures, frequencies are tallied. Sometimes the process can be computerized (such as content analysis of readability of textbooks), but most of the time researchers still rely on coders to complete the work. In many cases, it is a good idea to have coders who are not aware of the researcher's hypotheses actually record the results. Regardless of the individuals involved, the messages are presented to the coders (in some written, audio, or visual form) who then record their observations on tally sheets.

    Researchers are expected to show that the categories are used consistently and in meaningful ways (along with statistics to show the degree of consistency or **reliability** in using the categories). It is important to describe the methods used to train content analysts since incompetent coding of communication can result in meaningless data. If several coders are involved, their degree of agreement sometimes is called "intercoder reliability." Standard formulae appear in chapter 13 for computing such consistency among different raters. If consistency is not very high (if coders disagree with each other too often) the inconsistency should be noted, but the data should not be included as part of the data set formally analyzed.

Analyzing the Data.   The data are usually analyzed by reporting simple descriptive statistics. Sometimes, however, advanced statistical tests might be applied to the data to spot key patterns and underlying factors of interest. It is typical for content analysts to report tables of results, such as the one for our study in table 7.1. As can be seen here, the types of jobs people had in television commercials showed a wide range for men and a very limited range for women. In other data in this study, women were shown indoors twice as often as they were shown outside (19 percent versus 44 percent for men). The simple descriptive statistics tell much of the story in these data.

Interpreting Results.   Content analyses are completed to illuminate the research question and to help evaluate whether communication patterns are as they should

4. coding message treatment or content

training and reliability indicated for coding

5. analysis of data

6. interpret results

TABLE 7.1 Content Analysis Example			

Occupations of Men and Women in Television Commercials*

Females (Number of women = 230)	Percent	Men (Number of men = 155)	Percent
Housewife/mother	56	Husband/father	14
Airline cabin attendant	8	Professional athlete	12
Model	7		
Celebrity/singer/dancer	5	Celebrity	8
Cook/maid/servant	3		
Secretary/clerical worker	3		
		Construction worker	7
		Airline pilot	6
		Businessperson	6
		Sales representative	6
		Criminal	5
		Lawyer	3
		Mechanic	3
		Radio/TV interviewer	3
Other	18		27

*adapted from Dominick and Rauch (1972)

be. Yet, describing results can be troublesome. Roger Wimmer and Joseph Dominick (1983) warned about one aspect of this problem:

> Researchers are often faced with a "fully-only" dilemma. Suppose, for example, that a content analysis of children's television programs reveals that 30% of the commercials in these programs were for snacks and candy. What is the researcher to conclude? Is this a high or low amount? Should the researcher report, "*Fully* 30% of the commercials fell into this category," or should he or she present this same percentage in a different light: "*Only* 30% of the commercials fell into this category"? The point is that the investigator needs some benchmark for comparison. Thirty percent may indeed be a high figure when compared to commercials for other products or those shown during adult programs. (p. 152)

Thus, as with other types of research, interpreting results is a vital but challenging process.

Limitations of the Approach

Limitations:

1. cannot draw cause-effect conclusions

Naturally, there are some limits on content analysis methods.[3] Some questions can be answered by content analyses and some cannot. Though these methods are useful in describing major communication trends, they are restricted to descriptions. Thus, the first limitation is that content analyses do not permit one to draw cause and effect conclusions. One may describe the amount of anti-Iraqi references in newspapers, but content analysis does not reveal the impact of those references on people. Of course some content analysts make causal statements anyway. But you should recognize that such conclusions are examples of drawing conclusions from irrelevant evidence—hasty generalizations, at best.

A second limitation involves the difficulty of finding representative examples of communication. Searching through newspapers and watching video tapes of television programs may sound simple, but it can be very tedious. Sometimes researchers select convenient examples and, hence, miss important matters. Unfortunately, it is not easy to tell if researchers have made this mistake just by reading their articles. Scholars can be very clever in vaguely describing the exhaustiveness of their searches. In other situations, such as content analysis of the notes left at the Vietnam War memorial, access to such materials might be difficult or ethically controversial to obtain. Thus, gaining access to important communication examples can be difficult.

2. difficulty finding representative sample

A third limitation is that the results of one content analysis cannot be generally applied to others that use different categories. The systems that have been used by scholars to study violence on television, for instance, have been very different—some include threats as violence, some include only overt violent acts, some include good-natured roughhousing, some include contact sports, some include psychological violence, some include references to off-screen violence, some include slapstick comedy. Comparing different analyses may be very troublesome since similar units may not be used. In general, one must be prudent when trying to generalize results from one content analysis to another.

3. cannot generalize to other categories of content analysis

Interaction and Relational Analyses

Scholars of interpersonal communication often look at examples of messages people have exchanged to see if they can discover something about the nature of the relationship between the people. The messages give clues regarding who is in charge and who is controlling the exchange. In a general sense, **interaction and relational analyses** are forms of content analysis designed to describe the continuing oral communication between people. These methods apply categories to conversations and discussions to find out how people affect and control each other.

interaction and relational analyses defined

Interaction Analysis

Interaction analysis focuses on ways of tracking individual acts of communicators. Scholars studying interpersonal and small group communication have often looked at such communication examples. One of the most popular early forms was Robert Bales's Interaction Process analysis (see figure 7.1). The method involves recording a group as it deliberates and listening to each statement a person makes. Those statements, in turn, are counted in each of the categories listed in the figure. Bales himself dropped Interaction Process Analysis in favor of a more complicated system called SYMLOG (see Bales & Cohen, 1979), and researchers in communication have been interested in developing uses of the SYMLOG system (Cegala, Wall & Rippet, 1987). Yet, the notion of interaction analysis can be demonstrated by looking at Bales's initial approach. He was able to explain that successful

interaction analysis distinguished

Figure 7.1

Interaction Process
Analysis Categories

Adapted from Robert
Freed Bales. "A Set of
Categories for the
Analysis of Small Group
Interaction." *American
Sociological Review,* 15
(1948): p. 59. Courtesy
of American Sociological
Association.

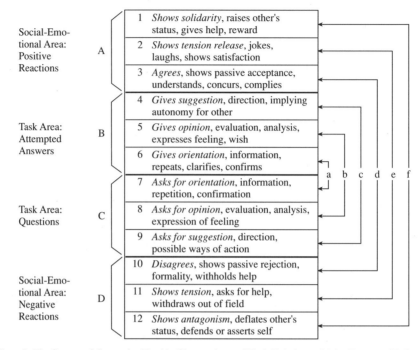

Chart. I. The System of Categories Used in Observation and Their Relation to Major Frames of Reference.

Key:

a. Problems of orientation   c. Problems of control   e. Problems of tension-management
b. Problems of evaluation   d. Problems of decision   f. Problems of integration

people need to balance the task dimension of their work with the social-emotional dimension. This chart allows you to identify the sorts of activities that take place from one phase of group decision making to another.

**study of acts and
double interacts**

B. Aubrey Fisher and his associates contributed a variation of the Interaction Process Analysis approach (Fisher & Drexel, 1983). They urged that the interaction between people, especially people taken two at a time (called dyads), be studied by looking at what were called "interacts" and "double interacts." The researcher looks at one person's conversation and the reaction of another—an interact. The researcher also looks at the first person's response to the other's reaction—the double interact. Though the concept was originally associated with management theorist Karl Weick (esp. 1969, p. 46), Fisher's work extended this method to discover how people develop a sense of belongingness in groups and how leaders emerge in groups (Fisher, Glover & Ellis, 1977; Fisher & Hawes, 1971) and how people conduct themselves during formal interviews (Hawes, 1972). As a whole, the method of interaction analysis has taken researchers in some interesting directions.

SPECIAL DISCUSSION 7–2
Conversational and Discourse Analyses

Conversational and discourse analyses are forms of content analysis in which the categories are suggested from naturally occurring conversations and their settings. Yet, these approaches do not produce numerical information. The structure or organization of conversations is examined along with functions that conversations perform for communicators. A somewhat fluid distinction is often drawn between conversational analysis, which tends to analyze macroscopic message characteristics such as themes and stories and the rules they suggest, and discourse analysis, which tends to analyze microscopic message components in a pattern much like traditional linguistic analysis or translation (see Levinson, 1983).

In conversational analysis, researchers sample conversations (from the laboratory or from the field). Historical, literary, or mass media conversations can be examined. Conversational analysis then attempts to identify "turns" taken by people during the exchange. What a person actually says in conversation is called an **utterance.** Both nonverbal and verbal cues are coded from transcriptions of the conversation, complete with symbols to indicate vocal inflections and pauses. Eventually researchers attempt to extract rules for conversational structures. Anita Pomerantz (1990) explained the sorts of claims drawn from conversational analysis. The first form asserts

> that interactants are "doing" particular social actions, identities, and/or roles. For example, we may assert an utterance is "agreeing," "rejecting an invitation," "fishing for information," "being an expert," "being a teacher," etc. A second type of claim is when we offer analyses of methods that interactants use in accomplishing particular actions, roles, or identities. The third type of claim is when we proposed how methods work: their sequential features and interactional consequences. I will refer to the first type of claim as a *characterization* of the action, the second type as a *proposed method,* and to the third type as its *proposed features* (pp. 231–232).

This full array of conclusion-drawing permits one to determine communication rules.

Discourse analysis is sometimes distinguished from conversational analysis (see Levinson, 1983). In this view, discourse analysis considers naturally occurring messages to examine "sequential and hierarchical organization, system and structure" using methods that are fairly "standard in phonology and linguistics" (Stubbs, 1981, p. 107). These studies tend to get very specific in identifying ways that guide using language and symbols. For instance, Labov and Fanshel (1977) examined the discourse between psychotherapists and patients. Among other things, they found that the exchanges were distinguished by the use of indirect requests as substitutes for direct statements. Discourse analysis attempts to discover the structures that underlie messages people use.

Relational Control Analysis

relational control analysis distinguished

Relational control analysis tracks message sequences to determine the relative patterns of position and control in the relationship. L. Edna Rogers and Richard Farace (1975) developed a set of methods to categorize who is "in charge" in personal exchanges. Thus, researchers check communication to see who seems to be in control of interpersonal exchanges. This method records people in conversations, usually in groups of two, but sometimes in increased numbers (DeStephen, 1982; Ellis, 1979). Statements made in these conversations are coded into categories called "one-up," "one-down," and "one-across." A "one-up" statement is one in which somebody is dominant over another because he or she asserts one's "definitional rights." A "one-down" message communicates that a person submits to the opinions or definitional rights of another. A "one-across" message extends the discussion without increasing assertions or accepting others' statements. The most obvious method simply counts the number of messages that fall into each category so that the general exchange can be characterized. The number of statements in each category indicates who is in charge and, over time, what types of people are in charge.

categories of relational control

Using the Interaction and Relational Control Analysis Methods

steps in interaction and relational control studies:

Using the interaction and relational control analysis methods involves deciding on a coding system to use, training people to code messages, gathering samples of communication, coding message content, and analyzing and interpreting message content.

1. deciding on a coding system

Researchers have several choices when selecting the coding system. For interaction analyses, the classification systems developed by Bales might be contrasted with modifications developed by others. For instance, some researchers want to focus attention on the impact of interaction in different time units (Amidon & Hough, 1967; Hawes, 1972). These researchers rely on methods that code the behavior at specific time intervals (such as ten–second intervals in the Hawes study). Other researchers have decided to look at each "speech act" during an interaction. For researchers of relational control, the coding systems can be fairly complicated. A popular checksheet was developed by Rogers and Farace (1975). Others have modified this form to improve validity. In their criticism of the coding methods, Joseph Folger and Marshall Scott Poole (1982) suggested that coding should be checked with individual communicators' reports of whether *they* believe their own messages indicate "one-up," "one-down," or "one-across" relationships. This method is recommended to assure "representational validity." Researchers following this advice add an interview with communicators as part of their research. Whether such a step is necessary is controversial, but the use of alternative approaches must be explained and justified.

The second step involves training people to code communication examples. Researchers do not do this sort of research alone. Instead, they work with other people to make sure that there is some consistency in using the categories. Thus, raters must be trained so that they know how to use coding check sheets and charts. Regardless of whether interaction or relational control analysis is involved, researchers are expected to explain how the training was completed. Furthermore, researchers are expected to reveal how consistently different people rated the same communication behavior.

2. training coders

The third step in interaction and relational control analysis is sampling communication transactions. Though one can attempt to get very scientific in such sampling, the reality of the matter is that sampling conversations and group discussions tends to involve a lot of compromises. A researcher must get permission to record deliberations of a group. Securing signed consent forms is typically required. Sometimes researchers ask people to come to a specially prepared room and carry on a discussion. Sometimes people are sampled in a naturally occurring environment. Researchers report the number of conversations sampled, the number of people involved, their ages, their sex, the length of the conversations, and the topics discussed. These days, researchers are expected to interview participants after the project, explain any purposes of the research, and ask for feedback. Any information from these "debriefing" sessions is made part of the final research report. The best analyses are those for which the researcher can provide some argument for the representativeness of the samples drawn.

3. gathering samples

Fourth, the message content is coded. Researchers find that they must spend most of their time listening to tapes (or reading transcripts) and coding messages by using the rating sheets or check sheets that they have chosen. Some analyses are simple tallies of the numbers of statements that fall into each category. Most relational control research has used this sort of method. Other times researchers can look at combinations of sequences of messages. In one outing, researchers found that marital satisfaction was most highly associated with the frequency of "one-across" messages between husbands and wives (Vanlear & Zeitlow, 1990). Work in interactional analysis occasionally has been fairly subtle. For instance, in a piece of classic research in small group communication, Thomas Scheidel and Laura Crowell (1964) adapted Bales's Interaction Process Analysis by adding a few specific categories and completed what they called "contiguity analysis." Contiguity analysis asks what sort of message *follows* immediately after another message type. They observed that the first reaction to a statement was another

4. coding message content

person's *repeating* the same sort of statement. Instead of group members responding to another's "asking for information" by "giving information" (which would seem logical), someone else in the group first repeated the request for information in different words. Groups seemed to do everything twice before making progress! Scheidel and Crowell suggested that group interactions might be described as a spiral in which progress is anchored in a backward spiral. (Put another way, groups take two steps forward and one step backward.) Coding the message content and relationship can be as simple or as sophisticated as the imagination of the researcher.

5. analyzing and interpreting message content

The last step in interactional and relational analysis is interpretation. Researchers try to develop theoretic explanations for their findings. Interactional and relational analyses do not tell whether the communication is "good" or "bad," but describe how people use messages. Relationships with other variables can be drawn, but explaining *why* those patterns exist requires researchers to develop ideas and suggest models. Most often researchers explain how current theories are supported or challenged by their work. Yet, some studies lead researchers to suggest new directions for theories.

Limitations of the Approach

Limitations:
1. may not be useful to assess perception or interpretation of others

2. cannot yield cause-effect statements

The interaction and relational analysis approach has two limitations that focus on the validity of the information measured. First, the methods may not be useful if the researcher's theoretical or explanatory basis is the perception or shared interpretation of individuals. Rather, these procedures are most appropriate when individual motivations are considered less important than other bases for understanding or explaining human behavior (Tardy, 1988, pp. 292–293). Such a limitation may make these methods impossible for attempts to answer many mainstream research questions. Second, since the method takes actual communication and observes relationships with other variables, it cannot be used to draw conclusions about cause-and-effect relationships. Variables related to interaction or relational categories can be assessed, but the method does not allow one to determine which came first.

SUMMARY

Researchers sometimes focus on message qualities that are unique, rather than generic. Thus, researchers distinguish nomothetic research (designed to find general laws that apply to many instances) from idiographic research (designed to develop a full understanding of a particular event or individual).

Rhetorical criticism uses standards to interpret and evaluate communication (rhetoric is the study of the available means of persuasion). Impressionistic criticism refers to opinions (or personal impressions) made by reviewers. Criticism involves: (1) presenting standards of excellence;

(2) contrasting the messages against the standards; and (3) explaining the degree to which the data meet or fall short of the standards (critical statements tell the difference between an actual message and the ideal). Neo-Aristotelian criticism relies on the following canons of rhetoric: invention, which involves the types and sources of ideas, including ethos (ethical appeal or the speaker's credibility), pathos (pathetic appeals or the use of emotion), and logos (logical appeals); arrangement (message organization); style (choice and use of words);

delivery (use of nonverbal cues). Though helpful when examining significant speeches, the method strains when applied to messages that rely chiefly on extralogical strategies. Burke's dramatistic criticism method places the concept of identification (uniting people by the use of ideas, images, critical methods constantly are being developed, including systems based on the "mythic perspective," comparisons with religious models, the narrative paradigm, and the use of creative analogies. and attitudes shared in common) central to the system. The dramatistic pentad examines act (the symbols actually exchanged); scene (the setting for the act); agent (the actor or rhetor); agency (symbolic and linguistic strategies used to secure identification); and purpose (intention of the rhetor). Though the approach is flexible, messages are judged largely by their effects, and the method occasionally may be difficult to replicate. Other critical methods constantly are being developed, including systems based on the "mythic perspective," comparisons with religious models, the narrative paradigm, and the use of creative analogies.

Content analysis is a systematic method designed to analyze the content and treatment of communication. Content analysis steps include: (1) defining and limiting the communication population to be studied; (2) selecting coding units and classification systems (coding units are the categories used to count the communication forms); (3) sampling messages; (4) coding message content (including determining consistency of coders and providing adequate training); (5) analyzing data, usually by reporting simple descriptive statistics; and (6) interpreting results. Limitations of the method are (1) inability to draw cause and effect conclusions; (2) difficulties in finding representative communication examples; and (3) generalizing from one content analysis to another.

Interactional and relational analyses are forms of content analysis designed to describe the continuous oral communication between people. Interaction analysis focuses on ways of tracking individual acts of communicators. A variation of direct coding approaches (such as Bales's Interaction Process Analysis) is the examination of "interacts" (one person's conversation and the reaction of another) and "double interacts" (which add the first person's response to the other's reaction). Relational control analysis tracks message sequences to determine the relative patterns of position and control in the relationship. Statements made in these conversations are coded into categories called "one-up" (in which somebody is dominant over another because he or she asserts one's "definitional rights"), "one-down" (in which a person submits to the opinions or definitional rights of another), and "one-across" (message extensions that extend discussions without increasing assertions or accepting others' statements). Using these methods involves deciding on a coding system to use; training people to code messages; gathering samples of communication; coding message content; and analyzing and interpreting message content. These methods are limited by the facts that they might not be useful if the researcher's theoretical or explanatory basis is the perception or shared interpretation of individuals and they cannot be used to draw conclusions about cause-and-effect relationships.

TERMS FOR REVIEW

nomothetic research
idiographic research
rhetorical criticism
rhetoric
criticism
impressionistic criticism
invention

ethos
pathos
logos
arrangement
style

delivery
memory
identification
act
scene
agent
agency

purpose
content analysis
coding units
reliability
interaction analysis
relational control analysis

NOTES

[1]Used through courtesy of Ava C. English.

[2]These three categories occasionally have been called the Three Musketeers of Rhetoric because of the main characters in the novel by Alexandre Dumas. As a rather dry joke, Dumas named his three Musketeers, Athos, Porthos (*ethos, pathos,* get it?), and Aramis.

[3]The first and third limitations benefit from the discussion completed by Wimmer & Dominick (1983, pp. 141–142) whereas the second limitation is drawn from Berg (1989, p. 125).

CHAPTER 8

Participant Observation and Naturalistic Research

The way to do research is to attack the facts at the point of greatest astonishment.

–Celia Green

ROLE OF PARTICIPANT OBSERVATION STUDIES IN COMMUNICATION RESEARCH
    Purposes of Participant Observation Methods
    Suitability of Participant Observation Methods to Research Questions

FORMS OF PARTICIPANT OBSERVATION STUDIES
    The Position of the Observer
    Ethnography
THE FLUID PROCESS OF PARTICIPANT OBSERVATION STUDY
    Steps in Participant Observation
    Limitations of the Approach

BEFORE WE GET STARTED . . .

Communication researchers often become active participants in the research setting. They may join Alcoholics Anonymous to learn of the informal communication that reinforces the famous ''12 step'' program, they may work in a car dealership to study special methods of influence, or they may live with the Tasaday ''stone age'' people of the Philippines to learn how legends are communicated. They ''get their hands dirty'' by gathering data in the natural environment rather than relying on formal questionnaires or experiments. This type of active inquiry is the subject of this chapter.

ROLE OF PARTICIPANT OBSERVATION STUDIES IN COMMUNICATION RESEARCH

Participant observation studies are based on a desire to focus on communication behavior that is not affected by the research process. The researcher explores communication by engaging in the natural environment. Many terms are used to describe this form of research, including fieldwork, participant observation, naturalistic study, and qualitative research. **Fieldwork** may be defined as "the study of people acting in the natural courses of their daily lives. The fieldworker ventures into the worlds of others in order to learn firsthand about how they live, how they talk and behave, and what captivates and distresses them" (Emerson, 1983, p. 1). For our purposes, fieldwork and naturalistic studies are interchangeable terms. **Naturalistic studies** are nonexperimental inquiries completed as subjects are involved in the natural course of their lives. **Participant observation** is the most well-known form of fieldwork in which researchers study groups by gaining membership or close relationships with them (see Wax, 1968, p. 238). In this chapter we will not equate naturalistic studies with qualitative research. Some fieldwork may yield quantitative data, though most of it does not. Thus, naturalistic/fieldwork designs are used to gather information, regardless of whether it is qualitative or quantitative. This chapter's applications focus on naturalistic fieldwork with special emphasis on participant observation.

fieldwork defined

naturalistic and participant observation distinguished

Purposes of Participant Observation Methods

Participant observation methods are characterized by the attempt to use nonintrusive ways to gather information.[1] Rather than asking individuals to complete questionnaires reporting about themselves, as they might in a survey, participant observation researchers join with groups of people to *observe* them from within the group. Scholars who use naturalist methods look at such things as how people say good-bye at airports, the stories people tell each other at work, and ways newscasters choose stories to cover. Though researchers who complete laboratory experiments try to get some distance from the subjects in the research, participant observation researchers try to get "up close and personal" with the people they study, short of passing out questionnaires or conducting structured interviews.

purposes: 1. when questionnaires inappropriate

Fieldwork studies have three major purposes. First, they try to answer questions in settings where use of questionnaires and direct reports would be inappropriate or impractical. In studies of health communication, for example, it is often not possible for a nurse to conduct research by asking several hundreds of patients detailed questions about the "bedside manner" of physicians. Yet, a nurse might watch patients who try to explain their medical problems to apparently uninterested physicians. Patterns may be identified in conversations between patients and doctors. Such naturalistic studies may explore questions where tight survey or experimental methods are impossible.

2. setting so new that hypotheses are undeveloped

Second, fieldwork is often undertaken when a setting has been so unexplored that formal hypotheses may not have been developed. Though this invitation to research is not unique to participant observation work, it is true that by immersing yourself in the field setting you might be able to acquire insight that cannot be gained as well in other ways. By looking for unexpected events, researchers can develop intriguing hypotheses to be explored in other inquiries.

Third, these studies are completed by researchers who wish to develop grounded theory. **Grounded theory** is a set of explanations that has immediate relevance to a specific field setting under investigation. Using this method, participant observers attempt to discover categories to describe their observations after they have entered the field. Then researchers make additional observations to refine and modify these categories. Eventually, a theory may emerge. An alternative approach called **analytic induction** involves researchers starting with some tentative hypotheses that they apply in fieldwork. If these hypotheses are inadequate they may be abandoned or reformulated. Though distinctions can be drawn between these views, many participant observer researchers find that their practical work involves some features of both.

3. developing grounded theory

analytic induction identified

Thus, the chief difference between participant observation methods and other studies is the method of gathering data. This approach still argues from information to conclusions. The data are empirical (empirical means "observable") and can be examined by others. Hence, solid participant observation fieldwork is at least as demanding as any other research.

such studies still empirically grounded

Suitability of Participant Observation Methods to Research Questions

Fieldwork and participant observation methods are invited when a researcher is interested in naturally arising behavior that has not always been shown to have regularities that can be produced in the laboratory. Sometimes researchers try to find the answers to such questions as: When is the insanity defense accepted by juries? When does the use of threat by a manager increase productivity? When do reporters choose to stick to a newspaper story despite threats on their lives? By working in the field, researchers might find examples of each situation. Then, by examining such occurrences, they might find explanations.

research questions involve: naturally arising behavior not consistently produced in laboratories

By recording conversations and exchanges, researchers can gain special insight. As three scholars of the subject explained (Judd, Smith, & Kidder, 1991, p. 299):

> Field-workers and participant observers become engaged in the conversations, actions, and lives of the people they study. And unlike the standardized questions and procedures used by experimenters and survey researchers, the questions and actions of a field-worker may vary from one person and setting to the next. Instead of approaching each respondent with the same list of questions, a field-worker engages in conversations and observations that may last several hours or continue for several days, weeks, or months. The conversations move in directions that cannot be anticipated, so the researcher's questions cannot be duplicated from one person to the next. To the extent that the researcher participates in the lives of the people under study, each day will provide new opportunities as a result of the previous day's activities.
>
> How can field research be systematic if the procedures vary so from one person or day to the next? The systematization occurs not by having uniform procedures but by recording faithfully what is seen and heard.

SPECIAL DISCUSSION 8–1
Observational Studies

Researchers who look at naturally occurring communication but avoid direct involvement with the phenomena are engaged in observational studies. In such work, one may take the view of a complete observer or unobtrusive measurer.

A *complete observer* has no contact with the individuals he or she is observing. Research of this form typically occurs when scholars go to field settings such as airports or bus stations and watch behaviors of interest from a distance. They may record behavior with photographs or by taking detailed notes. For instance, one scholar watched overweight students in a college cafeteria (Krantz, 1979). It was found that heavy people selected less food to eat when they were going to carry on a conversation with others during lunch.

Unobtrusive measurement uses artifacts that do not influence the behavior being studied. These unobtrusive methods include accretions and erosions, though some lists of these methods include other techniques as well (see Webb, et al. [1981] who include archival information, private records, simple observations, and contrived observations).

Accretions are deposits of material left by some action. Sometimes layers are placed down naturally, but often communicators deposit remnants of their own. Much work on accretion resembles archaeology. Two researchers examined the graffiti left on the walls of a juvenile corrections facility in New England (Klofas & Cutshall, 1985). The language and kinds of remarks revealed that the young people in the facilities had been socialized into a unique "incarceratory culture," in which the outside world and authority were viewed as objects to manipulate and where ordinary trust was viewed very suspiciously. Thus, by looking at deposits, researchers can find some interesting clues.

One area of study that examines artifacts is called **urban archaeology.** These studies survey objects created by humans as "leftovers" of communication activity. Searching trash cans in a neighborhood to find evidence of the rate of alcoholism is an example of the sort of work that often passes for such inquiry. Of course, such artifacts can be sketchy or misleading (one might have many liquor bottles in a trash can because of a recently held party for a large number of people; or someone might have run out of room and deposited liquor bottles in a neighbor's trash can). Thus, researchers usually try to find several signs before interpreting results.

SPECIAL DISCUSSION 8–1
Continued

Erosions are evidence of the wear or use of objects. One of the most popularly cited erosion studies involved inquiry into attention paid to different exhibits at the Chicago Museum of Science and Industry.

The vinyl tiles around the exhibit containing live, hatching chicks had to be replaced every six weeks or so; tiles in other areas of the museum went for years without replacement. A comparative study of the rate of the replacement around the various museum exhibits could give a rough ordering of the popularity of the exhibits (Webb et al., 1981, p. 7).

Though such information could have more than one explanation, there was reason to believe that the chick exhibit had attracted a larger amount of traffic (and attention) than many others. By finding examples of such erosions, it is possible to gather interesting circumstantial evidence related to answering key questions of interest.

Unobtrusive methods can be used in many sorts of studies. For example, an experimental study in the laboratory could use erosion measures (such as the amount of scratch paper used in a discussion as an indicator of the amount of thoughtful activity used in the group). Yet, unobtrusive methods are most often associated with naturalistic research.

Though most methods described in this chapter are techniques you might spot in nearly any communication journal, some naturalistic methods are derived from a special background and way of approaching knowledge. Despite any extra baggage they may have, all these methods are undertaken when the research problem statement demands fieldwork exploration of questions for which use of standardized forms or tools would not be appropriate.

FORMS OF PARTICIPANT OBSERVATION STUDIES

The role and the approach of the researcher can differ greatly among participant observers. In fact, to do such inquiry, you must decide what position to take, the advantages of different levels of participation, and the wisdom of taking an ethnographic approach.

The Position of the Observer

Researchers can observe communication at a distance, or they can attempt to become involved in the communication activities themselves. The sort of involvement scholars have affects their ability to acquire highly subjective information that otherwise might be lost. Yet, the level of participation the researcher has with groups studied can also affect his or her objectivity and the degree to which conclusions drawn are free from undue bias. There are two general ways to enter the field.

Full Participation Observation

Full participant observation research is characterized by the investigator's gathering data while taking part in the activities of a group—and while concealing one's research identity. In short, people are studied when they do not know it. A researcher might join an organization and follow its activities as an insider. He or she might record conversations with others in the organization. Rather than just observe a political campaign or activities in a speech clinic, the researcher might work within them. The reports might suggest interesting interpretations since the full participant can gain as intimate information as the opportunity invites.

Full participation observation is not easy. In a famous participant observation study, Leon Festinger, Henry W. Rieken, and Stanley Schachter (1956) studied a woman they called Mrs. Keech who had predicted the end of the world by a mighty flood. After reading about Mrs. Keech in a newspaper, Festinger's group joined her followers to see what would happen when the world did not, in fact, come to an end. Mrs. Keech claimed to have been receiving messages from a group called the Omnipotent Guardians from the planet Clarion. They had sent her messages through a combination of telepathy, automatic writing, and crystal ball gazing to indicate that at midnight on a particular December evening the world would be destroyed, killing all humanity except for Mrs. Keech's group. They were to be rescued by flying saucers sent from Clarion to Mrs. Keech's home. During the weeks before the "end of the world," several of the group members quit their jobs and spent their savings in preparation for the end. Messages continued to arrive daily to Mrs. Keech. At meetings Festinger and his associates frequently would excuse themselves and write down their notes while in the bathroom. At one meeting, the members were asked to look into a crystal ball and report any new pieces of information. One member of Festinger's group was forced to participate, even though he was hesitant to take a vocal role in meetings. After he remained silent for a time, Mrs. Keech demanded that he report what he saw. Choosing a single word response, he truthfully announced, "Nothing." Mrs. Keech reacted theatrically, "That's not nothing. That's the void." On the final evening, members of the group waited for midnight. During the evening other instructions arrived. Cultists were told to remove their shoelaces and belt buckles since these were unsafe aboard flying saucers. When midnight passed without any end of the world in sight—and without any flying saucers visible—members of the group began questioning whether they had misunderstood the instructions. Mrs. Keech began to cry and whimpered that none of the group believed in her. A few of the group comforted her and reasserted their belief in her. Some members reread past messages and many others sat silently with stony expressions on their faces. Finally in the wee hours of the morning, Mrs. Keech returned to the group with a new "automatically written" message from the Omnipotent Guardians. Because of the faith of the group, the earth had been spared. The cult members were exuberant and during the weeks that followed actually attempted to secure additional converts. One can find both insight and some entertainment in such a participant observation study. To Festinger's group of scholars, the experience permitted them to provide a field study examination of the theory of cognitive dissonance that they were trying to develop at the time—a theory that later became a major force in communication and social psychology.

Though the ability to get involved in groups that otherwise would not welcome a researcher permits gathering data, the method creates obvious ethical difficulties. The invasion of privacy of others is an obvious objection that may not have a satisfactory defense. In addition, concealing the researcher's identity has been charged with introducing "false and hypocritical interpersonal relationships between the actual participants and the participant observers" (Fox, 1969, p. 513).

ethical problems with the full participant approach

Participant as Observer

Most participant observation research follows the **participant as observer** method in which the group to be studied is made aware of the researcher's role. Upon agreeing to permit the researcher's participation, other group members typically become resources who explain and help interpret that group's actions. In one such study, Martin S. Weinberg (1965) visited three nudist camps to study nonverbal behavior of participants. In each case, he first identified himself as a researcher to each of the camps and requested permission to attend the camps as a nudist during the summer months. When attending the camps Weinberg identified himself as a researcher to the nudists. He reported that the nudists seemed uninfluenced by his presence, and they were willing to discuss matters with him. He had two potential hypotheses to guide his work, each one of which was opposite of the other. Perhaps people in nudist camps might be as unrestrained in their language and gestures as in their clothing. Or, perhaps since displays of the body are obvious, nudists might compensate by increased restraint in their language and gestures. He found strong support for his second hypothesis. He noticed that "verbal modesty" was common—there were few dirty jokes told, and sexual innuendo in conversation was frowned upon. Staring and body contact were discouraged. Similarly, use of alcohol was strictly forbidden. When Weinberg later interviewed 101 nudists in the Chicago area, he found that they were harsh in their judgments of others who violated their very strict norms. Furthermore, nudists lived a lifestyle in which nudity and sexuality were largely unrelated matters. As this example illustrates, the participant as observer does not hide his or her identity (or much of anything else). Instead, the observer becomes an active participant and develops increased appreciation for the actions and communication of the group.

participant as observer method defined

Balancing Involvement

The two approaches involve some trade-offs. Figure 8.1 shows the relationship between the researcher's approach and the types of claims drawn. When the researcher tends toward complete participation, interpretations become subjective, the researcher shares sympathy and concern for the communicators studied, plays an active role in the communication to be studied, and usually goes into the research setting in disguise to get close to the data. On the other hand, researchers who tend toward complete observational research are objective, unsympathetic, detached, and usually candid about the sorts of research completed. Since the

FIGURE 8.1
Ideal Typical
Continuum of
Fieldworker Roles
Figure from
STRATEGIES OF
SOCIAL RESEARCH,
3rd ed., by Herman W.
Smith. p. 332, copyright
© 1991 by Holt, Rinehart
and Winston, Inc.
Reprinted by permission
of the publisher.

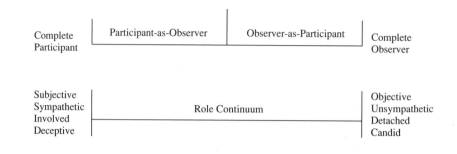

fieldwork of the participant observer tends to emphasize the involvement in the setting, his or her work may be tipped more toward one side of the continuum than the other. Participant observers must weigh the advantages and disadvantages of each approach to balance some of the benefits of one position against the costs that go with the levels of involvement.

Ethnography

ethnography defined

Ethnography is research in which the investigator participates, overtly or covertly, in people's lives for an extended period of time, collecting whatever data are available to describe behavior. As can be seen, ethnography is a broad term that includes a great deal, including most participant observation research (though participant observation work need not occur over very long time periods). The sorts of studies completed by Margaret Mead while living with the Samoan people or the natives of New Guinea are archetypes of ethnography, even though it appears that in some cases she may have been hoaxed by some native groups. By living with a group for an extended time, even with periodical breaks along the way, it is possible to acquire knowledge that is unexpected and often exciting. Ethnography has been used quite a bit in communication and educational studies. For instance, by "hanging around" a high school and neighboring community for a full year, Herve Varenne (1988) noticed that students began to use spaces to form cliques almost immediately, even in the regimented lines of the cafeteria, the library, or the study hall.

most participant
observation as a
special case of
ethnography

> By extraordinary right, most often by virtue of membership in some special "club," students could be found in the private offices in the back of the library, in the coordinator's office, in the room where the audiovisual equipment was kept. . . . By self-proclaimed right, students might also be found in the bathrooms for very long periods of times not solely dedicated to the satisfaction of biological functions or on the stairway from which the roof could be reached (p. 216).

Despite efforts to create a setting that minimized student differences, cliques made creative use of official and unofficial space to organize informal forums for communicating with each other.

ethnomethodology
distinguished from
ethnography

It sometimes is confusing to hear ethnography mentioned because so many researchers have used the term in very different senses (see Agar, 1988). **Ethnomethodology,** sometimes is used as though it were interchangeable with

---

SPECIAL DISCUSSION 8–2
Other Qualitative-Naturalistic Methods

Though the naturalistic methods used in communication are common enough, other qualitative tools sometimes appear. Some of the most frequently used methods are the following:

- "A 'life-history' or 'life story' is the autobiography of a person which has been obtained though interview and guided conversation" (McNeill, 1990, p. 85). The term "oral history" often is used as a synonym for the life-history study. This method does not result in composing an autobiography, but it uses life-histories (usually witnesses to major communication events) to gather information on significant times or events. Such studies are useful since collecting many such studies allows one to reconstruct a sense of a time period and the practice of communication across time.
- Time-budgeting studies are inquiries in which "the researcher asks the subjects of the research to keep a detailed diary over a given period" (McNeill, 1990, p. 88). Time-budgeting studies are often used in organizational communication and communication education to help determine whether professionals are using their time in ways that are most constructive and expected given their job descriptions. The maps constructed by time-budgeting studies can help identify areas of dominant focus and areas where readjustments might be advised.
- Community studies "involve a researcher or a team of researchers in studying a whole community of people, usually in a small town or village, or possibly part of a larger town" (McNeill, 1990, p. 90). Unlike ordinary ethnographic research, a variety of methods are used, including such tools as direct observation, use of informants, and informal and formal interviews with individuals.

---

ethnography, when, in fact, it is a distinct specialty. The "new ethnography" (Berg, 1989, pp. 51–52) is the study of the mundane and ordinary activities of everyday life, concentrating on the methods used by people to report their common sense practical actions to others in acceptable rational terms. Ethnomethodology attempts to impose a rational scheme onto essentially practical activities (practical reasoning). When it works properly, one can find patterns to explain the implicit rules or guidelines that people use to make sense of exchanges with each other. Although ethnomethodology occasionally has been criticized for being "almost wilfully obscure" (McNeill, 1990, p. 94), it has grown in popularity among students of communication since it focuses on how people use messages to perceive the world as they do.

THE FLUID PROCESS OF PARTICIPANT OBSERVATION STUDY

As with other research approaches, participant observation studies follow some fairly consistent methods. Furthermore, they have some limitations of which researchers should be aware.

Steps in Participant Observation

Participant observation studies are completed by steps that often overlap and cycle back and forth. The entire method has a fluid quality about it, though a protocol has established some clear phases in the research.

Selecting Settings and Cases

Researchers often choose research settings and fields that appeal to their personal interests. Thus, one researcher might focus on observing people at airports, another might attempt to spy on private conversations, and still another might try to have long visits with subjects. There is some disagreement about whether it is more desirable to study unusual and exotic settings or to stick to the ordinary and mundane. Those who urge study of exotic practices believe that looking at unusual activities may reveal things that challenge conventional wisdom. Those who want researchers to emphasize ordinary behavior hold that regularities in communication can be identified most efficiently by looking at typical, rather than aberrant, behaviors.

Getting into the Setting

Participant observers must take time to define their levels of activity. A passive observer may have difficulty getting a group's permission to observe key behavior. Yet, a researcher who does not reveal his or her own purposes to the individuals under study may face some dangers. Laud Humphreys (1970) studied the practice of casual homosexual sexual encounters. Without identifying himself as a researcher, and without choosing to participate, Humphreys agreed to serve as a ''lookout'' at a public restroom where men had brief homosexual affairs. He was presumed to be a voyeur or ''watch queen.'' He found that many of the men were married and led otherwise heterosexual lives. Yet, such research proved dangerous. Humphreys was arrested once and was beaten up by a gang of kids.

The ethical difficulties of concealing one's identity can be great. One research team (Berg, Ksander, Loughlin, & Johnson, 1983) studied a group of teenagers' criminal activities. Along the way, they acquired information about plans for car robberies, burglaries, assaults, shoplifting, and drug deals. These clearly illegal and violent activities never were reported to police, nor were victims warned. Did the researchers owe society or the victims anything? They apparently did not think so—nor was their own property stolen, nor were they assaulted. The authors possessed a Federal Certificate of Confidentiality that guaranteed that individuals involved in research studies would not have their records subpoenaed, and which required that confidential materials not be revealed. The ethics involved in learning more than one wishes to know constitute a major challenge in much, but not all, naturalistic study.

Sampling within the Case: Selecting the Types of Behaviors to Monitor

Based on their knowledge and theoretic interests, researchers gather data that they believe will be most meaningful. Though some researchers keep their early observations relatively unstructured, all seem to give attention to information about the physical setting, relationships among people, information that is overheard, and

Steps: 1. selecting settings and cases

controversy over study of exotic or ordinary behavior

2. getting into the setting

ethical challenges in research

3. selecting types of behaviors to monitor

locating guides who can help explain the new surroundings (Berg, 1989, p. 68). Researchers usually begin by noting nearly everything that they can identify as a potentially useful piece of information. Most, however, choose behaviors to track based on a combination of personal interest and the level of talk they notice other participants giving the concepts. When examining behavior, many participant observers ask themselves the following key questions to isolate and describe key behavior (Nachmias & Nachmias, 1987, p. 301, after Lofland & Lofland, 1984):

1. What type of behavior is it?
2. What is its structure?
3. How frequent is it?
4. What are its causes?
5. What are its processes?
6. What are its consequences?
7. What are people's strategies?

By a combination of direct observation and asking questions, meaningful communication processes and variables can be identified.

Keeping Records and Observations

While attempting not to distract participants from their ordinary actions, researchers maintain records of the things they have recalled and observed. These pieces of information are the hard data to be analyzed later. Often the setting requires that they keep records "on the run." Researchers try to record words and phrases they hear, the sequences of events, and their impressions. Though some researchers seem to invest a small lifetime into making observations, others set time limits on their entry into a setting. They frequently leave the setting and attempt to give themselves some room to "clear their minds" and organize their thoughts. The quality of a participant observation study is only as good as the records kept by researchers. Hence, the following questions are often raised to decide whether reports are sound ones (after Lofland & Lofland, 1984, p. 51):

4. keeping records and observations

Question:	Evaluation of Answer:
1. Is the report firsthand?	Hearsay may be very inaccurate.
2. Where was the observer?	The observer should be in a position to see or hear what is described.
3. Did the participant have a reason to give false or biased information?	Information from biased sources is unreliable. Participants who cannot tell the truth cannot give solid information to draw conclusions.
4. Is the report internally consistent?	Equivocal information prevents drawing clear conclusions.
5. Can the report be validated by other independent reports?	Reliance on isolated reports from participants may be unreliable.

As with all other kinds of data, researchers must show the validity of the information they use to make meaningful interpretations.

Interpretive Analysis of Data

The results of participant observation studies involve descriptions of communication settings. Scholars often rely on references to transcendent perspectives (such as phenomenology or symbolic interactionism) to explain their results. Other times they may look at the language of communicators to find the underlying structures or "grammars." Researchers may look at the so-called "surface devices" that people use to express themselves. Or they may search for evidence of "deep devices" that underlie language use. In reality, there is no real limit on the imagination of researchers in finding creative ways to assess their results.

One of the most popular methods has been the development of the "interpretive approach" (Denzin, 1983). This method identifies communicators' interactions to determine such things as the situations in which people find themselves, the structures within which they work, and the practical features of their world. These researchers frequently hang around communicators and listen to the stories they tell and their use of language. One such study was completed by Nick Trujillo and George Dionisopoulos (1987) on "Cop Talk." By accompanying police officers on calls for four months, they found that police used a vocabulary that emphasized their own sense of drama or excitement about their jobs.

> The drama of police work is also a social construction, enacted in the everyday communicative performances of the officers. The job of law enforcement, thus, may involve forms, tickets, false alarms, but the experience of being a cop involves motorcycle maggots, crushed esophaguses, and grilled assholes. And so as they call the public names, talk tough at the station, and share stories about what went down, cops create and maintain the organization drama of police work (p. 207).

By looking at the language and stories of communicators, one can interpret the function of messages to structure reality in specific social settings.

Exiting the Field Setting

Though it may seem obvious, participant observers need to set a time at which they exit the setting (at least as researchers). Yet, many participant observation researchers develop personal attachments to other participants and have a difficult time leaving the research setting. Moreover, if researchers "go native" and never leave the setting, they may lose their ability to make scholarly contributions. Participant observation researchers are usually expected to make arrangements in advance to terminate the research process. Researchers who end the experience unexpectedly and abruptly may create additional troubles. Participants may feel used and irritated. If the researcher wishes to renew contact at another time, he or she might find the participants to be reluctant. Thus, the timing and manner of exiting the research setting should be scheduled at the time the research is begun. Though many fieldworkers ignore this part of the project, they soon learn how important it is.

Limitations of the Approach

Though participant observation methods have many benefits, there are limits on the approach.[2] First, these methods are very time consuming and expensive. The amount of labor and required finances make them impractical for many research outings.

limitations: **1. time consuming and expensive**

Second and perhaps most obvious, is the fact that such work tends to rest on unreliable measurement. Since researchers rarely have the privilege of using standardized research tools, inquiries may suffer from measurement deficiencies. Furthermore, lessons learned in one naturalistic study may be highly unstable since observation methods may have unknown reliability.

2. unreliable measurement

Third, the participant observers can become overidentified with a group. By becoming an active participant, a researcher may develop biases and sympathies that color the fairness and accuracy of reports or interpretations. A researcher may begin subconsciously to report what he or she expected or what may put the studied group in the best light. Moreover, though they may try to avoid influencing the group, the behavior of participant observers might alter actions seen in the natural setting. The prudent researcher must be careful of such tendencies.

3. researcher bias

Fourth, naturalistic studies cannot reach comprehensive conclusions without combining many different sorts of data. There is a tendency to draw fascinating conclusions from sketchy evidence. Yet, in participant observation work, conclusions probably cannot be argued successfully unless many different sorts of information are available.

4. cannot reach comprehensive conclusions alone

SUMMARY

Participant observation studies are based on a desire to examine communication behavior that is not affected by the research process. Fieldwork is the study of people acting in the natural courses of their daily lives. Participant observers study groups by gaining membership or close relationships with them. Naturalistic studies are nonexperimental inquiries completed as subjects are involved in the natural course of their lives. Fieldwork studies have two major purposes: (1) answering questions in settings where use of questionnaires and direct reports would be inappropriate or impractical; and (2) examining a setting that has been so unexplored that formal hypotheses may not have been developed. Such research still argues from empirical facts to conclusions.

One can enter the field in two ways. Full participant observation research is characterized by the investigator's gathering data while taking part in the activities of a group—and while concealing his or her research identity. The method creates obvious ethical difficulties. The researcher may not satisfactorily be able to defend the invasion of privacy of others. In addition, concealing the researcher's identity can introduce potentially harmful interpersonal relationships. Most participant observation research follows the participant as observer method in which the group to be studied is made aware of the researcher's role. The different approaches involve some trade-offs. As the researcher tends toward becoming a complete participant, interpretations become subjective, the researcher shares sympathy and concern for the communicators studied, the researcher plays an active role in the communication studied, and the researcher usually goes into the research setting in disguise. Ethnography is research in which the investigator participates, overtly or covertly, in people's lives for an extended period of time, collecting whatever data are available to describe behavior. Ethnography is a broad term that includes a great deal including most participant observation research (though participant observation work need not occur over very long time periods). Ethnomethodology or the "new ethnography" is the study of the mundane and ordinary activities of everyday life, concentrating on the methods used by people to report their common sense practical actions to others in acceptable rational terms.

The steps of participant observation include: (1) selecting settings and cases; (2) getting into the setting; (3) sampling within the case by selecting the types of behaviors to monitor; (4) keeping records and observations; (5) interpreting data; and (6) exiting the field setting. Limitations in the use of the approach include: (1) the methods are very time consuming and expensive; (2) the work tends to rest on unreliable measurement; (3) researchers can become overidentified with a group and develop biases and sympathies that color the fairness and accuracy of reports or interpretations; and (4) such studies cannot reach comprehensive conclusions alone.

TERMS FOR REVIEW

fieldwork
participant observation
naturalistic studies
grounded theory
analytic induction

full participant observation
participant as observer
ethnography
ethnomethodology

NOTES

[1]Some writers like to emphasize three qualities that must exist in naturalistic settings. Kraut and Johnston (1979) explain that naturalistic research involves unobtrusive ways of gathering information, of natural events, in a natural setting, stimulated by naturally occurring events. Yet, some work included in the categories of naturalistic studies actually has employed unnatural settings and artificial stimuli (e.g., Byrne, Ervin, & Lamberth, 1970). Thus, for purposes of accuracy, we will limit naturalistic studies to situations in which, at minimum, natural behavior is studied through unobtrusive means.

[2] The first three limits are drawn from the discussion by Berg (1989, pp. 83–84).

CHAPTER 9

Descriptive Empirical Research

"A science is any discipline in which the fool of this generation can go beyond the point reached by the genius of the last generation."

—Max Gluckman

INVITATIONS TO EMPIRICAL RESEARCH
DESIGNING SURVEY RESEARCH

The Questionnaire Survey
The Interview Survey
Network Analysis

BEFORE WE GET STARTED . . .

Descriptive empirical research in communication tends to rely on quantitative methods, though empirical observations are also involved in other types of studies. The tools discussed in this chapter involve collecting data and summarizing them in numbers. Hence, this chapter deals with the very basic issue of how descriptive empirical research is completed. It will introduce you to the forms of such research and give you some details about survey research.

INVITATIONS TO EMPIRICAL RESEARCH

The study of communication often relies on empirical research. The term **empirical** actually means "observable" and thus applies to nearly all communication research that tests statements against data. It involves gathering fresh data to test statements. Descriptive empirical research is invited when problem questions ask

questions asked in attempts to describe matters

about current descriptions of things and explore explanations that characterize things as they are now. J. Jeffrey Auer explained that such questions may have three emphases (1959, p. 147):

1. Ascertaining norms: Where are we? What is the current situation?
2. Establishing goals: Where should we be? What is best?
3. Developing methods: How do we advance from norm to goal? What is best to do?

Surveys, content analyses, and observational studies can help researchers understand what is occurring. Surveying attitudes and opinions can show sentiments about directions to move. Scholars who attempt to develop new research methods and measurement tools can promote other studies to help solve practical problems.

experiments show causal relationships experiment defined

Some questions ask about cause and effect relationships between variables. Although historical research can answer such questions, the only way to get contemporaneous evidence of cause and effect relationships is through experimentation. An **experiment** introduces a variable and determines its effects while controlling all other variables. Achieving such control is difficult, but if successful, experiments provide immediate evidence of cause and effect relationships. This chapter focuses attention on nonexperimental methods, and the next chapter explores experimental research.

DESIGNING SURVEY RESEARCH

survey research defined

The term **survey** means the process of looking at something in its entirety. In quantitative research, a survey is an empirical study that uses questionnaires or interviews to discover descriptive characteristics of phenomena. We often think of surveys as polls, questionnaire studies, and interviews in which large groups of people are asked their views. Yet, relatively small groups of people such as employees of a company or a plant can be surveyed. Their responses may be used to identify employee sentiment. Or their responses could form the basis of a network analysis.

surveys are used in all branches of communication

Surveys are used across communication studies. In fact, students often find that after graduating they are asked to construct questionnaires in their jobs. Professionals also use this method actively. In speech and hearing science, Barbara Lewis (1990) surveyed family histories of children who had phonological disorders to discover the presence of dyslexia, learning disabilities, and speech disorders across generations. Leslie Rescourla (1989) used the survey method to validate two new measurement instruments to diagnose delayed language development in preschool children. In mass communication, Barnett and his associates (1989) surveyed students from rural areas in northern Belize (formerly British Honduras), and found strong associations between students' English speaking ability and their frequency of watching broadcasts of American television. In communication theory, Rod Troester and Cathy Sargent Mester (1990, p. 424) surveyed chairs of communication departments and found that although "student interest in [the area of] peace communication is waning," faculty members believed it to be appropriate for study. As you can see, survey research can add intriguing

SPECIAL DISCUSSION 9–1
Forms of Descriptive Studies

Though surveys are the dominant form of descriptive studies, several additional forms of such studies exist and are discussed below (after Auer, ch. 6).

Studies of Behavior: Facts and Opinions. These studies are designed to determine the current status of conditions or attitudes. In addition to surveying with questionnaires and interviews, researchers may make direct observations of communicators. Sometimes the observation can rely on special technologies, such as special screening rooms equipped with "wiggle-meters" (that measure how attentive television viewers are by tracking how often they shift weight [wiggle] during a broadcast).

Studies of Status and Development. Intensive detailed study of individual cases and events often reveals information that can be used to develop other hypotheses or to answer practical questions, including case studies or genetic studies (inquiries into the "growth and development among individuals and groups" [Auer, 1959, pp. 151–152]). These studies are usually long-term inquiries that trace the genesis and change of a group of people throughout a life cycle.

Methodological Studies. These studies deal with the development and validation of new tools and measuring instruments. Some studies examine the integrity of research approaches generally, such as Burgoon, Hall, and Pfau's (1991) check on the validity of persuasion studies that employ only one persuasive message topic (they found no major statistical or logical difficulty when different studies had provided replications across topics). Another type of methodological study develops research instruments, such as McCroskey's (1992) validation of a new scale to measure a person's "willingness to communicate" with others.

information to our store of knowledge. The three general forms of survey studies are questionnaire studies, interview studies, and network analysis.

The Questionnaire Survey

Completing a questionnaire study involves the six steps described below. At each point along the way, researchers explain and justify their choices.

**questionnaires
defined**

Selecting Questions and Providing Instructions

Questionnaires are survey forms in which individuals respond to written items. Questionnaires ask people to report their understanding of things, often including their own behavior.

Developing the questions is often difficult for students. In general there are three ways to develop survey items. Early in your own research you might want to rely on the first two, and as you become more experienced you can learn to use the third option.

**guides for
developing
questions**

1. Find standard forms in resource works. Collections of measures in such sources as *Measurement of Communication Behavior,* by Emmert and Barker (1989), *Measures of Personality and Social Psychological Attitudes,* by Robinson, Shaver, and Wrightsman (1991), *A Handbook for the Study of Human Communication,* by Tardy (1988). *Mental Measurements Yearbook* is a multi-volume set including references to hundreds of measures, though most of them must be purchased from private companies. These resources can help you find ways to measure communication concepts.
2. Select measurement forms that have been used in research articles you read. Researchers often provide copies of their items in research articles. If not, they will often cite sources from which their measures were drawn.
3. Develop them yourself by: (a) reading on the subject, (b) composing a rough draft of items based on your reading of statements on the issue, (c) putting them into a suitable format, such as those found in this chapter, and (d) evaluating them against the standards discussed below.

Researchers face several tactical challenges when phrasing questions and preparing survey forms. People must cooperate in completing questionnaires. Moreover, respondents must report the way they *honestly* perceive things. This reporting can be difficult since respondents sometimes do not *know* how they perceive things. Other times, respondents may feel pressure to respond in ways they believe the researcher wants. Naturally, these matters are not to be taken lightly. Thus, researchers try to use methods that avoid contaminating data.

In general, preparing questionnaires and interview schedules requires researchers to observe three criteria (Tuckman, 1978, p. 197):

1. To what extent might a question influence respondents to show themselves in a good light?
2. To what extent might a question influence respondents to be unduly helpful by attempting to anticipate what researchers want to hear or find out?
3. To what extent might a question be asking for information about respondents that they are not certain, and perhaps not likely, to know about themselves?

There are several options for designing survey items. Table 9.1 shows the sorts of questionnaire forms that communication researchers typically use.

Researchers must also decide on a format for their questions. Alternatives include the following.

- Direct or indirect questions (Tuckman, 1979, p. 198). Though direct questions ask for obvious reports, indirect questions ask respondents to react in ways that imply information. Instead of asking whether people enjoy programs on public television, a researcher might ask subjects to describe the quality of programs on public television. Speech and hearing therapists may ask clients to describe their communication problems, rather than asking them to identify the disorder they believe they have. Though it usually requires more indirect questions than direct questions to obtain information, these

TABLE 9.1 Types of Questions

Type and Description	Example	Useful When
Open-ended questions: Questions to which people respond in their own words	12. What fringe benefits offered by this company are most important to you? _____ _____ _____	1. Respondents may not have information on the topic 2. Respondents are motivated to communicate and spend time with the project
Closed-ended questions: Questions to which people respond in fixed categories of answers	12. The fringe benefits at this company are: (check one) [　] superior [　] excellent [　] good [　] fair [　] poor	1. Possible answers are limited in number 2. Respondents are known to possess information on the topic 3. Terms are commonly understood by respondents
Paired-comparison questions: Questions that ask respondents to make a judgment between alternatives taken two at a time	12. If you had to choose between the following two options, which one would you prefer in your career? [　] enjoyable work [　] high income 13. If you had to choose between the following two options, which one would you prefer in your professional career? [　] good people to work with [　] high income	1. Items to be rated are very close in desirability and simple ranking is difficult 2. Options are fairly limited in number 3. It is practical to contrast all options against each other
Contingency questions: Questions asked only of some respondents, determined by their responses to some other question (Babbie 1992, p. G2).	12. Have you given a speech in the last three months? [　] Yes (If yes, please go to question 13) [　] No (If no, please go to question 20)	1. Situations in which responses from only certain subjects are desired 2. Questions apply only to some people
Ranking questions: Closed-ended questions that ask respondents to rank a set of options	12. Which sources of news do you rely on most? (rank your first choice number 1, your second choice number 2, and so forth until you have ranked all five sources) _____ television _____ newspapers _____ radio _____ magazines _____ friends	1. A small number of items are to be ranked 2. All categories to be ranked are applicable to all subjects 3. When priority information is desired, rather than information about degree of differences in evaluations

TABLE 9.1—*Continued*

Type and Description	Example	Useful When
Inventory Questions: Closed-ended questions that ask respondents to list all responses that apply to them	12. How did you hear about the speech and hearing clinic services? (check all that apply) [ ] newspapers [ ] school officials [ ] health professionals [ ] friends [ ] radio [ ] television [ ] yellow pages listing	1. Respondents differ in their backgrounds in items on the inventory 2. Categories are fairly well known 3. Categories are not mutually exclusive of others
Matrix questions: Closed-ended questions that ask respondents to use the same categories to supply information	For each of the following statements, circle SA if you strongly agree with the statement, A if you agree with the statement, N if you neither agree nor disagree with the statement, D if you disagree with the statement, and DS if you disagree strongly with the statement. 12. Management is SA A N D DS competent 13. Management is SA A N D DS inept 14. Management is SA A N D DS trustworthy	1. Standard methods such as Likert scaling are invited 2. Many reliable statements are known to measure the domain of interest 3. Items can be reasonably added together to create a logical scale
Multiple-choice questions: Closed-ended questions that ask respondents to select a category response from a range of possible responses	12. How long have you been a major in your current field? [ ] 0–1 semesters [ ] 2–3 semesters [ ] 3–4 semesters [ ] 5–6 semesters [ ] over 6 semesters	1. It is desirable to group responses into meaningful underlying units 2. Exclusive categories can be found

questions often can yield honest responses when topics involve sensitive matters or issues people may try to answer in ways that put them in the best light.

• Specific or general questions. Specific questions focus on individual activities, whereas general questions ask about global evaluations. In organizational communication, employees are often asked about their satisfaction with the physical work environment. They may be asked specific questions regarding how satisfied they are with the temperature of the work environment, the cleanliness of the workplace, and the ease of operating equipment. General questions may ask about their overall view of the work environment, for example, "How satisfied are you with the company's physical work environment?" Though specific questions are used extensively by researchers to get precise information, in some cases individuals may grow unusually "cautious or guarded and give less-than-honest answers. Nonspecific questions may lead circuitously to the desired information but with less alarm by the respondent" (Tuckman, 1979, p. 198).

- Questions versus statements (Tuckman, 1979, p. 199). Some questionnaire items ask questions. Others make statements and ask subjects to indicate how much they agree or disagree with them. Both methods are useful. Yet, researchers typically select one mode or the other to minimize the number of different instructions that respondents must follow.

Of course, researchers often combine forms on a single questionnaire. Thus, questionnaires may include a broad repertoire of response modes.

Phrasing items on a questionnaire is a major challenge. Through tricky phrasing, a researcher can "rig" a survey to produce results that he or she wants. Thus, one must carefully look at survey items to make sure that they are worded appropriately. Table 9.2 lists generally accepted requirements for wording items. These requirements are standards that you may use to double-check questionnaires you compose or read. **phrasing items on questionnaires**

Questionnaire instructions are designed to enlist involvement of respondents and to explain how they are to answer questions. The instructions must be clear and should explain to people how they are to complete the questionnaire. As a matter of routine, many researchers find it useful to provide a category where the respondent can indicate "no response" or "not applicable." This strategy is useful since researchers can separate incomplete responses from thoughtful refusals to respond. Table 9.3 shows some typical instruction methods for some major response formats. Although instructions usually take a fairly standard form, experienced researchers learn the wisdom of running a pilot study on the instructions and survey items. Such a study helps find problems and eliminate potential confusion before completing the full inquiry. **use of questionnaire instructions**

Formatting

The actual composition of the survey tends to be fairly direct. Most survey forms begin with a brief statement of introduction to announce the survey, request participation, assure confidentiality (if appropriate), and indicate how to return the survey form. A letter of introduction is included, with mailed survey forms, though sometimes such letters are used in other settings as well. **format issues: introduction**

The meat of the survey form usually includes the questions or statements to which respondents must react. In practice, most questionnaires place demographic questions (sex, age, academic major, etc.) first. Yet, some argue that demographics should be placed last to avoid boring people with dull background questions at the outset (Babbie, 1992, p. 157). Next, questions that rely on the same sort of response mode are grouped together, preceded by instructions for completing the **order of questions**

grouping of items

TABLE 9.2 Problems in Wording Questions		
Difficulty	**Example**	**Comment and Suggestions**
Double-barreled questions	Do you favor expanded bus and fixed rail mass transit systems?	If you want only one option, you must answer "no" to this question. Instead, two questions should be asked, one for each alternative.
Loaded language	Do you favor reduced military expenditures in light of the reduced world threat from the Soviet Union?	The justification for the position is advanced along with the question itself. Questions should leave out the arguments for one side or another.
Improper grammar	Do you know anyone who wants their taxes raised?	Some questionnaire respondents will detect the incorrect grammar and will be distracted from the content. The question should read, "Do you know people who want their taxes raised?"
Incompleteness	Do you believe that more money should be spent on public higher education?	More than what? Technically, this wording is a fragment, rather than a complete interrogative sentence.
Vagueness	What do you think of your local cable TV company?	Such a question makes it impossible to get at specific, interpretable information. Researchers should ask questions that help them gather information they want.
Ambigious terms	Do you believe that women get their due at your company?	The term "get their due" is subject to many different interpretations. If the researcher wants specific information, unambigious language must be used.
Lengthy items	When engaged in special project teams, do members of management rely on responsive listening techniques prior to giving reactions to suggestions made by subordinates?	Questions should be asked as briefly as possible, but no briefer.
Complex questions	Should serious communication students be required to take a foreign language?	If one disagrees with requiring communication students to take a foreign language, the answer still would be "yes." The question only asks about "serious" students—an extra weasel word that restricts the question to a small group.
Averaging or restrictive questions	In the average week, how many hours of television news do you watch?	It may be difficult for a person to come up with an average. Instead one should ask about a limited time period, such as a week.
Leading questions	Do you agree with most Americans who believe that the quality of public argument is poor?	Such a question creates pressure to go along with the wishes of the questioner. Such prompts as "wouldn't you agree with me that . . ." similarly are dangerous examples of leading questions.
Abbreviations	Should the city council approve the construction of an interactive CATV system? (Wimmer & Dominick, 1983, p. 113)	Abbreviations and acronyms may not be universally understood. It is best to preface this question with a brief explanation of the meaning of the abbreviated term.

TABLE 9.2—*Continued*

Difficulty	Example	Comment and Suggestions
Imprecise questions	Does your cable TV company leave something to be desired?	Such imprecise language guarantees useless data. Whether a person is satisfied or dissatisfied with a local cable TV company, the answer would be "yes" since there is *always* something more that one could desire.
Misspelling	Should children with cleft palates increase there time spent on drills?	Questionnaires are communication encounters. Misspellings show contempt for readers who notice them.
Awkward construction	How many students do you have broken down by sex?	Drinking is more of a problem with my students.
Items with only one logical answer	Can television programs promote acquisition of language skills among immigrants?	Anything is possible in the future. Thus, questions that ask if something "can" or "might" occur have only one logical answer.
Presumptive questions	How severe is your child's stuttering?	Assuming information in a question makes it impossible to answer fairly. This example is much like the famous "wife beating" question. One might ask a man, "Have you stopped beating your wife?" Whether he answers yes or no, you've got him cornered.
Elevated vocabulary	Is the personal life of a presidential candidate germane to your choice of a candidate?	Simple words should be used where possible. Surprisingly, many people do not know that germane means relevant. Though one should not condescend to respondents, simple language should be used whenever possible.
Imprecise agents of action	Should we adopt a guaranteed income to replace welfare?	Who is "we?" Items should specify the active agency, as in the question, "Should the federal government adopt a guaranteed income to replace welfare?"
False bipolar	Do you like coffee with or without caffeine?	Such a question misleads since it assumes that the respondent likes coffee.

items. Some researchers recommend that questions that deal with the same issue should be grouped together. Yet this ordering sometimes can create bias in response. People may try to respond in ways that are consistent with early statements on the survey. For instance, suppose subjects are asked to evaluate the quality of teaching in communication classes. At a later point in the survey they may be asked to state what they believe are the most important needs at their school. It is quite likely that they will mention the quality of teaching—perhaps more than they would have otherwise. There is no simple way around this difficulty.

> The safest solution is sensitivity to the problem. Though you cannot avoid the effect of question order, you should attempt to estimate what the effect will be. Thus, you will be able to interpret results in a meaningful fashion. If the order of questions seems an especially important issue in a given study, you might construct more than one version of the questionnaire containing the different possible ordering of questions. You would then be able to determine the effects. At the very least, you should pretest your questionnaire in the different forms (Babbie, 1992, p. 157).

TABLE 9.3 Sample Instructions

Example 1
Please help us by rating a number of behaviors related to your communication on the job. Using the scales provided, please indicate how frequently you perform each behavior on the job, and your confidence in your ability to perform the behavior. Just circle the number that best reflects your response to each item. If the statement does not apply to you, circle NA.

	I perform this skill on my job	**My confidence in my ability to perform this behavior successfully**
	very rarely *very frequently*	*very low* *very high*
Encouraging others to communicate problems before they turn into major issues.	1 2 3 4 5 NA	1 2 3 4 5 NA
Using communication patterns that promote a supportive climate.	1 2 3 4 5 NA	1 2 3 4 5 NA

Example 2
Please use the scales below to indicate your evaluation of the underlined term. For each scale, place a check mark on the position that best reflects your feelings. If you believe that the concept applies extremely to the concept, check the positions closest to the adjective as in the following example:

         bad   _X_:___:___:___:___:___   good

or   bad   ___:___:___:___:___:_X_   good

If you believe that the concept applies quite a bit to the concept, check the positions indicated as follows:

         bad   ___:_X_:___:___:___:___   good

or   bad   ___:___:___:___:_X_:___   good

If you believe that the concept applies slightly to the concept, check the positions indicated as follows:

         bad   ___:___:_X_:___:___:___   good

or   bad   ___:___:___:_X_:___:___   good

If you are undecided or if you believe the scale does not apply to the concept, check the central position. Check only one position for each scale. Please work quickly. We are most interested in your first impressions.

<u>Management of This TV Station</u>

       positive ___:___:___:___:___:___ negative

       unfair ___:___:___:___:___:___ fair

       friendly ___:___:___:___:___:___ unfriendly

Example 3
Please look at the items below. Place a check mark next to all statements that apply to you.

If a suggestion box program were adopted at this speech clinic,

____ I would be willing to participate if cash awards were given for outstanding suggestions.

____ I would be willing to participate if noncash awards were given for outstanding suggestions.

____ I would be willing to participate if additional vacation time were awarded for outstanding suggestions.

____ I would be willing to participate if no awards were given for outstanding suggestions.

Though similar classes of questions may be grouped together, it does not follow that all the items within each category should be grouped together. For instance, if you wished to evaluate the credibility of management at a company, you might group all these ratings together. But since there are at least two dimensions of credibility, character and competence, it makes some sense to mix the order of such credibility items within the same section of the survey form.

scale items can be placed in random order

Determining the appropriate length for a survey form is a continuing struggle for researchers. In general, brief surveys are preferred to lengthy ones. But sometimes researchers may be stuck with long questionnaires. If you use standard measures of some personality traits, you may have to include many questions. In addition, when developing measures of your own, you may wish to use at least three scale items for each concept. It is difficult to determine the reliability of a single question or item. Hence, if you use three items to measure a concept (such as example 2 on table 9.3), you have some insurance. If one of the items proves unacceptable, you will still have two items left to complete analyses. If you use only a single item, however, and it proves unacceptable, you might wind up with a fistful of air. Even so, you should be careful about using very lengthy questionnaires and avoid the temptation to "throw in" scales to measure other, unrelated matters. If you use a lengthy survey, it is a good idea to prepare several questionnaire forms that put the scales groups in different orders to control for subject fatigue.

length of questionnaires

use of at least three items to measure a concept

Determining Reliability and Validity

Researchers must evaluate questionnaires to determine whether they are valid measures of the concepts under question. **Validity** is the degree to which a measure actually measures what is claimed. To show that a set of questions is valid, we first must show that it is stable. This requirement, called **reliability,** is the consistency of a measure with itself. In chapter 12 you will find specific methods used to determine validity and reliability.

validity defined

reliability defined

In addition to formal methods to establish validity, researchers often include other controls in their surveys. Sometimes they try to detect when people are not responding consistently or accurately. Three types of controls are check questions, test taking measures, and alternating polarity of items. A **check question** involves asking the same question twice at different locations in the questionnaire, usually once positively worded and once negatively worded, such as:

additional controls:

1. check questions

The physical working conditions are good.	SA A N D DS
The physical working conditions are poor.	SA A N D DS

If people pay attention, they should answer the items consistently. If they answer in very different ways, then they are not really alert when completing the survey. Check questions help identify people who are not responding consistently so that they can be discarded from the final sample.

A second control method is the use of measures of test-taking behavior. Scales have been developed to reveal whether an individual is responding in unrealistic ways to survey items. Table 9.4 shows some of these popular measures. A

2. measures of test-taking behavior

TABLE 9.4 Measures of Test-Taking Behavior

Type and Description	Example	Comment
Social Desirability A measure of the degree to which people attempt to describe themselves in ways that they think are acceptable, desirable, or approved by others (Crowne & Marlowe, 1960)	Circle T if the statement is true for you and circle F if the statement is false for you. T F 3.* It is sometimes hard for me to go on with my work if I am not encouraged. T F 4. I have never intensely disliked anyone. T F 5.* On occasion I have had doubts about my ability to succeed in life. *Credit for socially desirable response scored if person answers false.	• The scale consists of thirty three items, but researchers sometimes choose a subset, such as the examples provided here to identify any responses that indicate answering in socially desirable ways. • If a person scores high on these items (the mean for nondepressed people is approximately 14 [Tanaka-Matsumi & Kameoka, 1986]), he or she is answering in ways to put him- or herself in the best light, rather than giving a candid reaction. Many researchers delete such respondents from their final samples, though others prefer to study this effect directly. • Some researchers view this scale as measuring a general tendency to seek approval (Strickland 1977) or, at least, to avoid disapproval (Millham & Jacobson 1978).
MMPI Lie (L) Scale A scale to identify respondents who are attempting to avoid being candid and honest in their responses (not a general personality disposition toward dishonesty) (Meehl & Hathaway, 1946)	Circle T if the statement is true for you and circle F if the statement is false for you.* T F At times I feel like swearing. T F I get angry sometimes. T F Sometimes when I am not feeling well I am cross. *Any answer of "false" is scored as a lie.	• The scale consists of fifteen items interspersed in the Minnesota Multiphasic Personality Inventory (the most popular general personality test in the world). • Scoring high on these items (mean = 4.2 for males and 4.8 for females [Swenson, Pearson & Osbourne, 1973]) often requires a minimum score of 8. Such respondents can be deleted from the sample. • Some believe that the lie scale can be faked by test wise respondents (Dahlstrom, Welsh, & Dahlstrom, 1972).
Infrequency Index A measure of the inconsistency of response, indicative of a person giving random responses (Jackson, 1973)	Circle T if the statement is true for you and circle F if the statement is false for you.* T F Sometimes I get hungry or thirsty. **T F I make all my own clothes and shoes. T F I can run a mile in under three minutes. *Credit for infrequency response if a person answers false. **Credit for infrequency if a person answers true.	• The full scale includes twenty items systematically dispersed through the Jackson Personality Inventory. • For each item there is only one correct answer. Thus, individuals who respond incorrectly are not responding consistently to items on the research instrument. • Though the infrequency index is useful for identifying those who are answering questions in random ways, attentive respondents sometimes are surprised at being asked such stupid questions.

survey researcher can sprinkle these types of measures throughout a questionnaire. Then, scoring these subscales will reveal biases among respondents.

A third method of control is the use of **polarity rotation** of items. This process means (1) avoiding phrasing all items positively and (2) avoiding placing all positive adjectives on the same side of the measurement items. Researchers often are concerned about **response set,** which is a tendency for subjects to follow predictable patterns of responding to test items. If a person gets in the habit of responding positively to items on a survey form, he or she may not be attentive to the content. Furthermore, at one time research reported (probably apocryphal) that when right-handed people got tired they tended to check positions toward the right sides of questionnaires, whereas when left-handed people got tired they tended to check positions toward the left sides of questionnaires. A way to break these habits is by changing the wording of questions and shifting polarity of items. Every so often researchers might ask questions that are worded negatively. If bipolar adjective scales are used, the locations of positively and negatively oriented adjectives might be switched to break up the pattern.

polarity rotation
and control for
response set

Sampling Subjects

Researchers carefully select groups of respondents by defining the universe they wish to sample. After identifying important population characteristics, researchers must define the sampling units. He or she decides whether to sample reports, actual behavior, or examples of communication. In each case, the researcher tries to secure a sample that is representative of the population. Often this requirement means that a random sample is drawn, but other times he or she must use a nonrandom sample. Regardless of the methods they use, researchers are expected to describe and justify their sampling methods and their choice of a sample size.

samples are drawn
to be representative

Administering the Questionnaire

In questionnaire studies, people are given survey instruments along with instructions and left to provide their answers in writing. In experimental studies, the questionnaires may be accompanied by some sort of variable the researcher introduces, but in typical survey research, the respondent is pretty much left alone. Questionnaires can be administered through the mail, by fax, or even in classrooms. In each case, the researcher is guided by limits of subject willingness and the expense of such methods. People do not participate in survey research just because they are asked. Some people will not participate—for any number of reasons. Researchers face sampling biases when people choose not to respond to a survey. For mailed questionnaires, one popular guideline is that ''a response rate of at least 50 percent is *adequate* for analysis and reporting. A response rate of at least 60 percent is *good*. And a response rate of 70 percent is *very good*'' (Babbie, 1992, p. 267). Though these guidelines are just suggestions, they highlight the sorts of choices that researchers frequently make and potential ways to evaluate their efforts. After collecting the questionnaires, it is typical for the researcher to explain—in person or in writing—what the study was about and to offer additional feedback to subjects who wish it. This ''debriefing'' is not just a nicety—it is required of all ethical research.

administering the
questionnaire

response rates

Analyzing and Interpreting Results

Survey research establishes information about relationships, but not about *causal* relationships (we need experiments or long-term historical studies to make those sorts of claims). In particular, researchers use statistical tools to analyze the data. They can use simple descriptive statistics showing averages and spread of data. They can also use additional statistics to measure associations and to identify significant relationships.

Regardless of the extent of statistical analyses, questionnaire studies—and interview survey studies for that matter—interpret results to reveal answers to problem statements and hypotheses that focus on descriptions of current affairs and relationships. In each case, the emphasis is on describing patterns, rather than asserting cause and effect relations.

The Interview Survey

Though questionnaires can be handy, researchers sometimes find interview methods most useful for a couple of reasons. First, though it is easy for many people to ignore a cold questionnaire, it may be difficult for them to ignore a live person who asks questions. Of course, the interviewer may arouse some suspicions, but it is part of the job to involve respondents in the task. Second, the interviewer may record information (such as a respondent's manner and nonverbal actions) that might be lost with the questionnaire method. Of course, there is some art involved in completing interview studies. Thus, when you read studies that use the interview method, you can imagine the give and take involved in the interviews and the sorts of pressures the researcher and respondent felt.

Selecting Questions

First and foremost, interviews are ways for researchers to get answers to questions. Thus, the same question formats used in questionnaires may be employed in interviews. Indeed, most major polling organizations use formats that make their interviews sound like oral questionnaires. These interviews are called **structured interviews** since they use specific lists of questions. In contrast, **unstructured interviews** permit respondents to indicate their reactions to general issues without guidance from highly detailed questions. Furthermore, unstructured interviews allow interviewers to participate in extended exploration and follow up on new matters introduced by the respondent.

Interviews sometimes use special strategies to organize their questions. Unlike questionnaires that may place demographic questions at the end of the survey, interviewers place these items first to help respondents get comfortable with the interview process. Five major strategies can be used for both initial and follow-up questions during interviews. Table 9.5 shows these strategies along with examples and explanations of applications. Good advice on the phrasing of interview questions has been around for some time. As far back as 1940, the Gallup

TABLE 9.5 Major Interview Question Strategies

Type and Description	Example	Comment
I. STRATEGIES FOR INITIAL QUESTIONING		
A. *Funnel Questions:* Start with an open-ended question and follow up with increasingly narrow questions.	Q: How do you feel about the newspapers in your city? Q. How would you rate coverage of business news by the newspapers in your city? Q: How would you rate coverage of the stock market by the newspapers in your city?	This question format is useful when • Respondents must be screened to determine whether a question area applies to them • Respondents may need to think about the general issue before answering thoughtfully • Respondents "know the topic, feel free to talk about it, and want to express their feelings . . . open questions are easier to answer, pose less threat to interviewees, and get interviewees talking" (Cash & Stewart, 1988, p. 75)
B. *Inverted Funnel Questions:* Start with a very specific question and expand by asking increasingly general questions.	Q: What is your favorite TV show? Q: Do you like other shows that have the same format? Q: What types of TV shows do you like?	This question format is useful when • The larger issue is so broad that vague answers might be given if the final question were asked at first • Respondents need specific referents to answer logically • Respondents need encouragement to talk
II. STRATEGIES FOR FOLLOW-UP QUESTIONING		
A. *Mirror Questions:* Questions repeating previous responses to gain additional information	Q: What types of news programs do you watch on television? A: Nontabloid shows. Q: Nontabloid shows?	This question is useful when the interviewer • Does not understand what the respondent means or simply wants to double-check • Wishes to get further explanation without making judgmental statements
B. *Probing Questions:* Questions that ask directly for elaboration and explanation	Q: Why did you seek speech therapy for your son? A: He was having problems with other kids at school. Q: In what way? Could you explain that?	This question is useful when • Specific areas require definition • It is important to elicit examples
C. *Climate Questions:* Questions asking respondents to explain how they feel about the interview	Q: You seem to become uncomfortable when I ask about the reasons you want speech therapy for your son. Is there some problem with talking about this matter?	This question is useful when • The respondent is acting in ways that indicate an unwillingness to be candid • The interviewer senses difficulty in completing the interview with the subject

organization, which runs the Gallup polls, advanced these six recommendations for interviewers (Gallup & Rae, 1940, p. 101):

1. The question should be brief and to the point. Long conditional or dependent clauses tend to confuse people.
2. The words and phrases should be simple and in common day-to-day use among all groups in the community.
3. The question should not include words which have strong emotional content.
4. The question must avoid all possible bias or suggestion in favor of or against a particular point of view.
5. The question should include all the important alternatives which may emerge on a given issue.
6. When the individual is being asked to choose between different alternatives, this choice of alternatives must be given as early in the interview as possible.

Training and Controlling Behavior of Interviewers

training of interviewers necessary

Interview data can be strongly affected by the interviewer. Thus, if several people conduct interviews, researchers must train them to avoid actions that might bias results. Interviewers are trained to use the same introductions, the same answers to respondent questions, and the same manner of asking questions. Typically, the training instructs interviewers on ways to provide common instructions and ways to deal with typical problems that they might face in the field.

selection of interviewers can bias results

Sometimes the very selection of interviewers can bias results. For instance, following the Watts riots of August 1965, H. Edward Ransford completed some survey work in the area (1968). When Ransford and other white interviewers conducted door-to-door surveys in south-central Los Angeles, results indicated great sadness about the riots among the predominantly black community. Yet, when Ransford hired black interviewers, he found very different results. Respondents told black interviewers that they thought the riots were proud symbols of anger and perhaps even inevitable. Furthermore, the black interviewers found that the likelihood of one's participation in the riots was linked to isolation from whites and a deep sense of powerlessness. In contrast, the McCone Commission, which investigated the riots on behalf of the City of Los Angeles, employed white interviewers to complete its work. That commission concluded that the riot was an aberration and was regretted in the black community. Their major recommendations included hiring increased numbers of black police officers and installation of two-way radios in ambulances. Obviously, the interviewers can make a difference in the data collected.

Determining Reliability and Validity

interviewers look for additional clues of reliable and valid responses

In structured interviews the methods for determining reliability and validity are identical to those for questionnaires. Interviewers are also expected to make notes on the nature of the interview so that responses can be put in context. If a respondent seems distracted, the interviewer is expected to provide such a report on the interview form. If a respondent indicates difficulty in understanding questions, such information should be recorded. Check questions frequently are added to interviews to make sure that consistent responses are received. Thus, signs of reliability may be found from several different sources.

When an interview goes properly, validity claims often are quite strong. Since interviews permit use of follow-up questions, researchers often can tell whether the respondents are reacting to the questions as the researcher intended. In fact, interpreting items may be quite clear. The interviewer attempts to figure out what the subject is "driving at" in addition to getting simple answers to questions. Thus, validity claims are a natural counterpart of sound interview methods.

Sampling Subjects

As with questionnaire studies, interviewees should be selected to represent the population. Interviewers must isolate populations, decide on methods to sample events, and select an appropriate number. To secure a useful sample, individuals must be contacted to get their permission to be interviewed. Thus, interviewers must take time to promote participation before the sample can be taken. Face-to-face interviews may have a higher completion rate than questionnaires since most people have difficulty refusing to talk to another person. For interview studies, response rates in the neighborhood of 70 percent or more are quite common (McNeill, 1990, p. 40). Thus, collecting a sample may be as involving for interviews as it is for questionnaire methods.

Analyzing and Interpreting Results

Interview studies typically employ statistical tools to analyze results. Since some information—such as comments and explanations made by respondents—may be qualitative data, researchers might use special tools for these data. Sometimes content analyses or special statistics are employed. Regardless of the methods, however, the researcher tries to interpret results to reveal relationships among variables. **interpretation**

Unlike many questionnaire studies, interviews can produce interpretations for the reasons behind answers. By reporting on the results of follow-up questions and funnel question patterns, interviewers often gain insight to explain previously unknown reasons. Of course, the interviewer may report what he or she expects to see rather than the facts of the matter. But interviews can also yield information that might otherwise "fall between the cracks" of formal questions. It should be emphasized that research using interviews is not somehow superior to questionnaire research. In many ways, questionnaires provide controls on investigator behavior that interviews do not. Whether a particular study should use questionnaires or interviews must be decided by considering the purpose of the research and the degree of maturity of the research area. **reasons behind answers**

Network Analysis

Network analyses are most often used in studies of organizational communication, though studies of interpersonal and group networks have also been popular. The flow of communication through a company or organization may be traced to gain insights about the ways people use information. We will consider the approach of network analysis, the method, and its limitations.

Some researchers question whether we can trust information from questionnaires and interviews (Nisbett & Wilson, 1977a, b; Wilson & Nisbett, 1978). There are two general concerns. First, they doubt whether respondents are aware enough to give useful reactions. Sometimes people may not know how they feel about topics. Though there have been responses to such attacks (e.g., White, 1980), there is little doubt that it is not sensible to ask people questions that they cannot answer. Researchers have tried to deal with this problem by including questions that test whether respondents are responding accurately and with awareness. Martin Orne (1970) recommended checking accuracy of respondent reports by the use of "sacrifice groups." These groups are interrupted during the interview or questionnaire process to see if they really understand what is meant by specific questions. Since these respondents have been distracted somewhat, they are "sacrificed," and their responses are used only to validate the survey question content.

A second problem involves subjects' *recall* of information. Researchers often ask people to remember such things as a conversation with a friend or a recent argument with a parent. But people often recall things inaccurately. Researchers sometimes have dealt with this difficulty by asking more than one person to describe the same event—such as a conversation—and obtaining a common description. Another method involves using carefully designed "funnel questions" that start very broadly and then move to increasingly specific details. This method appears to enhance the accuracy of recalled information from respondents (Adair & Spinner, 1981). Sometimes simply instructing the respondents to respond honestly and accurately can enhance accuracy (Bowers, 1967).

The Approach of Network Analysis

network analysis
defined

Network analysis is a method that obtains individuals' reports of their communication activities with others for the purpose of observing and describing the flow of information in a particular organizational system. In a network, some people are "in the loop" of information and others are "out of the loop." Network analysis identifies such patterns so that the situation might be described and improved. Network analysis often results in a complicated chart showing the actual flow of messages.

purposes: 1. to
construct a map of
the interaction

There are three general purposes for network analyses. First, they are used to construct a map of the interaction among people in an organization. Whereas business scholars ask, "Who has the power in the organization?" communication scholars using network analysis ask "Who has the information?" Granted, information is a major source of power, but communication scholars focus primary attention on the nature of the message and information flow. A second purpose of such network analysis involves diagnosing problems in communication flow. Oftentimes there are failures (we hesitate to call them communication breakdowns because that term is technically contradictory) in the flow of messages, and people who are supposed to get information do not. By finding the roadblocks, researchers can identify these sources of difficulty so that action can be taken. In one factory in the Midwest where the author completed an applied project, changes in company procedures on sick leave and lateness policy were communicated to employees in writing on a bulletin board located outside the break room (a room with vending machines and a microwave oven). Since many employees did not read very well, checking the written messages was a chore for them—a chore they ignored during their short breaks. The block in the flow of information was identified and the plant manager adopted a system to make oral announcements to the incoming shift, rather than relying on the bulletin board alone. A third purpose of network analysis is to identify the roles played by different group members. Informal methods of communication exist in organizations. Network analyses can help identify these "grapevines." Sometimes small groups or cliques talk almost exclusively with each other. Yet, some people serve as bridges or "liaisons" between these groups, keeping up communication between them. With a knowledge of such informal communication channels, organizations may look at ways to spread critical information and methods for spotting problems before they turn into major crunches.

The margin notes appear alongside:
2. diagnosing problems in communication flow

identify roles played by different group members

The Method of Network Analysis

Network analysis involves gathering data to construct a communication map or diagram. Choosing important categories may be a challenge for researchers. Networks are not "things" that can be touched. They are patterns of communication that people use as they work with each other. Thus, networks are abstract matters that are "constructed" by people to organize information about the structure of communication. Peter Monge explained:

choosing categories challenging

> All communication networks are constructed out of two elements: a set of communicators and one or more relations among the communicators. The relations define the nature of the connections among the communicators. Many forms of relations can be used to study societal networks. For example, a kinship relationship could be "is the partner of," "is the sister of," or "is married to." An authority relationship could be of the form "reports to" or "supervises"; a resource relation might be "shares workers with" (Monge & Miller, 1985). Communication networks are constructed out of communication relations, which describe the nature of information flow among people. Typical communication relations are "shares information with," "talks to," "receives reports from," and "discusses new ideas with." (Monge, 1987, p. 243)

Finding the structure of communication flow requires carrying out four steps. First, network analysts select communication variables of interest consistent with the problem question that guides all inquiry. Such elements often are the frequency people communicate with each other, the importance (or perceived importance) of the information, the direction of the communication flow, and types of communication exchanged.

steps: 1. selecting communication variables

2. securing individual reports

Second, the researcher secures individual reports from all members of the group. Questionnaires are often constructed for group members to identify their communication with others. But sometimes actual uses of messages can be traced (such as numbers of telephone calls placed to a given location, or numbers of memos sent *to* a person as a ratio of the number of memos sent *from* a person). Thus, network analysis may use observational or self-report data.

3. construct network map

Third, researchers construct network maps and track information flow. Developing the network patterns can be complex since the flow of information among many people can become nested and quite involved. Even so, as figure 9.1 shows, some general patterns may emerge. Each pattern has some predictable communication effects. For instance, the chain pattern tends to be efficient when direct orders are to be given along a strict command structure, but the overall member satisfaction can be low since often only a limited picture of the entire project is possible for most group members. On the other hand, the all channel pattern permits individuals to coordinate their activities with others, but if there is a struggle for leadership or power within the group, or if any network members are hostile to any others, the all channel model may not be particularly useful.

interpreting network patterns: reciprocal,

liaison,

isolate

The reciprocal, liaison, and isolate patterns are interesting. A reciprocal pattern is one in which individuals share a nearly identical network pattern among themselves. People who are personally close or who have similar sorts of positions that include a lot of teamwork are examples of such a pattern. The liaison person links people of different networks. In figure 9.1 the liaison between two groups (identified by the X) is performed by one person who—officially or unofficially—is a member of both groups. The isolate is an individual who is not actively involved in any established communication network. This person usually is bypassed and occasionally may not even be aware that he or she is an isolate in the eyes of others. These individuals are out of the communication flow and, thus, may not hold potential for making productive contributions until their involvement levels are altered. These patterns may be interpreted and the description used to help make improvements.

results by comparing the network with a desired standard

A final step in network analysis involves interpreting results by comparing the network with a desired standard, such as an organizational chart. Checking whether people who *should* be communicating with each other really *are* allows evaluation of the flow of information. By contrasting the network against the organizational chart, the logic of the organization's structure can be verified—or questioned. By finding that people who are not expected to communicate actively with each other actually are involved in extensive conversation, it is possible to identify where informal channels emerge. These channels may be nurtured and attempts to explain them explored.

Limitations of the Approach

limitations:

Though most often used in studies of organizations and bureaucracies, network analyses have looked at communication within families, job networking groups, social networks, organizational networks, and links among people of different organizations. Even so, there also are two major limitations to network studies. First,

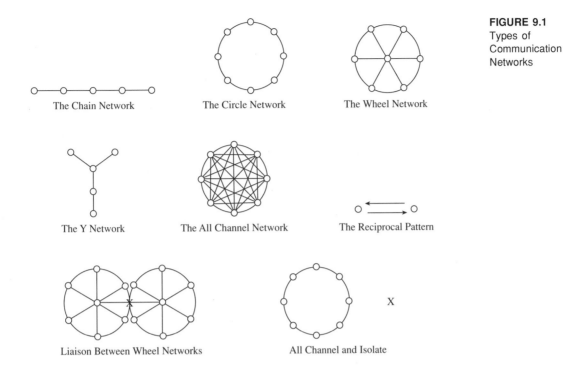

FIGURE 9.1
Types of
Communication
Networks

The Chain Network

The Circle Network

The Wheel Network

The Y Network

The All Channel Network

The Reciprocal Pattern

Liaison Between Wheel Networks

All Channel and Isolate

they emphasize structural information rather than content information. Though we can identify who is talking with whom, it is difficult to know the content of the information. People could be socializing, or they could be working on common projects. We may not know. Some researchers attempt to get additional information about the dominant sort of information exchanged, but structure of communication flow is dominant in network analyses. Second, network analysis allows researchers to identify relationships among communicators, but the technique does not permit the researcher to make claims about the reasons for the relationships. We cannot know for sure why a person was bypassed in the network, though the network may show that bypassing has occurred. We cannot identify why someone became a liaison between groups. But one can identify relationships to be explored with other research methods.

1. emphasis on structural information rather than content

2. reasons for the relationships not known

SUMMARY

The term "empirical" actually means "observable." Descriptive empirical research involves gathering data to test statements. It is most invited when problem questions ask about current descriptions of things and explore explanations that characterize things as they are now. Surveys cannot answer questions about cause and effect relationships, though experiments can (an experiment introduces a variable and determines its effects while controlling all other variables). A survey is an empirical study that uses questionnaires or interviews to discover descriptive characteristics of phenomena.

Questionnaires are survey forms in which individuals respond to items they have read. There are six steps in completing a questionnaire survey: (1) selecting questions and instructions (including developing questions, facing tactical issues in phrasing questions, and preparing survey forms); (2) formatting questionnaires to promote response; (3) determining reliability (the consistency of a measure) and validity (the degree to which a measure actually measures what is claimed) includes other controls such as check questions that ask the same question twice (once phrased positively and once phrased negatively) at different locations, measures of test-taking behavior, and polarity rotation of items (to avoid response set, or the tendency for subjects to follow predictable patterns of responding to test items); (4) sampling; (5) administering the questionnaire; and (6) analyzing and interpreting results.

Interview methods are completed to increase respondents' willingness to participate and to gather information that might be lost with the questionnaire method. The steps of interview studies includes the following: (1) selecting questions (structured interviews use specific lists of questions; unstructured interviews permit respondents to indicate their reactions to general issues without guidance from highly detailed questions);

(2) training and controlling behavior of interviewers; (3) determining reliability and validity; (4) sampling subjects; and (5) analyzing and interpreting results.

Network analysis is a method that obtains individuals' reports of their communication activities with others for the purpose of observing and describing the flow of information in a particular organizational system. There are three general purposes for network analyses: (1) to construct a map of the interaction among people in an organization; (2) to diagnose problems in communication flow; and (3) to identify the roles played by different group members. Informal methods of communication exist in organizations. Network analyses involve four steps: (1) selecting communication variables consistent with the problem question; (2) securing individual reports from members of the group; (3) constructing network maps and tracking information flow; and (4) interpreting results by comparing the network with a desired standard, such as an organizational chart. There are two major limitations to network studies: (1) they emphasize structural information rather than content information; and (2) they allow researchers to identify relationships among communicators but not the reasons for the relationships.

TERMS FOR REVIEW

experiment
empirical
survey
questionnaires
validity
reliability

check questions
polarity rotation
response set
structured interviews
unstructured interviews
network analysis

CHAPTER 10

Experimental Research

"Experiment is the consummation of the marriage of reason and experience, and although it is not in itself the life of the mind, it is the most passionate and fruitful expression of our intellectual life and loves."

–Abraham Kaplan

BEFORE WE GET STARTED ...

This chapter defines experiments, explains how they are designed, and discusses sources of invalidity and strategies to deal with special problems. It also explains the sorts of ''hidden codes'' and research abbreviations that experimenters use to examine hypotheses.

THE NOTION OF AN EXPERIMENT

Most people think that an experiment is just another name for a carefully completed study. But experiments involve much more than being careful. It is helpful to understand the logic of an experiment, the concept of control, and the sorts of research questions that are suitable for experimental research.

experiment defined

An **experiment** is the study of the effects of variables manipulated by the researcher, in a situation in which all other variables are controlled, and completed for the purpose of establishing causal relationships. It might help to break that definition down into its parts. First, experiments study "the effects of variables manipulated by

1. manipulating variables

the researcher." Unlike surveys, experimenters introduce variables (called "manipulating variables") that were not present to begin with. Then, they can assess the impact of these variables. Survey studies just try to identify associations among variables, but experiments add *new* experimental variables to the existing setting to

2. control of variables

see what *effects* might be found. The second part of the definition states that "all other variables are controlled." This requirement is the hard part. Most of the topics covered in this chapter involve ways to exercise experimental control. The third part

3. attempt to find causal relations

of this definition states that we complete experiments "for the purpose of establishing causal relationships." Though the method of history can permit researchers to draw long-term cause-and-effect relationships, only experiments can provide immediate evidence. If we can control other sources of variation and introduce one new experimental variable, then any effects must have been caused by the experimental variable.

As is mentioned above, exercising control is not easy. When introducing variables, a careless researcher might manipulate other variables by accident. For instance, in a study on the impact of evidence on persuasion, researchers may manipulate message length or language as well. Thus, the evidence manipulation may be mixed up with other sources of variation. This situation is called **confounding** and occurs when

confounding defined

variation from one source is mixed (or confused) with variation from another source so that it is impossible to know whether effects are due to the impact of either variable separately or some combination of the two. Such confounding may mislead researchers. A hypothesis may deal with only one experimental variable, but the actual experiment might involve a complex of independent variables. Confounding hides another variable in the hypothesis that makes the inference impossible.

The Concept of Control

control defined

Control refers to methods researchers use to remove or hold constant the effects of nuisance variables. The effort to improve control increases the ability of researchers to make clear statements that experimental variables are responsible for observed effects. To make sure that all elements in an experiment are controlled except for the new variables introduced by the experimenter, several major approaches are used: elimination, holding constant, matching, blocking, randomization, and statistical control.[1]

- *Elimination and removal.* We are rarely able to study the impact of one variable by itself. Other "nuisance" or "intervening" variables often get in the way. Careful researchers try to control these influences. The most

SPECIAL DISCUSSION 10–1
Mill's Canons of Causality

The philosopher John Stuart Mill developed tests to identify cause-and-effect relationships in experiments. He employed five canons (or standards) that could be used to disprove a causal relationship.

1. *The method of agreement.* "If two or more instances of the phenomenon under investigation have only one circumstance in common, the circumstance in which alone all the instances agree is the cause (or effect) of the given phenomenon." Thus, the cause must be present each time the phenomenon occurs.
2. *The method of difference.* "If an instance in which the phenomenon under investigation occurs and an instance in which it does not occur have every circumstance in common save one, the one occurring only in the former, the circumstance in which alone the two instances differ, is the effect, or the cause, or an indispensable part of the cause of the phenomenon." This canon virtually describes the methods of experimental studies using control groups.
3. *The joint method of agreement and difference.* "If two or more instances in which the phenomenon occurs have only one circumstance in common, while two or more instances in which it does not occur have nothing in common save the absence of that circumstance, the circumstance in which alone the two sets of instances differ, is the effect, or the cause, or an indispensable part of the cause, of the phenomenon." This canon combines the first two.
4. *Method of concomitant variation.* "Whatever phenomenon varies in any manner, whenever another phenomenon varies in some particular manner, is either a cause or an effect of that phenomenon, or is connected with it through some act of causation." Causal items must be highly correlated.
5. *The method of residues.* "Subduct from any phenomenon such part as is known by previous inductions to be the effect of certain intecedents, and the residue of the phenomenon is the effect of the remaining antecedents." Causal relationships may be found by a "detective-like" process of elimination.

obvious way to control for a nuisance variable is to remove it from the experimental setting. For instance, researchers often control extraneous variables such as temperature and illumination problems by collecting data in classroom "laboratory" settings where these sources of distraction may be eliminated completely.

• *Holding constant.* Technically, all control methods involve taking nuisance variables and holding them constant. When we eliminate variables, the nuisance variables are held constant at "zero influence." Sometimes researchers control for other variables by limiting the range of intervening variables so that they are equal across studies. There are three major ways to hold variables constant in experiments. First, limiting the population may control a nuisance variable (for instance, in very early self-disclosure research, results showed wild variation when men and women were paired with each other—to control for the sex composition of pairs, researchers soon learned to limit their studies only to populations of people of the same sex self-disclosing to each other). Second, using subjects as their own controls may control for the impact of nuisance variables (people may be sampled before and after some experimental treatment to identify their average amount of improvement despite any differences they may have had at the outset). Third, **counterbalancing** rotates the sequence in which experimental treatments are introduced to subjects in an effort to control for extraneous variables, such as fatigue or cumulative learning effects. With this method, the fatigue effects do not go away, but the variation produced is distributed across the experiment equally—hence, the term, "counter*balanced.*"

- *Matching.* The method of **matching** involves pairing subjects on some variable on which they share equal levels and then assigning one of them to an experimental group and the other to a control condition. Researchers sometimes use this method to control for initial differences people bring to a study. For instance, people might be matched because they share the same age, sex, job classification, intelligence level, or the like. In a study of attention to content of commercials by children, it might be important to control for sex of the child since girls tend to develop verbal abilities earlier than boys. Thus, a researcher might identify the number of boys and girls in a sample and then assign half of the girls to one experimental condition and half to a control group. Similarly half the boys might be assigned to each group in the experiment. Researchers can match individuals or groups of people (the most frequent use of matching). Even so, you should know that some researchers consider many applications of matching doubtful since they can introduce distortions. One can "overmatch" subjects so that they no longer represent the population. Furthermore, when matching on several nuisance variables, one may begin to lose subjects. As Fred Kerlinger explained: "If one decides to match intelligence, sex, and social class, one may be fairly successful in matching the first two variables but not in finding pairs that are fairly equal on all three variables. Add a fourth variable and the problem becomes difficult, often impossible to solve" (1986, p. 289).

- *Blocking.* **Blocking** adds a nuisance variable into the design as another independent variable of interest.[2] In a study of the impact of a female source's physical attractiveness on the persuasiveness of a message, the sex of the respondents might make a big difference in the results obtained. Thus, one might include the sex of the respondents into the study as another variable. Blocking permits one to draw conclusions about the impact of each independent variable separately or as part of an interaction. Of course, adding variables into a study requires that researchers have fairly sizable samples to permit the subdivisions. If such samples are available, however, this method may be among the most desirable options for control.

- *Randomization.* **Randomization,** a basic requirement for sound experimental control and subsequent inferential statistical analyses, involves assigning subjects so that each event is equally likely to belong to any experimental or control condition. In short, randomization involves using the rules of chance to balance groups of subjects. Respondents may be *selected* at random from the population and they also may be *assigned* at random to experimental or control conditions. The ways in which groups of people can differ from each other is almost infinite. Yet, randomization increases the likelihood that groups of people in different conditions will be comparable in ways that researchers might otherwise never imagine. Fred Kerlinger explained the importance of randomization:

    The *principle of randomization* may be stated thus: Since, in random procedures every member of a population has an equal chance of being selected, members with certain distinguishing characteristics—male or female, high or low intelligence, conservative or liberal, and so on and on—will, if selected, probably be offset in the long run by the selection of other members of the population with counterbalancing quantities or qualities of the characteristics. (1986, p. 115)

    Another way to phrase it is: if randomization has been accomplished, then the experimental groups can be considered statistically equal in all possible ways. This does not mean, of course, that the groups *are* equal in all the possible variables. We already know that by chance the groups can be unequal, but the probability of their being equal is greater, with proper randomization, than the probability of their not being equal. For this reason control of the extraneous variance by randomization is a powerful method of control. All other methods leave many possibilities of inequality. . . . A precept that springs from this equalizing power of randomization, then, is: *Whenever it is possible to do so, randomly assign subjects to experimental groups and conditions, and randomly assign conditions and other factors to experimental groups.* (p. 288)

It should be noted that individual differences do not go away when randomization is used. Instead, these sources of variation appear as random variation or background noise across conditions.[3] Thus, randomization controls a host of sources of variation so that they do not influence one experimental condition more than any other.

- *Statistical control.* If one can measure a nuisance variable, it is possible to use statistical tools to hold it constant. ''Analysis of covariance'' and ''partial correlation'' are two common methods of statistical control. They compute the variation associated with each nuisance variable and then separate it from the remaining total variation in the experiment. Analysis of covariance is used when the independent variables are broken down into nominal categories (such as experimental group vs. control group).

(margin notes)

randomization defined

random selection and assignment

analysis of covariance and partial correlation as methods of statistical control

---

SPECIAL DISCUSSION 10–2
Additional Control Issues

Experiments require control over all sources of variation. The major sources of invalidity deal with failures to exhibit such strong control. Some other common sources of error in experiments are discussed below (after Isaac & Michael, 1981, pp. 85–89).

The halo effect. Sometimes strong positive or negative impressions of a source of communication may affect all ratings that follow. Researchers may find that their credibility creates pressure in the minds of subjects to respond positively or negatively, regardless of experimental treatments used.

The placebo effect. In medical research, a placebo is a stimulus containing no medicine or no experimental treatment at all. In nonmedical work, subjects may show changes even in the absence of treatments, in reaction to the mental suggestion that they may have been given some stimulus. Thus, researchers attempt to use control groups and to exercise control over methods of providing treatments to groups.

The John Henry effect. Named after the folklore hero who died trying to outwork a machine, this effect describes the actions of people who try to perform extra hard when they participate in an experiment. Their behavior may not be consistent with their normal activity.

The pitfall of "do nothing" control groups. "Control groups ordinarily should experience *all things* in common with the treatment group *except* the critical factor, per se. Control groups that 'do nothing' are apt to differ from the treatment groups in more ways than just the isolated treatment variable." (Isaac & Michael, 1981, p. 88).

The nuisance variable is called a "covariate" and is used as the basis for adjusting output variable scores. When studies investigate correlations among variables, partial correlations are used to explore the relationship between two variables while holding a third one constant. Though all methods of control are related to some statistical model (blocking and analysis of covariance methods are equivalent, for instance) the major tactical differences described here should help you understand the options available to researchers.

Questions and Hypotheses in Experimental Designs

experimental designs permit drawing causal claims about variables that can be manipulated

Experiments are designed to answer research questions that deal with cause-and-effect relationships. But there is a slight catch. The causes must be matters that can be manipulated by the researcher. Thus, you cannot complete an experiment to show that being a woman causes a person to be more persuaded by a fear appeal than does being a man, because you cannot reasonably manipulate the sex of subjects. You can conclude that the sex of the receiver is *related* to persuasiveness of fear appeals, but there is no way to say that the sex of the receiver *caused* the effect (as opposed to differences in self-esteem or levels of submissiveness). On the other hand, it is possible to find out if messages that use internal organizers (previews and summaries) cause more attitude change than messages that omit them. Messages can be prepared by the experimenter with and without internal organizers and then presented to randomly selected audiences. Thus, experiments are limited to dealing with causal relationships stemming from *experimental independent variables.*

experimental independent variables

Hypotheses in experiments are phrased to explore such causal relationships. Typical experimental hypotheses in our field have included the following:

experimental hypotheses probe causal relationships

> During early adolescence (12 to 15 years), the presence of a label [a label on a recording warning of potentially offensive material] should, other things being equal, make a given song or album less attractive rather than more so (Christenson, 1992, p. 107).
> Mirroring behavior [mimicking the nonverbal behavior of another person] that is attributed as deliberate will be read as sending greater relational messages of similarity and interest than will behaviors seen to [be] intentional (Manusov, 1992, p. 73).
> As the level of sexual imagery in rock music videos increases, subjects will find both the visual and music content more appealing (Hansen & Hansen, 1990, p. 213).

In each case, the hypotheses suggested cause-and-effect relationships that were manipulated successfully in experimental research.[4]

EXPERIMENTAL VALIDITY AND INVALIDITY

Experiments can blow up in a researcher's face. When experiments fall apart, they have fallen prey to sources of invalidity. Sources of **experimental invalidity** are errors that prevent researchers from drawing unequivocal conclusions. There are two families of invalidity in experiments, internal and external.

experimental invalidity defined

Internal Invalidity

Internal invalidity is the presence of contamination that prevents the experimenter from concluding that a study's experimental variable is responsible for the observed effects. Table 10.1 lists the major sources of internal invalidity in experiments. To argue for cause-and-effect relationships, these sources of invalidity must be controlled or removed. If a researcher completes an experiment that controls for seven out of the eight sources of internal invalidity, the experiment still cannot lead to an unequivocal statement of experimental effect. That is, if all sources of internal invalidity are not controlled, it is not possible to claim that any observed effects were caused by the independent variable in the experiment. Instead, researchers have to add equivocating terms (ifs and maybes) as they draw their conclusions.

internal invalidity defined

External Invalidity

External invalidity refers to the degree to which experimental results may not be generalized to other similar circumstances. In a strict sense, study findings can be generalized only to the sample groups from which they were drawn. Yet, researchers often carefully sample so that some generalization of results may be possible. Regrettably, experiments sometimes are completed in ways that make it difficult, if not

external invalidity defined

TABLE 10.1 Sources of Internal Invalidity

History: Events not controlled by the researcher that occur during the experiment between any pretest and posttest

Selection: Sampling biases in selecting or assigning subjects to experimental or control conditions (in essence rigging the study by taking samples capriciously)

Maturation: Changes that occur naturally over time (including fatigue or suspicion), even if subjects are left alone

Testing: Alterations that occur when subjects are tested and made test wise or anxious in ways that affect them when they are given a second test

Instrumentation: Changes in the use of measuring instruments from the pretest to the posttest including changes in raters or interviewers who collect the data under different conditions

Statistical regression: Shifts produced when subjects are selected due to very high or very low scores on a particular test (such as selecting a group of people who score high in communication apprehension for participation in some experimental treatment) and then changes on that measurement are tracked in the experiment; statistical regression holds that people will "regress toward the mean" even if they are simply left alone

Experimental mortality: Biases introduced when subjects differentially (nonrandomly) drop out of the experiment (for instance, subjects may drop out of a weight reduction program if they receive disappointing results—thus, the remaining subjects will show inflated levels of improvement)

Interaction of elements: Effects created by the interaction of selection biases with differential levels of maturation, history, or any other source of variation.

impossible, to generalize results to general populations without severe limitations. These sources of external validity do not mean that the experimental variable did not produce the alleged effects—internal validity assesses *that* issue. Instead, external invalidity sets *limits* on the sorts of populations to which results may be generalized. The major sources of external invalidity are found in table 10.2.

Ideally, an experiment should have both internal and external validity. But researchers actually give greatest attention to internal validity issues. The concern is natural. If a study does not have internal validity, its findings cannot be generalized. Even so, researchers often comment about external invalidity when reporting their work. Research articles usually include some statements that limit research findings and call for replications to test generalizability of results to other population groups.

SPECIFIC EXPERIMENTAL DESIGNS

Experimental designs tend to follow a protocol of notation, methods, and applications, terms that tend to be mentioned without explanation in research articles. This section will help you decipher these terms.

TABLE 10.2 Sources of External Invalidity

Interaction of testing and the experimental variable: Also called pretest sensitization, this defect is created when the pretesting makes subjects either more or less sensitive to the experimental variable.
Interaction of selection and the experimental variable: Effects created by sampling groups in such a way that they are not representative of the population since they are more or less sensitive to the experimental variable than other subsamples from the same population (such as sampling college students in communication studies even though they may be more or less sensitive to the independent variable than the general population of people).

Reactive arrangements: Elements in the experimental setting that make subjects react differentially to the experimental arrangements rather than to the experimental variable alone (such matters as awareness of participation in an experiment may alter normal reactions of people).
Multiple treatment interference: Depending on the design, if subjects are exposed to repeated additional experimental treatments they may react in ways that are not generalizable to subjects who are uncontaminated by such additional independent variables.

Notation for Experimental Designs

To show what goes on in a research design, a notation system has been developed, much like notation used to sketch out a football play. Three terms are prominent. The first of these terms is

notation:

$$O.$$

O is an abbreviation for an *observation* a researcher makes of the study's dependent variable. If several observations are made, researchers sometimes add subscript numbers to keep things straight, such as

observation

$$O_1 \quad O_2 \quad O_3 \quad O_4.$$

These are translated, "observation one," "observation two," "observation three," and "observation four."[5] Regardless of the ways in which measurement of observations is handled, the observations are made to help the researcher identify the effects that are found in a study.

A second term used in experimental design is

$$X.$$

This abbreviation stands for the *experimental variable* used by researchers. When there is more than one experimental variable, some researchers add subscript numbers to help keep exact conditions clear. For this introductory treatment, however, we will not clutter up our notation with subscripts.

experimental variable

The final term used is

$$R.$$

	Sources of Invalidity											
	Internal								External			
	History	Maturation	Testing	Instrumentation	Regression	Selection	Mortality	Interaction of Selection and Maturation, etc.	Interaction of Testing and X	Interaction of Selection and X	Reactive Arrangements	Multiple-X Interference
Pre-Experimental Designs:												
1. One-Shot Case Study X O	−	−				−	−				−	
2. One-Group Pretest-Posttest Design O X O	−	−	−	−	?	+	+	−	−	−	?	
3. Static-Group Comparison X O / O	+	?	+	+	+	−	−	−	−		−	
True Experimental Designs:												
4. Pretest-Posttest Control Group Design R O X O / R O O	+	+	+	+	+	+	+	+	−	?	?	
5. Solomon Four-Group Design R O X O / R O O / R X O / R O	+	+	+	+	+	+	+	+	+	?	?	
6. Posttest-Only Control Group Design R X O / R O	+	+	+	+	+	+	+	+	+	?	?	

Note: In the tables, a minus indicates a definite weakness, a plus indicates that the factor is controlled, a question mark indicates a possible source of concern, and a blank indicates that the factor is not relevant.

It is with extreme reluctance that these summary tables are presented because they are apt to be "too helpful," and to be depended upon in place of the more complex and qualified presentation in the text. No + or − indicator should be respected unless the reader comprehends why it is placed there. In particular it is against the spirit of this presentation to create uncomprehended fears of, or confidence in, specific designs.

Figure 10.1
Experimental Design Validity Factors

Source: Campbell, D. T., & J. C. Stanley. *Experimental and Quasi-Experimental Designs for Research.* © 1966 by Houghton Mifflin Company. Used with permission.

This letter stands for *randomization*. Those experiments that include randomization (either random assignment or random sampling) include this notation promi-
nently. Randomization is the most effective means for controlling systematic
biases. Thus, it plays a strong role in sound experimentation.

Pre-experimental Designs

Some designs have good intentions but do not really exercise the control necessary
for a solid experiment. They are considered here because they reflect the thinking
that leads to full experiments and because they often are used by researchers who
feel the need to make compromises.

- *One-shot case study.* In these studies, an experimental treatment is introduced and researchers look at effects on some output (dependent) variable.
  Unfortunately, as figure 10.1 shows, this design does not really control for
  any source of experimental invalidity. You may have seen case studies
  used as teaching aids in classes you have taken. Often researchers complete case studies so that they can develop hypotheses for formal testing at
  a later time.
- *One-group pretest-posttest.* As an improvement over the one-shot case
  study, researchers sometimes add a pretest. Thus, subjects in an experiment can serve as their own controls. This method is a step in the right
  direction—and the method frequently has been used in evaluation studies—
  but the design does not really control for enough sources of invalidity to
  permit drawing clear conclusions of experimental effect.
- *Static-group comparisons.* This design attempts to use a control group, but
  the two groups are not known to be comparable. A researcher may sample
  students in a sophomore class at 10:00 AM and expose them to an experimental message. The researcher also might sample students in a graduate
  class at 7:00 PM for a control group. These groups are ''in tact'' and cannot be presumed to be comparable at the outset. The differences between
  the groups can throw a monkey wrench into the entire design. Sometimes
  researchers will complete a random sampling of a smaller subgroup from
  each in tact group. Yet, to assure comparability, researchers should also
  randomly assign subjects to experimental or control conditions.

True Experimental Designs

The three true experimental designs discussed below serve as the basis for increasingly
complicated factorial designs used in formal experiments.

Pretest-Posttest Control Group Design

Surely the most popular design for communication experiments, the pretest-posttest control group design is composed of an experimental group and a control
group. Subjects in the experimental group are pretested. They are then exposed to the
experimental variable and posttested. Subjects in the control group are treated the
same way except, of course, they are not presented with the experimental variable.

change scores are
not advised

You might suppose that researchers simply subtract pretests from posttests to observe the amount of change. Although this practice may seem to make sense, there are statistical problems with analyzing "change scores." First, change scores may not have distributions that make them easy to interpret with standard statistical tools. Second, by definition, change scores will have lower reliability than the original measures (Allen & Yen, 1979). Thus, prudent researchers usually try to use alternatives to change scores. Most often, researchers use a method of statistical control in which the posttest scores of experimental and control groups are compared with the pretest scores used as a covariate.

As you can see on figure 10.1, this design controls for all sources of internal invalidity. But the story is different when you consider external validity. Sometimes pretesting people can affect the way they respond to experimental variables. Rather than responding freshly to experimental variables, people may try to recall

pretest sensitization
described

what they did on the pretest and respond in the same way (perhaps to avoid being "wishy-washy"). Thus, the pretest may "sensitize" people and cause them to respond inhibitedly. The internal validity of the experiment is just fine, of course, since the experimental variable is the cause of observed effects. But the results of the experiment can only be generalized directly to populations of people who also have been sensitized by a pretest. To overcome the problems with pretest sensitization, two other approaches have been suggested.

Solomon Four-Group Design

You can add control groups to examine pretesting effects directly. This design actually uses three control groups. To check for pretest sensitization, one may compare the groups that have received a pretest with the groups that have not. If pretesting inhibited responses, the design will reveal it.[6] The problem with this design, however, is that it requires doubling the sample. Thus, it may be expensive.

Posttest-Only Control Group Design

Another way to avoid pretest sensitization is to delete the pretest entirely. If the researcher does not need to pretest subjects, this design is preferred. Take a look at the static-group comparison design. Do you see the difference between it and the posttest-only control group design? The difference is randomization. With this extra step, the experimental and control groups are made comparable. The result is dramatic. Rather than facing the limitations of the static group comparison, the pretest-posttest control group design introduces control over the major sources of experimental invalidity found on table 10.1.

Factorial Designs

So far we have dealt with situations in which single experimental groups are compared to control groups. Yet, these days, you will not see as many single variable experiments as once filled communication journals. When more than one independent variable is used in an experiment, it is called a factorial design.

SPECIAL DISCUSSION 10–3
Single-Subject Experiments

Much research in speech and hearing science has involved the "single-subject" design (Herson & Barlow, 1976; Kratochwill 1978), though the design has long been used in manufacturing under the rubric of the "component search" or "comparative experiments." Therapists attempting to find the best treatment for a patient often use the single subject design. The researcher starts by getting baseline information as a control. These observations are often abbreviated with the letter "A." Then the new treatment—perhaps a drug or a particular type of therapy—is introduced and effects measured. The new treatment may be identified as a "B" condition (standing for a "better" option, perhaps). Then researchers withdraw the treatment and see what happens. If a new treatment is effective, one would expect to see improvements with its presence and worsening with its withdrawal. To control for potential cyclical effects that have nothing to do with treatments, the researcher can alter the order of interventions, as in the design

A B A B B A.

To see if differences exist, researchers compare all of the "A" conditions with all of the "B" conditions. The formula for combinations can be used to assess how often such improvement patterns could be expected to occur by chance alone.

The approach can—and has been—extended to studies involving two, three, or more treatment options. Though of great value in therapeutic and medical settings, the use of single-subject designs has limitations in communication including: (1) it is most applicable to questions of individual difference, rather than patterns that occur across people; (2) its limited generalizability prevents examining hypotheses of social significance to most communication researchers; (3) it limits the sorts of statistical tools that might be used to help analyze results.

Uses of Factorial Designs in Research

When a variable is broken down into levels (such as high self-esteem vs. low self-esteem, high readability vs. low readability, or high dysfluency vs. low dysfluency) they are called variable factors or just **factors.** These levels of variables are used in factorial designs to introduce independent variables. The categories of each factor are called **levels.** It is important not to confuse levels of a factor with a factor itself. If a researcher compares men and women's interest in headline news stories, ''men'' and ''women'' are not variables. Instead, they are simply the levels of the variable factor ''sex of respondent.'' When factors are used, researchers are actually creating nominal categories for the independent variables involved. As an abbreviation of sorts, researchers often list the number of levels of their variables when describing the designs. Thus, if a study involves two

factors defined

levels defined

**abbreviation for
design structure by
levels**

Figure 10.2
Designs in Factorial
Modes

A. Posttest Only Control Group Design with a Single Independent Variable

R   X   O
R   O

B. Factorial Design with Two Independent Variables Using a Posttest Only Control
Group Design

Independent Variable 1

		Low	High
Independent Variable 2	Low	R X O R O	R X O R O
	High	R X O R O	R X O R O

C. Factorial Design with Two Independent Variables Using a Posttest Only Control
Group Design with Offset Control Groups

Independent Variable 1

		Low	High
Independent Variable 2	Low	R X O	R X O
	High	R X O	R X O

Control: R O

D. Factorial Design with Two Independent Variables Using a Posttest Only Control
Group Design with Inclusive Control Groups

Independent Variable 1

		Without X	With X
Independent Variable 2	Without X	R O	R X O
	With X	R X O	R X O

independent variables, each of which has two levels, the design may be called a
"two-by-two factorial design." If one independent variable has three levels, it
may be called a "two-by-three factorial design," and so forth.

Researchers employ factorial designs when they have multiple independent
variables. They can also complete a series of single variable designs with different
input variables. Factorial designs allow researchers to put input variables together
to see whether special combinations of variables produce unique effects. Thus,
these designs examine *interactions* among independent variables that might be
missed if researchers did several single variable designs.

**factorial designs
allow analysis of
more than one
independent
variable**

Factorial designs really are extensions of the experimental designs described
above. An experiment with a single independent variable may be illustrated simply, as figure 10.2A shows. For a factorial design, researchers adapt the design to
fit their needs. Suppose that a researcher wishes to complete a study with two
independent variables in a factorial design. Each variable might be broken down

into two levels each—a high level and a low level, for instance. If the researcher wishes to use a posttest-only method, then each cell of the factorial design contains a little posttest-only control group design, as shown in figure 10.2B. In each case, the X is actually a combination of levels of each independent variable. After a time a researcher might notice that all of the control groups are treated pretty much the same. Thus, he or she might try to economize on data collection by gathering one control group sample rather than four. When this method is followed, the common control group may be placed outside the design for later comparisons. This technique is known as a factorial design with an offset control group and is illustrated in figure 10.2C. Yet another variation builds the control group directly into the design. If both independent variables are true experimental variables, it may be possible to have a condition in the design in which the independent variables are absent. Figure 10.2D shows this adaptation. As you can see, a factorial model is not really different from the designs previously described, but an extension of them.

specific designs may be placed in cells of the factorial design use of offset control groups

Interpreting Factorial Results

Experimenters use factorial designs to find evidence of the impact of independent variables together and separately.

Main effects are dependent variable effects from independent variables separately. In factorial designs these main effects are identified by looking at differences between levels of each independent variable across levels of the other variables in the study. Sometimes diagrams can help identify these effects. In figure 10.3A you can see the impact of one independent variable on a dependent variable. The main effect is indicated by the presence of a sloping line (upward in the example). The levels of the independent variable are indicated in the horizontal axis of the diagram. If there were no main effect, you would see a line running parallel to the horizontal axis. Since the line shows a clear slope, the presence of a main effect is evident.

main effects defined

When a second independent variable is added, it is necessary to draw two lines to represent each level of the second independent variable. Figure 10.3B shows how this process works. The lines are some distance apart from each other, indicating a main effect for the second independent variable. If there were no main effect, you would see no distance between the lines at all.

Interaction effects are dependent variable effects from independent variables taken together. They involve variation arising from special combinations of levels of independent variables. Factorial designs allow researchers to identify them directly. Figure 10.4 shows two major types of interactions that might occur in research. It is important to distinguish between the types of interactions that exist because they affect the kinds of conclusions you can draw.

interaction effects defined

When drawing pictures of effects, interactions are indicated by lines that are *not* parallel to each other. In figure 10.4A the lines are not parallel, but they do not cross each other. This sort of pattern is called an **ordinal interaction.** Across the board, the high level for each independent variable produced higher scores on the dependent measure than the low levels did. Two main effects seemed to emerge. But put together, the high levels of each independent variable produced

distinguishing interactions: 1. ordinal interactions

Figure 10.3
Main Effects

A. Example of a Main Effect with a Single Independent Variable

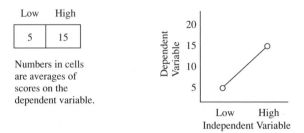

Low   High

| 5 | 15 |

Numbers in cells
are averages of
scores on the
dependent variable.

B. Example of Main Effects with Two Independent Variables

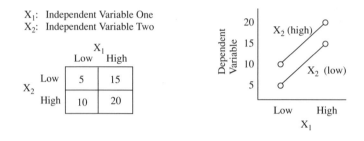

X_1: Independent Variable One
X_2: Independent Variable Two

the same effect—but more so! Thus, the interaction is in the same direction as the main effects, but with a bonus effect thrown in. In our particular example, when variable two is at its low level, changing the level of variable one produces no appreciable effect. But when variable two is at its high level, changing the level of variable one results in great increases in the dependent variable. Thus, if the researchers wanted to produce high scores on the dependent variables, they would recommend setting both independent variables at their high levels—any other combination would not be quite so good. When researchers are faced with an ordinal interaction it is permissible to interpret main effects for the variables involved in the interaction without fear of misrepresenting the facts. The interaction means that the real story lies in the special combinations of both variables.

2. disordinal interactions

A second sort of interaction effect has different lessons for researchers. A **disordinal interaction** occurs when the lines drawn for each independent variable cross each other.[7] Because of this pattern, the effect sometimes is called a "crossed interaction" for short. Figure 10.4B shows such a crossed interaction. When researchers find crossed interactions, as opposed to ordinal interactions, they are forbidden from interpreting the main effects for the variables involved since such interpretations would be misleading. Furthermore, if they plan to make recommendations or take action based on the experiment, they know that they must respond by looking at two variables at once. Thus, the type of interaction sets limits on the sorts of conclusions that researchers can draw.

not permitted to interpret main effects for variables in disordinal interactions

A. Example of an Ordinal Interaction Effect

Figure 10.4
Interaction Effects

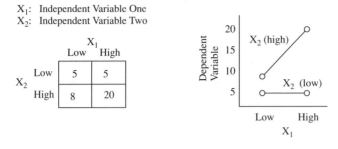

B. Example of a Disordinal or Crossed Interaction Effect

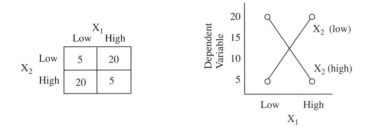

We have limited this introductory discussion to situations in which two variables are involved. But the number of variables in an interaction can include three, four, five, or potentially any number of variables. In such cases, separate diagrams are drawn for each level of the additional independent variables added. The number of diagrams can grow quite large. The problem is not really so troublesome, however. Experienced researchers know that whereas main effects and two-variable interaction effects are quite common, three-variable interactions are not as common, four-variable interactions seldom occur, and higher order interactions are quite rare (they can occur once in a while, however, and researchers carefully examine them).

ELEMENTS OF GOOD EXPERIMENTS

Sound experiments tend to include additional features that distinguish them from others. Some of these considerations will be considered next.

The Maxmincon Principle

To argue for clear claims of experimental effect, researchers must stay in command of all sources of variation. Fred Kerlinger phrased this need as the **maxmincon principle.** It is a reminder to experimenters to follow procedures of carefully designed experimentation. He explained:

the maxmincon
principle

> Maximize systematic variance, control extraneous systematic variance, and minimize error variance. In other words, we must *control variance*. According to this principle,

SPECIAL DISCUSSION 10–4
Quasi Experiments

Sometimes it is not possible for researchers to conduct experiments in which they have full control over all the variables in the design. Under such circumstances, they can employ an alternative called "quasi-experimental research" (Campbell & Stanley, 1963, pp. 34–63). In essence, quasi-experimental studies involve completion of experimental work where random assignment and control are not possible. Obviously, the sorts of conclusions that can be drawn are limited because no cause-and-effect statements can be demonstrated. But the method can be useful especially if the researcher is exploring a research field for potential hypotheses for later study, or if the researcher is not particularly interested in generalizing to larger populations than the sample group.

Three major forms of quasi-experimental designs are shown below (after Campbell & Stanley, 1963, p. 40).

Time series designs. A time series design measures subjects across different times. In the simplest form of this design, several observations are made before an experimental intervention, and several are made afterward. The design may be represented as follows:

$$O_1 \quad O_2 \quad O_3 \quad X \quad O_4 \quad O_5 \quad O_6.$$

This design is often used in research that tries to find cyclical trends or the decay of information retention. It controls for all sources of internal invalidity, with the possible exception of instrumentation depending on the procedures used by the researcher. Sometimes the researcher makes an effort to add control to this design but doing so requires the addition of another group that may not be equivalent to the first.

Separate sample posttest designs. Subjects might be sampled as part of another group of subjects that are close but not assured to be equivalent to the experimental group. For instance, a group of employees who complete a communication skills training seminar might be compared to a group of employees who are from the same pool but who have not yet had their training. One group would receive the experimental treatment (X) and the other would not. The basic form of these designs is illustrated as follows:

$$\frac{O \; X \; O}{O \quad O.}$$

This design resembles the static group comparison design, except that it includes a pretest. Yet, in this design the researcher tries to make the groups comparable—or at least as comparable as possible without randomization. This design controls for all sources of internal invalidity except for interaction of selection with other sources of invalidity and (possibly, depending on the design) the regression effect.

Counterbalanced designs. Counterbalanced designs introduce several experimental treatments that are presented to the subjects in different orders or sequences. Though not restricted only to quasi-experimentation as a method of control, the formal counterbalanced design allows for control of all sources of internal invalidity except for interaction of selection with other sources of invalidity.

by constructing an efficient research design the investigator attempts (1) to maximize the variance of the variable or variables of his [or her] substantive research hypothesis, (2) to control the variance of extraneous or "unwanted" variables that may have an effect on his [or her] experimental outcomes, and (3) to minimize the error or random variance, including so-called errors of measurement. (1986, p. 284)

This principle advises researchers to plan studies so that the impact of variables of interest will be recognizable while all others are held constant. Studies designed with this principle in mind tend to be rigorous and unambiguous. Thus, you should look for evidence that researchers attempted to exercise control over all sorts of variation in their experiments. A sloppy experiment will not control extraneous variance; a solid experiment will.

The Pilot Test

Sometimes what seems to be a beautiful experiment can blow up in a researcher's face. Many prudent experimenters complete dry runs or pilot studies to find existing problems. Though not all experiments are complicated enough to require a pilot study, in general, the more experienced researchers are, the more likely they are to complete one prior to full scale experimentation. These pilot studies usually involve small samples of people (sometimes as few as ten or twenty) who take part in an experiment. They are interviewed to find out if they had difficulty with experimental materials or in responding to measures. In addition, researchers often discover additional variables that—if left uncontrolled—may jeopardize the quality of study conclusions. After the pilot study, some modifications of the experiment can be made and additional controls added. Researchers cannot know in advance everything that might interfere with a successful experiment, and pilot studies reveal valuable information that helps guide worthwhile experiments.

usefulness of pilot studies in experiments

Manipulation Checks

It is one thing to introduce an independent variable, but quite another to make sure that it actually "took" in an experiment. To make sure that independent variables actually operated, researchers often include manipulation checks. A **manipulation check** is a researcher's measurement of a secondary variable to determine that an experimental variable actually operated in a study. For instance, if people in an experiment were asked to read a message with prominent use of internal summaries, the researcher might wish to check that people really attended to the message. Thus, a researcher might add a brief true-false test asking subjects to characterize information contained in the message. Depending on the needs of the researcher, the degree to which people perceived the message to have contained previews might also be tested. Solid experiments rarely ask readers to assume that all variables in the study were operating. Instead, good experiments often include manipulation checks to assure the presence of independent variables.

manipulation check defined

Care in Interpretation

Experimental research can be exciting and researchers sometimes get carried away when interpreting results. Yet, solid experiments avoid misstatements. The following three matters discussed below often guide the interpretations drawn by experimenters.

Resisting the Tendency to Infer Long-Term Effects from Short-Term Experiments

Occasionally an experiment will be completed over an extended time period, but most experiments are short-term affairs. Many researchers get carried away and draw conclusions about the long-term effects even though they collected only short-term data. For instance, many researchers have examined the persuasive effects of evidence. Early on it was found that evidence presented by a highly credible speaker did not seem as persuasive as evidence presented by a moderately or lowly credible speaker. Some other researchers found similar results. But this result was based on short-term findings. When long-term effects (at least two weeks) were examined, evidence proved to be persuasive for all speakers (McCroskey, 1967; Reynolds & Burgoon, 1983, p. 93). Thus, researchers must be very careful when drawing conclusions, because short-term and long-term results can differ greatly. Prudent researchers are careful to avoid the tendency to draw general or long-term conclusions based on short-term experiments.

Searching for Nonlinear Relationships

Many experiments compare two levels of a variable, often a "high" and a "low" level, and draw conclusions in an unqualified fashion. Unfortunately, many relationships between independent and dependent variables are not simple straight line relationships, but curved. That is, sometimes a low level of an experimental variable produces a low effect, a moderate level produces a high effect, and a high level produces a slightly lower effect. Unfortunately, if experimenters compare only two conditions, they will miss any curved relationships (since you cannot draw anything but a straight line between two plotted points). Prudent researchers do two things to avoid this difficulty. First, they carefully qualify their conclusions by noting that curved relationships have not been studied. Second, they follow initial experiments with other studies that include more than two levels of independent variables.

Using Multiple Dependent Variables

Experimental variables rarely produce effects on only one output variable. Yet some studies limit themselves to only one dependent measure. The experienced researcher knows that it is important to check for effects on additional related output measures. Hence, in studies on the impact of physical attractiveness of sources, researchers tend to look at a collection of influence variables, such as impact on interpersonal attraction, source credibility, and liking for the source. The underlying patterns behind research findings may be explored. Inexperienced researchers may look only at effects on one output variable, while experienced researchers tend to employ a collection of relevant dependent measures so that interpretations of results can be increasingly sophisticated.

SUMMARY

An experiment is the study of the effects of variables manipulated by the researcher, in a situation in which all other variables are controlled, and completed for the purpose of establishing causal relationships. Confounding occurs when variation from one source is mixed (or confused) with variation from another source so that it is impossible to know whether effects are due to the impact of either variable separately or some combination of the two. Control refers to methods researchers use to remove or hold constant the effects of nuisance variables. Several major control approaches include: (1) elimination and removal, in which a nuisance variable is removed from the experimental setting; (2) holding constant (by the methods of limiting the population, using subjects as their own controls, or counterbalancing, which rotates the sequence in which experimental treatments are introduced to subjects); (3) matching (pairing subjects on some variable on which they share equal levels and then assigning them to experimental or control conditions); (4) blocking (adding a nuisance variable into the design as another independent variable of interest); (5) randomization (assigning subjects so that each event is equally likely to belong to any experimental or control condition); and (6) statistical control, in which statistical tools are used to hold nuisance variables constant. Experiments are designed to answer research questions that deal with cause and effect relationships. But variables must be capable of manipulation.

Experimental invalidity prevents researchers from drawing alleged conclusions from the premises advanced. Internal invalidity is the presence of contamination that prevents the experimenter from concluding that a study's experimental variable is responsible for the observed effects. External invalidity refers to the degree to which experimental results cannot be generalized to other similar circumstances.

Experimental designs follow strict protocols. A notation system has been developed that includes O (an observation made by a researcher), X (the experimental variable), and R (randomization). Pre-experimental designs do not exercise the sort of control necessary for a solid experiment. In the one-shot case study, an experimental treatment is introduced and researchers look at effects on some output (dependent) variable. The one-group pretest-posttest design adds a pretest. Static-group comparisons attempt to use a control group as a baseline to compare with an experimental group. Yet, these designs do not meet the requirements of internal validity. True experimental designs control sources of internal invalidity. The pretest-posttest control group design involves a pretest of experimental and control subjects. Though change scores may be considered, difficulties with the distributions and reliability of using change scores make them inferior to other measures. This design fails to control the potential of pretest sensitization (an aspect of external invalidity). To control for pretest sensitization, one may use the Solomon four-group design (which tests for the impact of pretesting) or the posttest-only control group design (which omits the pretest). When more than one independent variable is used in an experiment, it is called a factorial design. When a variable is broken down into levels, the levels are called variable factors. The categories of each factor are called levels. Main effects are dependent variable effects produced from independent variables separately. Interaction effects are dependent variable effects from independent variables taken together. An ordinal interaction is an interaction in the same direction as the main effects. A disordinal interaction goes in a different direction from the main effects (indicated by graphs of effects that show nonparallel lines that cross).

Sound experiments should include the following features. First, they should follow the maxmincon principle (maximize systematic variance, control extraneous systematic variance, and minimize error variance). Second, they often include pilot studies to verify procedures and identify areas for improvements in experiments. Third, they include manipulation checks (a researcher's measurement of a secondary variable to determine that an experimental variable actually was operating in a study). Fourth, they include care in interpretation including: resisting the tendency to infer long-term effects from short-term experiments; searching for nonlinear relationships; and recognizing the desirability of multiple dependent variables.

TERMS FOR REVIEW

experiment
confounding
control
counterbalancing
matching
blocking
randomization
experimental invalidity
internal invalidity

external invalidity
factors
levels
main effects
interaction effects
ordinal interactions
disordinal interactions
maxmincon
manipulation check

NOTES

[1]This division of methods of control benefits from and expands on the categories developed by Kerlinger (1986, pp. 287–289).

[2]Some writers prefer that we reserve the term ''blocking'' for situations in which the additional variable factor is on a nominal scale, such as the sex of respondents (Campbell & Stanley, 1970). When the additional variable is on a ranking scale, they suggest using the term ''stratifying'' rather than ''blocking.'' If the additional variable is measured on an interval or ratio scale (such as dividing groups into high, moderate, and low self-esteem groups), they recommend using the term ''leveling.''

[3]Technically, randomization causes assignable variation from nuisance variables to be confounded (or confused) with random variation.

[4]The third hypothesis was supported and the first two were not.

[5]Some might read these terms as ''O sub-one,'' ''O sub-two,'' and so forth. But we consider the technical affectation a barrier to understanding and advise that you use plain language whenever you can.

[6]If pretest sensitization is found, all is not lost. If the experimental variable still produced a significant effect, then pretest sensitization was not enough to prevent experimental effects. In such cases, the impact of pretest sensitization is minor in comparison with the experimental variable.

[7]Researchers sometimes just eyeball the averages of groups to determine what types of interactions occur. When drawing graphs to illustrate the relationships, researchers usually draw two graphs to switch the independent variable that is represented by lines and the independent variable that is indicated on the horizontal axis. Lines will often cross under one set of circumstances but not with the other. Nevertheless, if either graph produces a crossing, a disordinal interaction is concluded.

CHAPTER 11

Sampling

You don't have to eat the whole cow to know the steak is tough.

–Samuel Johnson

THE ROLE OF SAMPLING IN QUANTITATIVE RESEARCH
  Relating Sampling to Other Concepts
  Defining the Population
  Eliminating Bias
ESSENTIALS OF SAMPLING
  Representative Sampling: The Goal of Effective Sampling
  Sample Size

  Statistical Effects of Small Samples
FORMS OF SAMPLING
  Random Sampling
  Nonrandom Sampling
DEALING WITH SAMPLING PROBLEMS
  Subject Refusal to Participate
  Evidence of Randomization in Research Articles

BEFORE WE GET STARTED . . .

Collecting data in empirical research means sampling from populations of events. This chapter introduces you to the terms and methods used for sampling. In addition, it addresses some special issues that must be faced in selecting sample sizes and constructing so-called "confidence intervals." By the end of this chapter you will have some guidelines to use when making your own inquiries and reading those of others.

THE ROLE OF SAMPLING IN QUANTITATIVE RESEARCH

You do not have to gather data on every single event in a population to draw accurate conclusions. Careful sampling can often accurately identify population characteristics even with very small numbers of events. To understand the role of sampling in empirical research you need to understand how it fits into other concepts, its relationship to populations, and its purposes.

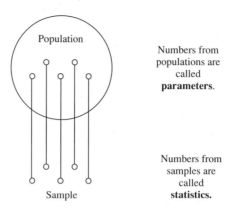

FIGURE 11.1
The
Population–Sample
Relationship

Relating Sampling to Other Concepts

sampling defined **Sampling** involves selecting events from a population. Researchers rarely sample all possible events, but they rely on a portion of all data to draw conclusions. Since a study's conclusions can be only as good as the data on which they are based, the sample must be gathered thoughtfully and with some solid reasoning behind choices. Anything less amounts to *non sequitur* thinking that threatens a study. It is helpful to define our terms to avoid this error.

population defined A **population** is the universe of events from which the sample is drawn. Figure 11.1 shows the relationship between a sample and population. As you can see, a sample is simply a selection of events from the population (the term "events" is used to permit including samples of people, messages, behavior, or things). Researchers can sample toward the center of the population, or they might accidentally sample at the periphery of the population. The actual individual

data defined events are called pieces of **data.**

statistic defined A number computed from a sample is called a **statistic,** sometimes also called "sample statistics" or "test statistics." Grammatically, a single number (in this sense) is called a statistic and more than one number is called a group of statistic*s*. You may have seen the term, "statistics" used to refer to the study of

"statistics" also quantitative information. In this latter sense, "statistics" is a singular term even refers to study of though it ends with an s. Thus, you have to be careful when reading studies. If quantitative researchers refer to computed "test statistics" then you know that conclusions information based on samples (and many events in the population) were omitted. If researchers talk about selecting statistics to analyze data, they mean the specific formulae they use in their studies. Almost always, communication researchers compute statistics because they gather samples to help analyze results.

parameter defined Suppose you were able to sample every single event in the population—leaving out none. These numbers would be called **parameters,** not statistics. A

parameter is the label for a number computed from a population. In practice, researchers rarely compute parameters. Instead they often inherit parameters from some other source. For instance, the federal government has told automobile manufacturers the maximum emissions that may be permitted for cars sold in the United States. Similarly, customers often tell manufacturers what specifications must be satisfied for a product to be accepted. In each case these parameters are defined in advance as descriptions of the population.

parameters rarely computed by researchers

Defining the Population

To draw samples from populations, researchers must first define the population. Suppose that you were interested in studying the degree to which senior citizens in the United States rely on televised news in preference to newspaper accounts. All senior citizens in the United States would be the population and you would want to make sure that any samples carefully represented them. Though the population may be defined quite broadly—including all people or all television programs in the world, for instance—they also may be defined quite narrowly, such as including only students at large western universities or only prime-time television programs from the three leading networks. The point is that populations are *defined* by the researcher as having certain characteristics.

populations defined by researchers

populations may be defined narrowly

Eliminating Bias

Bias in sampling is a tendency for the sample to err so that it fails to represent the population. Obviously, researchers work to eliminate or minimize bias. You may be mystified when you hear of the accuracy of some political polls or television rating services. They usually are able to give highly accurate reflections of the population based on what seem to be very small samples, often as few as 1,200 people. Such accuracy does not happen by accident. Controlling bias is critical and is handled by the direct action discussed below.

bias defined

ESSENTIALS OF SAMPLING

The basic concepts discussed below provide a framework for understanding sampling. This section also introduces ways to draw representative samples with appropriate sample sizes.

Representative Sampling: The Goal of Effective Sampling

A good sample must be representative of the population and big enough to permit reasonable analysis of data. These matters are related, of course. Yet, for researchers, the fundamental test of whether a sample is good is the degree to which it is representative. A **representative sample** is one that accurately reflects characteristics of the population from which it was drawn. Of course, unless researchers have the knowledge of gods, they will never know if samples are really representative. So, researchers take steps to prevent knowingly biasing samples. That way, they may presume that a sample is representative unless contrary evidence emerges.

representative sample defined

Sample Size

Collecting a representative sample involves having one large enough to make reasonable interpretations. Yet, large sample size is not enough to prove that a sample is representative of the population. Gathering a reasonably sized sample is just one step in collecting a representative sample. Research students often ask, ''How big should a sample be?'' To answer this question, they must decide on the amount of sampling error they are willing to accept, and consider the demands created by research tools employed.

Sampling Error

sampling error
defined

You probably have heard news reports that describe political polls. They often tell what percentage of the voters favor each candidate. They also often report a certain ''margin of error'' for the poll. This ''margin of error'' is the amount of sampling error associated with the sample. The term **sampling error** refers to the degree to which a sample differs from population characteristics on some measure. In general, as the sample size gets to be a larger and larger proportion of the population, the amount of sampling error is reduced. If you sample the entire population, there is no sampling error at all! Thus, a general piece of advice is to collect as big a sample as you can afford. But you often have to make some practical choices.

Sampling Guidelines

sizes should be
suitable to research
questions and design

Sample sizes should be suitable to the research questions and study designs. Thus, in pilot studies, small samples may be used. In speech and hearing science, samples of eight to fifteen subjects may be used in experiments in which physiological reactions are involved (and where few additional variables may need to be randomized). For studies attempting to validate new measurement instruments, researchers may be told to use quite a large sample, at least 200 events. To use some statistical tools, such as multiple correlation or factor analysis, researchers need a minimum number of events for every variable to be studied. Table 11.1 shows some of the popular guidelines suggested by students of research methods.

Guidelines Based on Sampling Error

confidence intervals
identified

If samples have been drawn at random, it is possible for researchers to report **confidence intervals** indicating the probability that sample statistics ''capture'' population parameters, within certain margins for error. This section will explain how these margins for error are used and calculated by researchers.

confidence intervals
for proportional
data

For instance, take the case of a poll you might complete with a sample of 100 people selected at random. Suppose you found that 60 percent reported anxiety about taking a communication course, and 40 percent did not. You might wonder how far from the true population proportions your sample data are—after all, a sample of 100 does not sound all that big. To plug numbers into the formula in table 11.2, you need only remember that proportions are numbers expressed with decimal points included (in other words, the proportion of anxious people is .6, not 60 percent). Then, you can fill in the blanks. As table 11.2 shows, the formula

TABLE 11.1 Sample Size Requirements for Different Research Traditions

Condition	Sample Size Requirements
Pilot studies	At least ten events in study (Isaac & Michael, 1981, p. 93)
Studies of physiological measures	At least eight events randomly selected (if individual response ratings are involved, the sample must be increased to ordinary sample sizes for experiments)
Validation or cross-validation studies	At least 200 events if standard methods of validation are used (such as multiple correlation or factor analysis); with other tools "N should be at least about 60, and preferably 100 or more, for this purpose" (Tatsuoka, 1969, p. 27)
Studies that use multiple correlation methods	Fifteen subjects for every predictor or independent variable (Stevens, 1986, p. 58)
Studies that use factor analysis	At least ten events for each variable item to be included in the factor analysis (Nunnally, 1978, p. 421)

reveals a ''margin of error'' in estimating how far from the true proportion of high-anxiety people in the population our sample may be 95 percent of the time. Put another way, this formula states that we are 95 percent confident that the sample proportion is equal to the population proportion, plus or minus 9.6 percent. We could also say that we are 95 percent confident that the true population proportion of people anxious about taking a communication class is somewhere between 50.4 percent and 69.6 percent. Of course, in our example, there is a 5 percent chance that our sample is *way off*—not even close to the range we have reported. At least people know the odds and can make sensible choices about interpreting study results.

Not all data deal with proportions or percentages, of course. For studies that deal with means and averages, confidence intervals can also be constructed. To estimate these intervals you need to have some measure of the amount of variation that exists in the population.[1] The standard deviation is a statistic that is most often used. Though it will be explained in chapter 13, for now let us just define **standard deviation** as a number that tells how far from the average the data are (on the average). The standard deviation is often abbreviated by the letter 's.' Suppose you want to know the margin for error you would have if you surveyed 100 people and found that the average number of hours they watched TV per week was 23. Table 11.2B shows this example. With a computed standard deviation of eight hours, you can construct a 95 percent confidence interval around the average. As the formula reveals, with such a sample size you can be 95 percent confident that the sample average is equal to the population average, plus or minus 1.57 hours. You can also say you are 95 percent confident that the true population average number of hours people watch TV per week is between 21.43 hours and 24.57 hours.

By doing a little algebra, you can use the formulae to help you choose the sample size for a study with different confidence intervals and margins for error.

confidence intervals
for averages

standard deviation
defined

TABLE 11.2 Confidence Intervals for Proportions and Means

Type of Measure	Formulae and Examples

A. For proportions (decimal point data) organized into two groups (such as 'yes' or 'no')

90% C.I. = observed proportion $\pm$ 1.645 $\quad * \quad \sqrt{\dfrac{p* (1-p)}{\text{sample size}}}$

95% C.I. = observed proportion $\pm$ 1.96 $\quad * \quad \sqrt{\dfrac{p* (1-p)}{\text{sample size}}}$

99% C.I. = observed proportion $\pm$ 2.58 $\quad * \quad \sqrt{\dfrac{p* (1-p)}{\text{sample size}}}$

where p = proportion of responses for one category

EXAMPLE: With a sample of 100 people selected at random, if 60 percent were anxious about taking a communication class, how far from the population proportion would the sample proportion be 95 percent of the time?

95% C.I. = observed proportion $\pm$ 1.96 $\quad * \quad \sqrt{\dfrac{p* (1-p)}{\text{sample size}}}$

$\quad = \quad$ .60 $\quad \pm$ 1.96 $\quad * \quad \sqrt{\dfrac{.6* (1-.6)}{100}}$

$\quad = \quad$ .60 $\quad \pm$ 1.96 $\quad * \quad \sqrt{\dfrac{.24}{100}}$

$\quad = \quad$ .60 $\quad \pm$ 1.96 $\quad * \quad \sqrt{.0024}$

$\quad = \quad$ .60 $\quad \pm$ 1.96 $\quad * \quad$ .049

95% C.I. $\quad = \quad$ .60 $\quad \pm$ .096

B. For means

90% C.I. = Observed Mean $\pm$ 1.645 $\quad * \quad (s / \sqrt{\text{sample size}})$

95% C.I. = Observed Mean $\pm$ 1.96 $\quad * \quad (s / \sqrt{\text{sample size}})$

99% C.I. = Observed Mean $\pm$ 2.58 $\quad * \quad (s / \sqrt{\text{sample size}})$

where s = an estimate of variability in the population called the "standard deviation" (see chapter 13 for computation of s)

EXAMPLE: With a sample of 100 people selected at random, if the average number of hours of TV watched per week were 23 hours with a standard deviation observed of 8 hours, how far would the population mean be from the sample proportion 95% of the time?

95% C.I. $\quad = \quad$ Observed Mean $\pm$ 1.96 $\quad * \quad (s / \sqrt{\text{sample size}})$

$\quad = \quad$ 23 hours $\pm$ 1.96 $\quad * \quad (8 / \sqrt{100} \quad)$

$\quad = \quad$ 23 hours $\pm$ 1.96 $\quad * \quad (8 / \quad 10 \quad)$

$\quad = \quad$ 23 hours $\pm$ 1.96 $\quad * \quad$ .8

95% C. I. $\quad = \quad$ 23 hours $\pm$ 1.57 hours

Table 11.3A shows what sample sizes might be required for different situations involving the use of proportional data. On occasion, researchers do not have measures (or even estimates) of variability but have to make some choices anyway. Fortunately there are some guidelines. Table 11.3B shows such a table for a 95 percent confidence interval and a margin for error expressed as a 5 percent range of variation, provided you know the size of the population. In national polling additional adaptations must be made. Assuming very large variability in the population, increased sample sizes have been suggested to control for the additional background variation that usually exists (Yamane, 1967). Such tables indicate that a national poll would require only 100 respondents for a 10 percent margin of error. To reduce error to 5 percent you would need a sample of 400. To reduce error to 3 percent (typical among national polls) a sample of 1,111 would be needed. To trim the margin for error to one percent would require a sample of 10,000! As you can see, reducing margins of error or increasing confidence requires increasing sample sizes.

other methods to compute confidence intervals

Statistical Effects of Small Samples

In general, small samples increase sampling error. Yet, another aspect of small samples may not have occurred to you. Because of the ways statistics are computed and distributions entered, it is difficult for researchers to find evidence of relationships when sample sizes are small. It is easiest to spot differences when large samples are used because the relationships tend to stand out from the background noise and variability. When small samples are used, only very big effects stand out. Thus, the impact of small samples creates a double whammy for the researcher. Not only may the sample be thrown off, but a small sample may inhibit the chances of relationships being identified by most statistical tools.

small samples invite sampling bias and make it difficult to find relationships

But isn't there a point at which a small sample turns into a large one? In reality, most statisticians have observed that samples of thirty or more events tend to produce identical distributions. Without getting into the detailed background of this statement, we will mention that different distributions used in statistical analysis tend to diverge from each other when the samples drop below thirty events.[2] In fact, Leonard Kazmier (1988, p. 132) recommended that any actual sample size should be at least thirty events when estimating averages since the standard formulae for data analysis presume normal distributions. When sample sizes grow above thirty, the distributions used by researchers and statisticians to help make decisions become fairly comparable to each other. So, big samples start somewhere near thirty events—but there is a catch. The events themselves in the sample must be drawn at random. To balance out other sampling concerns, researchers may need increased sample sizes.

sample sizes of thirty or more invite reasonable use of statistical tools

FORMS OF SAMPLING

When sampling events from a population, researchers make critical choices. To give you an idea of those choices, this section discusses categories of sampling that presume randomization and those that do not involve randomization.

TABLE 11.3 Sample Sizes Required for Proportional Data

A. For proportional data and an estimate of variability

SITUATION: This table presumes a single (dichotomous) stratification variable, conservative proportions of .5 and .5 (for maximum heterogeneity and to assume maximum internal sampling error), an unlimited population size, and truly random sampling.

		\multicolumn{4}{c}{**With margin for error of:**}			
		.10	.05	.025	.01
Confidence interval	90%	68	272	1089	6806
	95%	96	384	1537	9604
	99%	166	666	2663	16641

B. For proportional data from a population of known size and no estimate of population variability

SITUATION: This table presumes random samples of proportions drawn from populations of a known size so as to be within 5 percent of the population proportion at a 95 percent confidence interval (after Krejcie & Morgan, 1970).

Population Size	**Sample Size**
under 10	NA
10	10
15	14
20	19
30	28
40	36
50	44
75	63
100	80
250	152
500	217
1000	278
5000	357
10000	370
50000	381
100000	384

You probably have been in classes in which you participated in a study by completing a questionnaire or interview. In a technical sense, then, you were volunteering your participation. But you were asked to participate. You did not ask the researcher to permit you to be a part of the sample group. Yet some research actually relies on subjects who are volunteers for such research. Sometimes researchers place ads in newspapers asking people to participate in research, and they get a fair number of volunteers—especially if they offer to pay subjects. A question that faces researchers, however, is whether the volunteers give reactions that are typical of the population.

Many people are greatly concerned that volunteers differ from other members of the population. After all, people volunteer for a reason. If their reasons are not shared by the entire population, there is little reason to believe that the results from the volunteers are representative. Some scholars have noticed that volunteers tend to differ from the rest of the general population because they have increased needs for social approval, increased socioeconomic status, increased intelligence, and reduced conformity to authority figures (Rosenthal & Rosnow, 1969). The *Journal of Volunteerism,* is a journal dedicated to identifying ways in which volunteers behave, both in and out of research settings. Though the reasons volunteers choose to engage in research may be randomly distributed (Kruglanski, 1973)—and hence not a systematic source of variation in research—in many research settings there is no doubt that the use of volunteers can introduce great bias in studies. Thus prudent researchers tend to be wary of relying exclusively on volunteers as the chief evidence to draw meaningful conclusions.

Random Sampling

Sometimes called "probability sampling," randomization plays an important part in research. To understand random sampling, it is helpful to grasp key terms and to understand its key role.

Random sampling is the selecting of data in such a way that each event in the population has an equal chance of selection.[3] Random sampling is presumed for nearly all statistical tools that may be applied to data. You can use distributions of randomly occurring events to figure the odds that a sample truly reflects what goes on in the population. When students hear of random sampling they often mistakenly imagine that it is a hit or miss activity ("random" sounds a lot like "accidental"). The truth is that randomization is time-consuming and many researchers try to take shortcuts. But the shortcuts throw off the whole sample and make it impossible to enter distributions accurately to decide whether research findings represent anything other than sampling error.

Obtaining a random draw of events is not a haphazard matter. One might imagine sampling a bunch of people at a nearby shopping mall. These places fre-

*random sampling
defined*

*randomness not
accidental*

quently are the stomping grounds for researchers who wish to find out people's reactions to commercials, promotional campaigns, and marketing strategies (you may have been approached at a mall by a person carrying a clipboard who asked you to answer questions or participate in a focus group meeting). Yet, sampling people at a mall is usually not random. People conducting surveys are usually told to gather data from the first set of people they can find who fall into a target population (sometimes limited to women under thirty, people with children, or senior citizens). People arriving at the mall at a later time do not have the same chance to be sampled as those in the first grouping. Though researchers may claim to have been relatively unbiased in selecting individuals, they cannot claim that the study was truly random.

To improve their studies, some researchers attempt to sample according to a schedule. They might select the first five people to enter the main entrance of the shopping mall each hour. Or, they might approach every tenth person entering the mall. Though this is a step in the right direction, it is still not random since there is bias in favor of those who arrive promptly at the beginning of the hour. Thus, this method cannot claim all the advantages of random sampling. It is best

systematic or periodic sampling distinguished from random sampling

described as **systematic** or **periodic sampling** since it selects respondents according to a predetermined schedule other than a random sequence. You should be warned that many researchers actually use some form of systematic sampling and call it "random sampling" in passing.

Random sampling methods attempt to remove the human element from biasing the study. In the simplest sense, obtaining a random draw of events can be accomplished by taking care to insure that each event has an equal chance of selection. For instance, if you wished to expose a random sample of students to speech from a severe stutterer, you might write class members' names on pieces of paper and put them in a hat. After tossing the pieces of paper around for a while, you might sample by pulling names from the hat. If you are successful, you might gather a fairly random sample. But if the population is fairly large, it may not be practical to draw names from your hat.

using random numbers

There is a superior way. Suppose you wanted to sample a group of voters in your city. No problem. Voters must register and their names and addresses are matters of public record. You might assign each voter a number and then turn to a table of random numbers to select voters whose numbers have "randomly" come up. These tools of randomization help you effectively eliminate your own biases in data collection. Random sampling permits you to feel confident that the sample is as representative of the population—as free of bias—as possible. Randomization increases the chances that differences from one person to another in a sample will be random rather than systematic. Thus, random sampling allows you to control a host of background differences in sample groups that otherwise might foul up a study's meaningfulness.

methods of random sampling

There is more than one way to use random sampling. Table 11.4 shows the major random sampling methods—simple random sampling, stratified random sampling, and cluster sampling—and describes the ways in which they are frequently used. Since researchers often abbreviate their descriptions of methods, it is valuable to understand the labels used for these random sampling tools.

SPECIAL DISCUSSION 11–2
How to Use a Table of Random Numbers

Random number tables are often used to help researchers draw random samples and to assign subjects to various conditions at random. Table 11.A contains a list of random two-digit numbers that actually came out of a computer as single digits (the publisher arranged them into two digit numbers for convenience—thus, a good sized table can be used by researchers for nearly any number of digits desired). Though there are several options, here is one way to use a random number table to select a sample:

1. Give every event in the population a number. To keep it simple, suppose you wanted to draw a sample of thirty college debaters from three universities with a total of ninety debaters. The possible range of numbers would be 01 through 90—thus, a two digit table would do nicely (if you had to deal with three digit numbers, you might add a third column of numbers).
2. Enter the number table at random. Don't just close your eyes and point your finger somewhere on the page (right-handed people tend to let their hands drop toward the right side the page, and lefties tend to drop their hands toward the left side; the corners might as well not be on the page, given their chance of being selected!). As an alternative, one could cut cards (let aces equal 1 and face cards equal 0) or throw dice to find the column number and the row number to start with, but who carries around playing cards or dice? Instead, you can use one of the following techniques (adapted from Leedy, 1989, pp. 154–55): You can ask people to give you their social security numbers (let the first two digits identify the table column to start with; and let the last two digits be the row). You could check the daily stock quotations to find the last two digits for the Dow Jones Industrial Average high and low (to represent the starting column and row). One of the easiest methods involves pulling a dollar bill from your pocket and checking the serial number. Suppose yours is L 38 7321 14 G. The first two-digit number is 38 and the final two-digit number is 14. To decide which number is the row and which is the column reference, you can flip a coin. If the coin is heads, the first number will be the column. If the toss is tails, the last number will be the column. Say the coin came up tails. You would turn to the random number table and find the point where column 14 and row 38 intersect. On the table, the number at this intersection is 42 (find it for yourself!). If the row or column numbers are greater than the number of rows or columns on your table, just add the numbers together and use the sum as your new starting number.
3. Now, you need to know whether you will read the numbers by going across the page to the right, to the left, up, or down (don't mess with diagonals, it's too confusing). You can take out our coin and flip it twice (two heads mean you read to the right; two tails means you read to the left; heads followed by tails means you read up the column; tails followed by heads means you read down the column). Say your flips give you two heads, so you read to the right.

SPECIAL DISCUSSION 11–2
(Continued)

TABLE 11.A A Random Number Table

60 36 59 46 53	35 07 53 39 49	42 61 42 92 97	01 91 82 83 16
83 79 94 24 02	56 62 33 44 42	34 99 44 13 74	70 07 11 47 36
32 96 00 74 05	36 40 98 32 32	99 38 54 16 00	11 13 30 75 86
19 32 25 38 45	57 62 05 26 06	66 49 76 86 46	78 13 86 65 59
11 22 09 47 47	07 39 93 74 08	48 50 92 39 29	27 48 24 54 76
31 75 15 72 60	68 98 00 53 39	15 47 04 83 55	88 65 12 25 96
88 49 29 93 82	14 45 40 45 04	20 09 49 89 77	74 84 39 34 13
30 93 44 77 44	07 48 18 38 28	73 78 80 65 33	28 59 72 04 05
22 88 84 88 93	27 49 99 87 48	60 53 04 51 28	74 02 28 46 17
78 21 21 69 93	35 90 29 13 86	44 37 21 54 86	65 74 11 40 14
41 84 98 45 47	46 85 05 23 26	34 67 75 83 00	74 91 06 43 45
46 35 23 30 49	69 24 89 34 60	45 30 50 75 21	61 31 83 18 55
11 08 79 62 94	14 01 33 17 92	59 74 76 72 77	76 50 33 45 13
52 70 10 83 37	56 30 38 73 15	16 52 06 96 76	11 65 49 98 93
57 27 53 68 98	81 30 44 85 85	68 65 22 73 76	92 85 25 58 66
20 85 77 31 56	70 28 42 43 26	79 37 59 52 20	01 15 96 32 67
15 63 38 49 24	90 41 59 36 14	33 52 12 66 65	55 82 34 76 41
92 69 44 82 97	39 90 40 21 15	59 58 94 90 67	66 82 14 15 75
77 61 31 90 19	88 15 20 00 80	20 55 49 14 09	96 27 74 82 57
38 68 83 24 86	45 13 46 35 45	59 40 47 20 59	43 94 75 16 80
25 16 30 18 89	70 01 41 50 21	41 29 06 73 12	71 85 71 59 57
65 25 10 76 29	37 23 93 32 95	05 87 00 11 19	92 78 42 63 40
36 81 54 36 25	18 63 73 75 09	82 44 49 90 05	04 92 17 37 01
64 39 71 16 92	05 32 78 21 62	20 24 78 17 59	45 19 72 53 32
04 51 52 56 24	95 09 66 79 46	48 46 08 55 58	15 19 11 87 82
83 76 16 08 73	43 25 38 41 45	60 83 32 59 83	01 29 14 13 49
10 38 70 63 45	80 85 40 92 79	43 52 90 63 18	38 38 47 47 61
51 32 19 22 46	80 08 87 70 74	88 72 25 67 36	66 16 44 94 31
72 47 20 00 08	80 89 01 80 02	94 81 33 19 00	54 15 58 34 36
05 46 65 53 06	93 12 81 84 64	74 45 79 05 61	72 84 81 18 34
39 52 87 24 84	82 47 42 55 93	48 54 53 52 47	18 61 91 36 74
81 61 61 87 11	53 34 24 42 76	75 12 21 17 24	74 62 77 37 07
07 58 61 61 20	82 64 12 28 20	92 90 41 31 41	32 39 21 97 63
90 76 70 42 35	13 57 41 72 00	69 90 26 37 42	78 46 42 25 01
40 18 82 81 93	29 59 38 86 27	94 97 21 15 98	62 09 53 67 87
34 41 48 21 57	86 88 75 50 87	19 15 20 00 23	12 30 28 07 83
63 43 97 53 63	44 98 91 68 22	36 02 40 08 67	76 37 84 16 05
67 04 90 90 70	93 39 94 55 47	94 45 87 42 84	05 04 14 98 07
79 49 50 41 46	52 16 29 02 86	54 15 83 42 43	46 97 83 54 82
91 70 43 05 52	04 73 72 10 31	75 05 19 30 29	47 66 56 43 82

Source: *A Million Random Digits with 100,000 Normal Deviates* (New York: Free Press, 1955), with permission of the RAND Corporation.

SPECIAL DISCUSSION 11–2
(Continued)

4. Since you want to sample thirty debaters, you simply take the individuals whose numbers "come up." In your case, you select person 42, person 84, person 05, person 04, person 14, person 98 (ignore it since it does not exist in this population), person 07, and so forth until you have your sample. If the same number is repeated, you simply ignore it the second time.

There is another way to obtain random numbers, of course. These days, many inexpensive hand calculators have random number keys on them. If you purchase such a calculator, you need only press a button to generate random numbers.

Nonrandom Sampling

Despite its advantages, sometimes random sampling simply is not possible. It would not be possible for you to do an experiment in which you randomly assign a group of people to have cleft palates and another group of people not to have cleft palates. In this situation you pretty much have to take people as they are available to you. It would be unthinkable to create people with cleft palates for the purpose of maintaining the purity of a random sample. Yet, people with cleft palates also may have some other sorts of individual characteristics that are not shared to the same degree by the general population. They tend to show slightly higher levels of communication apprehension than others. They also may tend to experience lower levels of self-esteem than members of the general population. So, a researcher has a choice: give up, or go with the available data but qualify your conclusions carefully. The second option is obviously superior. You may remember John Paul Jones's famous advice: "Do the best you can with the means available to you." Sometimes random sampling is not feasible. So, you must do the best you can with the available methods of nonrandom sampling.

> randomization is
> not always possible

There are several different forms of nonrandom sampling. Table 11.5 describes their application to research. The four general categories include convenience sampling, quota sampling, purposive or known group sampling, and snowball sampling, although other specific varieties may be added to the listing if it were further subdivided. All of these methods have been used in the broad spectrum of communication studies and may be particularly invited in some studies.

Naturally, strengths and weaknesses are associated with all methods of nonrandom sampling. Some of each probably have occurred to you. A first strength of such methods is that they often allow the researcher to get samples that would be otherwise unavailable. If you wanted to study the communication strategies employed by drug dealers to sell their products, you could not very easily put an ad in the newspaper asking drug dealers to call you for an appointment to be interviewed. You probably would hear only from police officers and narcotics agents.

> strengths of
> nonrandom
> sampling

TABLE 11.4 Species of Random Sampling

	Simple Random Sampling	Stratified Random Sampling	Cluster Sampling
Definition and Description	Selection of data such that each event in the population has an equal chance of selection.	Samples are defined based on the known proportions within the population and random sampling is completed within each group.	Groups or areas (clusters) are randomly selected and an actual sample is drawn from them.
Method for Sampling	—Pulling names out of a hat or fishbowl —Assigning numbers to each event in the population and then using a table of random numbers or random number generator to call numbers that can be included in the final sample.	Population characteristics are identified (such as the number of men and women in the population); after deciding on the sample size to be drawn, a random sample is drawn from each level of the population stratification variable (using one of the methods of simple random sampling) to meet the proportion of the population that sample subgroup represents.	Whereas stratified random sampling selects *events* proportionately from each population group, cluster sampling progressively selects events among *clusters* that have been randomly selected. The method involves —identifying large groupings (such as newspaper editors) and preparing a listing of clusters of large city and small town newspapers —taking a random or stratified random sample in each cluster (e.g., selecting big city and small town newspapers) —taking a sample within the identified clusters of events (e.g., contacting newspaper editors in the cluster subgroup for sampling)
Applications	1. Experiments in which random assignment is feasible 2. Research problems that do not have meaningful subcategories in the population that affect responses	1. Major political polls and popularly reported surveys 2. Studies in which stratification variables are important elements for which blocking is possible	1. Most large-scale status surveys where it is easier to obtain lists of clusters than individuals within a population 2. Many surveys that include geographically based samples

TABLE 11.4—*Continued*

	Simple Random Sampling	Stratified Random Sampling	Cluster Sampling
Strengths	1. Sampling error can be computed 2. Controls of individual differences among subjects in the sample 3. Increases representativeness	1. Permits analysis by subdivision of strata, rather than just randomizing across them 2. Increased sample size and weighting of strata mean that population characteristics are most likely to be identified	1. Practical solution to problems of gaining access to many settings generally 2. Cost of sampling usually is minimized in large scale surveys
Weaknesses	1. Difficult to use in many field settings when a list of all events in the population does not exist 2. Time-consuming	1. Increased expense since stratification involves increasing sample size 2. Weights for each strata may be difficult to know in many settings 3. Carries same disadvantages as simple random sampling	1. Clustering requires larger samples than simple random sampling 2. Since stratification is a stage the method carries the same disadvantages as for stratified random sampling

If the activity involves issues that are intimate, private, or deviant, nonrandom sampling may be the only way to gather any information. A second strength is that nonrandom sampling methods are often invited by field and quasi-experimental research. Researchers may want to sample naturally occurring events—such as nonverbal displays of affection people show when saying good-bye at airports.[4]

Despite any advantages involved in nonrandom samples, they have severe limitations. Most of these matters are technical issues and involve the rigor that can be claimed for a study. First, nonrandom samples tend to show great biases. Respondents cannot be presumed to be a random draw from the population because they are not selected in ways that provide each event in the population with an equal chance of selection. Thus, without randomization, the sample may have clear biases. Sometimes researchers can take steps to describe these biases, but there are so many potential sources of bias that this strategy can only be partially successful. Second, since there is no distribution for nonprobability samples, no sampling error computation is possible. Thus, it is not possible to compute a

general disadvantages of nonrandom samples

TABLE 11.5 Species of Nonrandom Sampling

	Accidental or Convenience Sampling	Quota Sampling
Definition and Description	Selection of events that are most readily available.	Samples are defined based on the known proportions within the population and nonrandom sampling is completed within each group.
Methods for Sampling	In tact groups that are readily available are sampled; no attempt at randomization is made.	Population characteristics are identified (such as the number of men and women in the population); after deciding on the sample size to be drawn, an accidental or convenience sample is drawn from each level of the population stratification variable.
Applications	Used for TV "call in" polls that invite viewers to participate for a modest toll charge; though found in many studies, these samples are most useful in case studies and in pilot studies that identify problems with research materials.	Studies in which researchers desire to balance out a clearly unbalanced sample of convenience; often used in case studies in which individuals who are known to differ in some respect might not be sampled proportionately in those categories.
Strengths	Accidental samples tend to be economical to gather.	Attempts to make sure that important parts of the population are not omitted in sampling.
Weaknesses	1. No way to compute sampling biases. 2. No claims of control of extraneous variance from subjects can be made. 3. Not possible to generalize to the population.	1. Biases introduced when data collectors contact friends or cohorts to fill quotas. 2. Groups of individuals systematically excluded on the basis of convenience. 3. Carries same disadvantages as convenience sample since this method actually is convenience sampling within quota categories.

confidence interval and estimate how closely our data probably are to population parameters. This limitation means that the researcher cannot use standard tools to determine the accuracy with which the sample captures population parameters. Third, the use of nonrandom samples severely limits conclusions that researchers can draw. The impact of experimental variables can be very different from one

Purposive or Known Group Sampling	Snowball Sampling
Selection of events from groups that are known to possess a particular characteristic under investigation.	Selection of events based on referrals from initial informants.
Groups of individuals who are known to have certain characteristics are identified as a sample population (for instance to find people with high intelligence, a researcher might decide to sample members of Mensa, the organization of people who share high I.Q. scores).	A population is defined (usually people who engage in deviant or illegal behavior, such as street gang members, prostitutes or criminals); after contact for participation in the study (and trust built), the subject is requested to refer the researcher to other individuals in the population group; these people are also requested to refer the researcher to additional subjects.
Experiments or surveys where a criterion for admission to the sample clearly exists.	Highly useful in studies of behavior that is deviant, illegal, or part of a subculture where random sampling is not a possible option (such as Bryan's study of ways in which call girls are recruited and trained [1965]).
Studies that try to validate new measurement tools.	
On occasion, key states have been used by some political polling organizations to forecast the results of national elections.	
Usually a convenient and economical sampling method when key population characteristics are identified.	1. Useful when it is not really possible to identify all members of the population from the outset. 2. Very useful in case study work with unknown populations.
1. Does not yield trustworthy results when the known characteristic is subjective or not clear cut. 2. Groups of individuals selected as known groups may not be independent of each other (e.g., not every intelligent person is invited or interested in joining Mensa). 3. Carries same disadvantages as convenience sampling.	1. Difficult to identify whether sufficient referrals exist to penetrate beyond the periphery of a population group. 2. Referrals introduce bias since limited social groupings can be probed by those in the initial contact from which other sample elements "snowballed." 3. Since snowball sampling involves finding a willing and convenient starting subject, this method is the ultimate convenience sample and carries same disadvantages as convenience sampling.

selected subgroup to another. Though nonrandom sampling provides analyses that apply to the single subgroup sampled, other subgroups cannot be generalized at all. In fact, the use of nonrandom sampling means that the conclusions a researcher can draw are limited to those suggesting relationships, but they exclude conclusions based on convincing evidence.

DEALING WITH SAMPLING PROBLEMS

Research books often describe sampling as though problems are rarities. The dismal truth is that the research craft is riddled with choices and compromises. Some of these matters are addressed here.

Subject Refusal to Participate

systematic reasons for refusal to participate as sampling error

It will come as no surprise to you that people often do not want to participate in surveys. But if too many people refuse to be part of a sample, randomization is jeopardized. People have reasons for refusing. If these reasons are systematically shared by the portion of the population that declines to become involved, then the remaining sample may not be truly random. Thus, researchers must report such information in their studies and qualify their results accordingly.

1. initial refusal
2. incomplete responding

Respondents may refuse to participate in two ways. They can decline initially to accept a questionnaire, answer any questions, or mail in a survey. Or they can provide incomplete responses. In each case, the researcher is expected to describe how many subjects refused to participate and any differences they may have had from others who agreed to participate. A little refusal here and there may not be a big deal, but large scale refusal suggests that something may be terribly wrong with the study research question or its procedures. David J. Fox explained:

systematic attrition is meaningful to the researcher

> When attrition reaches 25 percent or higher, even assuming that there are no statistically significant differences between accepting and data-producing samples, the researcher and reader must be concerned with the phenomena of nonparticipation. There is extensive evidence in the literature that . . . those who answer initially hold different opinions from those who do not. As we analyze data for any one study this means that we must continually evaluate the data, particularly any data of particular significance, to determine if the nonresponders could have affected the response pattern. For example, assume we find that 70 percent of the selected sample of 100 actually produced data. In studying data for a particular question, we find that of the 70 respondents, 52 answered "yes" and 18 answered "no." We can have good confidence in these data, for even if the 30 nonrespondents had the same opinion, and it was "no," the majority would still be on the "yes" opinion. However, if the 70 respondents split 39 to 31 on another question, we could have little confidence in these data, for if a majority of the nonrespondents held to either point of view they could alter the result. (1969, pp. 345–46)

Researchers need to examine potential sources of nonresponse to limit conclusions and to discover additional variables for future study.

Evidence of Randomization in Research Articles

Researchers who use randomization tend to describe it in great detail. Research articles usually either explain how they handled randomization, or they make some reference to a table of random numbers. If they do not use either method, then you cannot—and probably should not—assume that they used randomization. Randomization is a pain in the neck and researchers who do it properly often complain about it.

researchers show randomization by either describing methods or referencing random number tables

To some extent, the credibility of the research project may be tested by looking at the degree to which the researcher offers evidence of randomization. Highly skilled researchers spell out their methods in enough detail for the study to be replicated.

SUMMARY

Sampling involves selecting events from a population. A population is the universe of events from which the sample is drawn. The actual individual events are called pieces of data. A number computed from a sample is called a statistic, sometimes also called ''sample statistics'' or ''test statistics.'' A parameter is the label for a number computed from a population. To draw samples from populations, researchers must first define the population. Bias in sampling is a tendency for the sample to err so that it fails to represent the population. Obviously, researchers work to eliminate or minimize bias.

A good sample must be representative of the population and big enough to permit reasonable analysis of data. A representative sample is one that accurately reflects characteristics of the population from which it was drawn. Part of a representative sample involves having a large enough sample to make reasonable interpretations. The term sampling error refers to the degree to which a sample differs from population characteristics on some measure. In general, as the sample size gets to be an increased proportion of the population, the amount of sampling error is reduced. Sample sizes should be suitable to the research questions and study designs. If samples have been drawn at random, it is possible to report confidence intervals indicating the probability that sample statistics ''capture'' popula-

tion parameters, within certain margins for error. Small samples often invite sampling bias. In addition, because of the ways statistics are computed and distributions entered, it is very difficult for researchers to find evidence of relationships when sample sizes get small. Yet, statisticians have observed that samples of thirty or more events tend to produce identical distributions.

Sometimes called ''probability sampling'' techniques, the use of randomization plays an important part in research. Random sampling is selection of data such that each event in the population has an equal chance of selection. Obtaining a random draw of events is not a haphazard matter. Systematic or periodic sampling is not true random sampling because it selects respondents according to a predetermined schedule rather than a random sequence. To select a sample, events can be assigned numbers and chosen by reference to a table of random numbers. Random sampling permits you to feel confident that the sample is representative of the population and that differences from one person to another in a sample will be random rather than systematic. Thus, random sampling allows control of a host of background differences in sample groups. Sometimes random sampling is not possible. Four general categories of nonrandom sampling include convenience sampling, quota sampling, purposive or known group sampling, and snowball sampling. These methods often allow the researcher to get samples that might otherwise be unavailable and are often invited by field and quasi-experimental research. They have severe limitations, however: (1) they tend to show great biases; (2) since there is no distribution for nonprobability samples, no sampling error computation is possible; and (3) their use severely limits the conclusions that researchers can draw.

Researchers often face problems of sampling and sampling error. First, subjects may refuse to participate (either because they initially decline, or because they provide incomplete responses). Second, researchers must provide evidence of randomization (either by explaining how they handled randomization, or by referencing a table of random numbers).

TERMS FOR REVIEW

sampling
population
data
statistic
parameter
bias
representative sample

sampling error
confidence intervals
standard deviation
random sampling
systematic or periodic sampling
accidental or convenience sampling

NOTES

[1]Actually this measure should be the variation known to exist in the population. But if the researcher does not have this information, the amount of variation in the sample may be substituted since the major measures of sample variability (standard deviation and variance) are unbiased estimators of population variability.

[2]This statement is not a casual one. When sample sizes grow beyond thirty, the t distribution, the binomial distribution, and the standard normal curve are, in essence, the same distribution. Comparisons of distributions tend to show a consistency among them as sample size increases.

[3]In a mathematic sense, randomization means that the probability of any event following any other is equal to zero. But the mathematic definition presumes an infinite population. Thus, for practical purposes, a quasi-random method might be involved. To say that the chance for event sampling is equal is close enough for the purposes of this book.

[4]Actually, some combination of randomization methods might be added to this example. One might sample randomly selected months and randomly selected airports during randomly selected time periods. Then a reduced random sample might be selected from this large grouping by numbering all the people saying good-bye and randomly selecting a group of people to serve as the final sample. Such work is not likely to be completed by most researchers, however.

CHAPTER 12

Measurement in Communication Research

*When you cannot measure, your knowledge is meager and
unsatisfactory.*

–Lord Kelvin

**THE ROLE OF SOUND
MEASUREMENT**
  Measurement as a Foundation for
  Research
  Levels of Measurement
**OPERATIONAL DEFINITIONS
AND MEASURES**

The Requirement of Reliability
The Requirement of Validity
**POPULAR TOOLS OF
MEASUREMENT**
  Methods to Measure Judgments
  Methods to Measure Achievement

BEFORE WE GET STARTED ...

In communication research, if you can't measure variables of interest, it is difficult to investigate communication. Researchers are expected to describe the measurements they use and to provide evidence that the measures are good ones. This
chapter describes how variables are measured, how evidence of good measurement
is provided, and popular tools you will find in communication studies.

THE ROLE OF SOUND MEASUREMENT

The ways researchers identify and measure variables in empirical research are important factors in determining the integrity of a study. It is almost a cliché to say
that our conclusions are only as good as our data. Yet, there is much wisdom in
this statement. If researchers have sound and accurate data, they can draw meaningful conclusions. Poor measurement produces studies for which only weak
claims can be drawn.

Measurement as a Foundation for Research

measurement error
creates attenuation
of results

Another reason researchers cannot live with poor measurement is that less-than-accurate measurement works against researchers—it never works in their favor. The reason for this fact is that measurement imperfections introduce additional variation or background noise into a study in addition to variation that already exists in samples. Thus, relationships that truly exist in the data may get lost in the background noise. This problem is called **attenuation** of results and means that there is a reduction of the size of observed effects because of errors in measurement. The imperfect measurement of variables, then, creates a bias against the researcher's finding of relationships (even if they really exist in the population).

Levels of Measurement

Measurement involves assigning numbers to variables according to some system. It is important to understand the many ways in which these numbers can be assigned because the levels of measurement dictate the sorts of statistical tools that can be used to analyze data.

nominal level
measurement
defined

- **Nominal level measurement.** The term "nominal" comes from the Latin word *nomen,* which means "name." Hence, nominal level measurement uses numbers as simple identifications of variables. Numbers are used to identify or "name" categories. Numbers on football jerseys are examples of nominal level measurement since the numbers are used just to name the players. Studies that compare men to women, stutterers and nonstutterers, speeches with evidence to speeches without evidence, or newspapers to television broadcasts all use the nominal level of measurement. One could assign numbers to each category (such as calling men "category 1" and women "category 2"), but the numbers are only labels for the categories. There is no measure of the *degree* to which a variable is present. Nominal level measurement often is called the lowest level of measurement because it uses numbers to identify categories. You might suppose that nominal level measurement is of limited use to researchers. But you should avoid this judgment. Experiments take nominal categories (an experimental group vs. a control group) and check for effects on an output variable.

ordinal level
measurement
defined

- **Ordinal level measurement** uses rank order to determine differences. Thus, if you were ranking a speech competition, you could rank the best speaker as "number 1," the second best as "number 2," the third best as "number 3," and so forth. But this method would not tell you *how much* of a difference existed between speakers. Thus, you might wish to add a rating scale to evaluate the speakers.

interval level
measurement
defined

- **Interval level measurement** identifies items as a matter of degree. "Specifically, the intervals between the numbers are *equal* in size" [Cozby, 1989, p. 149]. Most exams you have taken fall into this category. Most rating scales tend to be interval data as well.

ratio level
measurement defined

- **Ratio level measurement** extends interval measurement to include an "absolute zero." An absolute zero means that a score of 0 indicates that the property measured is completely absent. For instance, if you measured your weight, you would have ratio level measurement since a score of 0 would mean that you had no weight at all. Suppose you got up one morning and the outdoor temperature were 0 degrees Fahrenheit. Would that number mean indicate "no temperature" outside? Of course not—even though it might feel like it. But 0 on the Kelvin scale is the complete absence of heat since, among other things, electrons will not spin at 0 Kelvin.

Interval and ratio levels of measurement allow us to use meaningful arithmetic to examine data. Even so, some writers have been suspicious that most popular measurement tools actually use scales with equal intervals (Stevens, 1951). Yet, when other researchers (e.g., Baker, Hardyck & Petrinovich, 1966) have studied the impact of violating assumptions of pure intervals on statistical analyses, the alleged difficulties were found to be trivial. At least, we can follow the lead of scholars who have decided to call most of our popular tools "quasi-interval" measures (Hopkins & Glass, 1978, p. 13), because they act enough like interval measures to permit using statistical tools designed for them.

many of our measures are "quasi-interval"

It should be mentioned that measurement levels depend on the available tools. For instance, a speaker's voice pitch could be identified in simple nominal categories (speakers with high pitched voices and speakers with low pitched voices) or voice pitch could be measured by using an oscilloscope to identify ratio level cycles. In factorial experimental (and descriptive) designs, researchers often start with interval level variables and then group them down into nominal level categories. For instance, groups of highly intelligent and lowly intelligent people might be created out of a sample that originally measured everybody's I.Q. on an interval scale. Thus, measurement levels are often determined by the methods researchers choose.

researchers often collapse variables into lower levels of measurement

OPERATIONAL DEFINITIONS AND MEASURES

Once researchers have chosen variables to study, they select operational definitions for them. To determine if prudent selections have been made, two interrelated characteristics must be demonstrated for the operational definitions: reliability and validity.

The Requirement of Reliability

As a standard requirement in scholarly journals, empirical researchers are expected to produce evidence that their measures are reliable.

Defining Reliability

Reliability is the internal consistency of a measure. A consistent measure should tend to produce the same measurements over time. Thus, reliability is really a test of the stability of a measure. Unreliability can be introduced many ways. Items on a measure may be inconsistent because they are vague, confusing, or simply irrelevant to common concepts. But individuals who take a test can also introduce sources of unreliability. Bruce Tuckman explained (1978):

reliability defined

> Among the factors which contribute to the unreliability of a test are (1) familiarity with the particular test form (such as a multiple choice question), (2) fatigue, (3) emotional strain, (4) physical conditions of the room in which the test is given,

ways unreliability is introduced

SPECIAL DISCUSSION 12–1
The Fallacy of Misplaced Precision

Researchers know that the results of a study can only be as good as the data themselves. But some researchers may claim precision that goes beyond the data. Sometimes labeled "false precision" (Kaplan, 1964, p. 204), the basic idea is that researchers claim more precision in analyzing data than was present in the original data.

Suppose a researcher collects data from 500 people to find out how they feel about the statement: "Third-party candidates should not be elected U.S. president." Subjects may give their reactions on five point scales ranging from "strongly disagree" (scored as 1) to "strongly agree" (scored as 5). The researcher might report an average response in absurd detail. He or she might find that the average response was 4.26667. But, in reality, this precision is bogus since the original rating system was only a 1 to 5 scale. Carrying out general data to incredibly precise points is meaningless. It is false precision because the numbers researchers compute cannot be better than the data themselves.

So what should researchers do? One school of thought holds that researchers should round back to the level of precision in the original data. But this method may introduce great rounding error when other statistics are computed from the data. A second method advises carrying out computations no more than two digits beyond the level of precision in the original measures. In the example above, the researcher could carry out computations no more than two decimal places, thus, reporting an average of 4.27. Researchers are warned to avoid the temptation to commit the fallacy of misplaced precision.

(5) health of the test taker, (6) fluctuations of human memory, (7) amount of practice or experience by the test taker of the specific skill being measured, and (8) specific knowledge that has been gained outside of the experience being evaluated by the test. A test which is overly sensitive to these unpredictable (and often uncontrollable) sources of error is not a reliable test. Test unreliability creates *instrumentation bias,* a source of internal invalidity in an experiment (p. 161).

For the most part, standardized tests—such as I.Q. tests, personality tests, and placement tests sold by commercial testing firms—have been examined for reliability. The tests are often accompanied by reports and manuals that describe how such reliability has been established. Though there is controversy about the accuracy or validity of some of these measures, there has been enough evidence to permit researchers to use them.

Assessing Reliability

Researchers can determine a measure's reliability several ways. Despite differences, it is helpful to realize that all the methods discussed below are comparable. The methods really differ in their data collection methods, rather than in the sorts of information they provide. All these methods take information about the consistency of a measure with itself and compute a **reliability coefficient.** This coefficient actually is a correlation, which measures the amount of association or coincidence of things. Without getting into the details here, let it suffice to say that a reliability coefficient can range from 0 (no reliability) to 1 (perfect reliability). But you will not see many coefficients of 0 or 1. Instead, you will see numbers with decimal points, such as .82, .91, or .77. A measure with *really* good consistency will have reliability of .9 or higher. A good measure may have reliability in the .80 to .89 range. A fair measure should have reliability of at least .7. As a matter of publication policy, the American Psychological Association has decided that tests with coefficients below .6 should not be analyzed in studies.

reliability coefficients identified and interpreted

methods to assess reliability

- **Test-retest** reliability involves giving the measure twice and reporting consistency between scores. If a measure is consistent, then people should have pretty much the same scores both times. Of course, people can change from one testing time to another. But a reliable test should give tolerably consistent results from one occasion to the next. An audiometer used in speech and hearing science might be tested one week against standard pitches. The next week the process might be repeated. If the observed pitch drifted, this degree of unreliability might be noted and an adjustment made in the machine. Test-retest reliability is time-consuming since two data collections are involved. But this method often is useful when measures contain single items or when test items combine matters that are largely independent of others on the same measure.
- **Alternate forms** reliability involves constructing different forms of the same test from a common pool of measurement items. Then, the different forms are given to the *same* group of people. If the forms show consistency, then the scores on one form should be close to scores on the alternate form. You may remember taking standard achievement tests in high school or before attending college. You may have noticed that the tests had different forms (such as Form A, Form B, and Form C) so that people sitting next to each other did not have the same test. Professional test designers often combine alternate-forms reliability with other reliability methods.
- **Split half** reliability divides a test into two parts, scores them separately, and checks the consistency between the two scores. You might suppose that researchers with a forty-item true-false test create halves by scoring the first twenty items as one test and the second twenty items as the second test. But they don't. People may become fatigued near the end of a test and score worse than they did on the first part. So, researchers often create halves by scoring the even-numbered items as one test and the odd-numbered items as the other test. Hence, sometimes this method is called odd-even reliability.
- **Item to total** computes the correlation of items with the total test. If you take an exam in research methods and answer the first test question correctly, then you would expect to get a higher overall test score than

somebody who got the first answer wrong. There should be a high correspondence or correlation between your score on a test *item* and your score on the *total* test. Using this method, researchers drop unreliable items and keep the remaining test (often recomputing reliability). Under what circumstances could your score on a test item not correlate at all (0) with the total? That's exactly zero—no rounding. There are two ways such a thing is possible: either everybody passed the item or everybody failed it. In either case, your score on that item would give no information about whether you did well or poorly on the test as a whole. Sometimes a test item is related inversely with the total test score. This condition means that if you pass an item you are likely to get a lower score on the rest of the test than did someone who failed the item. These sorts of test items must be measuring something completely apart from the rest of the test. Therefore, researchers automatically delete them from their final measures.

Cohen's kappa and Scott's pi for reliability of content analysis categories

- **Intercoder reliability** takes a slightly different approach to reliability. Sometimes people will look at behavior and categorize it by using some sort of check sheet. The basic question becomes, "Do different people rate things the same way?" If a researcher completes a content analysis of communication, the check sheet categories can be examined for reliability. Though several forms have been used, prudent researchers tend to rely on either Cohen's *kappa* (Cohen, 1960), which compensates for the number of times rating categories are used, or Scott's *pi* (Scott, 1955), which also compensates for the rates of agreement that would be expected by chance alone. Table 12.1A illustrates the use of Scott's *pi* with a typical example. Though this example involves a case of two coders, the formula can be extended to any number of coders (see Fleiss, 1971). This method permits researchers to identify how reliably content analysis check sheets are used to code communication. Since Cohen's *kappa* involves some cumbersome computation, it is not included in this introductory treatment (a good review of these methods is found in Fleiss, 1981).

K-R 20 identified for tests with correct or incorrect answers

- **Statistical shortcuts** are not really different forms of reliability. They are simply ways to get reliability coefficients rapidly, especially when major computer programs are used. You should remember, however, that these tools are mathematically equivalent and can be interpreted similarly.[1] Two options are most often used. As table 12.1B shows, one tool is called **K-R 20**, which is shorthand for Kuder-Richardson formula 20 for reliability. This method is used when researchers want to determine the reliability of a measure with items scored as "correct" or "incorrect" answers. Most in-class exams and tests of comprehension and skills use this sort of method for reliability. But suppose we measure perceptions or ratings that people may have—such as attitudes, self-esteem, ratings of speech intelligibility, or ratings of newspaper sensationalism. Although under these conditions there is no "correct" answer, the consistency with which people react to the items on the measure may be tapped by using **Cronbach's coefficient alpha** (α) (Cronbach, 1970, p. 160–61)[2] as illustrated in table 12.1C.

coefficient alpha

TABLE 12.1 Statistical Reliability Formulae

A. Intercoder reliability for content analysis or diagnostic categories: (Scott's *pi*)
Formula

$$pi = \frac{\text{proportion observed agreement} - \text{proportion expected agreement}}{1 - \text{proportion expected agreement}}$$

where:

proportion observed agreement = $\dfrac{(\text{number of raters}) \times (\text{number of same ratings made})}{\text{total number of ratings by all raters}}$

proportion expected agreement = sum of the squared proportions in each category

EXAMPLE: Coders rated the proportion of violence in children's TV programs observed during a two-week period. They reported the proportion of agreement among themselves at .80 (leave in the decimal point). The violence was categorized into five categories:

threatening violence	.40
punching others	.10
slapping	.30
using weapons	.10
off-screen violence	.10

$$pi = \frac{\text{proportion observed agreement} - \text{proportion expected agreement}}{1 - \text{proportion expected agreement}}$$

$$= \frac{.80 - (.40^2 + .10^2 + .30^2 + .10^2 + .10^2)}{1 - (.40^2 + .10^2 + .30^2 + .10^2 + .10^2)}$$

$$= \frac{.80 - (.28)}{1 - (.28)}$$

$$= \frac{.52}{.72}$$

$$pi = .72$$

B. K-R 20: used when a test deals with "correct" and "incorrect" answers
Formula

$$\text{K-R 20} = \frac{k}{k-1} * \left(\frac{1 - \text{sum of P * Q of each test item}}{s^2 \text{ of the total test score}} \right)$$

where:

k = the number of items on the test
P = the proportion (keep the decimal point in) of people who answered the item correctly
Q = the proportion (keep the decimal point in) of people who answered the item incorrectly
s^2 = the variance (a measure of variability [see ch. 13])

EXAMPLE: A measure of retention of information in radio ads was assessed by use of a five-item true-false test. The first item was answered correctly (P) by 70% of the people, the second item was passed by 65%, the third

TABLE 12.1—*Continued*

item was passed by 50%, the fourth item was passed by 60%, and the last item was passed by 80%. The variance of the total test was 2.4.

$$= \quad \frac{k}{k-1} * \left(1 - \frac{\text{sum of P} * \text{Q of each test item}}{s^2 \text{ of the total test score}} \right)$$

$$= \quad \frac{s}{5-1} * \left(1 - \frac{(.7 * .3) + (.65 * .35) + (.50 * .50) + (.60 * .40) + (.80 * .20)}{2.4} \right)$$

$$= \quad 1.25 * \left(1 - \frac{(.21) + (.23) + (.25) + (.24) + (.16)}{2.4} \right)$$

$$= \quad 1.25 * \left(1 - \frac{1.09}{2.4} \right)$$

$$= \quad 1.25 * (1 - .45)$$
$$= \quad 1.25 * (.55)$$
$$\text{K-R 20} = \quad .69$$

C. Coefficient alpha: used when a test does not have "correct" and "incorrect" answers

Formula

$$\alpha \quad = \quad \frac{k}{k-1} * 1 - \left(\frac{\text{sum of } s^2 \text{ of each test item}}{s^2 \text{ of the total test score}} \right)$$

where:
  k = the number of items on the test
  s^2 = the variance (a measure of variability [see ch. 13])
EXAMPLE: A measure of speech fluency on a rating scale containing five seven-point scales. The variance for the first scale item was 3.2, the variance for the second item was 3, the variance for the third item was 3.8, the variance for the fourth item was 2.5, and the variance for the fifth item was 3.4. The variance of the total test was 38.

$$= \quad \frac{k}{k-1} * \left(1 - \frac{\text{sum of } s^2 \text{ of each test item}}{s^2 \text{ of the total test score}} \right)$$

$$= \quad \frac{5}{5-1} * \left(1 - \frac{3.2 + 3 + 3.8 + 2.5 + 3.4}{38} \right)$$

$$= \quad 1.25 * \left(1 - \frac{15.9}{38} \right)$$

$$= \quad 1.25 * (1 - .42)$$
$$= \quad 1.25 * (.58)$$
$$= \quad .73$$

James C. McCroskey, *An Introduction to Rhetorical Communication,* 4th ed. (Englewood Cliffs, NJ: Prentice-Hall, 1982). Used with permission of James C. McCroskey.

Reliability is computed for measures that deal with the same dimension. But how do researchers know if test items really represent only one dimension or many? Factor analysis is a commonly used statistical method that helps "the researcher discover and identify the unities or dimensions, called factors, behind many measures" (Kerlinger, 1986, p. 138). Largely because convenient computer programs are widespread, researchers routinely report results of factor analyses for scales as part of their reports of measurement reliability.

Though factor analysis has many complicated applications and some detailed math, when the method is used in measurement, researchers follow a rather consistent pattern. Factor analysis begins with a researcher giving the measure of interest to a group of subjects. Then, all the items on the measure are correlated with each other (sometimes using alternatives to correlations). Items that tend to be highly interrelated are identified as measuring common dimensions.

As a second step, factor analysis mathematically extracts chief factors underlying the larger number of measures. Though there are other options, the most common method is the principal components solution, which attempts to identify the number of common centers of variation that underlie the manifest variables. If one factor emerges as the center of variation for a set of test items, then the test items appear to measure that one dimension. If two factors are found, the test items would appear to measure two different things. If three factors emerge, three dimensions would appear to underlie the test items. For each emerging factor, the association of the test items to the common factor is identified by a set of "item loadings" that reveal how closely the items are related to each factor.

As a third step, the factors are interpreted. To help interpret factor loadings, the factors are "rotated" (contrary to popular confusion about the matter, "rotation" does not affect the factor analysis solution but is only an aid to interpret factors). Rotations are usually made orthogonally so that the nature of factor loadings can be identified with greatest separation (i.e., a 90 degree rotation system is used). Next, one decides what each factor really measures (if no theory is otherwise ready to guide the researcher). The item loadings are checked to see which ones "load" or "define" each factor. As a protocol of sorts, researchers usually interpret rotated item scores as loaded on a factor if the item has a score of at least .60 and no loading on another factor of .40 or greater. The following example shows a typical loading pattern:

	Factor I	Factor II
Test Item 1	.80	.18
Test Item 2	.77	.22
Test Item 3	.45	.45
Test Item 4	.31	.66
Test Item 5	.28	.71
Test Item 6	.44	.62

As can be seen, items one and two measure factor one, and items four and five measure factor two. These two dimensions are to be scored as separate measures for which reliability is assessed. By examining available theory and the properties shared in common by items on each factor, the researcher identifies an appropriate label to use to refer to the scores produced on each factor.

The Requirement of Validity

Imagine that you had a stairway in your home. If the stairway were not firm and stable, you would not get to your destination because the stairs would become shaky when you tried to stand on them. That's an example of an unreliable stairway. When a measure is unreliable, it is unstable, and you can't use it to get where you want to go. Now, suppose the stairway were sturdy. It would be reliable and you could use it the same way every time you walked on it. But if the carpenters built it to lead to the roof, rather than to the upstairs rooms, it could not get you where you wanted to go. This stairway is not a valid path to the upstairs rooms because it is pointed in the wrong direction. That's the notion of reliability and validity in a nutshell: reliability means the measure is stable; validity means the stable test truly measures what you intend.

Validity Defined

validity defined

Validity is the consistency of a measure with a criterion. In plain terms, it is the degree to which a measure actually measures what is claimed.[3] Reliability is determined by looking at the *internal* consistency of a measure. But looking at internal consistency will not reveal if a measure is "pointed in the right direction." To assess validity, researchers need *external* evidence to believe that they are measuring what they intended. Thus, we say that validity is the consistency of a measure with some outside criterion or standard by which to judge the test.

Reliability versus Validity

validity presumes reliability

As you can tell, it is possible to have a reliable test without having a valid one (you can have a stable stairway that does not go where you intended). But you cannot have a valid measure without its first being reliable. Thus, validity presumes reliability. Hence if a person has a valid test, that person is telling us that the measure is also reliable.

Assessing Validity

methods to assess validity

There are four major ways to determine validity, though researchers usually combine some of them to argue for their measures. Each of the major methods is discussed below.

Face validity involves researchers looking at the content of the measurement items and advancing an argument that, on its face, the measure seems to identify what it claims. Though this form of validation lacks additional empirical evidence as support, sometimes arguments about content can be quite reasonable. This method is the most common approach taken by researchers to argue the validity of their measures. It is limited, however, by the absence of additional evidence and, of course, by the reasoning powers of the researcher.

Expert jury validity involves having a group of experts on the subject matter examine the measurement device and judge its merit. Researchers sometimes list the number of positive assessments received from the experts. But most often, experts offer advice to help the researcher improve measurement tools. Thus, expert juries frequently are consulted to help develop measures. As a method of validation, the expert jury method is actually face validity that involves additional people.

Criterion validity consists of two methods that assess a measure's worth by examining its relation to some outside criterion.

- **Concurrent validity** correlates a new measure with a previously validated measure of the same thing. This method is commonly used when a traditional research area is extended with updated measures. For example, Brinberg and his associates (1980) validated their measure of ''interpersonal attraction'' by concurrent validity with Donn Byrne's ''Interpersonal Judgment Scale'' (1971).
- **Predictive validity** is the degree to which a measure predicts known groups in which the construct must exist. Thus, if you were developing a measure of people's tendency to self-disclose private information about themselves, you might find a group of people and see if this test predicts whether self-disclosure actually occurs. Rubin and Shenker (1978) used this technique to show that their self-disclosure scale successfully predicted whether college students' roommates actually heard any self-disclosures. If you developed an instrument to measure successful sales communication, you might find a group of successful salespeople and a group of not-so-successful salespeople. After administering the test to both groups, you could see if it distinguished between the two known groups. If so, then a claim of predictive validity could be made.

Construct validity studies are among the most impressive works in communication research. Construct validation requires that a new measure be administered to subjects along with at least two other measures. One of these measures should be a valid measure of a construct that is known conceptually to be directly related to the new measure (that is, as scores on the new measure increase, scores on the related construct should also increase). For instance, ''if a physiological measure of heartbeat is supposed to be indicative of communication anxiety, then it would be reasonable to expect people in high stress communication situations to have more rapid heartbeats (higher measured communication anxiety) than would be expected of people in low stress communication settings'' (Emmert, 1989, p. 114). Another of these measures should be a valid measure of a construct known conceptually to be inversely related to the new measure (that is, as scores on the new measure *increase,* scores on the related construct should *decrease*).[4] If the new measure is valid, it should produce significant findings in the correct directions. Obviously, the conceptual bases for the measures must be very well understood and the theoretic foundations clear. Such studies are not easy and they are major inquiries in and of themselves. One influential effort was completed by James McCroskey (1978) to validate the ''Personal Report of Communication Apprehension'' (also known as the PRCA).[5] Since communication apprehension is one's ''fear or anxiety associated with either real or anticipated (oral) communication with another person or persons'' (McCroskey, 1977, p. 78), he isolated a valid measure of ''verbal reticence,'' which was known to have a direct relationship with communication apprehension. He also found valid measures of three constructs that were known to have theoretically inverse relationships with communication apprehension: extroversion, self-esteem, and self-acceptance. When all the measures were administered, the patterns were as predicted. Though it does not always work out so well for researchers, construct validation was completed for the PRCA, and it has become a very popular research tool.

POPULAR TOOLS OF MEASUREMENT

Two major techniques for measurement that have been popular in our field are measures that express judgments of some kind and measures that identify achievement.

Methods to Measure Judgments

Communication researchers often ask people to report their attitudes or rate some behavior. These judgments can be measured in many ways, but the most popular tools in communication have been Thurstone scales, Likert scales, Guttman scales, and semantic differential-type scales.

Thurstone Equal Appearing Interval Scales

Thurstone scales identified

Named for their creator, L. L. Thurstone, these scales are actually called equal appearing interval scales. They are composed of statements related to some topic. For instance, if you wanted to rate the bias in newspaper coverage of political campaigns, you might have a Thurstone scale with statements such as: "Newspapers are very biased," "Newspapers do not tell the truth," and "Newspapers have a hard time being impartial." Respondents are asked to indicate which statements they agree with. Then, unbeknownst to the subjects, a total score is determined by adding up the point values for each of the statements with which subjects agreed. Getting the point values is the time-consuming part. The researcher typically puts together a list of 50 to 100 statements (on cards) and then asks a group of people (from the population who later will use the scales) to sort the cards on a scale ranging from 1 to 11, indicating how extreme the statements are. For instance, the statement "Newspapers are very biased" is more extreme than the statement "Newspapers have a hard time being impartial." So, these statements would be placed at different locations on the scale. After the raters are finished, the researcher identifies statements that have consistent ratings. These statements are given an average score based on their ratings. When using the scales in a later study, the researcher simply tallies up the total points of the statements with which each person agreed. Table 12.2 shows such a scale.

applications, advantages, and limitations

The method is quite sound and is used in many communication studies. Researchers who study effects of stress on communication often use a Thurstone rating scale of stressful life events (Reinard & Boster, 1978). Subjects receive a total stress score by adding up the points associated with the events that they report happening to them in the recent past. Yet, the method can often be tedious, time-consuming, and expensive. The scales also must be done anew every time the topic of evaluation is changed.

Likert Scales

This technique consists of statements that reflect clear positions on an issue and then asking subjects to indicate their responses on 1 to 5 point scales: Strongly Agree, Agree, Neither Agree nor Disagree, Disagree, Disagree Strongly. A few researchers use four point scales, leaving out the middle position entirely. Occasionally researchers have added additional scale positions (Disagree Slightly and Agree Slightly), but the basic system is not defined by the number of points used. Instead, items that have high reliability with each other are combined by adding up the ratings that respondents give. Unlike Thurstone scales, which assign a value for each item with which a person agrees, Likert scales simply gauge the degree to which there is agreement or disagreement with statements representing a common issue.

      You have probably filled out Likert scales on teacher evaluation forms and on other surveys in your classes. These scales are very popular because of the ease of developing them (a researcher can determine reliability at the same time the data are collected, for instance). Yet, a total score sometimes hides specific details of the response from a person. Moreover, if researchers change their topics, the items on the Likert scale may have to be composed all over again.

Likert scales distinguished

applications, advantages, and limitations

Guttman Scalogram

Developed by Louis Guttman, this scale involves a series of statements dealing with one topic and arranged according to their level of intensity. Surely the most popular Guttman scale has been the Bogardus "Social Distance" scale (see table 12.2). This scale often has been featured in studies on racial and ethnic prejudice. The more prejudice a person has, the reasoning goes, the fewer circumstances this person would find acceptable. Because the statements are arranged on a single continuum, if we know the number of statements with which a person agreed, we probably also know which statements the person accepted. For instance, if a respondent rated it acceptable for a person to have employment in one's profession, that respondent also probably would find it acceptable for the target person to be a citizen in the country and to visit the country. Thus, the number of statements with which a person agrees also probably lets us know *which* particular statements they were.

      The Guttman scale is scored by counting the number of statements with which a respondent agrees. In our example the fewer items circled, the more "socially distant" the respondent is from others. Of course, some people may not follow a set pattern in their responses. Thus, Guttman developed a criterion called the "coefficient of reproducibility" to assess the reliability of these scalograms. To compute a coefficient of reproducibility, the researcher arranges the statements according to the most frequently agreed to items in a sample through the least frequently agreed to items. Then the researcher looks at each subject's total score to count the proportion of the time that the respondent answered as expected. That is, if people agreed with three statements, they should have answered the three most frequently accepted statements. Any time an answer appears outside the predicted pattern, an exception is noted. Guttman recommended that consistent responses be observed at least 90 percent of the time, or a coefficient of reproducibility of .90.[6]

Guttman scales distinguished

scoring

use of the coefficient of reproducibility

TABLE 12.2 Examples of Rating Scales

Thurstone Scales

Place a check mark in the blank next to each statement with which you agree.
_____ 1. This class in research methods is more challenging than other courses I am taking this term. (9.8)
_____ 2. This class in research methods teaches me valuable information. (10.1)
_____ 3. This class in research methods is what I expected. (6.0)
_____ 4. This class in research methods provides interesting, valuable information. (8.9)

NOTE: Numbers in parentheses indicate the point value for each statement. The scale is scored by adding the points for all items with which the respondent indicated agreement.

Semantic Differential-type Scales

Rate the concept "The President" according to the way you perceive it or feel about it by placing an X on each of the seven point scales to indicate your evaluation.

The President

reliable	___ : ___ : ___ : ___ : ___ : ___ : ___	unreliable*
uninformed	___ : ___ : ___ : ___ : ___ : ___ : ___	informed
unqualified	___ : ___ : ___ : ___ : ___ : ___ : ___	qualified
intelligent	___ : ___ : ___ : ___ : ___ : ___ : ___	unintelligent*
valuable	___ : ___ : ___ : ___ : ___ : ___ : ___	worthless*
expert	___ : ___ : ___ : ___ : ___ : ___ : ___	inexpert
honest	___ : ___ : ___ : ___ : ___ : ___ : ___	dishonest*
unfriendly	___ : ___ : ___ : ___ : ___ : ___ : ___	friendly
pleasant	___ : ___ : ___ : ___ : ___ : ___ : ___	unpleasant*
selfish	___ : ___ : ___ : ___ : ___ : ___ : ___	unselfish
awful	___ : ___ : ___ : ___ : ___ : ___ : ___	nice
virtuous	___ : ___ : ___ : ___ : ___ : ___ : ___	sinful

NOTE: Items followed by asterisks (*) indicate reverse scoring. Scores on the first six items are added together to produce a "competence" score. The remaining items are added together to produce a "character" score.
Source: McCroskey, J. C. (1966). Scales for the measurement of ethos. *Speech Monographs, 33,* 72. Copyright by Speech Communication Association. Reprinted by permission of the publisher and James C. McCroskey.

Guttman Scale

Consider a person who is Chinese, and circle the number next to each of the situations listed below in which you would accept a person from this group.
1. as a visitor to my country
2. to citizenship in my country
3. to employment in my occupation
4. to my street as a neighbor
5. to my club as a personal friend
6. to close kinship by marriage

NOTE: This scale is an adapted version of the Bogardus Social Distance scale (Bogardus, 1933). The number of items circled is the score received by the individual.

TABLE 12.2—*Continued*

Likert Scale

Personal Report of Communication Apprehension (PRCA-24)

Directions: This instrument is composed of 24 statements concerning your feelings about communication with other people. Please indicate in the space provided the degree to which each statement applies to you by marking whether you (1) Strongly Agree, (2) Agree, (3) Are Undecided, (4) Disagree, or (5) Strongly Disagree with each statement. There are no right or wrong answers. Many of the statements are similar to other statements. Do not be concerned about this. Work quickly, just record your first impression.

_____ 1. I dislike participating in group discussions.
_____ 2. Generally, I am comfortable while participating in a group discussion.
_____ 3. I am tense and nervous while participating in group discussions.
_____ 4. I like to get involved in group discussions.
_____ 5. Engaging in a group discussion with new people makes me tense and nervous.
_____ 6. I am calm and relaxed while participating in group discussions.
_____ 7. Generally, I am nervous when I have to participate in a meeting.
_____ 8. Usually I am calm and relaxed while participating in meetings.
_____ 9. I am very calm and relaxed when I am called upon to express an opinion at a meeting.
_____ 10. I am afraid to express myself at meetings.
_____ 11. Communicating at meetings usually makes me uncomfortable.
_____ 12. I am very relaxed when answering questions at a meeting.
_____ 13. While participating in a conversation with a new acquaintance, I feel very nervous.
_____ 14. I have no fear of speaking up in conversations.
_____ 15. Ordinarily I am very tense and nervous in conversations.
_____ 16. Ordinarily I am very calm and relaxed in conversations.
_____ 17. While conversing with a new acquaintance, I feel very relaxed.
_____ 18. I'm afraid to speak up in conversations.
_____ 19. I have no fear of giving a speech.
_____ 20. Certain parts of my body feel very tense and rigid while giving a speech.
_____ 21. I feel relaxed while giving a speech.
_____ 22. My thoughts become confused and jumbled when I am giving a speech.
_____ 23. I face the prospect of giving a speech with confidence.
_____ 24. While giving a speech I get so nervous, I forget facts I really know.

SCORING
Group = 18 − (1) + (2) − (3) + (4) − (5) + (6)
Meeting = 18 − (7) + (8) + (9) − (10) − (11) + (12)
Dyadic = 18 − (13) + (14) − (15) + (16) + (17) − (18)
Public = 18 + (19) − (20) + (21) − (22) + (23) − (24)
Overall CA = Group + Meeting + Dyadic + Public

applications,
advantages, and
limitations

This scaling method is highly useful when there is a clear continuum of responses that people could make on some issue. Yet, the stringent requirements for such a scale may make it challenging to come up with new Guttman scales. Furthermore, they are specific to topics and must be developed from scratch each time a new topic is investigated.

Semantic Differential-type Scales

semantic
differential-type
scales distinguished

In 1957, Charles Osgood, George Suci, and Percy Tannenbaum wrote *The Measurement of Meaning* in which they reported their efforts to determine how people assign meaning to words. To help them along the way, they developed a scale that involved using pairs of adjectives (often separated by seven points, sometimes six, sometimes five) that could be used by people to indicate their reactions (see table 12.2). Since they were studying semantics (the study of the relationship between words and their meanings), they called their scale the ''semantic differential.'' The method became popular among researchers who were not studying semantics. Thus, applications of these scales to other subjects resulted in semantic differential-*type* scales.

This scale method has become the most popular measurement approach in communication studies. An object of evaluation is presented to people who indicate their responses by checking or circling scale positions. A total score is obtained by assigning values from 1 to 7 to each item and simply adding up items on the same dimension. To measure a concept—such as competence or character perceptions of a source—researchers use a set of adjective pairs. Then they use standard tools to show reliability for the items used to measure each common dimension.

applications,
advantages, and
limitations

This method is very convenient to use and, unlike other tools, can be employed almost regardless of the topic under evaluation. For instance, the same scales can be used to assess credibility of any source. The researcher need not construct new scales to evaluate each different source. Yet, the responses on each dimension give only a composite reaction, rather than information about the contours of responses. For instance, suppose a person received a score of 16 on four semantic differential-type scales. The person might have ''flip-flopped'' from one extreme positive position to an extreme negative position and back again. Or, the score might have emerged if the person neither agreed nor disagreed on all items. A simple total may miss such differences in response patterns. Overall, however, the method seems to have gained popularity because of its great versatility.

Methods to Measure Achievement

Researchers often want to obtain data on achievement or knowledge of some content. The formats for measuring such information provide a repertoire that researchers can use. On one level, achievement or knowledge of content can be tested by such methods as true-false or multiple-choice tests. Sometimes researchers give respondents questions that request them to choose between two alternatives. Called the ''forced choice format,'' the researcher gives subjects two statements, one of which they must choose. This method is useful to help identify how individuals make choices, but sometimes the choices are difficult for respondents to complete accurately (Hale, Boster, & Mongeau, 1991).

A variation of sorts is the paired-comparison method, in which subjects receive alternatives with all possible combinations given two at a time. This method is invaluable for ranking alternatives that may seem to have a great overlap in quality. If you were asked to rank a list of ten newspapers for general credibility, it might be difficult to do the rating all at once. Instead, you could be given two newspapers and asked to choose which of the two is the most credible. Then all other combinations would follow, a pair at a time. The final ranking could be found by counting the number of times each paper was preferred.

SUMMARY

Accurate measurement is vital to sound research. Measurement imperfections introduce additional variation or background noise into a study in addition to variation that already exists in samples. This problem is called attenuation of results, which means that there is a reduction of the size of observed effects because of errors in measurement. There are four levels of measurement for data: (1) nominal level uses numbers as simple identification of variables; (2) ordinal level uses rank order to determine differences; (3) interval level identifies items as a matter of degree (the intervals between the numbers are equal in size); and (4) ratio level extends interval measurement to include an ''absolute zero'' (in which a score of 0 indicates that the property measured is completely absent).

Reliability is the internal consistency of a measure. There are several ways researchers can determine a measure's reliability. All these methods take information about the consistency of a measure with itself and compute a reliability coefficient, which is a correlation that measures the amount of association or coincidence of things. Test-retest reliability involves giving the measure twice and reporting consistency between scores (this method is time-consuming but often useful when measures contain single items or when test items combine matters that are largely independent of others on the same measure). Alternate forms reliability involves constructing different forms of the same test from a common pool of measurement items and correlating scores that sample groups receive on both. Split half reliability divides a test into two parts, scores them separately, and checks the consistency between the two scores for a sample group (often this method employs odd-even reliability). Item to total reliability computes the correlation of items with the total test. Intercoder reliability examines the degree to which different raters consistently categorize things by using some sort of check sheet (in content analysis of communication, prudent researchers tend to rely on either Cohen's *kappa,* which compensates for the number of times rating categories are used, or Scott's *pi,* which also compensates for the rates of agreement that would be expected by chance alone). Statistical shortcuts are ways to get reliability coefficients rapidly using such methods as K-R 20 (used when researchers want to determine the reliability of a measure that has items that are scored as ''correct'' or ''incorrect'') or coefficient alpha (when correct answers are not identified).

Validity is the consistency of a measure with a criterion. In plain terms, validity is the degree to which a measure actually measures what is claimed. Though it is possible to have a reliable test without having a valid one, one cannot have a valid measure without its first being reliable. Thus, validity presumes reliability. There are four major ways to determine validity. Face validity involves researchers looking at the content of the measurement items and advancing an argument that, on its face, the measure seems to identify what it claimed. Expert jury validity involves having a group of experts on the subject matter examine the, measurement device and judge its merit. Criterion validity assesses a measure's worth by examining its relation to some outside criterion, such as concurrent validity (which correlates a new measure with a previously validated measure of the same thing), and predictive validity (which is the degree to which a measure predicts known groups in which the construct must exist). Construct validation requires that a new measure be administered to subjects along with at least two other measures, one of which is known to be directly related to the concept and one of which is known to be inversely related to the concept (if the new measure is valid, it should produce significant findings in the correct directions).

Communication researchers often ask people to report their attitudes, or rate some behavior. The most popular measurement tools are Thurstone equal appearing interval scales (that assign point values for each of the statements with which subjects agree), Likert scales (that consist of statements for which subjects indicate their agreement or disagreement on 5-point scales); Guttman scalograms (involving a series of statements dealing with one topic and arranged according to their level of intensity); and semantic differential-type scales (seven point scales bounded by bipolar adjectives). Researchers often obtain data on achievement or knowledge of some content by using such formats as true-false or multiple-choice tests. Sometimes researchers give respondents forced-choice format items that request them to choose between two alternatives. A variation is the paired-comparison method, in which subjects receive alternatives in all possible combinations given two at a time.

TERMS FOR REVIEW

attenuation
nominal level measurement
ordinal level measurement
interval level measurement
ratio level measurement
reliability
reliability coefficient
intercoder reliability
test-retest
alternate-forms
split-half
item-to-total

K-R 20
coefficient alpha
validity
face validity
expert jury validity
concurrent validity
predictive validity
construct validity
Thurstone equal appearing interval scales
Likert scales
Guttman scalogram
semantic differential-type scales

NOTES

[1]An interesting fact about measurement is that the longer a test is, the more reliable it becomes. With increasing length, variation from item to item has an increased chance of balancing out. A mathematic proof of this relationship is called the Spearman-Brown prophecy formula. Thus, major statistical formulas for reliability tend to be "corrected" for test length so that comparisons of different measures can be made.

[2]Cronbach developed a shortcut formula called coefficient alpha$_k$ to deal with the reliability of tests that have correct and incorrect answers. In fact, as Cronbach explained (p. 161) this formula is the same as K-R 20. Similarly, Kuder and Richardson developed a formula called K-R 21, which is virtually the same as Cronbach's coefficient alpha. Yet, most researchers report coefficient alpha for measures *without* correct and incorrect answers and reserve K-R 20 for tests that include correct and incorrect answers.

[3]When discussing experimental design, "validity" referred to "experimental validity" or the soundness of research designs. In this chapter we are concerned with "measurement validity."

[4]Some researchers add a third variable known to be unrelated to the construct measured by the new instrument. Yet, most construct validation studies exclude this final comparison.

[5]This study actually relied on information from other published and unpublished works to make its case. Furthermore, a section on personality correlates is excluded from this description.

[6]The coefficient of reproducibility is computed by counting the number of "errors" and dividing by the total number of responses. Then this proportion is subtracted from 1.0. Originally Guttman (1944) stated that a coefficient of .90 was required for an acceptable scale. At a later time, Guttman permitted the scale to be used if the coefficient of reproducibility were .80 or higher, but the requirement of .9 has remained the most typical standard.

Statistical Analysis of Data

13

Descriptive Statistics

14

Introductory Inferential Statistics I: Hypothesis Testing with Two Means

15

Inferential Statistics II: Beyond Two Means

CHAPTER 13

Descriptive Statistics

Then there is the man who drowned crossing a stream with an average depth of six inches.

–W. I. E. Gates

STATISTICS IN COMMUNICATION RESEARCH
  Measures of Central Tendency
  Measures of Variability or
    Dispersion

DISTRIBUTIONS
  Non-normal and Skewed
    Distributions
  Standard Normal Distribution
MEASURES OF ASSOCIATION
  Interpreting Correlations
  Forms of Correlations

BEFORE WE GET STARTED . . .

Many students think that "research methods" is another term for statistics. But as you have seen, statistics are just tools used by scholars to understand information. In this chapter you will learn the language of descriptive statistics and the basic methods used to help characterize quantitative data. You will find that statistical analyses involve a lot of common sense. You do not have to remember your high school math to understand statistics. Instead, this chapter does not presume that you have any background in the subject.

STATISTICS IN COMMUNICATION RESEARCH

importance of
statistical
understanding

These days you cannot read the literature of the field without some basic knowledge of statistical tools. Thus, you must understand how to use different families of statistics because they are all around you. Furthermore, a knowledge of statistical tools allows you to think critically about research and to assess the worth of different studies.

There are two general types of statistics. **Descriptive statistics** consist of numbers that are designed to characterize information. Averages, variability, and correlations are examples of descriptions. The second type is called **inferential statistics** and refers to tools that help researchers draw conclusions about the probable populations from which samples did or did not belong. This chapter discusses descriptive statistics and the next two chapters cover major inferential statistical tools.

descriptive and inferential statistics distinguished

It is helpful to realize that statisticians use the Greek alphabet to represent population parameters (remember that parameters are numbers that characterize populations) and when they discuss conceptual formulae. To balance things out, statisticians use the Roman alphabet (the one used in English) to symbolize sample statistics. This distinction will help you keep things straight.

Measures of Central Tendency

Measures of **central tendency** tell what is going on within sample groups or populations *on the average.*. You may hear people talk about the ''average'' rainfall, ''average'' levels of communication apprehension, or ''average'' numbers of hours people watch TV. But researchers tend to use specific terms to describe *types* of averages. Let's take an example. Suppose that you gave a sample of eight classmates a ten-point rating scale to find out how much they liked the instruction of the research methods class they were taking (10 would be the most exciting course ever, and 1 would be the worst course ever). Suppose you received the following data:

measures of central tendency identified

$$3 \quad 4 \quad 5 \quad 6 \quad 6 \quad 7 \quad 8 \quad 9.$$

There are several ways to describe the central tendency of these data. The **arithmetic mean** is the number most people call ''the average.'' It adds a set of scores (represented as Xs in formulae) and divides by the number of scores. Other types of means are used in different situations,[1] but if you hear someone refer to ''the mean,'' the word ''the'' is a definite article indicating the arithmetic mean. The population mean is computed by using this formula:

arithmetic mean identified

$$\mu = \frac{\Sigma X}{N}.$$

The symbol μ is the Greek letter mu (''mew'') and represents the population mean. The capital N stands for the number of events in the population. The Σ is called ''sigma'' and is a math symbol instructing us to ''sum'' or add up everything that follows. For the sample mean, the formula is

$$\overline{X} = \frac{\Sigma X}{n}.$$

The sample mean is represented by $\overline{X}$, which is read ''X bar.'' The lower case n indicates the number of events in the sample. If you plug the numbers from the sample into the formula you will find that the mean is 6. The formulae for sample

unbiased estimators

and population means are very similar. In fact, the sample mean is said to be an **unbiased estimator** of the population mean. This statement asserts that a representative sample mean is likely to approximate the population mean. Certainly, it is *more likely* to equal the population mean than any other measure we can find. Hence, if researchers do not have the population mean for a formula that requires it, the sample mean may be substituted. Though the mean is a very useful number, it can be thrown off by a small number of extreme scores. So, other methods of central tendency may be examined.

the median identified

The **median** is a score that appears in the middle of an ordered list of scores. As such, the median separates one half of the data from the other half. For the above data, eight scores are listed from lowest to highest. So, there is no score in the "middle." To identify the median, you "split the difference" between the two scores surrounding the middle. In this case, the two scores that surround the middle are 6 and 6. Hence, splitting the difference between these two numbers yields a score of 6.

the mode identified
bimodal
distributions

The **mode** is the most commonly occurring score. In this example, the score 6 appears most often. Sometimes data have more than one mode. When data have two modes, they are called **bimodal.** But if data have many modes, the mode may not be a meaningful way to depict central tendency.

Measures of Variability or Dispersion

In addition to characterizing the averages of scores, researchers may want to determine how close the data are to the mean. This matter can be important. Suppose you were on a bowling team and one of your players got ill and you needed a substitute. If you had a choice between Pat (whose last three games were 155, 175, and 210) and Merle (whose last three games were 172, 180, and 188), which substitute bowler would you ask first? Each bowler has exactly the same average! Yet, most people would ask Merle first. Consistency with the average matters. Measures of dispersion or variability tell how far from the average the data tend to be.

Range

the range identified

The **range** is the difference between the highest and lowest scores. In our example, Pat has a range of 55 pins, and Merle's range is only 16. Sometimes researchers further divide the range into quartiles to describe additional divisions. The range is often used to summarize data, but since the range does not deal with the spread of scores *around* a measure of central tendency, researchers may not be able to compare ranges very usefully. Furthermore, the range is greatly affected by extreme scores.

Variance

variance identified

The **variance** is a measure of the average of squared differences of scores from the mean. As a matter of notation, the symbol s^2 represents the variance of a sample. The symbol σ^2 (sigma squared—that's lowercase sigma) represents the variance of the population. But these definitions do not give you much of a feeling for these highly useful measures of variability.

SPECIAL DISCUSSION 13–1
How to Read a Statistical Formula

It is often helpful to read statistical formulae by using shorthand symbols. Let's look at the formula for sample variance:

$$s^2 = \frac{\Sigma (X - \overline{X})^2}{n - 1}.$$

To read such a formula, you start with items inside the parentheses. In this case, you are told to take an X score, subtract the sample mean ($\overline{X}$) from it, and square the difference. Because of the presence of the sigma sign, you know that you are going to continue this process for all the other X scores as well.

The sigma sign (Σ) tells you to sum—or add up—the values you have computed. This sigma sign is shown here in its abbreviated form, but you should know that it actually has subscripts and superscripts that may be used. For instance, the following form is fairly standard:

$$\sum_{i=1}^{n,1} X_i$$

This statement still means that you sum the X scores that follow, but there is additional detail. The $i = 1$ statement below the sigma sign means that you are to start summation with the first instance. The $n, 1$ above the sigma means that you are to continue through the total number of events in the data set by intervals of one. Suppose you wanted to add up the even-numbered events out of the first twenty events. The sigma would indicate

$$\sum_{i=2}^{20,2} X_i$$

Notice that the X score has an i to indicate that it represents instances of X scores that are to be included in the summation. If you see a sigma sign without the additional symbols, it is shorthand for summing up scores starting with the first instance and moving through all of them by intervals of one.

Other symbols frequently used in statistical discussions include the following:

* multiplied by
/ divided by
> greater than
< less or fewer than
≥ equal to or greater than
≤ equal to or less (or fewer) than
≠ not equal to

In each case, these symbols can help summarize a great deal of information in statistical calculations.

Let's use some common sense. You want to find a number that tells the average distance of data from the mean. For now, pretend you have a data set that includes the entire population of events. If you want to tell people how far from the mean your data happen to be, you should find out how far *each* data point is from the mean; then you can average the distances. Do it one step at a time; it is important to understand the common sense of this statistic.

You could start by subtracting the mean (μ) from each score (X). If you used the data discussed earlier in the chapter, it would appear as:

X	μ	$(X - \mu)$
3 − 6		−3
4 − 6		−2
5 − 6		−1
6 − 6		0
6 − 6		0
7 − 6		1
8 − 6		2
9 − 6		3

Now, you just need to average these differences, right? Try it!

It doesn't work, does it? When you add up all the difference scores, the plus and minus signs cancel out the differences. When you add up the positive and negative numbers, you get 0. It happens every time you subtract a mean from the data you used to compute that mean. So, you need to get rid of the negative numbers on a temporary basis. You could accomplish this objective by squaring the differences (multiplying each difference score by itself). Then you could average these "squared differences" and finish up by "unsquaring" the average so that you get back to the kinds of cardinal numbers you started with. Try it.

X	μ	$(X - \mu)$	$(X - \mu)^2$
3 − 6		−3	9
4 − 6		−2	4
5 − 6		−1	1
6 − 6		0	0
6 − 6		0	0
7 − 6		1	1
8 − 6		2	4
9 − 6		3	9
		sum =	28

Sometimes this sum is called the "sum of squares" (short for the "sum of squared differences of scores from their mean"). Now, you take the average of this sum. Twenty-eight divided by 8 is 3.5. This number is called the variance. Thus, the variance really is just the average of squared differences of scores from the mean. It is all common sense, but the plus and minus signs caused you to take an additional step or two.

When the pieces are put together, the formula for variance may be symbolized as follows:

$$\sigma^2 = \frac{\Sigma (X - \mu)^2}{N}.$$

This formula reads ''sigma squared (the population variance) equals the sum of the squared differences of the population mean subtracted from each of the scores, and divided by the number of scores in the population.''

You have been pretending to have the entire population of events. Suppose you had only a sample from the population. Then things change a little. You see, the mean of the sample $(\bar{X})$ is an unbiased estimator of the population mean (μ). But it is only an estimator. It probably is close, but it is not exact. Thus, if you acted as if the sample mean perfectly identified the population mean, you would not only fool yourself, but you would ''low ball'' the amount of variation that truly exists in the population. Furthermore, your sample variance (s^2) would become a biased estimator of the population variance (σ^2). That won't do.

Permit an explanation (see also Aczel, 1989, pp. 171–75). You could have computed variation many ways. You might have subtracted each score from every other score. But you did not. You used a fixed point—the sample mean—around which to make comparisons. Selecting that starting point meant that the range of variability of the individual scores was artificially restricted to average out to the sample mean. The degrees of freedom of the first data points in the sample to take on any values were unrestricted. But by the time the last data point was reached, the only way the mean could be as reported is if the last data point had no degree of freedom in taking a value. Think of it this way. Suppose you offered to three friends their choice of candy bars: Milky Way, Three Musketeers, and Snickers. The first friend you ask has a choice (she chooses Snickers). The second person also has a choice (he chooses Milky Way). But by the time you get to your third friend, there is no choice left at all. Similarly, when you have an arbitrary point around which to make comparisons of events in a sample, the freedom of the events to take on values is restricted by the time you get to the last data point. If you had the entire population, you could live with it, since there would be no error in estimating the population mean. But every time you compute a *sample* variance, you ''lose a degree of freedom'' equal to the number of means you computed to make comparisons. Thus, statisticians say that every time one ''estimates a parameter from a sample'' (a sample mean is an unbiased estimator of the population mean, remember?), a degree of freedom is lost. It always works that way—every time you estimate a population mean, you lose a degree of freedom.[2]

losing a degree of freedom every time you estimate a parameter from samples

To estimate a population mean legitimately from a sample mean, you have to ''pay the kitty'' for the privilege. To use the sample mean in the formula for the variance, you must ''ante up'' by altering the way you compute the variance: divide the sum of squared differences of scores from the sample mean by the number of events *minus one for the mean you estimated from the sample.* Thus, the formula for sample variance is

$$s^2 = \frac{\Sigma (X - \overline{X})^2}{n - 1} \; .$$

The sample variance in this case would be a little different, since the divisor of this formula is n − 1 (8 − 1). Thus, if you divided 28 by 7, you would get a variance (s²) of 4.

The variance is—with some adjusting for using sample means—the average squared difference of scores from the mean. But this number is difficult to interpret. To return to cardinal numbers, researchers need to remove the effect of squared differences on averaging. This step leads to the last part of our common sense way of measuring variability.

Standard Deviation

standard deviation distinguished

The **standard deviation** shows how far the average of the scores deviates from the mean. Since the variance is the average of squared deviations of differences of scores from the mean, to get to "unsquared" differences (the cardinal numbers with which you started), you simply take the square root of the variance, using these formulae:[3]

Sample Standard Deviation	Population Standard Deviation
$s = \sqrt{\dfrac{(X - \overline{X})^2}{n - 1}}$	$\sigma = \sqrt{\dfrac{\Sigma (X - \mu)^2}{N}}$

The standard deviation is, in essence, an average of "unsquared" deviations of scores from their own mean. It tells the average difference of scores from the mean. In the example, the variance (s²) was 4. Thus, the sample standard deviation would be the square root of 4. Hence the sample standard deviation (s) is 2. Since the population variance (σ²) is 3.5, the population standard deviation (σ) is 1.87.

standard deviations permit use of the standard normal curve

Another quality makes standard deviations so valuable to researchers. These numbers make it possible for researchers to use the standard normal curve to help make decisions. To grasp this matter, you must understand the notion of distributions.

DISTRIBUTIONS

Data tend to form distributions that have different appearances. A knowledge of the patterns they form can help researchers understand what the data really are saying. This section looks at two types of distributions: data distributions and the standard normal curve.

Non-normal and Skewed Distributions

The location of the median, mean, and mode can indicate quite a bit about the nature of underlying data patterns. Several different patterns might be found in the data. In each, the data are "talking" to the researcher; he or she just has to know how to listen.

Types of Skew

An off-center distribution is **skewed.** Contrary to popular belief, skewness does skewness identified not tell where data are. Instead, it indicates where the long tail away from the "hump" of the data is located. There are formulae to compute skewness, but for this discussion it is most important just to understand the basic ideas.[4] If the distribution is perfectly centered and symmetrical, there is no skew at all (and formulae report skewness coefficients of 0). The tails on each side of the mean would start at the same location and be equally as long. If skewness is negative, the long negative or leftward skew tail is "below" the mean (our "ground zero"). Then, you could say that the distribution is "skewed to the left" or has "negative skew." Figure 13.1A shows such a pattern. If the skewness is positive, then the long tail is "above" the rightward or positive skew "ground zero" mean. As figure 13.1B shows, positive skew means that the distribution is "skewed to the right." In the sample of class ratings, the distribution is not skewed one way any more than the other. A bimodal distribution, such as that found in figure 13.1C, exaggerates skew because the hump in data is found at two different locations.

Peakedness of Distributions

In addition to measures of "centeredness," there are ways to find out how peaked kurtosis identified a distribution is. The measure of peakedness is called **kurtosis.** Since the formula is a bit cumbersome, we will not present it here. But here is the basic idea: In a perfect normal distribution, the distribution is as high as three standard deviations is wide. If the peak is higher than three standard deviations is wide, then the kurtosis is greater than 3. If the peak is shorter than three standard deviations is wide, kurtosis is lower than 3. This explanation does not give credit to the computation methods for kurtosis. Furthermore, you should know that many popular computer programs now subtract 3 from the kurtosis formula. So, you must be careful when looking at kurtosis numbers to make sure you do not misinterpret them.

Figure 13.1D shows a distribution that has a kurtosis lower than three. It is distributions: very flat and its profile looks almost as though someone turned over a plate onto the baseline. This distribution is called, by coincidence, **platykurtic.** Figure 13.1E platykurtic shows a distribution that has a peak that is neither very high nor very low (kurtosis of 3). This distribution is called **mesokurtic.** The last figure (13.1F) shows an mesokurtic extremely peaked distribution, which seems to leap upward. This pattern is called **leptokurtic.** By looking at both skewness and kurtosis, the researcher can get a leptokurtic good picture of the data.

Standard Normal Distribution

One of the basic tools used by researchers is called the **standard normal curve.** Because this distribution is the basis for many other distributions and statistics, we should understand something about it.

The Gaussian Curve

The standard normal curve is a mathematic ideal. It is a **probability distribution** probability distributions that tells the expected value that would be obtained by sampling at random. Data

FIGURE 13.1
Distribution Forms

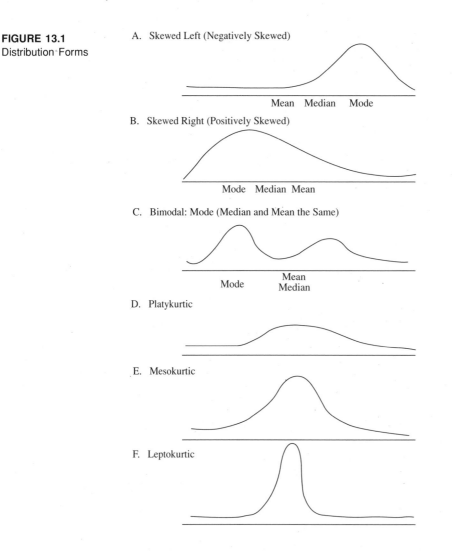

A. Skewed Left (Negatively Skewed)

Mean   Median   Mode

B. Skewed Right (Positively Skewed)

Mode   Median Mean

C. Bimodal: Mode (Median and Mean the Same)

Mode   Mean
              Median

D. Platykurtic

E. Mesokurtic

F. Leptokurtic

data distributions

you collect (**data distributions**) can form normal curves, but they cannot be the standard normal curve unless they meet the exact definitions for this kind of distribution. In the early part of the nineteenth century, mathematician Carl Friedrich Gauss (1777–1855) and the Marquis de Laplace (1749–1827) developed the language of the standard normal curve (Pearson, 1924). Though at the time, Gauss was trying to find clues to the normal deviations in orbits and polar ''wobbles'' of planets, he also found that many types of ordinary data tended to cluster around their averages with fewer and fewer pieces of data at the extremes. As you can see on figure 13.2, the standard normal curve is perfectly centered and peaked. The median, mean, and mode are all at the same place on the distribution. The skewness is 0 since the distribution is completely centered. The kurtosis of the standard normal curve is 3. You also can see that the tails of the standard normal curve never really touch bottom—they go out forever.

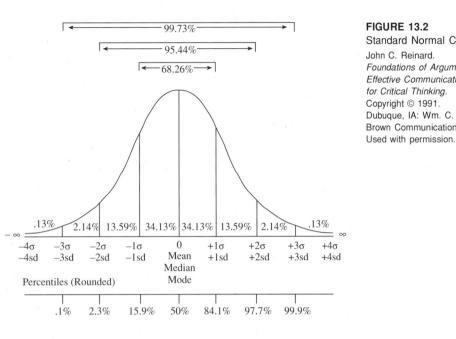

FIGURE 13.2
Standard Normal Curve

John C. Reinard.
*Foundations of Argument:
Effective Communication
for Critical Thinking.*
Copyright © 1991.
Dubuque, IA: Wm. C.
Brown Communications Inc.
Used with permission.

Starting at the top of the curve, Gauss observed the point where the slope changed direction. To identify this location on the curve, he dropped a line down to the baseline. Then he noticed that there was a second point where the slope changed direction again. He dropped another line to mark the spot and soon he observed that the intervals between his lines were identical whether he followed the curve above the mean or below the mean. He called these points deviations of slope on the standard normal curve or "standard deviations" for short.

naming the
standard deviation
on the standard
normal curve

The mean, median, and mode are symbolized by the letter mu (μ). The standard deviation is symbolized by the Greek lowercase letter sigma (σ). Figuring that numbers might be needed, statisticians defined the center of the distribution as ground zero, or just 0. Each standard deviation is set to be one unit wide. Hence σ is defined to be equal to 1. A standard deviation below ground zero has a negative sign in front of it and a standard deviation above ground zero has a positive number. Researchers often collect data that have normal distributions. But if they do not have a mean of 0, a standard deviation of 1, a skewness of 0, a kurtosis of 3, and tails that stretch to infinity, they do not have *standard* normal curves. Yet, we can compare data to a standard normal curve to help identify long range expectations and to make sound decisions. The section below shows how researchers use this curve.

requirements of a
standard normal
curve

Interpreting Areas under the Normal Curve

Gauss reported the density function for the standard normal curve, which indicates what percentage of the total area under the standard normal curve extends *from ground zero out* to a point of interest. As you can see, *approximately* two-thirds of the distribution exist from 1σ below the mean to 1σ above the mean (though the amount actually is 68.26 percent). Over 95 percent (actually 95.44 percent) of the

interpreting areas
under the standard
normal curve

FIGURE 13.3
Standard Normal
Curve Used in
Grading on the Curve
Portion of the Table
of Areas under the
Standard Normal
Curve

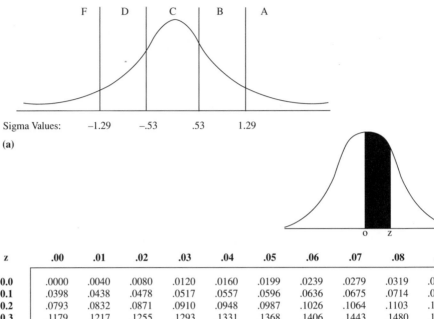

Sigma Values: −1.29   −.53   .53   1.29

(a)

z	.00	.01	.02	.03	.04	.05	.06	.07	.08	.09
0.0	.0000	.0040	.0080	.0120	.0160	.0199	.0239	.0279	.0319	.0359
0.1	.0398	.0438	.0478	.0517	.0557	.0596	.0636	.0675	.0714	.0753
0.2	.0793	.0832	.0871	.0910	.0948	.0987	.1026	.1064	.1103	.1141
0.3	.1179	.1217	.1255	.1293	.1331	.1368	.1406	.1443	.1480	.1517
0.4	.1554	.1591	.1628	.1664	.1700	.1736	.1772	.1808	.1844	.1879
0.5	.1915	.1950	.1985	.2019	.2054	.2088	.2123	.2157	.2190	.2224
0.6	.2257	.2291	.2324	.2357	.2389	.2422	.2454	.2486	.2517	.2549
0.7	.2580	.2611	.2642	.2673	.2704	.2734	.2764	.2794	.2823	.2852
0.8	.2881	.2910	.2939	.2967	.2995	.3023	.3051	.3078	.3106	.3133
0.9	.3159	.3186	.3212	.3238	.3264	.3289	.3315	.3340	.3365	.3389
1.0	.3413	.3438	.3461	.3485	.3508	.3531	.3554	.3577	.3599	.3621
1.1	.3643	.3665	.3686	.3708	.3729	.3749	.3770	.3790	.3810	.3830
1.2	.3849	.3869	.3888	.3907	.3925	.3944	.3962	.3980	.3997	.4015
1.3	.4032	.4049	.4066	.4082	.4099	.4115	.4131	.4147	.4162	.4177
1.4	.4192	.4207	.4222	.4236	.4251	.4265	.4279	.4292	.4306	.4319
1.5	.4332	.4345	.4357	.4370	.4382	.4394	.4406	.4418	.4429	.4441

(b)

**use of the standard
normal curve**

curve extends from −2σ to +2σ. All but .27 percent—that's "point 27 percent" not "27 percent") exists from −3σ to +3σ. The density function has been summarized on tables that are widely available (see appendix A). These tables have many uses. For instance, suppose you had an instructor who wished to "grade on the curve." Though few instructors really use a strict curve, the method submits that if you assume that grades have a generally normal distribution (and experience shows that grades generally do), then you should be able to slice off the top 10 percent of students to receive As and the bottom 10 percent to receive Fs. The next 20 percent in from each extreme would receive Bs and Ds, and the remaining 40 percent would receive Cs. Figure 13.3 shows how normally distributed scores are arranged when a teacher grades on the curve. The C range is in the middle of the distribution and approximately 40 percent of the curve extends from ground zero up to .53σ and down to −.53σ.

You may wish to look at appendix A to see what is going on here. We have reproduced a portion of it in figure 13.3. Here is how to use this table. The term *z* identifies the number of sigmas or standard deviations of interest. Read *down* the column marked *z* until you find 0.5. That brings you to the first decimal point. Now read across the top row to find the column identified .03. This column picks up the second decimal point: 0.53. Where this column and row intersect, you see the number .2019. This number means that 20.19 percent of the total area under the standard normal curve exists from ground zero out to .53 sigmas. The shaded area in the picture at the top of the table illustrates this relationship. This distribution is symmetrical. So, to figure out how much area exists from .53 sigmas *below* the mean up to .53 sigmas *above* the mean, simply double the area (.2019 * 2 = .4038). Thus, the amount of area from −.53σ to +.53σ is approximately 40 percent. To pick up an additional 20 percent of the grades around ''C,'' you would have to go out to 1.29σ in each direction. The 10% of the total area left over on each side of the distribution would be identified as A and F ranges.

using the table for the standard normal curve

As you can see, the standard normal curve can help identify long run expectations you might have for samples you draw. These distributions are used as probability distributions to help you understand when unusual patterns exist in the data—so that you can make appropriate decisions.

using the standard normal curve to identify unusual occurrences

Using z Scores

Researchers usually are not lucky enough to collect data that have a mean of zero and a standard deviation of 1. Yet, they can still use the standard normal curve to make decisions by changing data into **z scores.** Because z scores allow the use of the standard normal curve to help make decisions, they are called standard scores. Z scores permit you to represent data scores as units under the standard normal curve. Thus, you can use z scores to compare general patterns of scores to others. The formula for z is

z scores identified

$$z = \frac{X - \mu}{\sigma}$$

The *X* is a score of interest to the researcher. For example, much communication research examines the role of receiver intelligence on reactions to messages. Scores on the popular Stanford-Binet I.Q. test are normally distributed with a population mean (μ) of 100 and a population standard deviation (σ) of 15. Suppose you scored 115 on an I.Q. test. Assuming for the sake of argument that I.Q. tests measure something, how many people's scores would your score exceed? You might insert numbers as follows:

$$z = \frac{X - \mu}{\sigma}$$
$$= \frac{115 - 100}{15}$$
$$= \frac{15}{15}$$
$$= 1.00.$$

So, how many scores would yours exceed? You need only look at the table. On figure 13.3 find the column for z and identify the row corresponding to 1.0. To find the second decimal point value, continue across the top of the table to the column marked .00. The intersection of this column and this row reveals the number .3413, indicating that 34.13 percent of the area lies between the mean and a z value of 1.00.

How do you find out how many scores are below yours? You might suppose that you just double the value of .3413. DON'T DO IT! The 115 score is above average, right? So you have a higher score than all the people who were "below average." Since 50 percent of the area is below the mean (and 50 percent above the mean), you know that your score is automatically better than 50 percent of the below average scores. In addition, the z table shows that your score is greater than 34.13 of the scores that were average and above. Thus, your I.Q. score is greater than 50 percent + 34.13 percent, for a total of 84.13 percent. Your score is greater than those of approximately 84 percent of other I.Q. scores.

z scores when population mean and standard deviation are estimated from samples

Suppose you do not have the population mean (μ) or the population standard deviation (σ). No problem. The sample mean ($\overline{X}$) is an "unbiased estimator" of the population mean (μ). The sample standard deviation (s) is an "unbiased estimator" (provided the right formula was used for the sample standard deviation) of the population standard deviation (σ). So, you can substitute the sample means and standard deviations for population means and standard deviations to compute your answers. Let's return to the example of a teacher grading on the curve. Suppose the mean on the test is 50, your test score is 61, and the standard deviation is 10. What grade would you get, given the dividing points used in the example? We complete the following formula:

$$z = \frac{X - \overline{X}}{s}$$
$$= \frac{61 - 50}{10}$$
$$= \frac{11}{10}$$
$$= 1.10.$$

Look up this value on figure 13.3, and notice that you would get a B on this exam. If you wanted to know how many people got lower scores than you did, you could look at the z table. As the area under the normal curve shows, 36.43 percent of the scores on the normal distribution exists between the mean and 1.10 z scores. Thus, our test score is higher than the 50 percent of students who were below average, plus 36.43 percent, for a total of 86.43 percent.

uses of the standard normal curve

Despite its usefulness, you might wonder why so much fuss is made about the standard normal curve. Researchers often use the standard normal curve to describe the presumed way in which variables occur. They may gather samples and use the normal curve to learn how likely it is that such samples could be found at random from an underlying distribution in which only ordinary and random occurrences of variables exist. Suppose, for instance, that you gather some sample data whose typical z score is 2.6 or greater. By looking at the standard normal curve, you know that such data could be found very rarely if the distribution is normal and centered at its assumed mean. What would you do? You *could* conclude that you sampled data that just happened to come from the upper end of the underlying distribution. *Or,* you might conclude that the underlying distribution from which the sample was drawn is not really as ordinary as assumed. You might conclude—by looking at the odds of getting samples such as yours at random—that your data have been systematically influenced to make them different from the assumed "ordinary" distribution. By using the standard normal curve (and its variations) you can "play the odds" to see how likely new sample results could have occurred at random. This thinking is the basis for significance testing, which is described in the next chapter.

MEASURES OF ASSOCIATION

One major way to describe data statistically uses measures of association or correlation.[5] A **correlation** is just a measure of the coincidence of variables. Most people use the word "coincidence" to mean an "accidental" or "bogus" relationship. But in reality, a coincidence means simply that two variables "coincide" with each other. Correlations show the degree to which variables "coincide" with each other by use of formulas that show the amount of coincidence.

  For correlations, you must have data on two measures (though some correlations allow the use of more than two variables) from each event in the sample. For instance, your income and the number of magazines to which you subscribe can be correlated. You could check the association between the severity of articulation disorders among children and their school grades. Each situation requires that events in the sample include scores that can be plotted and analyzed to reveal associations. This section considers the ways that correlations are interpreted and two major methods used to determine correlations.

correlation defined

Interpreting Correlations

Correlation coefficients can have a range of values from -1.00 to 1.00, but you probably will not see many 1.00 correlations in research. Instead, you will see numbers behind decimal points. The closer the number is to 1 (regardless of the sign before it), the stronger is the correlation. Two types of relationships can be revealed. The first is called a **direct relationship,** which indicates that as one variable increases, the other variable also increases. Similarly, as one variable decreases, so does the other. Figure 13.4A shows the general pattern (called a scatterplot) that is indicated by direct relationships. As an aid to interpretation, researchers often add a line of "best fit" through the data. This line sometimes is called a "line of regression," because Karl Pearson, who refined correlation formulae, used data that investigated the "regression effect" when he drew *his* first line—and the name stuck. Both diagrams reveal high direct correlations since the line of "best fit" shows that as the variable on the horizontal axis increases, so does the variable on the vertical axis. The second illustration shows a perfect 1.00 correlation since all the data are exactly on the line. Though often misunderstood, the correlation is not the steepness of the line's slope—the slope is called "covariance."

direct relationships identified

line of best fit or regression noted

FIGURE 13.4
Forms of Correlations

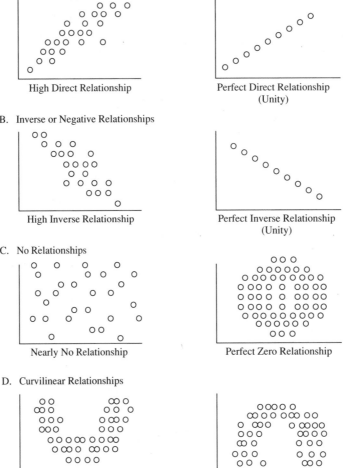

A. Direct or Positive Relationships

High Direct Relationship

Perfect Direct Relationship
(Unity)

B. Inverse or Negative Relationships

High Inverse Relationship

Perfect Inverse Relationship
(Unity)

C. No Relationships

Nearly No Relationship

Perfect Zero Relationship

D. Curvilinear Relationships

Instead, correlation size is shown by the closeness of the data to the line of best fit. If you look at figure 13.4C, you will see scatterplots showing no relationship. As you can tell, if a chart is drawn according to standard protocols, zero correlations are reflected in plots that form perfect circles (or lines that are perfectly horizontal or perfectly vertical, in the case of situations in which one "variable" has only one value in the data).

inverse relationships   An **inverse relationship** is one in which an increase in one variable corre-
identified   sponds to a decrease in the other. These correlations are identified by the use of negative signs, but you should *not* interpret negative signs as subtractions or "take away." A correlation of –.82 is a strong one. The negative sign does not mean that this correlation is "less than" a positive correlation of .15. The minus sign only indicates that as one variable increases, the other declines (see figure 13.4B). There are many such

**SPECIAL DISCUSSION 13–2
Correlation and Causality**

Though causal relationships should produce high correlations, a correlation cannot show causation by itself. To show cause-and-effect relationships directly, researchers must use the experimental method.[6] Researchers who think that correlations show cause-and-effect relationships can make some silly mistakes. Li (1975) reported a study of factors predicting birthrates among Taiwanese. The researchers observed that birthrate decreased as the number of small appliances one owned increased. Thus, it seemed that one could control population growth by sending toasters, hair dryers, and the like to Taiwan. Of course, owning small appliances does not cause one to have a small family. But it might work the other way around—if you don't have children you have additional money to purchase small appliances. Thus, the researchers made a double error. Not only did they assume a causal relationship, but they claimed a mistaken direction for the difference.

Glass and Hopkins explained the reasons that it is unwise to assume a causal relationship based on correlational information (1984, p. 104):

First, even when one can presume that a causal relationship does exist between two variables being correlated, r_{xy} can tell nothing by itself about whether X causes Y or Y causes X. Second, often variables other than the two under consideration could be responsible for the observed association. Third, the relationships that exist among variables in behavioral and social science are almost always too complex to be explained in terms of a single cause.

Experienced researchers resist the temptation to view correlations as identical to causal relationships.

examples in communication research. As the amount of conflict within a group increases, the amount of ambiguity the members feel about the issues declines. The higher one's intelligence, the fewer hours of television one might watch. Such patterns occur frequently in communication research and can be very interesting.

To understand how to judge the size of different correlations, statistician Robert Koenker developed this general guide (1961, p. 52):

**guidelines to
interpret correlations**

.80 to 1.00   highly dependable relationship
.60 to .79   moderate to marked relationship
.40 to .59   fair degree of relationship
.20 to .39   slight relationship
.00 to .19   negligible or chance relationship.

There are some common sense exceptions to this guideline, of course. If you examined questions searching for the last few contributors to effects, you might interpret a small coefficient more favorably than you would otherwise.

Let's see how the method works. Many communication students eventually pursue careers in law and they usually take the Law School Aptitude Test (LSAT). This test seems bothersome to most students, but the test scores correlate .50 with first year grades in law school. When a student's undergraduate grades are added to the mix, the combination correlates .70 with first year law school grades (Anastasi, 1968, pp. 431–432). Thus, it seems that the test alone is a "fair" predictor of first year law school grades, and when undergraduate grades are included, the combination becomes a "marked" predictor of success in law school.

not confusing correlations for percentages

Some students look at correlation coefficients as percentages. They think that a .80 correlation explains 80 percent of the effect. NOT TRUE! A correlation uses its own metric to identify correspondence between scores. To find out the percentage impact one variable has on another, you can simply square the correlation coefficient. This number is called a **coefficient of determination** and shows the percentage of variation in one variable that can be explained by a knowledge of the other variable alone. Hence a correlation of .80 means that 64 percent ($.80^2 = .64$) of the variation in one variable can be explained by the other one alone. In the example of LSAT tests, the combination of first year test scores and undergraduate grades explains 49 percent of total variability—slightly under half. This relation surely is better than intuition alone, but the coefficient of determination also reveals that there is plenty of room for improvement.

use of the coefficient of determination

curvilinear relationships

Sometimes the data show different patterns, as indicated on figure 13.4D. These relationships are curvilinear since the best fit of a line to the data is not a straight line. These curves invite the use of special correlations that can identify the magnitude of the curved effect (such as the correlation ratio, eta [η]). Furthermore, they tell the researcher that there is an optimal low point or high point that will be missed if the researcher is not careful.

Forms of Correlations

forms of correlations

There are many correlation formulae that have been developed for different sorts of data. Table 13.1 lists these major forms. As you can see, they differ most in the sorts of data they allow researchers to examine for relationships. Thus, the levels of measurement for the independent and dependent variables are listed. If you need to use any of these tools, you can find them explained in many comprehensive statistics books (e.g., Glass & Hopkins, 1984; Aczel, 1989). For the purposes of this book, only the two most commonly used tools will be described.

Pearson Product Moment Correlation

Pearson product moment correlation

Developed by Karl Pearson, the **Pearson product moment correlation** method is suitable for situations in which *both* the independent and dependent variables (identified as *X* and *Y* respectively in most notation) are *interval* or *ratio* level measures. Table 13.2 shows how to use the Pearson product moment formula. We compute the covariance and divide it by the product of the standard deviations of each variable. The "covariance" often is abbreviated s_{xy}, even though that symbol makes it look like some kind of standard deviation (s), which it is not.

TABLE 13.1 Forms of Association and Correlation Measures

Measures Designed for Two Variables

Levels of Measurement for:

One Variable	Other Variable	Correlation Method
	Nominal	Tetrachoric Correlation (for two false dichotomies)
	Nominal	Yule's Q (for use if both variables have only two categories)
	Nominal	Phi Coefficient (computed from chi square based on two variables with only two categories)
N	Nominal	Asymmetric lambda (computed from number of events in mode category and distinction made between independent and dependent variable)
O		
M	Nominal	Symmetric lambda (computed from number of events in mode category)
I	Nominal	Contingency Coefficient (for two or more categories in each variable; coefficient upper limit affected by category numbers)
N		
A	Nominal	Cramer's V (for two or more categories in each variable)
L	Interval or Ratio	Biserial r (for false dichotomy in nominal variable)
	Interval or Ratio	Point Biserial r (for true dichotomy in nominal variable)
	Ordinal	Spearman Rank Order Correlation
O	Ordinal	Goodman and Kruskal's gamma (for use with any sized tables)
R	Ordinal	Kendall's tau a, tau b, Kim's d (for use when many tied ranks are present)
D	Ordinal	Kendall's tau c (for use when variables have different numbers of categories)
I	Ordinal	Somers' d (for use when distinction made between independent and dependent variable)
N	Interval or Ratio	Jaspen's coefficient correlation of multiserial correlation (used when assuming that ordinal the variable is derived from a normally distributed interval variable)
A		
L	Interval or Ratio	Mayer and Robinson's M_{yu} (for assumption that the ordinal variable is composed of ordered levels of an underlying variable)
I	Interval or Ratio	Pearson Product Moment Correlation (for linear relationships)
N		
T R		Eta (a.k.a. correlation ratio) (for nonlinear relationships)
E o A		
R r T		
V I		
A O		
L		

Measures Designed for More Than Two Variables

Correlation Method	Application
Kendall's Coefficient of Concordance	correlation of more than two sets of rankings
Partial Correlation	correlation of an interval level dependent variable with one predictor variable while holding a third variable constant (the proportion of variance that is not associated with a third controlled variable)
Part Correlation (semipartial correlation)	correlation equalling the unique contribution made by a predictor variable (the variation between the predictor variable and other potential predictors is eliminated)
Multiple Linear Correlation (Multiple Regression Analysis)	correlation of a single interval level criterion variable with multiple predictor variables
Canonical Correlation	correlation of a set of multiple predictor variables with a set of criterion variables
Multiple Discriminant Analysis	correlational method used to predict group membership categories (measured on the nominal level) from a set of interval level variables
Multivariate Multiple Regression Analysis	an extension of multiple linear correlation for situations in which more than one criterion variable is treated as a common set

TABLE 13.2 Computing the Pearson Product Moment Correlation

Consider a study relating the average amount of time people spend watching sporting events on TV each week and the average number of bags of potato chips they purchase per month.

One simply computes the differences between each score and its own mean. The result is multiplied by the difference of the other score subtracted from its mean. Then, the sum of these products is divided by the number of samples minus one.

$$\frac{\Sigma[(X-\overline{X})*(Y-\overline{Y})]}{n-1}$$

This term is called the covariance.

To compute the Pearson product moment correlation for raw scores, use the following formula:

$$r = \frac{\text{Covariance (X,Y) or } s_{xy}}{s_x * s_y}$$

For this example, you could compute as follows:

Family	Hours Watching Sports on TV		Bags of Potato Chips Purchased Monthly		
	X	$(X - \overline{X})$	Y	$(Y-\overline{Y})$	$(X-\overline{X})*(Y-\overline{Y})$
Jones	3	−3	2	−4	12
Smith	4	−2	5	−1	2
Chan	6	0	6	0	0
King	9	3	4	−2	−6
Manson	5	−1	8	2	−2
Addams	7	1	7	1	1
Simpson	8	2	7	1	2
Mann	6	0	9	3	0
	$\overline{X} = 6$		$\overline{X} = 6$		sum = 9
	s = 2		s = 2.27		

The covariance is the sum of the differences multiplied by each other, divided by the number of scores minus one

$$\text{covariance (X,Y)} = \frac{\Sigma(X-\overline{X})*(Y-\overline{Y})}{n-1}$$

In our instance, this formula becomes

$$\text{covariance (X,Y)} = \frac{9}{8-1} = 1.29$$

The overall correlation becomes

$$r = \frac{\text{Covariance (X,Y) or } s_{xy}}{s_x * s_y}$$

$$= \frac{1.29}{2 * 2.27}$$

$$= .28$$

indicating a "slight" relationship.

Spearman Rank Order Correlation

Sometimes researchers have measures on the *ordinal* level. For instance, a manager might decide to explore whether there is a relationship between the number of successful salespeople and the number of hours they have spent in communication skills training classes. The scores on each variable would be expressed by ranks. For instance, the manager might rank nine salespeople from best (number "1") to worst (number "9"). Then, they might be ranked according to the amount of communication skills training classes they have received. Though the Pearson product moment correlation method may be adapted if there are no ties among the rankings, the **Spearman rank order correlation** formula is suitable across settings. Table 13.3 shows how this formula can be used with both untied and tied ranks.

Spearman rank order correlation

This method is usually abbreviated as r_s, though other notation often is used.[7] The Spearman rank order correlation coefficient is often used even when original data were measured on an interval scale but the researcher suspects that the underlying distributions are not normal. It may be interpreted as any other correlation, including computation of coefficients of determination.

notation for Spearman rank order correlation

TABLE 13.3 Computing the Spearman Rank Order Correlation

Examples without tied ranks

Here are data for a study relating the rankings of salespeople and rankings of the amount of communication skills training they received.

Person	Ranking of Salesperson Ability X	Ranking of Amount of Communication Training Y
Manny	1	1
Moe	2	4
Jack	3	3
Larry	4	7
Curly	5	2
Patty	6	5
Maxine	7	6
Laverne	8	8
Gallagher	9	9

TABLE 13.3—*Continued*

Differences between ranks are computed and these differences are squared, creating a term abbreviated as D^2. Then these squared difference scores are added up. Here is how it works in our example.

Person	Ranking of Salesperson Ability X	Ranking of Amount of Communication Training Y	Differences D	D^2
Manny	1	1	(1 − 1) = 0	0
Moe	2	4	(2 − 4) = −2	4
Jack	3	3	(3 − 3) = 0	0
Larry	4	7	(4 − 7) = −3	9
Curly	5	2	(5 − 2) = 3	9
Patty	6	5	(6 − 5) = 1	1
Maxine	7	6	(7 − 6) = 1	1
Laverne	8	8	(8 − 8) = 0	0
Gallagher	9	9	(9 − 9) = 0	0

sum of differences = 24

The formula for the Spearman rank order correlation is

$$r_s = 1 - \frac{6 * \Sigma D^2}{n * (n^2 - 1)}$$

In this formula, *n* is the number of events for which there are paired ranks. Employing our data, substitute the following numbers:

$$= 1 - \frac{6 * 24}{9 * (81 - 1)}$$

$$= 1 - \frac{144}{9 * (80)}$$

$$= 1 - \frac{144}{720}$$

$$= 1 - .20$$

$$= .80$$

which is a "highly dependable" relationship

TABLE 13.3—*Continued*

Example with tied ranks

Here are data for a study relating the rankings of salespeople and rankings of the amount of communication skills training they received in which some people had the same number of hours of training.

Person	Ranking of Salesperson Ability X	Ranking of Amount of Communication Training Y
Manny	1	tied
Moe	2	for
Jack	3	first
Larry	4	7
Curly	5	5
Patty	6	6
Maxine	7	4
Laverne	8	tied for
Gallagher	9	eighth

To deal with tied ranks, simply split the difference among the tied ranks and assign those values to all the tied ranks. Since three people are tied for first place (though they normally would receive ranks 1, 2, and 3), give them the average of the three ranks (2 is the average of ranks 1, 2, and 3). The tie between rank 8 and 9 is settled by giving each person an average rank of 8.5. Complete the computations as follows:

Person	Ranking of Salesperson Ability X	Ranking of Amount of Communication Training Y	Differences D	D^2
Manny	1	2	(1 − 2) = −1	1
Moe	2	2	(2 − 2) = 0	0
Jack	3	2	(3 − 2) = 1	1
Larry	4	7	(4 − 7) = −3	9
Curly	5	5	(5 − 5) = 0	0
Patty	6	6	(6 − 6) = 0	0
Maxine	7	4	(7 − 4) = 3	9
Laverne	8	8.5	(8 − 8) = −.5	.25
Gallagher	9	8.5	(9 − 9) = .5	.25
			sum of differences =	20.5

$$r_s = 1 - \frac{6 * \Sigma D^2}{n * (n^2 - 1)}$$

$$= 1 - \frac{6 * 20.5}{9 * (81 - 1)}$$

$$= 1 - \frac{123}{9 * (80)}$$

$$= 1 - \frac{123}{720}$$

$$= 1 - .17$$

$$= .83$$

which is a "highly dependable" relationship

SUMMARY

Descriptive statistics are numbers that characterize information. Inferential statistics are tools that help researchers draw conclusions about the probable populations from which samples did or did not belong. Statisticians use the Greek alphabet to represent population parameters and the Roman alphabet when describing samples.

Measures of central tendency tell what is going on within sample groups or populations on the average. The arithmetic mean adds a set of scores and divides by the number of scores. The sample mean is an unbiased estimator of the population mean. The median is a score that appears in the middle of an ordered list of scores and separates one half of the data from the other half. The mode is the most commonly occurring score. When data have two modes, they are called bimodal. But if data have many modes, the mode may not meaningfully depict central tendency.

Measures of variability or dispersion tell how close to the mean data are. The range is the difference between the highest and lowest score in a data set. The variance is a measure of the average of squared differences of scores from the mean (the symbol s^2 represents the variance of a sample and σ^2 represents the variance of the population). The formulae for sample variance and standard deviation are computed so that unbiased estimators of variance and standard deviation may be created. The standard deviation shows how far the average of the scores deviates from the mean.

Distributions of data often tend to be symmetrical around their averages, but sometimes it does not work that way. A distribution that is off-center is skewed. The measure of peakedness is called kurtosis. A very flat distribution is called platykurtic. A distribution with a peak that is neither very high nor very low is called mesokurtic. An extremely peaked distribution is called leptokurtic. The standard normal curve is a bell-shaped probability distribution that tells the expected value that would be obtained by sampling at random. Data distributions can form normal curves, but they cannot be "the standard normal curve" unless they meet the exact requirements for this special distribution (perfect centeredness and peakedness; median, mean, and mode equal to 0; standard deviation of 1). The areas under the standard normal curve are identified to reveal probabilities of drawing samples from one location on the distribution to another. z scores permit representing scores from data as units under the standard normal curve. By looking at the standard normal curve, we can estimate whether such data could be found very frequently or very rarely if the distribution is normal and centered at its assumed mean.

A correlation is a measure of the coincidence of variables. Direct relationships mean that as one variable increases, the other variable also increases. An inverse relationship indicates that an increase in one variable corresponds to a decrease in the other (identified by negative signs). Correlation coefficients are not percentages. To know the percentage impact one variable has on another, the square of the correlation coefficient (called a coefficient of determination) should be computed. Sometimes relationships show curvilinear patterns since the best fit of a line to the data is not a straight line. The Pearson product moment correlation is suitable for situations in which *both* the independent and dependent variables (identified as *X* and *Y* respectively in most notation) are *interval* or *ratio* level measures. The Spearman rank order correlation is suitable when variables are measured on the ordinal level.

TERMS FOR REVIEW

descriptive statistics
inferential statistics
central tendency
arithmetic mean
unbiased estimator
median
mode
bimodal
range
variance
standard deviation
skewness
kurtosis

platykurtic
mesokurtic
leptokurtic
probability distribution
data distribution
standard normal distribution
z scores
correlation
direct relationship
inverse relationship
coefficient of determination
Pearson product moment correlation
Spearman rank order correlation

NOTES

[1]For instance, the ''geometric mean'' is used to average ratios or proportions. If money deposited in a savings account grew from $100 to $300 in five years, the average percentage increase would *not* be computed by dividing the 200 percent increase by 5 (because of the presence of compounded interest). The *geometric mean* would be used. To find average miles per gallon for a car driven for 10 miles at 35 miles per hour, 5 miles at 20 miles per hour, and 8 miles at 40 miles per hour, the *harmonic mean* would be used to account for different speeds the gas mileage.

[2]It works with all parameters estimated from samples. For instance, in multiple correlation, a degree of freedom is lost each time a beta weight is computed.

[3]These formulae are the correct ones for standard deviation of samples and populations. Without naming names, it is the case that for nearly a quarter of a century some books in communication research methods have gotten the formulae for sigma and s confused with each other.

[4]The equation is called Pearson's first coefficient of skewness.

$$skewness = \frac{Mean - Mode}{Standard\ Deviation}$$

Pearson's second coefficient of skewness is calculated

$$skewness = \frac{3 * Mean - Mode}{Standard\ Deviation}$$

[5]Some writers reserve the term ''association'' for measures on the nominal or ordinal levels of measurement.

[6]The historical method also can produce such information, though one must wait a long time to identify the effects and responsible causes.

[7]Regrettably, some statistics books use rho (ρ) as the abbreviation for the Spearman rank order correlation.

CHAPTER 14

Introductory Inferential Statistics I: Hypothesis Testing with Two Means

To understand God's thoughts, we must study statistics, for these are the measure of His purpose.

–Florence Nightingale

BEFORE WE GET STARTED. . .

Inferential statistics help researchers figure out how likely their sample results may occur by chance. They play the odds by entering a distribution, such as the standard normal curve, to make comparisons. This chapter introduces some major tools researchers use with inferential statistics. This introduction stresses the logic behind using statistics to test hypotheses, with emphasis on making comparisons between means. The next chapter carries this notion further by looking at applications other than contrasting two means.

USING PROBABILITY DISTRIBUTIONS TO PLAY THE ODDS

To understand the process of statistical inference, you need to learn some basic ideas about ways that people can play the odds to figure out what to expect under normal circumstances. The section below examines what a probability distribution is and the ways in which it can be used.

Statistics of Probability and Inference

The so-called law of averages implies to many of us that anything that can happen will (the Chicago Cubs may win the World Series, for instance—don't laugh, it could happen). But in the ordinary course of events, some things happen more often than others. So, it would be wise to figure the odds before concluding that you have found something striking or unusual in your research. Suppose you had a coin and tossed heads five times in a row. You might think that this pattern is very unusual among fair coins. So, is it a fair coin? If you want a certain answer, you are out of luck. But if you want to see how *probable* such a pattern is, you can get some answers. **Probability** refers to the tendency or likelihood with which an event occurs in a population. You could figure the odds of getting five heads when tossing a fair coin five times. Here's how. The chance of getting heads on a single toss of a fair coin is fifty-fifty (excluding any chance of the coin landing on its edge). Thus, the probability of getting heads is .5 (point five).[1] What is the probability of getting heads if you toss a coin once, *and* heads again on the second toss, *and* heads again in the third toss, *and* heads again on the fourth toss, *and* heads again on the fifth toss? Compute it as

$$.5 * .5 * .5 * .5 * .5.$$

probability defined

The probability of getting all heads in five tosses of a fair coin is .03125. Hence, the odds are only about three chances out of a hundred that you could get your observed pattern from a fair coin. So, what do we decide? It is always *possible* that the tosses reflect something that *can happen* approximately three times out of a hundred among fair coins—in which case, the run of heads would mean that only dumb luck or random occurrence is at work. But, the odds of getting your run of heads by dumb luck from random tosses of a fair coin is so *improbable* that the "smart money" would bet the coin probably is *not* fair. You could decide that your coin is *unlikely* to be fair since your sample findings could be observed very, very rarely among fair coins.

This example illustrates the basic idea behind playing the odds to see if observed relationships are unlikely to occur by chance. Statisticians have investigated probability theory in some detail and have found ways to identify the odds of getting different sorts of results for various sorts of data (see Chung, 1975; Feller, 1968, 1971). Without getting into the fine details, this chapter will discuss how to use probability distributions, the roots of statistical inference methods.

Using Probability Distributions

Distributions such as the standard normal curve can be useful to determine the probability of underlying patterns. They can describe what you might expect to see ordinarily. **Probability distributions** represent the theoretical patterns of expected sample data. The standard normal curve is very much like most data in research. Despite limitations, you can often use the standard normal curve to figure the odds of various outcomes.

probability distributions identified

For instance, suppose that you and some of your friends buy some quarter-pound hamburgers from a fast food restaurant. You may have been told by the

FIGURE 14.1
Section from the
Z Table

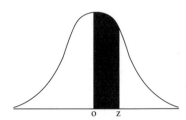

z	.00	.01	.02	.03	.04	.05	.06	.07	.08	.09
1.6	.4452	.4463	.4474	.4484	.4495	.4505	.4515	.4525	.4535	.4545
1.7	.4554	.4564	.4573	.4582	.4591	.4599	.4608	.4616	.4625	.4633
1.8	.4641	.4649	.4656	.4664	.4671	.4678	.4686	.4693	.4699	.4706
1.9	.4713	.4719	.4726	.4732	.4738	.4744	.4750	.4756	.4761	.4767
2.0	.4772	.4778	.4783	.4788	.4793	.4798	.4803	.4808	.4812	.4817
2.1	.4821	.4826	.4830	.4834	.4838	.4842	.4846	.4850	.4854	.4857
2.2	.4861	.4864	.4868	.4871	.4875	.4878	.4881	.4884	.4887	.4890
2.3	.4893	.4896	.4898	.4901	.4904	.4906	.4909	.4911	.4913	.4916

nutrition information posted at the restaurant that the mean weight of the burgers after cooking is .2 of a pound with a standard deviation of .04 of a pound. Since the burgers you have been eating seem to be well below the average, you and your friends suspect that you are not getting your money's worth. If the restaurant is living up to its word, you would expect the size of the burgers to vary at random around a mean of .2 pounds with a standard deviation of .04 of a pound.

using the standard normal curve to identify areas of unusual activity

How could you figure out whether to complain? You start by looking at the standard normal curve. You could say that if you regularly start finding hamburgers that weigh in at the bottom 5 percent of the area under the normal distribution of burgers, you would suspect that the current distribution of burgers is not what is alleged by the restaurant—and you could complain.

You need to look at the standard normal curve table (appendix A) to find the z value that covers 45 percent of the area from ground zero and leaves out the last 5 percent of the area. Figure 14.1 includes a portion of the z table. As you can see, when you compute z values to the second decimal point as this table does, no location indicates *exactly 45 percent* of the area from the mean to that location. But two numbers surround exactly 45 percent. A z of 1.64 covers 44.95 percent of the area, and a z of 1.65 covers 45.05 percent. So, if you carry out your z value one more decimal point, you can split the difference. This process is called "interpolating" a table. Thus, a z value of 1.645 corresponds to the location on the curve that includes 45 percent of the area from ground zero.

using z scores

To figure out how small the hamburgers are when they fall into the bottom 5 percent of a normal distribution, use the z score formula:

$$z = \frac{X - \mu}{\sigma}.$$

To identify the minimum size of hamburgers to complain about, we can solve the formula for X as follows:

$$X = \mu + (z * \sigma).$$

The z value may be positive or negative. In this example, you suspect that the hamburgers weigh *less* than promised. Thus, the z value has a negative sign in front of it. Putting the data into the formula, you have

$$X = \ .2 \text{ pounds} + (-1.645 * .04 \text{ pounds})$$
$$X = \ .2 \text{ pounds} - .0658 \text{ pounds}$$
$$X = .13 \text{ pounds}.$$

Thus, any burger weighing .13 pounds or under falls into the bottom 5 percent. If you find burgers this small, you can complain because it appears that the assumed population could produce such burgers no more than 5 percent of the time. Suppose your friends buy three quarter-pound hamburgers and weigh them. The first one is .12 pounds, the second one is .20 pounds, and the last one is .13 pounds. It would appear that two burgers are very unlikely to be found if the restaurant truly is meeting its promised standard. The two friends who got the undersized burgers might feel justified in asking for explanations. As you can see with these noncommunication examples, you can play the odds very effectively using probability notions and distributions.

REASONING WITH STATISTICAL HYPOTHESES TESTING

To test a statistical hypothesis, researchers need to have a formula and a distribution of the odds of finding different sorts of results.

Determining Statistical Hypotheses

When you use tests of statistical significance, you *do not* find evidence that proves that your research hypothesis is so. Instead, you gather evidence that tests whether assuming that your research hypothesis is untrue is improbable. This statement seems strange at first, but it is the way researchers handle such matters.

statistical hypotheses test that research hypotheses are improbable

To understand this idea, you need to recall the difference between the sorts of hypotheses used in research. A research **hypothesis** (H_1) is "an expectation about events based on generalizations of the assumed relationship between variables" (Tuckman, 1978, 27). It is the prediction that researchers hope to examine. Arguing for this hypothesis requires the use of a **null hypothesis** that is capable of being judged improbable by use of statistical methods. A null hypothesis (H_0) states that there is no relationship between variables. This null hypothesis is tested directly by statistical tools.

hypothesis identified

null hypothesis identified as used in testing: application to conclusions drawn

- If the null hypothesis is rejected, then the research hypothesis may be tenable and the researchers conclude that a relationship exists among variables.
- If the null hypothesis is not rejected (logically you cannot claim to "accept" a null hypothesis), then researchers make no claim that a relationship exists among variables.

Suppose you found a sample in which people who watch lots of television report being more fearful of violence than people who watch little TV. Does this sample prove that the amount of TV viewed is positively related to levels of fearfulness? The data are consistent with such a view, but how do you know for sure? Maybe you just got a weird sample—it happens sometimes even with randomization. Perhaps you have proof or perhaps you don't. The fact is, when you look for positive proof, there is little way to find out if you are right unless you are willing to wait a very long time for history to decide the matter.

So instead, for the sake of argument, you assume that there are no relationships among variables and that your samples reflect only differences due to the vagaries of random sampling. In short, you temporarily assume the null hypothesis (H_o) is true. *Then,* you look at the data and ask, "How likely is it that we could find results such as our observed in our samples if no relationships existed?" This reasoning is a very clever way to help you decide whether to reject null hypothesis:[2]

using probabilities to decide to reject the null hypothesis

- If finding results such as yours is *quite probable* when sampling from a population in which no relationships exist, you agree to continue assuming that any differences are just random.
- If it is very *improbable* that you could find results such as yours by sampling from a population in which no relationships exist, you reject the assumption that any differences are just random.

In short, you assume that nothing much is going on, and then you gather data that makes continuing that assumption unreasonable or improbable. Put another way, researchers collect data that show that "nothing" probably "is *not*" what's going on.[3]

Decision Making When Testing Statistical Hypotheses

To make decisions based on probability rather than intuition, researchers rely on probability distributions that presume no relationships. Then, researchers make decisions about their samples based on those distributions.

Finding Unusual Occurrences

unusual events usually identified if probability of occurrence by chance is .05 or lower

Researchers often look at distributions to isolate unusual patterns or unlikely events. In communication research it is typical to state that a pattern or event is unusual or improbable if it could be found at random only 5 percent of the time. This statement corresponds to a probability of .05 for finding such results by chance alone. Finding such results leads researchers to conclude that the sample probably *does not* come from a population of events in which no relationships exist among variables (this fact is the reason for calling these tools "inferential statistics").

Returning to the fast food example, suppose that you decided to do a "serious" study by randomly sampling thirty-six quarter-pound burgers. You could use the standard normal curve by slicing off a point of the distribution that separates the bottom 5 percent of the burgers from the rest. You could divide up the normal curve as shown in figure 14.2. The last five percent shaded in figure 14.2 is called

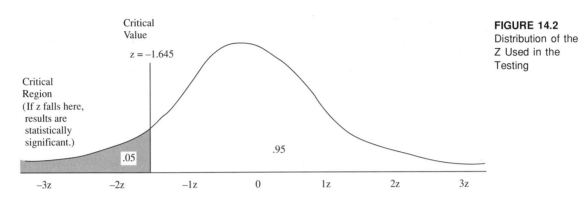

FIGURE 14.2
Distribution of the
Z Used in the
Testing

the **critical region** since if your test statistic puts you in that zone, you can claim to have found a "significant difference." A **significant difference or relationship** is one that is beyond what might be expected to occur by chance alone. Results that place you in the critical region will cause you to reject the null hypothesis. If your results do not place you in the critical region, you will not reject the null hypothesis. The line that divides the critical region from the rest of the distribution is called the **critical value.** Researchers want to find statistics that are equal to or beyond this number on the distribution. Test statistics that do not reach this point lead the researcher *not* to reject the null hypothesis. In figure 14.2, the critical region is shaded. The critical value is –1.645 (the negative sign is not subtraction; it means that the hamburgers in the sample are suspected of weighing less than the presumed population mean promised by the restaurant).

    You might compute a mean of .18 pounds for the sample of thirty-six quarter-pound hamburgers. You could enter the z distribution to compare the means of your two groups using the z formula:

$$z = \frac{\overline{X} - \mu}{\sigma} \; .$$

    But there is a slight problem. The new formula compares a couple of *means,* but divides these differences by a σ based on *raw scores.* That's like playing basketball on a football field. You have to put the measures on the same playing field if you want to divide like terms. The difference between means should be divided by a standard deviation of means. You could go out and complete a big study to find out the size of the standard deviation of a bunch of means—but who's got time for that? There is another way around it. The central limit theorem (see Special Discussion 14.1) shows that the standard deviation of a sampling distribution of means can be found by dividing the standard deviation of raw scores by the square root of the number of events. The standard deviation of a distribution of means is often called the **standard error of the mean.** Yet, you should *not think* "standard error" refers to mistakes. Whenever a standard deviation is based on

critical region
identified

significant
difference identified

critical value
identified

adaptations to
standard deviation
required to use z
when comparing
means

standard error of
the mean identified

SPECIAL DISCUSSION 14–1
The Central Limit Theorem

Data distributions in communication studies sometimes show abnormalities. Curiously though, a distribution of means does not work that way. This surprising finding is called the central limit theorem and states that a sampling distribution of means tends toward normal distribution with increased sample size regardless of the shape of the parent population. If you reached into a population and got a sample of two events and computed a mean for it and then did it again, and again, and again (say thirty or forty times), you could construct a histogram of these means. The distribution would tend to look pretty much like the underlying data—flaws and all. Suppose instead, you reached into a population and repeatedly sampled twenty events and computed means. The distribution would tend toward a normal distribution. The bigger the sample gets, the more normal the distribution of means gets. This pattern is beyond common sense, but it is a regular characteristic of distributions of means.

Because of the central limit theorem, studies comparing means can safely presume underlying normal distributions. Furthermore, the average of a distribution of means ought to come closer to identifying the population mean than any other estimation. Furthermore the central limit theorem is the backbone of the so-called "law of large numbers." A useful application of the central limit theorem is its expression of the relationship between the standard deviations of means and of raw scores (see proof for this statement in Glass & Hopkins, 1984, 188–191):

$$\sigma_{\bar{x}} = \frac{\sigma}{\sqrt{n}}.$$

This statement is used in formulae employed in tests that compare means.

---

measures other than raw scores, it is called the "standard error" of something, for example, standard error of the variance (for distributions of variances), standard error of the range (for distributions of ranges), and standard error of estimate (for distributions of predicted values). When you apply the standard deviation of the means as the key term, the resulting z formula takes this form:

$$z = \frac{\bar{X} - \mu}{\sigma_{\bar{x}}} \qquad \text{or} \qquad z = \frac{\bar{X} - \mu}{\sigma/\sqrt{n}}.$$

Now, you can compute the z value to see if the resulting number places you in the bottom five percent of the area. If so, you can conclude that the new sample probably is *not* from the population guaranteed by the restaurant.

TABLE 14.1 Decision Table

		Actual Situation (unknown)	
		H_0 is false	H_0 is true
Decision Based on Statistical Results	Reject H_0	Correct decision	Type I error
	Do not Reject H_0	Type II error	Correct decision

Run the numbers and you will find

$$z = \frac{\overline{X} - \mu}{\sigma / \sqrt{n}}$$

$$= \frac{.18 - .20}{.04 / \sqrt{36}}$$

$$= \frac{-.02}{.04 / 6}$$

$$= \frac{-.02}{.0067}$$

$$= -2.99.$$

This z value places the results into the area at the bottom 5 percent of the hamburgers. Thus, it would seem that differences between your sample of burgers and what is promised could be found no more than 5 percent of the time if the burgers really were cooked as promised by the restaurant. Thus, reasonable people might conclude that currently sold burgers probably are lighter than promised.

Choice and Errors in Testing Statistical Hypotheses

Researchers look at test statistics—such as z in our examples so far—and decide whether to reject the null hypothesis. This fact creates some interesting possibilities for the researcher, which are illustrated in table 14.1. Each row indicates the decision the researcher makes based on available sample statistics—either to reject or not to reject the null hypothesis. The columns show the reality of the matter. Of course, if you knew this reality, you would not have to complete a study. But at the time the research is completed, the researcher has only the sample data to go on.

using the decision table to identify errors and risks in hypothesis testing

    Suppose that you gather data that lead you to reject the null hypothesis (the first row). If the null hypothesis truly is false, you have made a correct decision. It also is possible for researchers to reject the null hypothesis when, in reality, it is true.

Type I error
identified

A **Type I error** occurs when sampling error gives the researcher samples that represent unusual—but randomly occurring events—and the researcher incorrectly rejects the null hypothesis. At the time a study is completed, you do not know whether this mistake has been made, but you can tell the *chances* that this error might be made. The probability of incorrectly rejecting the null hypothesis is called **alpha risk** (α risk). Alpha risk is announced by the researcher at the beginning of a study for all the world to see. The alpha level determines how much area under a distribution is in the critical region. For alpha risk of .05, 5 percent of the distribution is in the critical region. For alpha risk of .01, only 1 percent of the distribution is established as the critical region.

alpha risk identified

It is also possible that you could fail to reject the null hypothesis (fail to claim that a nonrandom relationship exists). As the second row shows, a researcher who fails to reject the null hypothesis when, in fact, there is a relationship in the population, commits a **Type II error.**[4] Though you cannot tell in advance if a Type II error has been made, the chances of such an error can be identified. This probability is called **beta risk** (β risk) and usually is associated with a study's use of samples that may not be large enough to permit existent relationships to cast a shadow big enough for statistical significance. **Power** of a statistical test is the probability of rejecting the null hypothesis correctly.

Type II error
identified
beta risk identified

Examining Statistical Hypotheses

steps in testing
statistical hypotheses

There are four major steps in testing statistical hypotheses. These steps will be considered in the order that researchers follow them.

1. Determining a Decision Rule for Rejecting Null Hypothesis

Before researchers collect data, they must decide the levels of alpha risk and beta risk. As a matter of convention—and *only* as a matter of convention—researchers usually set alpha risk at .05, often just announcing "alpha was set at .05" in their description of the statistical analyses. This statement sets a decision rule:

- If observed results could have been found by chance no more than 5 times out of 100, researchers will claim to have found real (nonrandom) differences.
- If observed results could have been found by chance *more* than 5 times out of 100, researchers will *not* claim to have found real (nonrandom) relationships.

Applying these decision rules, when differences are claimed, researchers report finding "statistically significant" differences. The term "statistical significance" does not mean that an important relationship has been found, but just that such results are not likely to be due to chance alone.

controlling alpha
risk

There are implications for selecting risk levels. By choosing an alpha risk of .05 researchers are telling others that 5 times out of 100, they *will* claim differences when it really is just sampling error playing jokes on them. This ratio works out to one test out of every twenty turning out to be "significant" by sampling error alone. Thus, researchers may replicate their studies to see if a pattern of results is stable. Beta risk is addressed by researchers' attempts to reduce background variation and by drawing sufficiently large samples.

and beta risk

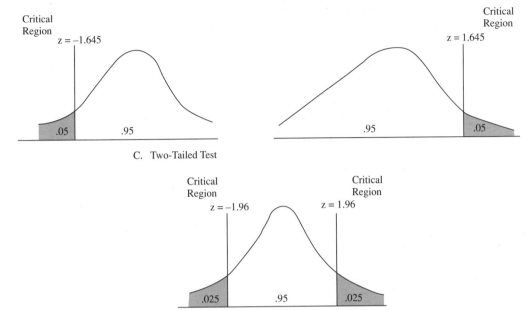

FIGURE 14.3
Using Distributions for One Tailed vs. Two Tailed Tests

2. Computing the Test Statistic

A **test statistic** is a number computed from a statistical formula to test the statistical hypothesis. So far, we have used the z statistic, but other formulae are also used.

test statistic identified

3. Finding the Critical Value

To find the critical region, the researcher must find the portion of the distribution corresponding to alpha risk. For most distributions, tables are available showing the critical value at which this critical region begins. When using a directional hypothesis, researchers are interested in only one side of the distribution. Any other location on the distribution (even the extreme opposite tail) would not support the research hypothesis. Figure 14.3 shows how this critical region is distinguished in one-tailed and two-tailed tests when using the standard normal curve. Figure 14.3A shows a left-tailed test and figure 14.3B shows a right-tailed test. These tests are called **one-tailed tests** since the critical region lies on only one side of a two-tailed distribution. The relevant side of the distribution is determined by the way the research hypothesis is stated. A directional hypothesis might state:

one-tailed tests distinguished

H_1: The current average amount of time children watch
television is greater than the average amount of
time children watched television in 1985.

SPECIAL DISCUSSION 14–2
Assumptions Underlying Parametric Tests

To use parametric statistical significance tests, researchers assume four things about the populations from which the samples were drawn:

1. Randomization in selecting events and/or assigning events drawn from populations
2. Measurement of the dependent variable on a interval or ratio level
3. Underlying normal distribution of events in a population
4. Homogeneous variances of the groups compared (any differences in variances should be within the limits of sampling error)

What happens if you do not meet these assumptions? The first two assumptions are quite firm. The remaining assumptions are the ones that you may wonder about.

Research indicates that the impact of non-normal distributions rarely is significant. Studies (Boneau, 1960; Hsu & Feldt, 1969) show that if sample sizes are five or below, the combination of a normal and skewed distribution and a rectangular and a skewed distribution can result in studies rejecting more null hypotheses than the announced alpha. Yet, when sample sizes are at least fifteen events in each group, statisticians have found that the actual proportion of Type I errors is within 1 percent of the announced alpha risk—close enough to make this assumption relatively unimportant for significance testing.

If the variances are not homogeneous, effects on Type I errors are insignificant if researchers keep sample sizes equal—or at least within a 4 to 5 ratio of each other (Glass, Peckham, & Sanders, 1972). If sample sizes are not equal, the true Type I error will be *less* than the announced alpha risk if the large variance comes from the large sample. If the large variance comes from the small sample, the true Type I error will be *greater* than the announced alpha risk. The bottom line is that the last two assumptions of parametric tests are not practical concerns in studies with roughly equal sample sizes.

The effects of unequal variances may reveal other interesting things for researchers. Unequal variances can stem from two families of causes: **ceiling or floor effects** in the data or **subjects by treatments interactions.** Ceiling or floor effects occur when scores are so high (or so low) in samples, that the data are "crunched up" (or down) near the end of the measurement range. Thus, variances for these samples are artificially reduced since they do not have the full room to spread. If ceiling or floor effects exist (measured by correlating cell means and variances with each other), the amount of explained variation made by the researcher is understated. The second family of causes for unequal variances is subjects by treatments interaction, which means that at least one additional variable uncontrolled by the researcher has introduced systematic variation influencing subjects in some conditions more than others. Thus, subjects by treatments interactions mean that researchers' studies have blown up in their faces. The researchers must reconsider their designs to find the additional variables that must be included in the study as it is reconsidered. Obviously, researchers who find unequal variances would prefer ceiling or floor effects as the explanation—otherwise they know that they have missed including at least one other significant moderating variable in their research design.

Expressed symbolically, this hypothesis states:

H_1: μ current $>$ μ amount in 1985

The direction sign lets us know that we have a right-tailed test. To support this hypothesis, the difference must be significant, *and* in the predicted direction.

A nondirectional hypothesis predicts *some* difference regardless of the direction. As figure 14.3C shows, the alpha risk must be divided equally for both sides of the distribution. Thus, the last 2.5 percent on the left tail and the last 2.5 percent on the right tail of the distribution are isolated as the critical regions that add up to the total alpha risk of .05. As you can see, for the directional hypothesis, the critical region begins closer to the center of the distribution than it does for nondirectional hypotheses. Thus, it should be easiest to find significant differences if researchers know enough to make directional predictions.

using distributions for two-tailed tests

4. Rejecting or Failing to Reject the Null Hypothesis

If a test statistic falls in the critical region, the null hypothesis is rejected. Sometimes researchers try to get fancy about this rather simple and mechanical step. For instance, after setting alpha risk at .05, they might observe that their test statistic placed them in the last 1 percent of the distribution, and they will report a significant difference at the .01 level. This step—though common—is unnecessary since the null hypothesis died as soon as the critical region was entered. It cannot be killed again after it has been rejected.

COMPARISONS OF TWO MEANS: THE t TEST

Among the tools used to examine how often observed results could have been found by chance alone are **parametric tests,** which make assumptions about populations from which the data were drawn. This section considers a family of parametric tests called the t test.

parametric tests isolated

The t test is used to compare observed means with those normally expected from a distribution of means. In short, the t test compares means to each other to check for statistical significance. This test was developed by William S. Gossett who was a chemist for Guinaess Stout Malt Liquor (the same people who publish the famous book of world records). He had to control the quality of the production, but he was not permitted to take large samples. So, he developed a distribution that described what happens to distributions of means as sample sizes get smaller and smaller. He also developed a formula to permit researchers to compare one mean to another. Because he was concerned with comparing *two* means, he called this test the t test, and the distribution of means the t distribution, it is easy to remember: it is called the t test because it means "t for two and two for t"[5] When Gossett made his discovery in 1908, Guinaess had a policy forbidding employees to publish under their own names. So, he used the pen-name "Student"—and to this day, the method is often called the "Student's t test."

developing the t test

Forms of the *t* Test

The three major forms of the *t* test are illustrated here with a formula for each and an example of its use in a little study.

One-Sample t *Test*

The "classic" form of the *t* test involves examining when a new sample mean differs from a known population mean (μ) under conditions when the population standard deviation is unavailable. This application uses the following formula:

$$t = \frac{\overline{X} - \mu}{s / \sqrt{n}} \ .$$

You may notice that this formula looks somewhat familiar. It is. In the example of testing for light-weight hamburgers, we used the standard normal curve (z) to help compare a mean to a standard. Aside from a different distribution, the only difference between that formula and this one is that this one uses the sample standard deviation (s) instead of sigma (σ). Thus, *t* really is a logical extension of the standard normal curve.

computing degrees of freedom (number of events minus number of new parameters estimated from samples)

On the *t* table (appendix B) there are many rows, corresponding to different "degrees of freedom" (found in the first column). Degrees of freedom are the number of events in a study minus the number of population parameters estimated from samples. Thus, for all *t* tests, one need only look at the formulae to determine degrees of freedom. For the one-sample *t* test, you can see that only *one* new sample mean is computed. Thus, degrees of freedom here are the number of events in the study minus one.

Table 14.2 shows an example in which the null hypothesis is rejected after using the one-sample *t* test. This method is useful to test if samples adequately identify the population means. In addition, if researchers find differences between population and sample means, they may conclude that the new sample probably does not come from the same population—or that the population is no longer described accurately by the presumed parameters. In short, the population may have changed from its previous form, perhaps inviting corrective action.

t *Test for Independent Samples*

The *t* test for independent samples is probably the most frequently used *t* test in communication research. Researchers often want to compare two sample groups to each other (one of which often is a control or current condition). These samples are independent because the events are not matched in advance, and there is no before-and-after scoring of the samples.

The conceptual test statistic for this *t* test is

$$t = \frac{\overline{X} - \overline{X}}{s_{diff}} \ .$$

The formula still looks like the previous formula, doesn't it? The population mean has been replaced by another sample for comparisons. Otherwise the only

TABLE 14.2 The One-Sample *t* Test

EXAMPLE A sample of twenty-five people are sampled from a Communication Research Methods class to find their level of math anxiety on a standardized measure, which has a known population mean of 50 for college students. The communication students produced a mean of 58 and a standard deviation of 20. Do the communication students have a higher level of math anxiety than the known population of college students?

With alpha risk set at .05, test the null hypothesis that the mean of the new sample is not different from the population mean of 50:

$$H_0: \mu \text{ indicated by new sample} = 50$$

The degrees of freedom for this test are: n − 1; 24 in this case.
Critical *t* value (for a one-tailed test) = 1.71.

COMPUTING THE TEST STATISTIC

$$t = \frac{\overline{X} - \mu}{s / \sqrt{n}}$$

$$t = \frac{58 - 50}{20 / \sqrt{25}}$$

$$t = \frac{8}{20 / 5}$$

$$t = \frac{8}{4}$$

$$t = 2$$

Since the *t* statistic (*t* = 2) was greater than the critical value (1.71), the null hypothesis was rejected. Thus, communication students were found to have significantly higher levels of math anxiety than the general population of students.

Effect size computation

$$r = \sqrt{\frac{t^2}{t^2 + \text{degrees of freedom}}}$$

$$r = \sqrt{\frac{4}{4 + 27}}$$

$$r = \sqrt{.13}$$

r = .36, a slight relationship

differences from one sample *t* test

standard error of the difference

pooled standard deviation

degrees of freedom for *t* test for independent samples

difference is that the standard deviation of means has been replaced by the standard deviation of the differences between means (s_{diff}). The term "s_{diff}" sometimes is called the "standard error of the difference" although, as you know, it has nothing whatsoever to do with making mistakes. To compute the standard deviation of the differences between means, a couple of steps should be explained.

You will remember that a standard deviation of means can be computed by taking the standard deviation of raw scores used to compute a mean and dividing it by the square root of the number of events, such as:

$$s_{\bar{x}} = \frac{s}{\sqrt{n}} .$$

But when you have two samples, you have more than one standard deviation and more than one sample size. What can you do? You could start by averaging together the standard deviations from each group to get a pooled standard deviation (abbreviated s_p for short). Yet, mathematically, you cannot average the standard deviations, since that would presume an ordered effect that does not apply here—instead, you have to average the variances (s^2) and then take the square root of that average, as in the following formula:

$$s_p = \sqrt{\text{average of variances}} = (\ (s^2 + s^2)/2\ ) .$$

This formula can be used if samples sizes are equal in both groups. If the sample sizes are not the same, a slightly longer formula is used:

$$s_p = \sqrt{\frac{(n-1)\,s^2 + (n-1)\,s^2}{(n-1) + (n-1)}} .$$

Regardless of computation, the logic is the same. You have a pooled standard deviation from both samples.

According to the original formula, you would expect to divide this pooled standard deviation by the number of events in the sample. But since there are two samples, you must make an adjustment. Instead of *dividing* the pooled standard deviation of the sample groups by $\sqrt{n}$, you could accomplish the same thing by *multiplying* the pooled standard deviation as follows:

$$s_p * \sqrt{\frac{1}{n} + \frac{1}{n}} .$$

This pattern yields the test statistic formula found in table 14.3. This example illustrates the case with unequal sample sizes—you may use the described shortcut if you have equal sample sizes in the compared groups.

For the *t* test for independent samples, degrees of freedom are the number of events in the total samples minus 2 (the number of new means that have been computed to estimate population parameters).

TABLE 14.3 *t* Test for Independent Samples

EXAMPLE A random sample of seven students read a news story that featured colored printing of the headline title. A sample of nine students in a control condition read the same message with a standard black headline. Comprehension of the information was rated on a ten-item true-false test. The mean comprehension score for the experimental condition was 8 (standard deviation of 1; variance = 1). The mean comprehension score for the control group was 6 (standard deviation of 2; variance = 4).

With alpha risk set at .05, test the null hypothesis that the mean of the color headline group is significantly different from the mean of the noncolor headline group:

H_0: μ color headline = μ standard headline

The degrees of freedom for this test are: n − 2 or 14
Critical *t* value (for a one-tailed test) = 1.76.

Computing the Test Statistic

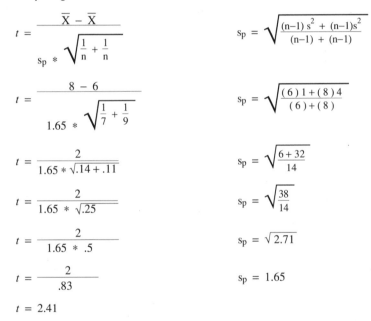

$$t = \frac{\overline{X} - \overline{X}}{s_p * \sqrt{\frac{1}{n} + \frac{1}{n}}}$$

$$s_p = \sqrt{\frac{(n-1)\,s^2 + (n-1)s^2}{(n-1) + (n-1)}}$$

$$t = \frac{8 - 6}{1.65 * \sqrt{\frac{1}{7} + \frac{1}{9}}}$$

$$s_p = \sqrt{\frac{(6)\,1 + (8)\,4}{(6) + (8)}}$$

$$t = \frac{2}{1.65 * \sqrt{.14 + .11}}$$

$$s_p = \sqrt{\frac{6 + 32}{14}}$$

$$t = \frac{2}{1.65 * \sqrt{.25}}$$

$$s_p = \sqrt{\frac{38}{14}}$$

$$t = \frac{2}{1.65 * .5}$$

$$s_p = \sqrt{2.71}$$

$$t = \frac{2}{.83}$$

$$s_p = 1.65$$

$t = 2.41$

Since the *t* statistic (*t* = 2.41) was greater than the critical value (1.76), the null hypothesis was rejected.
Effect size computation

$$r = \sqrt{\frac{t^2}{t^2 + \text{degrees of freedom}}}$$

$$r = \sqrt{\frac{5.81}{5.81 * 14}}$$

$r = \sqrt{.29}$
$r = .54$
A fair relationship.

t *Test for Dependent Samples*[6]

adaptations for the t test for dependent samples

Subjects are often matched or sampled twice. For instance, to find the impact of coupon advertising on grocery purchases, you could ask a sample of people to report the average amount spent on certain groceries during a month. Then, after exposing those same people to a newspaper advertising campaign using discount coupons for targeted products, you could ask them to report the amount spent on the targeted groceries they purchased in the *following* month. You could look at the differences in the amount spent on coupon advertised items in the months before and after the newspaper ads appeared. To employ this form, you use the following *t* test statistic:

$$t = \frac{\overline{X}_{diff}}{s_D / \sqrt{n}} .$$

In this formula, $\overline{X}_{diff}$ is the mean difference between two measures of the same individuals. The standard deviation in the denominator of this formula (s_D) is the simple standard deviation of the difference scores.

Degrees of freedom for this form of the *t* test are found by taking the total number of events in the sample (*not* the total number of scores) and subtracting one for the new mean that is computed in the formula ($\overline{X}_{diff}$). As table 14.4 shows, this method is a simple way to look at "before and after" changes, and it also is sensitive to differences that might get lost if data were clumped into groupings as in the *t* test for independent samples.

Determining Effect Sizes

other formulae required for effect size computation

Tests of statistical significance allow the researcher to rule out chance as the probable explanation of results. But significance testing does not reveal how big or small the nonchance relationships are. So a researcher is also expected (and required in professional journals) to report the magnitude of effects. One useful way to do so is to take information from a *t* test and determine what kind of correlation is indicated between the variables. Then, a large effect can be identified and distinguished from a small effect.

For the *t* test, the following formula will reveal the effect size

$$r = \sqrt{\frac{t^2}{t^2 + \text{degrees of freedom}}} .$$

This tool allows researchers to take the observed *t* value from the test statistic and compute a number that can be interpreted as any other correlation.

TABLE 14.4 t Test for Dependent Samples

EXAMPLE A sample of ten employees was tested for listening ability before and after attending a seminar in effective listening. Did the employees show significant improvements (increases in scores)? With alpha risk set at .05, test the null hypothesis that there was no significant improvement:

H_0: μ difference $= 0$

The degrees of freedom for this test are: n $-$ 1; 9 in this case.
Critical t value (for a one-tailed test) $= 1.83$.

Computing the Test Statistic (unequal sample sizes)
The data are as follows

Person	Posttest Score	Pretest Score	Difference
Larry	5	4	1
Moe	5	5	0
Curly	4	4	0
Manny	7	5	2
Moe	5	6	−1
Patty	6	4	2
Maxine	7	6	1
Laverne	8	6	2
Jerry	9	7	2
Dino	8	7	1

$$\overline{X}_{\text{diff}} = 1$$
$$s_D = 1.05$$

Test Statistic

$$t = \frac{\overline{X}_{\text{diff}}}{s_D / \sqrt{n}}$$

$$t = \frac{1}{1.05 / \sqrt{10}}$$

$$t = \frac{1}{1.05 / 3.16}$$

$$t = \frac{1}{.32}$$

$$t = 3.13$$

Effect Size Computation

$$r = \sqrt{\frac{t^2}{t^2 + \text{degrees of freedom}}} \text{ çM}$$

$$r = \sqrt{\frac{3.13^2}{3.13^2 + 9}}$$

$$r = \sqrt{\frac{9.8}{9.8 + 9}}$$

$$r = \sqrt{.52}$$

$$r = .72, \text{ a marked relationship}$$

Since the t statistic ($t = 3.13$) was greater than the critical value (1.83), the null hypothesis was rejected. Thus, there was a significant difference between the pretest and posttest scores.

SUMMARY

Probability refers to the tendency or likelihood with which an event occurs in a population. This notion is a foundation of statistical inference in which we attempt to see if observed relationships are unlikely to occur by chance. Distributions such as the standard normal curve can be useful. These distributions serve as probability distributions since they represent the theoretical patterns of expected sample data. The z distribution can be used to make statistical inferences.

When researchers use tests of statistical significance, they *do not* find evidence that proves that their research hypotheses are so. Instead, they gather evidence that tests whether assuming that their research hypotheses are untrue is improbable. The null hypothesis, which states that there is no relationship between variables, is the one actually tested statistically. If the null hypothesis is rejected, then the research hypothesis may be tenable and researchers conclude that a relationship exists among variables; if the null hypothesis is not rejected (logically we cannot claim to "accept" a null hypothesis), then researchers make no claim that a relationship exists among variables.

Researchers look at distributions and isolate unusual patterns or events. In communication research it is typical to state that a pattern or event is unusual or improbable if it could be found at random only 5 percent of the time. One location on distributions is called the critical region since if the test statistic falls in that zone, you can claim to have found a "significant difference." A significant difference or relationship is one that is beyond what might be expected to occur by chance alone. The line that divides the critical region from the rest of the distribution is called the critical value. The standard deviation of a distribution of means is often called the standard error of the mean and is used in formulae that compare means.

The ability of a statistical test to reject the null hypothesis correctly is called statistical power. Type I error involves incorrectly rejecting the null hypothesis (the probability of committing a Type I error is called alpha risk). Type II error means that researchers have failed to detect a relationship that is present (the probability of committing a Type II error is called beta risk).

There are four major steps in testing statistical hypotheses: (1) determining decision rule for rejecting null hypothesis (researchers usually set alpha risk at .05); the term "statistical significance" does not mean that an important relationship has been found, but that such results are not likely to be due to chance alone; (2) computing the test statistic (a number computed from a statistical formula to test the statistical hypothesis); (3) finding the critical value (when using a directional hypothesis only one side of the distribution is involved; one-tailed tests are identified as those in which the critical region lies on only one side of a two-tailed distribution; nondirectional hypotheses predict some difference regardless of the direction, requiring that critical regions be divided equally for both sides of the distribution); (4) rejecting or failing to reject the null hypothesis (if a test statistic falls in the critical region, the null hypothesis is rejected).

Parametric tests make assumptions about populations from which the data were drawn. In addition to the z distribution, this chapter considers another parametric test called the *t* test, which compares two means. The one-sample *t* test involves examining when a new sample mean differs from a known population mean when the population standard deviation is unavailable. For all *t* tests, degrees of freedom are the number of events in a study minus the number of population parameters estimated from the samples. The *t* test for independent samples compares two sample groups to each other (which are independent because the events are not matched in advance, and there is no before-and-after scoring of the samples). The *t* test for dependent samples is used when subjects are matched or sampled twice. After finding a significant difference, researchers may determine effect sizes by use of equivalent methods to compute correlations.

TERMS FOR REVIEW

probability
probability distributions
hypothesis
null hypothesis
critical region
significance
critical value
standard error of the mean
power
Type I error

alpha risk
Type II error
beta risk
test statistic
one-tailed tests
two-tailed tests
parametric tests
ceiling or floor effects
subjects by treatments interactions

NOTES

[1]Do not use the word "percent" when you speak about probability—it drives statisticians nuts. In probability, keep the decimal point. So, the probability of throwing heads is "point five," not "fifty percent."

[2]This reasoning method was not invented by statisticians. Thomas Aquinas used this method to argue for the existence of God. In *He Who Is,* Aquinas asked, "What would the world look like if God did not exist?" Then he concluded that the world was inconsistent with those explanations, leading to support for his claims. The application to scientific inquiry predates Aquinas. Aristotle explained how researchers reject chance as an explanation: "If then, it is agreed that things are either the result of coincidence or for an end, and these cannot be the result of coincidence or spontaneity it follows that they must be for an end" (*Physics*).

[3]This reasoning uses the conditional syllogism in the form:

MP: If p, then q	MP: If the null hypothesis is true, then data we collect will not be significantly different from each other.
mp: not q	mp: the data we collect are significantly different from each other.
C: (Therefore) not p	C: (Therefore) the null hypothesis is not true.

[4]The reason for these Type I and Type II labels stems from Aristotle's remark "To say about that which is true, that it is false, is false. To say about that which is untrue, that it is true, is false. The first is an error of the first type. The second is an error of the second type."

[5]The song "Tea for Two" had nothing to do with Gossett's labeling. The song was written for a 1926 musical called *No, No, Nanette.*

[6]Another name for this *t* test is the "*t* test for correlated groups." This method uses the product moment correlation to adjust scores that are correlated, though it is equivalent to the method of computing direct differences illustrated here.

CHAPTER 15

Inferential Statistics II: Beyond Two Means

Statistics are numbers used as arguments.

–Leonard Louis Levinson

SELECTING APPROPRIATE STATISTICAL TESTS
COMPARISONS OF MORE THAN TWO MEANS: ANALYSIS OF VARIANCE
  One-Way Analysis of Variance
  What to Do after Finding
    Statistical Significance

Factorial Analysis of Variance
BASIC NONPARAMETRIC TESTING
  The Nature of Nonparametric
    Tests: The Randomization
    Assumption
  Tests for Nominal Level
    Dependent Variables

BEFORE WE GET STARTED

This chapter extends consideration of hypothesis testing to two of the most frequently used tools found in research: analysis of variance, and the nonparametric statistic called chi square. Since the logic of other tools is consistent with those covered here, you should have little difficulty understanding other advanced applications you might encounter in your own work.

SELECTING APPROPRIATE STATISTICAL TESTS

To explore statistical significance, researchers need a test statistic or formula to help them enter a distribution and play the odds. Table 15.1 lists the major tests used to determine whether significant differences exist between groups. Methods that adapt these statistics to control for additional variables (such as analysis of covariance or analysis of variance with repeated measures) are not listed here since they are extensions of the tools listed.

TABLE 15.1 Selecting a Statistic to Test for Differences

	Measurement Level of Dependent Variable		
	Nominal Level	Ordinal Level	Interval or Ratio
Number of Sample Groups Compared for Independent Variables			
1 (sample compared to a theoretically presumed population value)	one sample chi square (goodness of fit test) binomial z test (for data that have only two possible values)	Kolmogorov-Smirnov one-sample test	Z test (if n ≥ 30 and σ known) one-sample *t* test
2 independent samples	chi square test of independence z test (difference between proportions) Fisher exact test (for expected frequencies <5)	Wilcoxon rank sum test Mann-Whitney *U* test (good for large samples) Kolmogorov-Smirnov two-sample test (for small samples) Wald-Wolfowitz runs test (detects any differences in central tendency *or* skew; assumes initially continuous output measures)	*t* test for independent groups
2 dependent samples	McNemar test for significance of changes (for dependent sample pairs)	Sign test (for matched sample pairs; does not show magnitude of differences) Wilcoxon matched pairs signed ranks test (for matched sample pairs)	Randomization test for matched pairs (for small n) *t* test for matched dependent sample pairs
more than 2	chi square of independence Cochran's Q test for (for matched or paired samples)	Kruskal-Wallis H test Median test (weak compared to Kruskal–Wallis) Friedman two–way analysis of variance	Analysis of variance Factorial analysis of variance (for two or more independent variables)

The statistics are listed by the type of data used for the dependent variable and the number of groups in the independent variable compared in a study. To select a tool to test for differences between groups, you start by finding the *column* that identifies the level of measurement for the dependent variable. Next you identify how many new sample groups of the independent variables are to be compared in the study and find the appropriate *row*. If the subjects in the study are pairs of sample data (such as pretest and posttests of the same subjects), or if subjects have been matched on some variable into pairs for comparison, special

using the table to select tests of statistical significance

sets of tools are available. For ordinary independent samples, the appropriate tools also are identified. Though many test statistics are listed, you will find that only one test really will be suitable for your particular needs in a given study.

Because covering the details of all these tests and their computation are beyond the scope of this introductory book, you are encouraged to check specific statistics books to find details about many of the formulae listed (some of the most readable of these books are Aczel, 1989; Wagner, 1992; Glass & Hopkins, 1984; Ott & Hildebrand, 1983; Champion, 1970). The rest of this chapter will illustrate some of the *most commonly used* tests found in communication research.

COMPARISONS OF MORE THAN TWO MEANS: ANALYSIS OF VARIANCE

ANOVA applied to more than two group means

When you have more than two groups, the *t* test is inappropriate. Thus, the statistic called analysis of variance (ANOVA) is invited.[1] Analysis of variance involves the use of the *F* distribution to compare results to those normally expected from a distribution of variances. In essence, the *F* distribution—named in honor of Sir Ronald Fisher—is a distribution of variances that have been divided into each other. You can use this distribution to test for differences among several means.

the notion of the *F* statistic

To compare means, researchers compute a variance (s^2) using several means as the data—just as if they were ordinary scores. Then, this variance is compared to the kind of background variation that already exists within each group. This idea is the backbone of the following conceptual formula:

$$F = \frac{\text{between groups variance}}{\text{within groups variance}} .$$

the logic of the *F* statistic: variances of means get big if the means differ from each other

This formula is not a computational guide. But the idea is simple enough. The "between groups" variance is computed using sample group means as the scores of interest (a variance of means $s_{\bar{X}}^2$). This difference is divided by a measure of background variation called "within groups" variance. Within groups variance is simply the average of the variances within each of the sample groups in the study. This measure is known to us as the "pooled variance" (s_p^2). The pooled variance is nothing more than the squared *pooled standard deviation* that we computed for the *t* test for independent samples (see chapter 14).

if the variances of means are beyond chance, they will be greater than background noise

The idea behind analysis of variance is simple. If there are no differences among group means, then the variance computed from them will be very small. In fact, if the means are all the same, a variance computed from them will be zero. But if there *are* differences among means, then the variance computed from the means will get bigger and bigger. If the differences are beyond chance, then this variance of means will be greater than the average amount of background noise within groups. That's what the *F* statistic does—divides a variance of means by background noise.

degrees of freedom for ANOVA

When using analysis of variance there are two sets of degrees of freedom: a set for the numerator of the fraction and a set for the denominator of the fraction. Indeed, if you look at the *F* table in appendix C, you will notice that the upper-left corner of the table shows the fraction from the conceptual formula. Thus, to find the degrees of freedom for the numerator, you move *left to right* to the appropriate column. In general, the degrees of freedom for the numerator are the number of means compared minus 1 (1 lost for the new mean parameter that must be computed to arrive at a variance from the sample means). To find the denominator degrees of freedom, one moves *down* the table to the appropriate row. The degrees of freedom for the numerator are the number of events in the study minus 1 for each of the means computed within each of the sample groups (to compute an estimate of variance within groups).

One-Way Analysis of Variance

To compare several means for one independent variable you use one-way analysis of variance. The number of levels for the independent variable is often included in listings of such studies. For instance, a researcher may describe a ''one-by-three analysis of variance.'' The term is shorthand for a one-way analysis of variance with three levels for the independent variable. This section describes one-way analysis of variance, the use of follow-up tests to find relationships, and how researchers may use the method to look for nonlinear relationships.

one-way analysis of variance and nomenclature

Let's suppose that three groups of ten people each were exposed to a message from a lowly, a moderately, and a highly credible source. Their attitudes might be illustrated on a 1 to 20 attitude scale as follows:

description of one-way ANOVA

Lowly Credible	Moderately Credible	Highly Credible
$\bar{x} = 5$	$\bar{x} = 10$	$\bar{x} = 15$
$s^2 = 15$	$s^2 = 25$	$s^2 = 35.$

The null hypothesis to be tested directly is

$$H_0: \mu_1 = \mu_2 = \mu_3.$$

You can compute a variance of the three means by entering the means as data into the formula for s^2 (see chapter 13). If you do so, the answer is 25. Since each group has equal sample sizes, to obtain the pooled variance s_p^2, you can just average the variances within groups. In this case—as you can see—the average of background variances in 25.

To compute F for these data, you actually use a formula that allows you to compare variances of means with averages of background variance. This appropriate adjustment leads to the following formula:

$$F = \frac{n * s_{\bar{x}}^2}{s_p^2}$$

$$= \frac{10 * 25}{25}$$

$$= \frac{250}{25}$$

$$= 10.$$

FIGURE 15.1
Examining the
F Distribution

Portion of the F Table

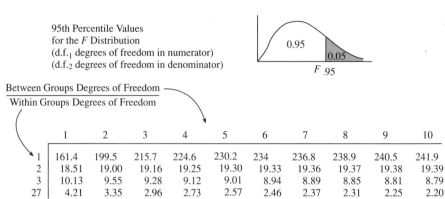

95th Percentile Values
for the F Distribution
(d.f.$_1$ degrees of freedom in numerator)
(d.f.$_2$ degrees of freedom in denominator)

Between Groups Degrees of Freedom
Within Groups Degrees of Freedom

	1	2	3	4	5	6	7	8	9	10
1	161.4	199.5	215.7	224.6	230.2	234	236.8	238.9	240.5	241.9
2	18.51	19.00	19.16	19.25	19.30	19.33	19.36	19.37	19.38	19.39
3	10.13	9.55	9.28	9.12	9.01	8.94	8.89	8.85	8.81	8.79
27	4.21	3.35	2.96	2.73	2.57	2.46	2.37	2.31	2.25	2.20

F Distribution and Example Test Statistic

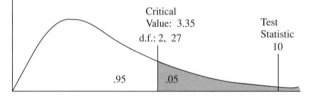

**using the F table to
interpret results**

To figure out what this test statistic means, you need to check how likely these results are to occur by chance alone. The degrees of freedom for this test are

2 for the numerator (number of group means minus one; 3 − 1 = 2); thus, you are on column two of the chart.
27 for the denominator (the number of events in the sample groups minus the number of means that were computed within each group to compute the variance; 10 + 10 + 10 − 1 − 1 − 1). Thus, you would go to row 27 on the F table.

To test for significance with alpha risk at .05, use the portion of the F table found in figure 15.1. The intersection of column 2 and row 27 gives a critical F value of 3.35 for alpha risk at .05. Since variances always are positive numbers, only one side of the F distribution is used to test hypotheses. As figure 15.1 also shows, the critical value at which the critical region begins is 3.35. To reject the null hypothesis, the test statistic must fall somewhere in the critical region—the test statistic must be equal to or greater than 3.35. Since the test statistic is 10, you can reject the null hypothesis.

The example had equal sample sizes. If there were *unequal* sample sizes, then you would compute the numerator of these fractions differently. The contribution to the total between groups variance must be weighed by the different

TABLE 15.2 One-Way Analysis of Variance Including Unequal Sample Sizes

EXAMPLE Researchers wanted to test whether groups of children, adults, or senior citizens were more persuaded by "negative campaign" ads. So, they contacted three groups of people and showed them a typical negative political ad. Their reactions were assessed on an attitude scale ranging from 3 (negative attitude) to 21 (positive attitude). The following list shows the cell means, variances, and sample sizes:

Children	Adults	Senior Citizens
$\overline{X} = 14$	$\overline{X} = 9$	$\overline{X} = 12$
$s^2 = 18$	$s^2 = 15$	$s^2 = 15$
$n = 15$	$n = 10$	$n = 20$

The first thing to do is compute a grand mean from *all* the data (you cannot just average the averages since the cell sizes are unequal). Compute it by multiplying each cell group mean by the number of events in each cell. Then add up all these numbers and divide by the total number of events in the study. In this case, the computation of the grand mean is

$$\overline{\overline{X}} = \frac{(n * \overline{X}_1) + (n * \overline{X}_2) + (n * \overline{X}_3)}{n_1 + n_2 + n_3}$$

In this example the following numbers may be substituted

$$\overline{\overline{X}} = \frac{(15 * 14) + (10 * 9) + (20 * 12)}{15 + 10 + 20}$$

$$\overline{\overline{X}} = 540/45$$

$$\overline{\overline{X}} = 12$$

To compute between groups variance, subtract each cell mean from this grand mean, square the difference, and multiply by the number of events in the cell. After completing this process for each cell, add up the totals. Then, divide this number by the degrees of freedom (number of groups minus one). Complete this process as follows

Between
Groups Variance $= \dfrac{\sum n_i (\overline{X}_i - \overline{\overline{X}})^2}{\text{degrees of freedom} = \text{groups} - 1}$

$$= \frac{[15 * (14 - 12)^2] + [10 * (9 - 12)^2] + [20 * (12 - 12)^2]}{3 - 1}$$

$$= \frac{150}{2}$$

$$= 75.$$

TABLE 15.2 —*Continued*

To compute within groups variance, use the long form of the formula for the pooled variance estimate

$$s_p{}^2 = \frac{(n-1)\ s^2 + (n-1)\ s^2 \ldots x}{(n-1) + (n-1) \ldots x}.$$

This pooled variance simply averages background variations after giving weights for different sample sizes. With these data, the numbers become:

$$s_p{}^2 = \frac{(14 * 18) + (9 * 15) + (19 * 15)}{14 + 9 + 19}$$

$$= \frac{672}{42}$$

$$= 16.$$

The degrees of freedom for this within group variance (the pooled variance) are 42. To find out if there is a difference among the means of these groups, the between groups variance is divided by the within groups variance as summarized below

ANOVA TABLE

Source	d.f.	Mean Square	F
Between Groups	2	75	4.69
Within Groups	42	16	

Since the critical value for 2 and 42 degrees of freedom is 3.22, the observed *F* value falls into the critical region with alpha risk of .05. Thus researchers would reject the null hypothesis and claim significant differences between the groups.

---

adjustments for unequal sample sizes   sample sizes. The grand mean of all the group means also must be computed from the total sample, rather than as a simple average of cell means. Otherwise the process is pretty much the same (using the long formula for the pooled variance). The example shown on table 15.2 shows how to compute and summarize ANOVA with unequal sample sizes. Of course, these formula can be used for equal sample sizes as well, though the extra steps involved are unnecessary.

What to Do after Finding Statistical Significance

Analysis of variance is not the end of the road. Additional follow-up work must be completed after finding a significant *F* ratio.

TABLE 15.3 Major Multiple Comparison Methods

Method	Application	Comment
Dunns'	Used when making comparisons that have been planned or hypothesized in advance; restricted to a small number of comparisons by the number of hypotheses.	Most powerful multiple comparison test (aside from running ts or Fs).
Dunnett's d'	Used to compare a control group against multiple treatment groups in the study.	Pairwise comparisons only.
Newman–Keuls	Used when you want a different critical value for comparisons of individual means with each other.	First comparisons very powerful, others less so; the method does not control for experimentwise alpha risk; requires equal sample sizes.
Duncan Multiple Range Test	Used when you want a different critical value for comparisons of means arranged in descending order.	Controversial since predicated on debatable notion that as number of conditions increases the probability of finding differences increases; first comparisons very powerful, others less so; the method does not control for experimentwise alpha risk; requires equal sample sizes.
Tukey's HSD	For pairwise comparisons; thus used as a follow-up test only.	Spreads out alpha risk for all possible comparisons; requires the use of equal sample sizes (for unequal sample sizes, use Spjøtvoll and Stoline's modification of HSD).
Scheffe's Critical S	Most useful for compound comparisons (e.g., two cells vs. four cells).	Most powerful for compound comparisons; but among least powerful when applied to pairwise comparisons.

Multiple Comparison Tests

The simple example produced evidence showing a significant difference among the groups. But where were the differences? Was one group different from the other two? Were all three significantly different from each other? To tease out these differences you can use some follow-up methods called **multiple comparison tests.** These methods are usually computed so that alpha risk is stretched out across comparisons.

multiple comparison tests isolated

Table 15.3 shows several major forms of multiple comparison tests and their uses. For the most part, in communication studies, researchers tend to use two tools; Tukey's HSD and Scheffe's S. Though they can be applied to the same data, the methods actually have different functions. **Tukey's HSD** (abbreviation for John Tukey's Honestly Significant Difference test) is used to make all possible comparisons of means, when the means are taken two at a time. It is the most powerful of the multiple comparison tests for making pairwise comparisons. For complex comparisons, such as comparing two cells against four others, **Scheffe's critical S** method is the most powerful tool. Each of these methods has its own method of computation and researchers should report the test statistics in their results. As table 15.3 shows, however, other tools are also suitable for multiple comparisons.

Of course, if only two levels are used in the analysis of variance, the *F* test is a direct comparison of the two conditions. Thus, no additional multiple comparison test is necessary to examine differences.

Determining Effect Sizes

Though analysis of variance permits researchers to identify nonchance differences, the size of those differences is not directly observed. Thus, differences could be big ones, little ones, or somewhere in between. The researcher needs to supplement the measure of statistical significance with a measure of effect size. Though more than one tool is available, perhaps the most readily interpretable are eta (η) and eta squared (η^2).[2] Eta, also known as the "correlation ratio," is directly interpreted as any correlation. An added advantage of the correlation ratio is that it can identify the size of nonlinear as well as linear effects. Thus, the overall correlation can be identified, regardless of its form.

**effect size
computation by eta
or eta squared**

The formula for eta is:

$$\eta = \sqrt{\frac{\text{between groups variance} * \text{degrees of freedom}}{\text{total of all mean squares multiplied by their degrees of freedom}}}$$

In our example using equal sample sizes, the numbers work out as follows:

$$= \sqrt{\frac{(10 * 25)}{25 * 27}}$$

$$= \sqrt{\frac{250}{675}}$$

$$= \sqrt{.37}$$
$$\eta = .61.$$

Thus, a correlation of .61—a "moderate to marked relationship"— appears to exist between the independent and dependent variables in this study. To report the percentage impact of one variable based on a knowledge of the other alone, eta squared (η^2) may be employed. In this example, η^2 is .37.

Looking for Nonlinear Relationships

So far, you have learned how to look for simple differences among the means of several groups. Yet, sometimes the underlying independent variable levels are arranged in some sort of continuum. This arrangement allows researchers to identify trends in the dependent variable.[3] For instance, suppose the independent variable involved low, moderate, and high amounts of information possessed by employees. The amount of employee satisfaction is the dependent measure. Given that you have three groups, you can use analysis of variance to detect any differences. You can also adapt analysis of variance to help reveal the exact contour of the relationship.

    After identifying a significant difference, researchers can use a method called **trend analysis.** Trend analysis isolates the nature of linear and nonlinear trends in effects identified as a significant by analysis of variance. Without getting into computational details, it is useful to see what a set of results might look like for hypothetical data from the example. Suppose that the means for the three levels are as follows:

trend analysis identified

Amounts of Communication

Low	Moderate	High
$\overline{X} = 5$	$\overline{X} = 15$	$\overline{X} = 10$
$s^2 = 15$	$s^2 = 25$	$s^2 = 35$
$n = 10$	$n = 10$	$n = 10.$

Obviously, these data look a great deal like the previous example, but the three means now seem to rise and fall as you move from low to high amounts of communication received by employees. If you drew a line to connect the means, it would show a curve. To identify this trend in the data, you can use trend analysis. The overall observed F value remains 10 (with 2 and 27 degrees of freedom), since the means are the same as in the previous example. Thus, there appear to be differences in satisfaction stemming from the three amounts of communication received by employees.

    Trend analysis multiplies the means by weights (called orthogonal polynomials) to reflect linear and nonlinear trends. After weighting the means, simple analysis of variance is computed again. Thus, you can tell if the significant differences stem from a linear or nonlinear trend. The result of this analysis is a set of results as follows:[4]

the method of trend analysis

Source of Variation	d.f.	(between groups variance) Mean Square	F
Amount of Communication	2	250	10
Linear trend	1	125	5
Nonlinear trend	1	375	15
Within Groups Variance	27	25	

The term "mean square" is a synonym for the variance (shorthand for "the mean of the squared differences of scores from their mean"). The linear (straight line) and nonlinear (curved) effects are tested directly. These are indented on the listing to indicate that they are not new independent variables, but just the main effect examined for trends. If you look at appendix C, you will find that for alpha risk at .05, the critical value is 4.21 for 1 and 27 degrees of freedom (the degrees of

"mean square" is a synonym for the variance

SPECIAL DISCUSSION 15–1
Interval Estimation Methods

The tools of statistical significance testing described here are called point estimation methods. This term derives from the estimating of a single value or point for a population based on the samples. When testing for significance, researchers hope (and have reason to do so) that the sample mean will lie very close to the population mean. Despite the usefulness of this method, it is not the only one available.

Some statisticians prefer to rely exclusively on interval estimates—that is, they like to report a range of values that they believe will capture population parameters. Though it may seem that both these methods are valuable (we have relied on interval estimation to describe confidence intervals around different sample estimates), some have used the logic of interval estimation as a basis for attacking standard methods of significance testing, such as are described in this introductory treatment.

Those who prefer to use interval estimation methods suggest that instead of computing whether there are significant differences between means of samples (point estimates), we should construct confidence intervals around means and contrast them. Thus, the probable range of population values could be identified. The most extreme members of this camp also have been known to write disapproving essays about what they view as faults with significance testing statistics.

There is no reason that a researcher could not do *both,* of course, but they generally do not. Mathematically, the methods of interval estimation and point estimate tests of statistical significance are equivalent. Thus, the interval estimation method also permits one to identify the presence of significant differences among groups. For instance, if a researcher found three means such as those in the following example, a sampling confidence interval could be constructed around each mean. In this case, the dots in the centers of the distributions are the means and the lines extending up and down reflect a 95 percent confidence interval:

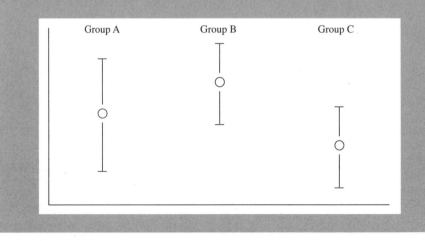

SPECIAL DISCUSSION 15–1 (Continued)

If the width of the confidence interval around one mean is large enough to include the mean of another group, then there is no difference (in this case no difference at the .05 level, two-tailed). If the mean of a group is outside the confidence interval of another group, then there is a significant difference (p = .05). In this example, there is a significant difference between Group B and Group C, indicated by the fact that the means are outside the other's confidence interval (the confidence intervals may overlap, but that does not matter). But there is no difference between Group A and the other groups since the confidence interval of Group A is so large that it includes the means of Group B and Group C. Thus, the use of interval estimation methods has been advanced as a subtle way to identify the location and form of differences, just as point estimation methods attempt to reveal them directly.

Single Factor Design

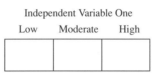

Two Factor Design

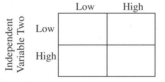

FIGURE 15.2
Variable Factors and
Cell Design

freedom we use for examining the trends). As you can see, both the linear and nonlinear trends are significant. This finding means that although the linear effect exists, the nonlinear or curved trend really tells the tale. Thus, the best fit of a trend to the data is a curved one.

Obviously, trend analysis can help identify whether curved or linear effects exist in the data. This example had three groups so only a simple nonlinear effect could be found. If there were more than three groups, you could examine additional types of trends in the data as well (such as cubic, quartic, quintic trends). Thus, this method can help researchers identify fairly subtle patterns in the data.

Factorial Analysis of Variance

We often ask questions that involve more than one independent variable of interest, each one with two or more levels. Factorial analysis of variance is invited for these sorts of situations. The term **variable factor** is used to identify a variable that has been broken down into levels or groups. Thus, "factorial analysis of variance" is analysis of variance applied to multiple independent variables that have been broken down into levels or groups.

Specifically, **factorial analysis of variance,** or factorial ANOVA, is a test of statistical significance that identifies main and interaction effects between independent variables. **Main effects** are dependent variable effects from independent variables separately. In factorial designs, these main effects are identified by looking at differences between levels of each independent variable across levels of the other variables in the study. **Interaction effects** are dependent variable effects from independent variables taken together. These interaction effects involve variation in the dependent variable arising from special combinations of levels of independent variables.

Rather than complete a bunch of studies on each independent variable separately, researchers may economize by sampling once and getting as much information as possible from the data. The language of factorial analysis of variance often describes the layout of a design. Figure 15.2 shows two designs. The first is a single factor design and the second is a two-factor design. Since the first has only one independent variable with three levels, it often is called a "one-by-three" design. This sort of design can only identify a main effect since only one variable is included. Furthermore, the design invites use of a one-way analysis of variance as its statistical test.

The second design features two independent variables, each of which has two levels. Depending on the preferences of the researcher, analysis of variance for this design is called a "two factor ANOVA," a "two-way ANOVA," a "two-by-two ANOVA," or a "two variable factorial ANOVA." The specific combinations of conditions are called "cells" of the design because they are framed by levels of independent variables. Though the figure shows only two independent variables, there is no limit to the number of independent variables that could be examined. Thus, you could have a "two-by-two-by-two design," a "three-by-six-by-two-by-four design," or any other combination of variable factors with different levels.

Computing Factorial ANOVA

Once the design of the factorial analysis of variance is decided, researchers may collect dependent measure data for each condition. ANOVA is computed to determine where the differences in dependent measures are found in the design. Though designs can be extended for three or more factors, a two-factor design for equal sample sizes is illustrated here (though, of course, the method can also be applied to unequal sample sizes). If a design has *radically* unequal sample sizes across cells, the researcher cannot really claim to have a balanced design, and the statistics may not be robust to violations of the assumptions of normal distribution and homogeneous variances.

Computing factorial analysis of variance is very much like one-way analysis of variance. An example may help. Let's look at a study to examine whether men and women differ in their scores of communication competence after taking a seminar on communication skills. The competence test has a possible range of scores from 1 to 50 (high scores indicate increased competence). Consider a study in which half of randomly selected groups of forty-two men and forty-two women at a large company are randomly assigned to take a standard training course in improving interpersonal communication, while the other half does not. Thus, the design has twenty-one subjects in each cell. Scores on the communication competence measure could be secured for each person. Table 15.4 shows the means $(\overline{X})$ and variances (s^2) for each cell. It also provides information about the column and row means $(\overline{\overline{X}}$—pronounced "X bar bar"). Furthermore, the **grand mean** or average of the averages is provided $(\overline{\overline{\overline{X}}}$—pronounced "X bar bar bar").

notation: grand mean identified

As table 15.4 shows, formulae produce answers that are placed in a summary table. Start by computing the within groups variance (sometimes this line is called "error" for "error variance," or "residual" for "residual variance"). Names notwithstanding, the within groups variance is simply the pooled variance (s_p^2). With equal sample sizes, the pooled variance is just the average of the variances within each cell. For this example, this number is 40. Degrees of freedom are the number of events in the study minus the number of cells (the number of mean parameters computed within each to obtain a variance). For this example, there is a total sample of 84 minus 4 cells, for a total of 80 degrees of freedom.

computing within groups variance

Thus, the row for within groups variance may be filled in as follows:

constructing the ANOVA summary table

ANOVA Table

Source	d.f.	Mean Square	F
Within Groups	80	40	

Now, you can look at the two main effects and the one interaction effect between the two variables. To compute the effect for the sex of the individuals who went through training

- Compute a variance using the two row means $(\overline{\overline{X}})$ for men and for women as the two pieces of data. The variance is 8.
- Multiply this variance by the number of events in each row grouping. Multiply 8 by 42 (there were forty-two men and forty-two women—forty-two events in each row). The result of this step is 336, which is placed in the "mean square" column.

computing between groups variance for sex variable

Degrees of freedom are the number of conditions (rows), minus 1. Here 2 rows minus 1 equals 1. This number is placed in the column marked d.f. To compute an *F* ratio

TABLE 15.4 Data for the Communication Competence Study

Completion of Communication Class

		Completed Class	**Did Not Take Class**	
S e x	**Men**	$\bar{X} = 30$ $s^2 = 40$ (cell 1)	$\bar{X} = 24$ $s^2 = 34$ (cell 2)	$\bar{\bar{X}} = 27$
	Women	$\bar{X} = 36$ $s^2 = 50$ (cell 3)	$\bar{X} = 26$ $s^2 = 36$ (cell 4)	$\bar{\bar{X}} = 31$
		$\bar{\bar{X}} = 33$	$\bar{\bar{X}} = 25$	$\bar{\bar{X}} = 29$

Table of Analysis of Variance with Computations

Source	d.f.	Mean Square	F
Main Effects			
Training	(columns − 1)	$\dfrac{n \text{ in column} * s_{\bar{X}}^2 \text{ column means}}{\text{degrees of freedom}}$	$\dfrac{\text{Mean Square for effect}}{\text{Within Groups Mean Square}}$
Sex	(rows − 1)	$\dfrac{n \text{ in row} * s_{\bar{X}}^2 \text{ row means}}{\text{degrees of freedom}}$	$\dfrac{\text{Mean Square for effect}}{\text{Within Groups Mean Square}}$
Interaction Effects			
Sex × Training	(rows − 1) × (columns − 1)	$\dfrac{n \text{ in each cell} * (\text{each cell} - \text{row mean} - \text{column mean} + \text{grand mean})^2}{\text{degrees of freedom}}$	$\dfrac{\text{Mean Square for effect}}{\text{Within Groups Mean Square}}$
Within Groups Variance	(total sample − number of cells)	s_p^2	

Portion of the *F* Table

FIGURE 15.3
Examining the *F*
Distribution

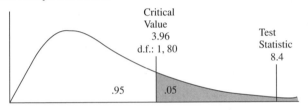

95th Percentile Values
for the *F* Distribution
(d.f.$_1$ degrees of freedom in numerator)
(d.f.$_2$ degrees of freedom in denominator)

0.95

0.05

$F_{.95}$

Between Groups Degrees of Freedom
Within Groups Degrees of Freedom

	1	2	3	4	5	6	7	8	9	10
1	161.4	199.5	215.7	224.6	230.2	234	236.8	238.9	240.5	241.9
2	18.51	19.00	19.16	19.25	19.30	19.33	19.36	19.37	19.38	19.39
3	10.13	9.55	9.28	9.12	9.01	8.94	8.89	8.85	8.81	8.79
80	3.96	3.11	2.72	2.48	2.33	2.21	2.12	2.05	1.99	1.95

F Distribution and Example Test Statistic

Critical
Value
3.96
d.f.: 1, 80

Test
Statistic
8.4

.95   .05

- Divide between groups variance (mean square) by within groups variance (mean square). In this case divide 336 by 40. The result is 8.4. Place this number in the column marked F, as follows:

Source	d.f.	Mean Square	F
Sex	1	336	8.4
Within Groups	80	40	

To learn whether this difference is beyond chance alone, you need only look at the *F* table in appendix C. For 1 degree of freedom in the numerator (column 1 on the table), and 80 degrees of freedom in the denominator (row 80), the critical *F* value for alpha risk at .05 is 3.96, as figure 15.3 shows. Since the calculated *F* exceeds this critical value, the observed *F* statistic falls in the *F* distribution's critical region. Thus, you can reject the null hypothesis and conclude that there is a significant difference between the competence scores of men and women. Women in the sample score higher in communication competence than do men.

computing between groups variance for training variable

To identify any main effects from training, you can follow the same general process. Start by

- Computing a variance from the two column means (across levels of the sex independent variable). With this step, you obtain 32.
- Multiplying by the number of events in each column (42). This action reveals the mean square for this source of variation: 1344.
- Identifying degrees of freedom as the number of columns minus one, yielding one degree of freedom in this example (2 − 1).

The *F* ratio is computed by dividing the treatment mean square by the within groups mean square, which produces a value of 33.6. When you enter it into the summary table, you get the following:

Source	d.f.	Mean Square	F
Sex	1	336	8.4
Training	1	1344	33.6
Within Groups	80	40	

computing interaction variance

This *F* value is also statistically significant with 1 and 80 degrees of freedom (column 1 and row 80 on the *F* table). By looking at the means, you can observe that people who take the communication skills training score higher in competence than those who do not take the training.

The computation of the interaction is accomplished by

- Taking each cell mean, subtracting the corresponding row mean, subtracting the corresponding column mean, and then adding grand mean into the mix.[5] For our example, we get the following numbers (cell 1 = −1; cell 2 = 1; cell 3 = 1; cell 4 = −1).
- Squaring the answer for each cell.
- Adding up these squared answers from all the cells (4 in this example).
- Multiplying this sum by the number of events in each cell. Multiplying 4 by 21 (the number of events in each cell) produces 84, which is placed in the mean square column.
- Computing degrees of freedom by multiplying the degrees of freedom for each of the main effects of the variables in the interaction. Since each variable in the interaction had one degree of freedom, the total degrees of freedom are $1 \times 1 = 1$.
- Computing the *F* ratio by dividing this mean square by the within groups variance and placing the answer in the column indicated as *F*.

Source	d.f.	Mean Square	F
Sex	1	336	8.4
Training	1	1344	33.6
Sex x Training Interaction	1	84	2.1
Within Groups	80	40	

As you can see, the interaction F ratio is smaller than the critical F ratio. Thus, no significant interaction effect can be claimed. Hence, it appears that women score higher in communication competence than men, and that those who attend the communication skills training score higher than those who do not take such training. Moreover, these effects are additive since there is no significant interaction between the two.

Examining Effect Patterns

As you recall from chapter 9, main effects indicate the impact of one variable across levels of others in the design. As such, main effects can be interpreted as if a simple one-way analysis of variance had been completed. But there is a catch. If there are significant interactions, the researcher may or may not be permitted to interpret main effects for involved independent variables. If the interaction effect is shown to be a crossed interaction (disordinal), then the researcher should not interpret main effects for variables involved, since such information would be misleading. Yet, if the interaction effect is uncrossed (ordinal), main effects may be interpreted without fear of misleading the reader. Thus, the interactions must be teased out, often using multiple comparison tests and even formal diagrams.

main effects not interpreted if disordinal interactions present

As in one-way ANOVA, it is important to identify the magnitude of the relationships observed. You can use the same eta statistic discussed previously. Thus, the comparative importance of each significant source of variation may be evaluated by the researcher.

BASIC NONPARAMETRIC TESTING

So far, this chapter has emphasized ways to compare the means of interval or ratio level dependent variables with each other. But sometimes the data are simple frequency counts in categories and require different tools.

The Nature of Nonparametric Tests: The Randomization Assumption

Nonparametric tests are statistical methods that do not make assumptions about population distributions or parameters. Thus, they are sometimes called "distribution-free" statistics. But, this statement does not mean that there are no assumptions made at all. On the contrary, one assumption is made when using nonparametric tests: randomization. If you want to examine how often a given set of categorical data or rankings could be found by chance, you must use randomization to begin figuring the odds of finding a set of results at random. Thus, as with parametric tests, randomization is a consistent requirement of statistical testing.

nonparametric tests identified

Nonparametric tests are required when researchers examine dependent measures on ordinal or nominal levels of measurement. Of course, the dependent variable data originally may have been measured on interval levels, but researchers can reduce the level of measurement to lower level data. For instance, a researcher might be interested in examining the impact of watching presidential debates on the credibility of candidates. People could fill out credibility scales before and after the debates. Instead of examining the degree of differences, researchers simply could count the number of people who rated the candidates more credible, less

required for nominal or ordinal dependent measures

SPECIAL DISCUSSION 15–2
Bells and Whistles: A Reader's Guide to Advanced Statistical Methods

Many statistical methods go far beyond an initial understanding of statistical tools. This guide defines some advanced techniques and identifies some things to look for when you read reports that use them.

Multiple Regression Correlation (a.k.a. multiple correlation): produces a correlation of multiple predictors with a single output variable. Beta weights tell the contribution made by each predictor to the overall correlation. Predictors are supposed to be uncorrelated with each other (called absence of multicollinearity).

Multiple Discriminant Analysis: predicts membership in particular groups from a knowledge of a number of predictor variables (measured on the interval or ratio level). Researchers report discriminant functions composed on linear combinations of variables which, in turn, are tested for significance. Prediction also is evaluated by using canonical correlation and hit ratio success.

Log-Linear Analysis: extension of chi-square testing for analysis of more than two variables measured on the nominal level. The method uses applications of maximizing methods (e.g., maximum likelihood estimation) to identify explanatory models and patterns.

MULTIVARIATE ANALYSES

Canonical Correlation: an extension of multiple regression correlating two sets of variables. Scholars interpret roots of canonical correlations (tested for significance using chi square) and identify components for each root (interpreted as meaningful the farther they are from zero). The redundancy index tells whether sets of variables should be interpreted differentially for additional canonical component roots (look for a redundancy index greater than .05).

MANOVA (Multivariate Analysis of Variance): extension of analysis of variance for multiple dependent variables. The method represents interrelated dependent variables (checked by a test of "sphericity") as a weighted linear combination. It tests to determine if effects are on some dependent variables more than others (such as Wilks's lambda) or whether effects are shared across dependent variables (such as Pillai's trace).

Multivariate Multiple Correlation: extension of multiple regression for many interrelated dependent measures. Canonical correlation, omnibus (Wilks's), and trace (e.g. Pillai's) statistics are combined to interpret results.

Multivariate Analysis of Covariance: extension of MANOVA to adapt analysis of covariance for multiple interrelated dependent variables (see MANOVA guides).

Hotelling's T2: t test for intercorrelated dependent variables

---

SPECIAL DISCUSSION 15–2
(Continued)

Modeling Methods

Path Models: use correlational tools to interpret relationships to identify causal models with exogenous (input variable) sources, endogenous (mediating) variables, and dependent (output or criterion) variables. Tests of fit often are expected in acceptable models.

LISREL (Linear Structural Relations): a computer program to isolate relationships by examining covariances among variables. The method develops simultaneous equations (usually employing a method such as maximum likelihood estimation to maximize the degree of relationship found) to represent relations among variables. Tests of fit using residual mean square and chi square tests usually are included.

---

credible, or unchanged after the debate. Of course when you move the level of measurement to a lower level, you lose the sensitivity contained in the original data. Thus, researchers tend to make such a choice only when practical matters of design or control of extraneous variables demand it.

Tests for Nominal Level Dependent Variables

The family of nonparametric tests applies to situations in which the dependent measures are on the ordinal or nominal level. Though there are many formulae in these categories, the most popular ones in communication research are variations of chi-square tests. Thus, this introductory treatment will focus on them. The chi-square test is designed to deal with "count" data. That is, chi square allows one to use categories and determine if there are differences between the number of data that fall into each category. The "count" of the number of events in each category is analyzed by using the applications of chi square described here: the one-sample test and the test for independence of samples.

use of the chi-square statistics: count data

The One-Sample Chi-Square Test

Also inelegantly called the "goodness of fit" test, the one-sample chi-square test allows a researcher to take a single independent variable that is broken down into nominal categories and identify whether the arrangement among categories is greater than would have been expected by chance alone.

one-sample or "goodness of fit" chi square

The chi-square (χ^2) distribution is enlisted to help play the odds. This distribution can be thought of as a probability distribution of squared differences of scores. Hence, it can be used to help assess differences among proportions and to identify when actual counts of data differ from counts that could have been expected by chance. As figure 15.4 shows, this chi-square distribution is not symmetrical, though it does tend to become more and more normal as degrees of

the chi-square distribution

Chi Square Distribution

Portion of the Chi Square Table

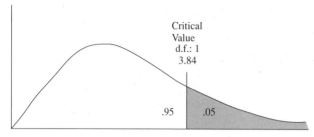

| | Critical
Value
d.f.: 1
3.84 | | | | | |
| | .95 | .05 | | | | |

| | Alpha Risk Levels
(indicating the proportion of the chi
square distribution that lies to the right
of the critical value) | | | | |
Degrees of Freedom	.95	.10	.05	.025	.01
1	.004	2.71	3.84	5.02	6.64
2	.10	4.61	5.99	7.38	9.21
3	.35	6.25	7.81	9.35	11.34
4	.71	7.78	9.49	11.14	13.28
5	1.15	9.24	11.07	12.83	15.09

FIGURE 15.4
Using the Chi Square Distribution

one-sample test used
when contrasts with
theoretically
expected frequencies
exist

freedom increase. This distribution's properties permit the identification of unusual differences by isolating the critical region, as is possible with other distributions.

The one-sample chi-square test is often used when researchers gather data that they believe can be contrasted with theoretically expected patterns. For instance, it is known that the proportion of children with speech handicaps is about 7 percent of the population. Suppose a teacher noticed that a surprising number of her pupils seemed to have speech defects. She might randomly sample a group of 100 children and find this pattern:

	Speech Handicapped	**Not Speech Handicapped**
Number of Children	15	85

To test whether this pattern is statistically significant, you can use the chi-square test with alpha risk set at .05. Using the symbol p for the probabilities of occurrence of events, the null hypothesis is

$$H_o : p_1 = p_2.$$

Since theory guides the teacher, those expectations can be compared against the actual observations. Since 7 percent of children have speech defects in the population, you would expect that 7 out of 100 children would have such defects, and 93 would not. This expectation would contrast with the observed frequencies as

	Speech Handicapped	**Not Speech Handicapped**
Number of children	15	85
Theoretic expectation	7	93

The test statistic for this case is shown by the following formula:

$$\chi^2 = \sum \frac{(f_{observed} - f_{expected})^2}{f_{expected}}$$

The f stands for the frequency or count. To use the formula, subtract the expected frequency from each observed frequency, square the difference (to get rid of minus numbers since chi square has no minus numbers), and divide by the expected frequency. Then repeat the process for all other groups. Finally, total the numbers and obtain a chi-square test statistic. In this case, you get the following numbers:

$$\chi^2 = \frac{(15-7)^2}{7} + \frac{(85-93)^2}{93}$$

$$\chi^2 = 9.14 + .69$$

$$\chi^2 = 9.83$$

degrees of freedom for chi square

Degrees of freedom are computed by looking at the number of groups − 1. Thus, in this example, degrees of freedom are 2 − 1, or 1. As figure 15.4 and appendix D show, the critical chi-square value for alpha risk at .05 and one degree of freedom is 3.84. Since our computed chi square of 9.83 is greater than 3.84, we enter the critical region—and the null hypothesis is rejected. It seems that the teacher's children have a higher rate of speech handicaps than the general population.

the equal probability hypothesis used

Sometimes researchers do not have theory to go on. Thus, they make use of the **equal probability hypothesis** to form expected frequencies. For instance, suppose that you sampled 300 people to find out if there were differences among their preference for reading the weekly news magazines *Time, Newsweek,* and *U.S. News and World Report.* You might find the following:

	Time	*Newsweek*	*U.S. News and World Report*
Number of People Preferring:	130	110	60

To find out if the observed pattern differs from what might be expected at random, you could hypothesize that if there were no preferences, each magazine would have an equal chance of selection. If each magazine were equally preferred, you would expect one-third of the sample to prefer each magazine. Thus, the equal probability hypothesis would lead you to the following comparisons:

	Time	*Newsweek*	*U.S. News and World Report*
Number of People Preferring:	130	110	60
Expected Frequencies	100	100	100

The test statistic for this case is:

$$\chi^2 = \sum \frac{(f_{observed} - f_{expected})^2}{f_{expected}}$$

$$\chi^2 = \frac{(130-100)^2}{100} + \frac{(110-100)^2}{100} + \frac{(60-100)^2}{100}$$

$$\chi^2 = 9 + 1 + 16$$

$$\chi^2 = 26$$

degrees of freedom for the one-sample chi-square test

Degrees of freedom are computed by looking at the number of groups − 1. Hence, the degrees of freedom are 3 − 1, or 2 degrees of freedom. Since at alpha risk of .05 the critical region of chi square begins at 5.99, the null hypothesis is rejected. Consequently, researchers would conclude that there is a difference among preferences of news magazines.

The Chi-Square Test of Independence

If you have two or more ways to classify variables, you can create what are called "contingency tables" to see if there is a relationship between the variables that compose the framework of the table. For instance, suppose you wanted to find out whether teams of male or female college debaters won more or fewer debates than each other. You could find a sample of debate teams composed of males and a sample of debate teams composed of women. Then, during the preliminary rounds of a tournament, you could count the number of debates each team won or lost. The null hypothesis in this case would be that the two classification variables are independent (unrelated to each other). After analyzing 150 debates by males and 150 debates by female debate teams (none involving the same pairs of debate teams debating against each other), you might find the following data:

using contingency tables with two classification variables

test of independence

	Number of Debates Won	Number of Debates Lost	
Debates by Males	90	60	150 (50%)
Debates by Females	80	70	150 (50%)
total	170	130	

computing expected frequencies for the chi-square test of independence

The formula for this chi-square test statistic is the same as the "goodness of fit" test. The only difference lies in the source of the expected frequencies. If the two classification variables are independent and unrelated to each other, then you would expect to see a roughly equal distribution of counts across conditions. In this case, look at the row percentages and the column totals. As you can see, each row includes 50 percent of the data. Thus, if there were no relationship between classification variables (sex of team and win-loss record), you would expect to see 50 percent of each column total composed of male debate teams and 50 percent composed of female debate teams. Thus, researchers compute the row percentages and use those percentages to identify the expected frequencies for each row. Now apply this logic to the example. The column for number of debates won was 170. Thus, you would expect to see 50 percent of this 170 on the row for women and 50 percent on the row for men. Similarly, the column indicating the number of debates lost was 130. Thus, you would expect to see 50 percent of this 130 on the row for women and 50 percent on the row for men. The results are shown on this revised table:

	Number of Debates Won	Number of Debates Lost	
Debates by Males expected frequency:	90 (85)	60 (65)	150 (50%)
Debates by Females expected frequency:	80 (85)	70 (65)	150 (50%)
total	170	130	

The test statistic uses the standard formula for chi square:

$$\chi^2 = \sum \frac{(f_{observed} - f_{expected})^2}{f_{expected}}$$

$$\chi^2 = \frac{(90 - 85)^2}{85} = \frac{(60 - 65)^2}{65} + \frac{(80 - 85)^2}{85} + \frac{(70 - 65)^2}{65}$$

$$\chi^2 = .29 + .38 + .29 + .38$$

$$\chi^2 = 1.34$$

Degrees of freedom are equal to the number of columns minus one multiplied by the number of rows minus one. In this case, you have $(2 - 1)$ times $(2 - 1)$, which yields one degree of freedom. Since the critical chi-square value is 3.84, it is clear that the test statistic did not fall into the critical region of the chi-square distribution. Thus, the researcher fails to reject the null hypothesis and concludes that there is no difference indicated by the data. Hence, there did not appear to be a relationship between the sex of the debaters and the win-loss record.

degrees of freedom for the chi-square test of independence

Determining Effect Sizes

The chi-square test permits you to determine whether you can eliminate chance to explain research findings. But the test does not identify how big the effects are. Thus, it is useful to assess effect size. Several methods for doing so are available, but among the most frequently employed is the contingency coefficient, which involves taking the observed chi-square value and computing the following formula:

$$C = \sqrt{\frac{\chi^2}{N + \chi^2}}$$

This formula permits individuals to identify the size of relationships between variables equivalent to a correlation. Thus, the contingency coefficient is an important counterpart to significance testing.

SUMMARY

Analysis of variance involves the use of the F distribution to compare more than two means. Researchers may compute a variance using sample means as the data (between groups variance) and compare this variance to the kind of background variation that already exists within each group (within groups variance). This latter term is represented by the "pooled variance" (the squared pooled standard deviation used for the t test). To compare several means for one independent variable one uses one-way analysis of variance. Additional follow-up work must be completed after finding a significant F ratio. To identify the location of differences, multiple comparison tests may be used (these methods are usually computed so that alpha risk is stretched out across comparisons). Tukey's HSD is used to make all possible comparisons of means, when the means are taken two at a time. For complex comparisons Scheffe's critical S method is recommended. The researcher needs to supplement the measure of statistical significance with measures of effect size, such as eta (η) and eta squared (η^2) (also called the "correlation ratio"). To identify nonlinear relationships, researchers may follow up by using trend analysis, a method that isolates the nature of linear and nonlinear effects by considering weighted means.

A variable factor is a variable that has been broken down into levels or groups. Factorial analysis of variance is analysis of variance applied to multiple independent variables that have been broken down into levels or groups. This test of significance identifies main and interaction effects between independent variables. Main effects are dependent variable effects from independent variables taken separately. Interaction effects are dependent variable effects from independent variables taken together. If there is a crossed interaction (disordinal), then the researcher should not interpret main effects for variables involved, since such information would be misleading.

Nonparametric tests are statistical methods that do not make assumptions about population distributions or population parameters. Yet, these methods make one assumption for use of these tests: randomization. The family of nonparametric tests applies to situations in which the dependent measures are on the ordinal or nominal level. The most popular ones in communication research are variations of chi-square tests. The chi-square test is designed to deal with "count" data. The one-sample chi-square test allows a researcher to take a single independent variable that is broken down into nominal categories and identify whether the arrangement among categories is greater than would have been expected by chance alone. It often is used when researchers gather data that they believe can be contrasted with theoretically expected patterns. When researchers do not have theory to go on, they make use of the "equal probability hypothesis" to form expected frequencies. The chi-square test of independence is used when there are two or more ways to classify variables that can be classed into "contingency tables." After finding a significant chi square, researchers follow up by using a measure of effect size, such as the contingency coefficient.

TERMS FOR REVIEW

multiple comparison tests
Tukey's HSD
Scheffe's critical S
trend analysis
factorial analysis of variance
variable factors

main effects
interaction effects
grand mean
nonparametric statistics
equal probability hypothesis

NOTES

[1]You might wonder what would happen if we used both F tests and t tests to compare two means. The answer is that under these circumstances, $F = t^2$.

[2]There are two other methods: the intraclass correlation $(\hat{\rho}_I)$, which applies to the "random effects" model of analysis of variance, and omega squared $(\hat{\omega}^2)$, which is suitable to the "fixed effects" model of analysis of variance. These methods adjust for expected variance within groups sums of squares and mean squares respectively (Kirk, 1982, pp. 161–63). For computational ease, eta is described here.

[3]Statisticians prefer that the spacing between the levels of the independent variable be equal. Provided that the levels are rationally chosen to cover the range of interest to the researcher, little difficulty is created by this requirement.

[4]Though discussing these computation methods is beyond the scope of this book, they are based on the discussion found in Kirk (1982, pp. 150–61). In this case the linear effect orthogonal polynomial weights were –1, 0, and 1; the nonlinear weights were 1, –2, and 1. The formula used to compute the effect was:

$$MS = \frac{\dfrac{n * [\Sigma\,(\text{weights} * \overline{X})]^2}{\Sigma\,\text{weights}^2}}{\text{degrees of freedom}}$$

[5]If you had three independent variables, you would compute the three variable interaction by taking the cell mean and subtracting the row mean, subtracting the column mean, subtracting the slice (that's what the third variable division is called) mean, and adding in the grand mean twice (to keep the numbers sensible).

Areas under the Standard Normal Curve

$$Z = \frac{X - mean}{standard\ deviation}$$

z	.00	.01	.02	.03	.04	.05	.06	.07	.08	.09
0.0	.0000	.0040	.0080	.0120	.0160	.0199	.0239	.0279	.0319	.0359
0.1	.0398	.0438	.0478	.0517	.0557	.0596	.0636	.0675	.0714	.0753
0.2	.0793	.0832	.0871	.0910	.0948	.0987	.1026	.1064	.1103	.1141
0.3	.1179	.1217	.1255	.1293	.1331	.1368	.1406	.1443	.1480	.1517
0.4	.1554	.1591	.1628	.1664	.1700	.1736	.1772	.1808	.1844	.1879
0.5	.1915	.1950	.1985	.2019	.2054	.2088	.2123	.2157	.2190	.2224
0.6	.2257	.2291	.2324	.2357	.2389	.2422	.2454	.2486	.2517	.2549
0.7	.2580	.2611	.2642	.2673	.2704	.2734	.2764	.2794	.2823	.2852
0.8	.2881	.2910	.2939	.2967	.2995	.3023	.3051	.3078	.3106	.3133
0.9	.3159	.3186	.3212	.3238	.3264	.3289	.3315	.3340	.3365	.3389
1.0	.3413	.3438	.3461	.3485	.3508	.3531	.3554	.3577	.3599	.3621
1.1	.3643	.3665	.3686	.3708	.3729	.3749	.3770	.3790	.3810	.3830
1.2	.3849	.3869	.3888	.3907	.3925	.3944	.3962	.3980	.3997	.4015
1.3	.4032	.4049	.4066	.4082	.4099	.4115	.4131	.4147	.4162	.4177
1.4	.4192	.4207	.4222	.4236	.4251	.4265	.4279	.4292	.4306	.4319
1.5	.4332	.4345	.4357	.4370	.4382	.4394	.4406	.4418	.4429	.4441
1.6	.4452	.4463	.4474	.4484	.4495	.4505	.4515	.4525	.4535	.4545
1.7	.4554	.4564	.4573	.4582	.4591	.4599	.4608	.4616	.4625	.4633
1.8	.4641	.4649	.4656	.4664	.4671	.4678	.4686	.4693	.4699	.4706
1.9	.4713	.4719	.4726	.4732	.4738	.4744	.4750	.4756	.4761	.4767
2.0	.4772	.4778	.4783	.4788	.4793	.4798	.4803	.4808	.4812	.4817
2.1	.4821	.4826	.4830	.4834	.4838	.4842	.4846	.4850	.4854	.4857
2.2	.4861	.4864	.4868	.4871	.4875	.4878	.4881	.4884	.4887	.4890
2.3	.4893	.4896	.4898	.4901	.4904	.4906	.4909	.4911	.4913	.4916
2.4	.4918	.4920	.4922	.4925	.4927	.2929	.4931	.4932	.4934	.4936
2.5	.4938	.4940	.4941	.4943	.4945	.4946	.4948	.4949	.4951	.4952
2.6	.4953	.4955	.4956	.4957	.4959	.4960	.4961	.4962	.4963	.4964
2.7	.4965	.4966	.4967	.4968	.4969	.4970	.4971	.4972	.4973	.4974
2.8	.4974	.4975	.4976	.4977	.4977	.4978	.4979	.4979	.4980	.4981
2.9	.4981	.4982	.4982	.4983	.4984	.4984	.4985	.4985	.4986	.4986
3.0	.4987	.4987	.4987	.4988	.4988	.4989	.4989	.4989	.4990	.4990
3.1	.4990	.4991	.4991	.4991	.4992	.4992	.4992	.4992	.4993	.4993
3.2	.4993	.4993	.4994	.4994	.4994	.4994	.4994	.4995	.4995	.4995
3.5	.4998									
4.0	.49997									
4.5	.499997									
5.0	.4999997									
6.0	.499999997									

Critical Values of t

Alpha risk for one-tailed tests

Alpha risk for two-tailed tests

	.05	.025	.01	.005
	.10	.05	.02	.01

Degrees of freedom:

(Number of events minus the number of new means computed in the numerator of the t statistic formula)

Example:

$$t = \frac{\bar{x} - \bar{x}}{s \, \text{diff}}$$

d.f. = n - 2

1	6.314	12.706	31.821	63.657
2	2.920	4.303	6.965	9.925
3	2.353	3.182	4.541	5.841
4	2.132	2.776	3.747	4.604
5	2.015	2.571	3.365	4.032
6	1.943	2.447	3.143	3.707
7	1.895	2.365	2.998	3.500
8	1.860	2.306	2.896	3.355
9	1.833	2.262	2.821	3.250
10	1.812	2.228	2.764	3.169
11	1.796	2.201	2.718	3.106
12	1.782	2.179	2.681	3.054
13	1.771	2.160	2.650	3.012
14	1.761	2.145	2.624	2.977
15	1.753	2.132	2.602	2.947
16	1.746	2.120	2.584	2.921
17	1.740	2.110	2.567	2.898
18	1.734	2.101	2.552	2.878
19	1.729	2.093	2.540	2.861
20	1.725	2.086	2.528	2.845
21	1.721	2.080	2.518	2.831
22	1.717	2.074	2.508	2.819
23	1.714	2.069	2.500	2.807
24	1.711	2.064	2.492	2.797
25	1.708	2.060	2.485	2.787
26	1.706	2.056	2.479	2.779
27	1.703	2.052	2.473	2.771
28	1.701	2.048	2.467	2.763
29	1.699	2.045	2.462	2.756
30	1.697	2.042	2.457	2.750
35	1.690	2.030	2.438	2.724
40	1.684	2.021	2.423	2.704
50	1.676	2.009	2.403	2.678
75	1.666	1.993	2.378	2.644
100	1.660	1.984	2.364	2.626
150	1.655	1.976	2.352	2.609
200	1.652	1.972	2.345	2.601
500	1.648	1.965	2.334	2.586
∞	1.645	1.960	2.326	2.576

Critical Values of *F*
with alpha risk = .05

between groups degrees of freedom

within groups degrees of freedom

	1	2	3	4	5	6	7	8	9	10	11	12	15	20	25
1	161.4	199.5	215.7	224.6	230.2	234	236.8	238.9	240.5	241.9	242.5	243.9	245.9	248.0	249.3
2	18.51	19.00	19.16	19.25	19.30	19.33	19.36	19.37	19.38	19.39	19.40	19.41	19.43	19.44	19.46
3	10.13	9.55	9.28	9.12	9.01	8.94	8.89	8.85	8.81	8.79	8.76	8.74	8.70	8.66	8.63
4	7.71	6.94	6.59	6.39	6.26	6.16	6.09	6.04	6.00	5.96	5.93	5.91	5.86	5.80	5.77
5	6.61	5.79	5.41	5.19	5.05	4.95	4.88	4.82	4.77	4.74	4.70	4.68	4.62	4.56	4.52
6	5.99	5.14	4.76	4.53	4.39	4.28	4.21	4.15	4.10	4.06	4.03	4.00	3.94	3.87	3.83
7	5.59	4.74	4.35	4.12	3.97	3.87	3.79	3.73	3.68	3.64	3.60	3.57	3.51	3.44	3.40
8	5.32	4.46	4.07	3.84	3.69	3.58	3.50	3.44	3.39	3.34	3.31	3.28	3.22	3.15	3.11
9	5.12	4.26	3.86	3.63	3.48	3.37	3.29	3.23	3.18	3.13	3.10	3.07	3.01	2.94	2.89
10	4.96	4.10	3.71	3.48	3.33	3.22	3.14	3.07	3.02	2.97	2.94	2.91	2.85	2.77	2.73
11	4.84	3.98	3.59	3.36	3.20	3.09	3.01	2.95	2.90	2.86	2.82	2.79	2.72	2.65	2.60
12	4.75	3.88	3.49	3.26	3.11	3.00	2.92	2.85	2.80	2.76	2.72	2.69	2.62	2.54	2.50
13	4.67	3.81	3.41	3.18	3.03	2.92	2.84	2.77	2.72	2.67	2.63	2.60	2.53	2.46	2.41
14	4.60	3.74	3.34	3.11	2.96	2.85	2.77	2.70	2.65	2.60	2.56	2.53	2.46	2.39	2.34
15	4.54	3.68	3.29	3.06	2.90	2.79	2.71	2.64	2.59	2.55	2.51	2.48	2.40	2.33	2.28
16	4.49	3.63	3.24	3.01	2.85	2.74	2.66	2.59	2.54	2.49	2.45	2.42	2.35	2.28	2.23
17	4.45	3.59	3.20	2.96	2.81	2.70	2.62	2.55	2.50	2.45	2.41	2.38	2.31	2.23	2.18
18	4.41	3.55	3.16	2.93	2.77	2.66	2.58	2.51	2.46	2.41	2.37	2.34	2.27	2.19	2.14
19	4.38	3.52	3.13	2.90	2.74	2.63	2.55	2.48	2.43	2.38	2.34	2.31	2.23	2.16	2.11
20	4.35	3.49	3.10	2.87	2.71	2.60	2.52	2.45	2.40	2.35	2.31	2.28	2.20	2.12	2.07
21	4.32	3.47	3.07	2.84	2.68	2.57	2.49	2.42	2.37	2.32	2.28	2.25	2.18	2.10	2.05
22	4.30	3.44	3.05	2.82	2.66	2.55	2.47	2.40	2.35	2.30	2.26	2.23	2.15	2.07	2.02
23	4.28	3.42	3.03	2.80	2.64	2.53	2.45	2.38	2.32	2.28	2.24	2.20	2.13	2.05	2.00
24	4.26	3.40	3.01	2.78	2.62	2.51	2.43	2.36	2.30	2.26	2.22	2.18	2.11	2.03	1.97
25	4.24	3.39	2.99	2.76	2.60	2.49	2.41	2.34	2.28	2.24	2.20	2.16	2.09	2.01	1.96
26	4.23	3.37	2.98	2.74	2.59	2.47	2.39	2.32	2.27	2.22	2.18	2.15	2.07	1.99	1.94
27	4.21	3.35	2.96	2.73	2.57	2.46	2.37	2.31	2.25	2.20	2.16	2.13	2.06	1.97	1.92
28	4.20	3.34	2.95	2.71	2.56	2.45	2.36	2.29	2.24	2.19	2.15	2.12	2.04	1.96	1.91
29	4.18	3.33	2.93	2.70	2.55	2.43	2.35	2.28	2.22	2.18	2.14	2.10	2.03	1.94	1.89
30	4.17	3.32	2.92	2.69	2.53	2.42	2.34	2.27	2.21	2.16	2.12	2.09	2.01	1.93	1.88
40	4.08	3.23	3.84	2.61	2.45	2.34	2.25	2.18	2.12	2.08	2.04	2.00	1.92	1.84	1.78
80	3.96	3.11	2.72	2.48	2.33	2.21	2.12	2.05	1.99	1.95	1.91	1.88	1.80	1.70	1.64
120	3.92	3.07	2.68	2.45	2.29	2.18	2.09	2.02	1.96	1.91	1.87	1.83	1.75	1.66	1.60
200	3.89	3.04	2.65	2.41	2.26	2.14	2.05	1.98	1.92	1.87	1.83	1.80	1.72	1.62	1.56
∞	3.84	3.00	2.61	2.37	2.21	2.10	2.01	1.94	1.88	1.83	1.79	1.75	1.67	1.57	1.51

Critical Values of Chi Square

	Alpha Risk Levels indicating the proportion of the chi square distribution that lies to the right of the critical value				
Degrees of freedom:	.95	.10	.05	.025	.01
1	.004	2.71	3.84	5.02	6.64
2	.10	4.61	5.99	7.38	9.21
3	.35	6.25	7.81	9.35	11.34
4	.71	7.78	9.49	11.14	13.28
5	1.15	9.24	11.07	12.83	15.09
6	1.64	10.64	12.59	14.45	16.81
7	2.17	12.02	14.07	16.01	18.48
8	2.73	13.36	15.51	17.53	20.09
9	3.33	14.68	16.92	19.02	21.67
10	3.94	15.99	18.31	20.48	23.21
11	4.57	17.28	19.68	21.92	24.72
12	5.23	18.55	21.03	23.34	26.22
13	5.89	19.81	22.36	24.74	27.69
14	6.57	21.06	23.68	26.12	29.14
15	7.26	22.31	24.99	27.49	30.58
16	7.96	23.54	26.30	28.85	32.00
17	8.67	24.77	27.59	30.19	33.41
18	9.39	25.99	28.87	31.53	34.81
19	10.12	27.20	30.14	32.85	36.19
20	10.85	28.41	31.41	34.17	37.57
21	11.59	29.62	32.67	35.48	38.93
22	12.34	30.81	33.92	36.78	40.29
23	13.09	32.01	35.17	38.08	41.64
24	13.85	33.20	36.42	39.26	42.98
25	14.61	34.38	37.65	40.65	44.31
26	15.38	35.56	38.89	41.92	45.61
27	16.15	36.74	40.11	43.19	46.96
28	16.93	37.92	41.34	44.46	48.28
29	17.71	39.09	42.56	45.72	49.59
30	18.49	40.26	43.77	46.98	50.89
40	26.51	51.81	55.76	59.34	63.69
50	34.76	63.17	67.50	71.42	76.15
75	56.07	91.06	96.21	100.83	103.60
100	77.93	118.50	124.34	129.56	135.81

GLOSSARY

absolute zero A score that indicates that the property measured is completely absent.

abstract bibliographic card Bibliographic cards featuring summaries of materials.

abstract calculus An element of theory, which is the logical structure of relationships (the word "calculus" refers to any deductive system).

accidental or convenience sampling Selection of events that are most readily available.

accretions Deposits of material left by some action.

act In Burke's dramatistic pentad, the symbolic action (the speech, for instance).

ad hoc **rescue** A fallacy of research in which support for a theory is claimed for a theory despite failed predictions.

advertising The study of mass media methods of influence to promote a product, service, or cause.

agency In Burke's dramatistic pentad, the symbolic and linguistic strategies used to secure identification.

agent In Burke's dramatistic pentad, the actor or rhetor who performs the act.

agreement, method of *See* method of agreement.

alpha *See* Cronbach's coefficient alpha.

alpha risk (α risk) The probability of committing a Type I error.

alternate forms test reliability Constructing different forms of the same test from a common pool of measurement items, giving them to the *same* group of people, and determining the degree of consistency.

analogy *See* argument from analogy.

analysis of covariance A method of statistical control that determines the variation associated with each nuisance variable and then separates it from the remaining total variation in the experiment by use of analysis of variance methods.

analysis of variance A test of statistical significance that compares the means of two or more groups.

analytic inductions Methods that involve researchers starting with some tentative hypotheses that they apply in fieldwork. If these hypotheses are inadequate they may be abandoned or reformulated.

annotations Additional explanations, comments, evaluations, or criticisms that clarify the material.

applied research Study completed to develop a product or solve an immediate practical problem.

a priori (Literally "from the earlier part"), a "way of knowing" that

claims knowledge before having any experience with events.

argumentation The study of reason giving communication.

argument from analogy A method of reasoning that compares "two things known to be alike in one or more features and . . . suggests that they will be alike in other features as well" (McDonald, 1980, p. 164).

argument from definition A method of reasoning in which people submit that things do or do not belong in a certain class.

argument from example and generalization A method of reasoning taking some particular cases and arguing that what is true of instances is generally true in the population of events.

arguments Claims advanced on the basis of reasoning from evidence.

arithmetic mean The number computed by adding a set of scores and dividing by the number of scores.

arrangement The canon of rhetoric concerning the organization of ideas.

association *See* correlation.

attenuation A reduction of the size of observed effects because of errors in measurement.

authority A way of knowing in which a claim is accepted because authority figures have accepted it.

averaging or reconstructive questions Questionnaire items that ask respondents to report an average or to recall typical past behavior.

basic research Studies completed to learn about relationships among variables, regardless of any immediate commercial product or service.

beta risk (β risk) The probability of committing a Type II error.

beta weights In multiple correlation, the contribution made by each predictor to the overall correlation.

bimodal A condition in which a distribution possesses two modes.

blocking Including a nuisance variable to the design as another independent variable of interest.

canonical correlation An extension of multiple regression correlating two sets of variables.

canons of rhetoric Five established major categories that help explain communication.

case studies and interpretive studies Intensive inquiries about single events, people, or social units (interpretive studies attempt to look for themes or stories that are helpful to 'interpret' or understand the case).

categorical syllogism A syllogism that starts with a categorical statement.

causal argument A method of reasoning asserting that "a given factor is responsible for producing certain other results" (Reinard, 1991, p. 197).

CD-ROM (Compac Disk—Read Only Memory) Database records recorded in CD format.

central limit theorem The statement that a sampling distribution of means tends toward normal distribution with increased sample size regardless of the shape of the parent population.

central tendency Measures that report averages.

check question A check on test-taking behavior that involves asking the same question twice at different locations in the questionnaire, usually once positively worded and once negatively worded.

chi-square distribution A probability distribution of squared differences of scores.

chi-square test of independence Adaptation of chi-square test to the analysis of contingency tables.

chronological summary A summary strategy that reviews literature by considering studies in their order of publication from the oldest study through the most recent one.

circularity A problem created when definitions simply repeat terms.

climate questions Follow-up interview questioning that asks respondents to explain how they feel about the interview.

closed-ended questions Questions to which people respond in fixed categories of answers.

cluster sampling 1. (In content analysis) sampling in which groups of messages exist in a cluster (such as the cluster of articles that appears in a single newspaper); 2. samples are defined based on the known proportions within the population and random sampling is completed within each group.

code systems The study of the uses of verbal and nonverbal symbols and signs in human communication.

coding units In content analysis, categories used to count the communication forms in the examples chosen.

coefficient alpha *See* Cronbach's coefficient alpha.

coefficient of determination A number that shows the percentage of variation in one variable that can be explained by a knowledge of the other variable alone; the square of a correlation coefficient.

coefficient of reproducibility In Guttman scales, a measure of reliability.

Cohen's *kappa* A measure of intercoder reliability, which compensates for the number of times rating categories are used.

communication The process by which participants transact and assign meaning to messages.

communication disorders *See* speech and hearing science.

communication education *See* speech communication education.

communication policy The study of public policy and regulation of mass media communication and freedom of speech.

communication research "Research in speech-communication focuses on the ways in which messages link participants during interactions" (Kibler & Barker, 1969, p. 33).

communication technology The study of the mechanisms and technologies of mass media.

complete observer Inquiry that observes individuals in settings in which there is no contact between the observed and the observer.

complex questions Questionnaire items that include extra qualifying words or phrases that render simple yes or no answers misleading.

concepts *See* hypothetical constructs.

conceptual (or constitutive) definitions Definitions that rely on other concepts to describe a term.

concomitant variation *See* method of concomitant variation.

concurrent validity A method of test validity that involves correlating a new measure with a previously validated measure of the same construct.

conditional syllogism A form of syllogism whose major premise makes an "if-then" statement.

confidence intervals Numbers indicating the probability that sample statistics "capture" population parameters, within certain margins for error.

confidentiality The requirement that all information gathered from individual subjects is secret.

conflict management The study of the role of communication in the creation and control of conflict and disputes.

confounding Mixing (or confusing) variation from one source with variation from another source so that it is impossible to know whether effects are due to the impact of either variable separately or some combination of them.

constant A symbol to which only one number may be assigned.

constitutive definition *See* conceptual definitions.

constructs "Generalizations about observables according to some common property" (Deutsch & Krauss, 1965, p. 9).

construct validity A method of test validity that involves correlating the new measure with at least two other measures, one of which is a valid measure of a construct that is known conceptually to be directly related to the new measure, and another one of which should be a valid measure of a construct that is known conceptually to be inversely related to the construct of interest.

content analysis "A systematic, quantitative study of verbally communicated material (articles, speeches, films) by determining the frequency of specific ideas concepts, or terms" (*Longman Dictionary of Psychology and Psychiatry,* 1984, p. 176).

contingency coefficient A method to determine effect sizes following a significant chi-square test.

contingency questions "Questions asked only of *some* respondents, determined by their responses to some other question" (Babbie 1992, p. G2).

control 1. (As a function of theory) the power to direct things; 2. (in research design) methods researchers use to remove or hold constant the effects of nuisance variables.

convenience sampling *See* accidental or convenience sampling.

conversational analysis Content analysis that attempts to identify "turns" taken by people during exchanges.

conversational and discourse analyses Forms of content analysis in which the categories are suggested from naturally occurring conversations and their settings. Yet, these approaches do not produce numerical information. The structure or organization of conversations is examined along with functions that conversations perform for communicators. A distinction often is drawn between conversational analysis (which tends to analyze macroscopic message characteristics such as themes and stories and the rules they suggest) and discourse analysis (which tends to analyze microscopic message components in a pattern much like traditional linguistic analysis or translation).

correlation A measure of the coincidence of variables.

counterbalanced designs Quasi-experiments that introduce several different experimental treatments presented to the subjects in different orders or sequences.

counterbalancing Rotating the sequence in which experimental treatments are introduced to subjects in an effort to control for extraneous variables, such as fatigue or cumulative learning effects.

creative studies Use of the method of performance or demonstration to explore an aesthetic or creative experience.

criterion validity Methods including concurrent and predictive validity that assess a measure's worth by examining its relation to some outside criterion.

critical region In significance testing, the portion of the probability distribution that would cause rejection of the null hypothesis if it were the area in which the test statistic fell.

critical value The line that divides the critical region from the rest of the probability distribution.

criticism Message evaluation in which standards of excellence are announced (which, in turn, can be argued as relevant or irrelevant) for application. To the extent that a message meets the standards, it is evaluated positively. The further away from the standard the message is, the harsher is the negative evaluation.

Cronbach's coefficient alpha A formula for reliability, used when researchers want to determine the reliability of a measure that has no "correct" answer.

crossed interaction *See* disordinal interaction.

curvilinear relationship In correlations, relationships in which the best fit of a line to the data is not a straight line.

daily definitions Statements generally adopted by members of a society.

data The actual individual events in a sample.

data distributions Distributions of data actually collected.

debate The study of decision making in which adversaries present arguments for decision by a third party.

deductive reasoning A form of reasoning in which a valid conclusion necessarily follows from premises.

deductive summary A summary strategy that reviews literature by considering what is known in general categories, followed by increasingly specific categories that are related to the topic.

definitions Statements asserting that one term may be substituted for another.

degrees of freedom The number of events in a study minus the number of population parameters estimated from samples; used to enter probability distributions.

delivery The canon of rhetoric concerning the use of voice and gesture.

Delphi fallacy A special fallacy of research involving the use of vague predictions as research claims.

dependent variables Variables whose values or activities are presumed to be conditioned upon (variables that are consequent to) the independent variable in the hypothesis.

description The lowest level of theorizing in which behavior is characterized into different forms.

descriptive or observational surveys Direct observations of behavior by use of some measurement (the researcher does not manipulate or change any variables).

descriptive statistics Numbers that are designed to characterize some information in a data set.

determination *See* coefficient of determination.

difference, method of *See* method of difference.

direct classification variables Operational definitions that rely on simple identification or classification of observable characteristics of information.

directional material hypotheses Hypotheses that state the form of predicted differences.

direct questions Questionnaire items that ask for obvious reports.

direct relationship A correlation showing that as one variable increases, the other variable also increases.

discourse analyses Considerations of naturally occurring messages to examine "sequential and hierarchical organization, system and structure" using methods that are fairly "standard in phonology and linguistics" (Stubbs, 1981, p. 107).

discourse/conversational analyses Methods of examining utterances people exchange for the purpose of discovering the rules and strategies people use to structure, sequence, and take turns in speaking to learn how

people manage their interactions with others.

discussion and conference The study of methods of decision making in which participants strive by consensus to discuss and explore an issue.

disinterestedness The norm of researchers, holding that "researchers must ban ulterior motives and be relatively free from bias" (Kerlinger, 1986, p. 9).

disjunctive syllogism A form of syllogism whose major premise makes an "either-or" statement.

disordinal interaction Dependent variable interaction effects that are not in the same direction as the main effects of the variables involved and that are diagrammatically revealed when lines drawn for each independent variable cross each other.

distributions Arrangements of scores along a continuum.

double-barreled questions Questionnaire items that include multiple objects of evaluation.

double interacts The combination of one person's conversation, a reaction by another, and the first person's response to the other's reaction.

Einstein syndrome A malady in which researchers fail to connect their "sudden breakthrough" with lessons from others.

elimination and removal A method of control that removes a nuisance variable from the experimental setting.

empirical Observable.

equal probability hypothesis A method of determining expected frequencies for the one-sample chi-square test.

erosions Observations of evidence of the wear or use of objects.

error variance Another name for within groups variance.

eta (η) Also known as the "correlation ratio," it is directly interpreted as any correlation and is

used to determine the size of effects following finding a significant *F*. Eta also may be used to identify nonlinear as well as linear effects.

eta squared (η^2) A coefficient of determination computed from eta.

ethical and rhetorical theories Principles that describe good and effective communication respectively.

ethnography Research in which the investigator participates, overtly or covertly, in people's lives for an extended period of time, collecting whatever data are available to describe behavior.

ethnomethodology (Also called the "new ethnography," originally developed by anthropologists to study societies of humans), an approach (rather than a rigorous method) in which researchers find an ethnic group, live within it, and attempt to develop insight into the culture; emphasis is placed on the mundane and ordinary activities of everyday life, concentrating on the methods used by people to report their common sense practical actions to others in acceptable rational terms.

ethos Sometimes called "ethical appeal," an element of the canon of invention (artistic proofs) referring to the speaker's credibility.

evidence Information used to support claims.

example *See* argument from example and generalization.

exemplary literature reviews Surveys of only the most important contributions to the literature.

exhaustive literature reviews Research surveys that include all material related to the subject.

experiment *See* experimental methods.

experimental invalidity Errors that prevent researchers from drawing unequivocal conclusions (*see also* internal invalidity; external invalidity).

experimental methods A method of studying the effect of variables manipulated by the researcher in situations where all other influences are held constant. Variables are manipulated or introduced by experimenters for the purpose of establishing causal relationships.

experimental mortality A source of internal invalidity involving biases introduced when subjects differentially (nonrandomly) drop out of the experiment.

experimental variable An independent variable manipulated in an experiment.

expert jury validity A method of test validity that involves having a group of experts in the subject matter examine the measurement device and judge its merit.

expert opinions Opinions from people who are experts in the field of inquiry.

explanation Taking an event and treating it as an instance of a larger system of things.

explication A literature review that makes an issue clear and comprehensive.

external invalidity The degree to which experimental results may not be generalized to other similar circumstances.

face validity A method of test validity that involves researchers looking at the content of the measurement items and advancing an argument that, on its face, the measure seems to identify what it claimed.

factor analysis A statistical method that helps ''the researcher discover and identify the unities or dimensions, called factors, behind many measures'' (Kerlinger, 1986, p. 138).

factorial analysis of variance Analysis of variance applied to multiple independent variables that have been broken down into levels or groups.

factorial designs Experimental designs in which more than one independent variable is used.

factors Variables broken down into levels.

factual evidence Descriptions and characterizations of things.

fallacy of misplaced precision Attempts by researchers to claim precision that goes beyond the data.

false precision *See* fallacy of misplaced precision.

falsification The requirement that any theory must deal with statements that could be falsified by data and information if the theories were untrue.

fantasy theme analysis A method of analyzing collections of communication to determine underlying ''world views'' that people hold, judging by the messages that they use.

***F* distribution** In essence, a distribution of variances that have been divided into each other.

figurative analogy An analogy that compares something to a hypothetical situation.

film as communication The study of the role of popular and technical cinema in society.

forced choice format A question system in which researchers give subjects two statements, one of which must be chosen.

full-participant observation research Fieldwork characterized by the investigator's gathering data while taking part in the activities of a group—and while concealing his or her research identity.

funnel questions A questioning strategy that starts with an open-ended question and follows up with increasingly narrow questions.

generalization *See* argument from example and generalization.

general questions Questions that ask about global evaluations.

general to specific A library search strategy in which one starts with general sources that lead to specific sources.

goodness of fit test *See* one-sample chi-square test.

grand mean The average of the averages computed in factorial analysis of variance.

grounded theory A set of explanations that has immediate relevance to a specific field setting under investigation. Participant observers attempt to discover categories to describe their observations after they have entered the field. Then, researchers make additional observations to refine and modify these categories and potentially develop theory.

Guttman scalogram A scale involving series of statements dealing with one topic and arranged according to their level of intensity.

halo effect A special source of experimental invalidity in which strong positive or negative impressions of a source of communication may affect all other ratings that follow.

historical-critical methods Research designed to describe a period, person, or phenomenon for the purpose of interpreting or evaluating communication and its effects.

history A source of internal invalidity in which events not controlled by the researcher occur during the experiment between any pretest and posttest.

holding constant Controlling for other variables by limiting the range of intervening variables so that they are equal across studies (technically, all control methods involve taking nuisance variables and holding them constant).

homogeneous variances The parametric test assumption that any differences in variances should be within the limits of sampling error.

Hotelling's T^2 *t* test for intercorrelated dependent variables.

hypothesis ''An expectation about events based on generalizations of the assumed relationship between variables'' (Tuckman, 1978, p. 27).

hypothetical constructs Concepts; constructs for which direct observations cannot be made.

identification The uniting of people by the use of ideas, images, and attitudes.

idiographic research Scholarship designed to develop a full understanding of "a particular event or individual" (English & English, 1958, p. 347).

impressionistic criticism Statements of opinion (or personal impression) made by reviewers.

independent variables Variables that predict outcomes (dependent variables) posited in hypotheses.

indirect questions Questionnaire items that ask respondents to react in ways that imply information.

inductive reasoning "The process by which we conclude that what is true of certain individuals is true of a class, what is true of part is true of the whole class, or what is true at certain times will be true in similar circumstances at all times" (Mill, in English & English, 1958, p. 259).

inductive summary A summary strategy that reviews literature by producing general propositions (laws or rules) that are demonstrated by each subcollection (studies are grouped largely by their findings, rather than their input variables).

inferential statistics Tools that help researchers draw conclusions about the probable populations from which samples did or did not belong.

informed consent Written agreement from people indicating their willingness to participate in a study.

infrequency index A measure of the inconsistency of response, indicative of a person given random responses.

instrumentation A source of internal invalidity involving changes in the use of measuring instruments from the pretest to the posttest including

changes in raters or interviewers who collect the data in different conditions.

item-to-total reliability Computation of the correlation of items with the total test.

interactional and relational analyses Forms of content analysis designed to describe the continuing oral communication between people.

interaction analyses Studies that focus on ways of tracking individual acts of communicators.

interaction effects Dependent variable effects from independent variables taken together and involving variation arising from special combinations of levels of independent variables.

interaction of elements A source of internal invalidity involving effects created by the interaction of selection biases with differential levels of maturation, history, or any other source of variation.

interaction of selection and the experimental variable Effects created by sampling groups in such a way that they are not representative of the population since they are more or less sensitive to the experimental variable than other subsamples from the same population (such as sampling college students in communication studies even though they may be more or less sensitive to the independent variable than the general population of people).

interaction of testing and the experimental variable Also called pretest sensitization, this source of experimental external invalidity is created when pretesting makes subjects either more or less sensitive to the experimental variable.

interacts The combination of one person's conversation and the reaction of another.

intercoder reliability Determining the consistency of different raters who respond to the same events by using some sort of check sheet.

intercultural communication The study of communication among

individuals of different cultural backgrounds.

internal invalidity The presence of contamination that prevents the experimenter from concluding that a study's experimental variable is responsible for the observed effects.

interpersonal communication The study of communication interactions occurring in person-to-person and small group situations.

interpretive analysis of data A naturalistic approach that identifies communicators' interactions, uses of themes, and uses of stories to determine such things as the situations in which people find themselves, the structures within which they work, and the practical features of their world. (*See also* case studies and interpretive studies.)

intersubjectivity The degree to which different researchers with essentially different beliefs draw essentially the same interpretations of the meaning of observations.

interval level measurement Assignment of numbers to items as a matter of degree ("the intervals between the numbers are *equal* in size [Cozby, 1989, p. 149]").

interval sampling Sampling by selecting instances of communication at specific units (such as coding every third commercial during prime time for a month).

interview surveys The use of personal contacts between a questioner and respondent in which the questions and answers are exchanged orally.

invention The canon of rhetoric concerning the types and sources of ideas.

inventory questions Closed-ended questions that ask respondents to list all responses that apply to them.

inverse relationship A correlation showing that as one variable increases, the other variable decreases.

inverted funnel questions A questioning strategy that starts with a very specific question and expands by asking increasingly general questions.

isolate   In network analysis, an individual who is not actively involved in any established communication network.

Jeanne Dixon fallacy   A special fallacy of research that involves making multiple predictions and claiming partial support.

John Henry effect   A special source of experimental invalidity in which subjects try to perform extra hard when they participate in an experiment.

joint method of agreement and difference   One of Mill's canons of causality, which holds that "If two or more instances in which the phenomenon occurs have only one circumstance in common, while two or more instances in which it does not occur have nothing in common save the absence of that circumstance, the circumstance in which alone the two sets of instances differ, is the effect, or the cause, or an indispensable part of the cause, of the phenomenon."

journalism   The study of the methods of reporting and organizing news for presentation in print media.

kappa   *See* Cohen's *kappa*.

keywords   Terms under which information about a topic may be found.

known to unknown summary   A summary strategy that reviews literature by considering what (little) is known separately about each variable in the research review question and then announces what remains to be learned.

K-R 20   Kuder-Richardson formula 20 for reliability, used when researchers want to determine the reliability of a measure that has items that are scored as "correct" or "incorrect" answers.

kurtosis   A measure of the peakedness of a distribution.

law   "A verbal statement, supported by such ample evidence as not to be open to doubt unless much further evidence is obtained, of the way events of a certain class consistently and uniformly occur" (English & English, 1958, p. 288).

law of large numbers   A rule that holds that the assumptions of statistical method are best satisfied by large samples.

leading questions   Questions that imply their answer.

leptokurtic   A distribution that is tall, with a kurtosis above 3.

levels   Categories of each factor.

liaison   In network analysis, a person linking together people of different networks.

lie scale   *See* MMPI lie (L) scale.

life-history or life story research   Naturalistic study that involves "the autobiography of a person which has been obtained through interview and guided conversation" (McNeill, 1990, p. 85).

Likert scales   Scales composed of statements that reflect clear positions on an issue, for which subjects indicate their agreement (typically) on 1 to 5 point scales.

line of regression   In correlations, a line of "best fit" through the data.

LISREL (Linear Structural Relations)   A computer program that isolates relationships by examining covariances among variables.

literal analogy   An analogy that compares something to an event or object that really exists.

literature reviews   *See* exhaustive literature reviews; exemplary literature reviews.

loaded language   Questionnaire items worded to imply an evaluation.

log-linear analysis   Extension of chi-square testing for analysis of more than two variables measured on the nominal level.

logos   Treated by most critics as logical appeals, *logos* is an element of the canon of invention (artistic proofs)

and refers to the use of rational appeals.

μ   The Greek letter mu, representing the population mean.

main effects   Dependent variable effects from independent variables separately.

manipulated independent variables   Sometimes called "stimulus variables" because researchers introduce and control them in experiments.

manipulation check   A researcher's measurement of a secondary variable to determine that an experimental variable actually was operating in a study.

MANOVA (multivariate analysis of variance)   Extension of analysis of variance for multiple dependent variables.

matching   Pairing subjects on some variable on which they share equal levels and then assigning them to experimental or control conditions.

material hypothesis   *See* hypothesis.

matrix questions   Closed-ended questions that ask respondents to use the same categories to supply information.

maturation   A source of internal invalidity involving changes that naturally occur over time (including fatigue or suspicion), even if subjects are left alone.

maxmincon principle   A reminder to experimenters to follow procedures that "maximize systematic variance, control extraneous systematic variance, and minimize error variance" (Kerlinger, 1986, p. 284).

mean   *See* arithmetic mean.

measured/assigned variables   Variables not introduced or controlled by the researcher, but carefully observed and/or measured.

measurement   Assigning numbers to variables according to some system.

median   A score that appears in the middle of an ordered list of scores.

memory The canon of rhetoric concerning the ability to recall passages and examples for utterance.

mesokurtic A distribution that is neither very high nor very low, with a kurtosis close to 3.

message The set of verbal and nonverbal cues communicators exchange.

meta-analysis A statistical method that combines quantitative results from many studies to reveal the overall sizes of effects that exist among variables.

metatheories Ways to think about theories (called ''metatheory'' to indicate notions ''beyond the theories'' themselves).

method of agreement One of Mill's canons of causality, which holds that ''If two or more instances of the phenomenon under investigation have only one circumstance in common, the circumstance in which alone all the instances agree is the cause (or effect) of the given phenomenon.''

method of agreement and difference *See* joint method of agreement and difference.

method of concomitant variation One of Mill's canons of causality, which holds that ''Whatever phenomenon varies in any manner, whenever another phenomenon varies in some particular manner, is either a cause or an effect of that phenomenon, or is connected with it through some act of causation.''

method of difference One of Mill's canons of causality, which holds that ''If an instance in which the phenomenon under investigation occurs and an instance in which it does not occur have every circumstance in common save one, the one occurring only in the former, the circumstance in which alone the two instances differ is the effect, or the cause, or an indispensable part of the cause of the phenomenon.''

method of residues One of Mill's canons of causality, which holds that ''Subduct from any phenomenon such part as is known by previous inductions to be the effect of certain antecedents, and the residue of the phenomenon is the effect of the remaining antecedents.''

methodological studies Inquiries that deal with the development and validation of new tools, measuring instruments, or research approaches.

mirror questions A strategy of follow-up interview questioning that repeats previous responses to gain additional information.

misplaced precision *See* fallacy of misplaced precision.

MMPI lie (L) scale A scale to identify respondents who are attempting to avoid being candid and honest in their responses (not a general personality disposition toward dishonesty).

mode The most commonly occurring score.

model An expression that not only states relationships, but exhibits them.

moderator variables Variables that mediate the independent variable's prediction of the dependent variable (in reality, moderator variables are just other independent variables that help input variables predict their effects).

mortality *See* experimental mortality.

multicollinearity In multiple correlation, the quality of predictors being uncorrelated with each other.

multimodal A condition in which a distribution possesses many modes.

multiple-choice questions Closed-ended questions that ask respondents to select a category response from a range of possible responses.

multiple comparison tests Tests completed after finding a significant analysis of variance effect for the purpose of determining the location of differences among groups.

multiple discriminant analysis A method that predicts membership in particular groups from a knowledge of a number of predictor variables (measured on the interval or ratio level).

multiple regression correlation (a.k.a. multiple correlation) A method that produces a correlation of multiple predictors with a single output variable.

multiple treatment interference A source of experimental external invalidity, in which subjects exposed to repeated additional experimental treatments react in ways that are not generalizable to subjects that are uncontaminated by such additional independent variables.

multistage sampling Sampling in which instances are selected sequentially (such as selecting commercials from one month, selecting one week from that month, selecting three hours from the days of the week, etc.).

multivariate analyses Statistical analyses in which multiple dependent variables are treated as a common set.

multivariate analysis of covariance Extension of MANOVA to adapt analysis of covariance for multiple interrelated dependent variables.

multivariate multiple correlation Extension of multiple regression for many interrelated dependent measures.

mythic perspective An approach to criticism that attempts to identify the underlying stories to which speakers appeal (a myth is defined as ''a story about a particular incident which is put forward as containing or suggesting some general truth'' [Sykes, 1970, p. 17]).

narrative fidelity In the narrative paradigm, the consistency of new accounts with other stories people have heard.

narrative paradigm An approach to criticism that analyzes messages by looking at them as stories.

naturalistic studies Nonexperimental inquiries completed as subjects are involved in the natural course of their lives.

negative skew Skewness in which the longest tail of the distribution lies to the left of the mean.

neo-Aristotelian criticism Criticism using Aristotelian standards and involving the canons of rhetoric.

network analysis A method that obtains individuals' reports of their communication activities with others for the purpose of observing and describing the flow of information in a particular organizational system.

nominal level measurement Use of numbers as simple identification of variables.

nomothetic research Scholarship designed to find general laws that apply to many instances.

nondirectional material hypotheses Hypotheses that state simply there will be *some kind* of relationship between variables (sometimes called "two-tailed" hypotheses because of the way statistics are used to test them).

nonlinear relationships Relationships between independent and dependent variables that are not simple straight line relationships, but curved.

nonparametric tests Statistical methods that do not make assumptions about population distributions or population parameters.

non sequitur A fallacy of reasoning in which a conclusion does not follow from premises because the necessary steps in between are omitted.

nonverbal cues Communication elements beyond the words themselves.

normative and prescriptive theories Theories whose principles involve defining the qualities that make communication meaningful or desirable.

normative science "A discipline that systematically studies man's attempts to determine what is correct, valuable, good, or beautiful" (English & English, 1958, p. 349), which has given rise to normative and prescriptive theories.

null hypotheses Statistical hypotheses that state that there is no relationship between variables.

O An abbreviation for an observation a researcher makes of the study's dependent variable.

observational surveys *See* descriptive or observational surveys.

"One-across" statement In relational control analysis, a statement in which one extends the discussion without increasing assertions or accepting others' statements.

"one-down" statement In relational control analysis, a statement in which one person submits to the opinions or definitional rights of another.

one-group pretest-posttest A pre-experimental design in which a pretest is added to a one-shot case study.

one-sample chi-square test A test of statistical significance for nominal level variables for which frequency data are obtained.

one-sample t test An application of the t test that examines when a new sample mean differs from a known population mean under conditions when the population standard deviation is unavailable.

one-shot case study A pre-experimental design in which an experimental treatment is introduced and researchers look at effects on some output (dependent) variable.

one-tailed hypotheses *See* directional material hypotheses.

"one-up" statement In relational control analysis, a statement in which one person is dominant over another because he or she asserts one's "definitional rights."

one-way analysis of variance Analysis of variance in which the groups are levels for the independent variable.

open-ended questions Questions to which people respond in their own words.

operational definition Isolation of a concept by specifying the steps researchers follow to make observations.

opinions Interpretations of the meaning of collections of facts.

opinion surveys Assessments of reports from individuals about topics of interest.

oral interpretation The study of literature through performance involving the development of skilled verbal and nonverbal expression based on critical analysis of written texts (including aesthetics of literature in performance, criticism of literature in performance, group performance, oral traditions).

ordinal interaction Dependent variable interaction effects in the same direction as the main effects of the variables involved.

ordinal level measurement Use of rank order to determine differences.

organizational communication The study of interrelated behaviors, technologies, and systems functioning within an organization.

organized skepticism The norm of researchers, holding that "researchers are responsible for verifying the results on which they base their work [Researchers do not accept claims blindly. They question research claims and offer criticism for each other.]" (Kerlinger, 1986, p. 9).

paired-comparison questions Questions that ask respondents to make a judgment between alternatives taken two at a time.

parameter A number computed from a population.

parametric testing Tests of statistical significance that make assumptions about populations from which the data were drawn.

parliamentary procedure The study of the means used to handle deliberation in large, legislative bodies through the use of formal rules and procedures to regulate debate and discussion.

partial correlation A method of statistical control that determines the variation associated with each nuisance variable and then separates it from the remaining total variation in the correlation.

participant as observer methods Fieldwork in which the group to be studied is made aware of the researcher's role.

participant observation Fieldwork in which researchers study groups by gaining membership or close relationships with them (see Wax, 1968, p. 238).

patchwork quilt fallacy A special fallacy of research in which no predictions are made, but explanations are offered after the fact.

path models Use of correlational tools to interpret relationships to identify causal models with exogenous (input variable) sources, endogenous (mediating) variables, and dependent (output or criterion) variables.

pathos Sometimes called ''pathetic appeals,'' *pathos* is an element of the canon of invention (artistic proofs) and refers to the use of emotional or motivational appeals.

Pearson product moment correlation A correlation method suitable for situations in which *both* the independent and dependent variables (identified as X and Y respectively in most notation) are interval or ratio level measures.

periodic sampling A method by which researchers select respondents according to a predetermined schedule other than a random sequence.

persuasion The study of communication used to influence the choices made by others.

pi *See* Scott's *pi*.

pilot studies Studies usually involving small samples of people (sometimes as few as ten or twenty people) who take part in an experiment as an aid in developing materials and protocols.

placebo effect A placebo is a stimulus containing no medicine or no experimental treatment at all; hence, a special source of experimental invalidity in which subjects show

changes even in the absence of any treatments at all, in reaction to the mental suggestion that they may have been given some stimulus.

plagiarism ''The act of using another person's ideas or expressions in your writing without acknowledging the source'' (Gibaldi & Achtert, 1988, p. 20).

platykurtic A flat distribution with kurtosis under 3.

poetic definitions Statements that involve figurative interpretations of objects.

polarity rotation A check on test-taking behavior that avoids response set by (1) avoiding phrasing all items positively and (2) avoiding placing all positive adjectives on the same side of the measurement items.

polymodal *See* multimodal.

pooled standard deviation (s_p) The square root of the average of variances in subgroups involved in comparisons.

population The universe of events from which the sample is drawn.

positive skew Skewness in which the longer tail of the distribution lies to the right of the mean.

posttest-only control group design A true experimental design that avoids pretest sensitization by deleting the pretest entirely.

power A statistical test's probability of rejecting the null hypothesis correctly.

pragmatic communication The study and practice of communication, the object of which is to influence or facilitate decision making.

prediction Descriptions of what can be expected in the future.

predictive validity The degree to which a measure predicts known groups in which the construct must exist.

premise A statement in a logical argument that is the foundation for others drawn from it.

presumptive questions Questions that assume information (e.g., ''Have you stopped beating your spouse?'').

pretest-posttest control group design A true experimental design that includes randomly selected experimental and control groups, each of which is given a pretest and a posttest.

primary sources Reports provided by individuals who have firsthand experience with the events reported.

principal components solution In factor analysis, a method to identify the number of common centers of variation that underlie the manifest variables.

probability The tendency or likelihood with which an event occurs in a population.

probability distributions The theoretical patterns of expected sample data.

probability sampling Techniques that use randomization to identify samples.

probing questions A strategy of follow-up interview questioning that directly asks for elaboration and explanation.

problems Questions for which we expect to find answers through research.

problem-solution summary A summary strategy that reviews literature by considering a problem and its cause, followed by a research suggestion that might solve the problem.

professional responsibility The requirement that researchers follow accepted rules of conduct with thoroughness and attention to concerns of subjects.

public address The study of speakers and speeches; including the historical and social context of platforms, campaigns, and movements.

public relations The study of methods of managing publicity and press relations for an organization, person, or cause.

purpose   In Burke's dramatistic pentad, the intention of the rhetor.

purposive or known group sampling   Selection of events from groups that are known to possess a particular characteristic under investigation.

qualitative methods   Research methods of study that use descriptions of observations expressed in predominantly non-numerical terms.

qualitative observational studies   Methods designed to use predominately attribute-type data when interpreting contemporaneous communication interactions.

quantitative methods   Inquiries in which observations are expressed predominantly in numerical terms.

quasi-experiments   Studies involving completion of experimental work where random assignment and control are not possible.

quasi-interval measures   Interval-like measures that have enough properties of true interval measures to permit using statistical tools designed for them.

questionnaires   Survey forms in which individuals respond to items they have read.

quota sampling   Samples are defined based on the known proportions within the population, and nonrandom sampling is completed within each group.

quotation bibliographic card   Bibliographic cards featuring quoted materials.

R   1. In experimental design, an abbreviation for randomization; 2. in statistics, an abbreviation for the coefficient of multiple correlation.

radio   The study of the methods and uses of radio communication.

random assignment   *See* randomization.

randomization   Assigning subjects so that each event is equally likely to belong to any experimental or control condition.

random sampling   Selection of data such that each event in the population has an equal chance of being selected.

range   The difference between the highest and lowest scores.

ranking questions   Closed-ended questions that ask respondents to rank a set of options.

ratio level measurement   Assignment of numbers to items as a matter of degree, including an "absolute zero."

reactive arrangements   A source of experimental external invalidity, consisting of elements in the experimental setting that make subjects react differentially to the experimental arrangements rather than to the experimental variable alone (such matters as awareness of participation in an experiment may alter normal reactions of people).

reciprocal pattern   In network analysis, a pattern in which individuals share nearly an identical network pattern.

reconstructive questions   *See* averaging or reconstructive questions.

redundancy index   In canonical correlation, a coefficient that tells whether sets of variables should be interpreted differentially for additional canonical component roots.

regression   *See:* 1. statistical regression; 2. line of regression; 3. multiple regression correlation.

relational control analysis   Studies that track message sequences to determine the relative patterns of position and control in the relationship.

reliability   The internal consistency of a measure.

reliability coefficient   Actually a correlation; a number indicating the degree of consistency of a measure.

replication   The ability of other scholars to reproduce research.

report   An account of what took place whether by a participant or by an outside observer.

representative sample   Sampling that accurately reflects characteristics of the population from which it was drawn.

research   (1) The systematic effort to secure answers to questions; (2) a way of knowing that makes claims by using the tools of scholarship and science.

research hypothesis   *See* hypothesis.

research prospectus   A complete proposal for a research activity to be completed at a future date.

residues, method of   *See* method of residues.

response set   A tendency for subjects to follow predictable patterns when responding to test items.

rhetor   One who practices rhetoric.

rhetoric   According to Aristotle, "The faculty of discovering in the particular case what are the available means of persuasion."

rhetorical and communication theory   The study of the principles that account for human communicative experiences and behavior.

rhetorical criticism   The use of standards of excellence to interpret and evaluate communication.

rhetorical visions   Images of the way the world is organized as perceived by groups of people.

rhetorician   One who studies rhetoric.

rotation   In factor analysis, an aid in interpretation that helps reveal the items that are used to understand a factor.

rule   "A theory that explains a pattern of effects by referring to human intentions, reasons, or goals" (M. J. Smith, 1988, p. 354).

rules of correspondence   The degree to which a theory's constructs and abstract calculus can be applied to actual experience.

s   A symbol that represents the standard deviation of a sample.

s^2   A symbol that represents the variance of a sample.

sacrifice groups A method to check the accuracy of respondent reports by interrupting groups during the interview or questionnaire process to see if they really understand what is meant by specific questions. Since these respondents have been distracted somewhat, they are "sacrificed" and their responses are used only to validate the survey question content.

sampling Selecting events from a population.

sampling error The degree to which a sample differs from the population on some measure.

scene In Burke's dramatistic pentad, the setting in which the act takes place.

Scheffé's critical S A multiple comparison test designed to contrast all possible comparisons of means, when the means are taken as part of complex comparisons.

scholarly definitions Highly specific statements that have technical meanings for a group of scholars.

science A way of testing statements by systematic application of the scientific method.

scientific method A method that involves collecting data and establishing "a functional relationship among these data" (Bachrach, 1981, p. 4); generally a method involving four steps: observation of facts, development of a working hypothesis or theoretical solution to guide the research, test of expectations against information, establishing a conclusion or functional relationship based on deciding whether the working hypothesis or theoretic solution is supported.

Scott's *pi* A measure of intercoder reliability, which also compensates for the rates of agreement that would be expected by chance alone.

secondary sources Reports provided by individuals who do not have firsthand experience with the events reported.

selection A source of internal invalidity involving sampling biases in selecting or assigning subjects to experimental or control conditions (in essence rigging the study by taking samples capriciously).

semantic differential-type scales Scales (often seven point intervals) bounded by pairs of bipolar adjectives.

separate sample posttest designs Quasi experiments in which subjects in control conditions are selected to be close, but not assured to be equivalent to the experimental group.

serendipity Researchers finding something of value while looking for something else.

significance A difference or relationship that is beyond what might be expected to occur by chance (sampling error) alone.

simple random sampling *See* random sampling.

single subject designs Also called component search studies, experimental designs that determine the effect of treatments by strategically repeated exposures for a single subject.

skewness A measure of the centeredness of distributions.

snowball sampling Selection of events based on referrals from initial informants.

social desirability A measure of the degree to which people attempt to describe themselves in ways that they think are acceptable, desirable, or approved by others.

Solomon four groups design A true experimental design that assesses the impact of pretesting by adding control groups.

sophists Teachers in ancient times who traveled around instructing people wherever there was a market.

Spearman rank order correlation A correlation method suitable for situations in which both the independent and dependent variables are ordinal level measures.

specific questions Questions that focus on individual activities.

specific to general A library search strategy in which one starts with a reference and writes down the citations to related research and theory identified in them. Then, the process is completed with the new sources until the information "snowballs" as one reference leads to others.

speech and hearing science The study of the physiology and acoustical aspects of speech and hearing (including biological, phonological, and physiological aspects of speech and hearing).

speech communication education The study of communication in pedagogical contexts (including communication development, oral communication skills, instructional communication).

speech pathology *See* speech and hearing science.

split half reliability Dividing a test into two parts, scoring them separately, and checking consistency between the two scores.

standard deviation A measure of how far the average of the scores deviates from the mean, symbolized for the sample standard deviation as s.

standard error The standard deviation of a distribution of elements other than raw scores.

standard error of the mean The standard deviation of a distribution of means.

standard normal curve A probability distribution that tells the expected value that would be obtained by sampling at random.

standard scores *See* z scores.

static group comparisons A pre-experimental design in which a control group is used, but the groups are not known to be comparable to begin with.

statistic A number computed from a sample.

statistical control Taking measures of nuisance variables and using statistical tools to hold them constant.

statistical regression A source of internal invalidity involving shifts produced when subjects are selected due to very high or very low scores on a test; statistical regression holds that people will "regress toward the mean" even if they simply are left alone.

statistics (1) Quantitative reports based on observations in a sample; (2) The study of quantitative information.

stimulus variables *See* manipulated independent variables.

stratification Sampling in which strata are identified (such as geographic region, type of radio station format, type of ad) and a random sample within each strata is proportionately selected.

stratified random sampling Population characteristics are identified (such as the number of men and women in the population); after deciding on the sample size to be drawn, a random sample is drawn from each level of the population stratification variable (using one of the methods of simple random sampling) to meet the proportion of the population in that sample subgroup.

structured interviews Interviews that use specific lists of questions.

studies of behavior, facts and opinions Studies designed to determine the current status of conditions or attitudes by using questionnaires, interviews, or direct observations of communicators.

studies of status and development Intensive detailed studies of individual cases over time.

style The canon of rhetoric concerning the use of words.

subject tracings Keywords that list other subject headings under which a book also is listed.

survey Empirical study that uses questionnaires or interviews to discover descriptive characteristics of phenomena; *see* opinion surveys.

syllogism A formal logical system in which the premises lead to a conclusion.

systematic sampling *See* periodic sampling.

tenacity A way of knowing in which we claim to know something because we have always believed it.

testing A source of internal invalidity involving alterations that occur when subjects are tested and made testwise or anxious in ways that affect them when they are given a second test.

test-retest reliability Giving the measure twice and reporting consistency between scores.

test statistic A number computed from a statistical formula to test the statistical hypothesis.

theoretic constructs Terms that are substituted into the abstract calculus of a theory (*see also* constructs).

theory "A body of interrelated principles that explain or predict" (*Longman Dictionary of Psychology*, 1984, p. 744).

Thurstone equal appearing interval scales Scales composed of statements with assigned point values.

time-budgeting studies Inquiries in which "the researcher asks the subjects of the research to keep a detailed diary over a given period" (McNeill, 1990, p. 88).

time series design A type of quasi-experiment that measures subjects at different times.

topical summary A summary strategy that reviews literature by reference to content categories into which the studies fall.

trend analysis A method that isolates the nature of linear and nonlinear trends in effects identified as significant by analysis of variance.

trial and error A "way of knowing" that claims knowledge by making repeated trials to eliminate unacceptable answers.

t test A test of statistical significance designed to assess the difference between the means of two groups.

t test for dependent samples An application of the *t* test that compares the means of two sample groups in which subjects are matched or sampled twice.

t test for independent samples An application of the *t* test that compares the means of two sample groups.

Tukey's HSD (John Tukey's Honestly Significant Difference test) a multiple comparison test designed to contrast all possible comparisons of means, when the means are taken two at a time.

two-tailed hypotheses *See* nondirectional material hypotheses.

Type I error Incorrectly rejecting the null hypothesis.

Type II error Failing to detect a relationship that is present; incorrectly failing to reject the null hypothesis.

unbiased estimator A sample statistic that is most likely to approximate the corresponding population parameter.

universalism The norm of researchers, holding that "scientific laws are the same everywhere" (Kerlinger, 1986, p. 9).

unobtrusive measurement Use of artifacts that do not hold the potential to influence the behavior being studied, including the use of accretions and erosions.

unstructured interviews Interviews that permit respondents to indicate their reactions to general issues without guidance from highly detailed questions.

urban archaeology Examination of modern artifacts of urban life (such as searching trash cans in a neighborhood to find evidence of alcoholism rates).

utterance In conversational analysis, what a person actually says in conversation.

validity   1. Test validity is the consistency of a measure with a criterion; the degree to which a measure actually measures what is claimed. 2. Experimental validity refers to the absence of errors that prevent researchers from drawing unequivocal conclusions.

variable   A symbol to which numbers may be assigned.

variance   A measure of the average of squared differences of scores from the mean, symbolized for the sample variance as s^2.

verbal cues   Words people use in communication.

X   An abbreviation for: 1. a score from a continuous distribution; 2. the experimental variable used by researchers.

$\overline{X}$ "X bar," representing the sample mean.

z scores   Scores represented as units under the standard normal curve.

WORKS CITED

Aczel, A. D. (1989). *Complete business statistics.* Homewood, IL: Irwin.

Adair, J. G., & Spinner, B. (1981). Subjects' access to cognitive processes: Demand characteristics and verbal report. *Journal for the Theory of Social Behavior, 11,* 31–52.

Agar, M. H. (1988). *Speaking of ethnography.* Newbury Park, CA: Sage.

Alcock, J. E. (1981). *Parapsychology: Science or magic? A psychological perspective.* Oxford, OK: Pergamon Press.

Allen, M. J., & Yen, W. M. (1979). *Introduction to measurement theory.* Monterey, CA: Brooks-Cole.

Amidon, E. J., & Hough, J. B. (1967). *Interaction analysis: Theory, research, and application.* Reading, MA: Addison-Wesley.

Anastasi, A. (1968). *Psychological testing* (3rd ed.). New York: Macmillan.

Auer, J. J. (1959). *An introduction to research in speech.* New York: Harper & Row.

Austin, B. A. (1986). Motivations for movie attendance. *Communication Quarterly, 34,* 115–126.

Babbie, E. R. (1992). *The practice of social research* (6th ed.). Belmont, CA: Wadsworth.

Bachrach, A. J. (1981). *Psychological research: An introduction* (4th ed.). New York: Random House.

Baker, B. O., Hardyck, C. D., & Petrinovich, L. F. (1966). Weak measurements vs. strong statistics: An empirical critique of S. S. Stevens' proscriptions on statistics. *Educational and Psychological Measurement, 26,* 291–309.

Baker, D. C. (1990). A qualitative and quantitative analysis of verbal style and the elimination of potential leaders in small groups. *Communication Quarterly, 38,* 13–26.

Bales, R. F. (1950). A set of categories for the analysis of small group interactions. *American Sociological Review, 15:* 257–263.

Bales, R. F., & Cohen, S. P. (1979). *SYMLOG: A system for the multilevel observation of groups.* New York: Free Press.

Barnett, G. A., Oliveira, O. S., & Johnson, J. D. (1989). Multilingual language use and television exposure and preferences: The case of Belize. *Communication Quarterly, 37,* 248–261.

Bastedo, R. W. (1981). An empirical test of popular astrology. In K. Frazier (Ed.), *Paranormal borderlands of science* (pp. 241–262). Buffalo, NY: Prometheus Books.

Beasley, D. (1988). *How to use a research library.* New York: Oxford University Press.

Benoit, W. L. (1991). Two tests of the mechanism of inoculation theory. *Southern Speech Communication Journal, 56,* 219–229.

Berg, B. L. (1989). *Qualitative research methods for the social sciences.* Boston: Allyn and Bacon.

Berg, B. L., Ksander, M., Loughlin, J., & Johnson, B. (1983, August). *Cliques and groups: Adolescent affective ties and criminal activities.* Paper presented at the Society for the Study of Social Problems Convention, Detroit.

Berger, C., & Calabrese, R. J. (1975). Some explorations in initial interaction and beyond: Toward a developmental theory of interpersonal communication. *Human Communication Research, 1,* 99–112.

Berlo, D. K. (1960). *The process of communication: An introduction to theory and practice.* San Francisco: Rinehart Press.

Berscheid, E. (1985). Interpersonal attraction. In G. Lindzey & E. Aaronson (Eds.), *Handbook of social psychology,* (3rd ed.) (pp. 413–484). New York: Random House.

Best, J. W. (1981). *Research in education* (4th ed.). Englewood Cliffs, NJ: Prentice-Hall.

Bogardus, E. S. (1933). A social distance scale. *Sociology and Social Research, 17,* 265–271.

Bokeno, R. M. (1987). The rhetorical understanding of science: An explication and critical commentary. *Southern Speech Communication Journal, 52,* 285–311.

Boneau, C. A. (1960). The effects of violations of assumption underlying the t-test. *Psychological Bulletin, 57:* 49–64.

Booth, W. C. (1964). *The rhetoric of fiction.* Chicago: University of Chicago Press.

Borg, W. R. (1963). *Educational research: An introduction.* New York: McKay.

Bormann, E. H. (1972). Fantasy and rhetorical vision: The rhetorical criticism of reality. *Quarterly Journal of Speech, 58,* 396–407.

Bormann, E. H. (1973). The Eagleton affair: A fantasy theme analysis. *Quarterly Journal of Speech, 54,* 143–159.

Bormann, E. H. (1982). Colloquy I: Fantasy and rhetorical vision: Ten years later. *Quarterly Journal of Speech, 68,* 288–305.

Bostdorff, D. M. (1967). Vice-presidential comedy and the traditional female role: An examination of the rhetorical characteristics of the vice presidency. *Western Journal of Speech Communication, 55,* 1–27.

Bowers, K. S. (1967). The effect of demands for honesty on reports of visual and auditory hallucinations. *International Journal of Clinical and Experimental Hypnosis, 15,* 31–36.

Brinberg, D., Coleman, J., Hoff, H., Newman, G., & Risk, L. (1980). Interpersonal attraction: A multitrait-multimethod analysis. *Representative Research in Social Psychology, 11,* 54–59.

Brown, L. M. (1961). A content analysis of anti-Catholic documents circulated through the mails during the 1960 presidential election campaign. Unpublished master's thesis, University of Iowa, Iowa City.

Budd, R. W., Thorp, R. K., & Donohew, L. (1967). *Content analysis of communications.* New York: Macmillan.

Bullock, A., & Stallybrass, O. (Eds.). (1977). *The Harper dictionary of modern thought.* New York: Harper & Row.

Burgoon, M., Hall, J., & Pfau, M. (1991). A test of the ''messages-as-fixed-effect fallacy'' argument: Empirical and theoretical implications of design choices. *Communication Quarterly, 39,* 18–34.

Burke, K. (1969). *A grammar of motives.* Reprint. Berkeley: University of California Press. (Original work published 1945.)

Burke, K. (1969). *A rhetoric of motives.* Reprint. Berkeley: University of California Press. (Original work published 1950.)

Burkholder, T. R. (1989). Kansas populism, woman suffrage, and the agrarian myth: A case study in the limits of mythic transcendence. *Communication Studies, 40,* 292–307.

Burleson, B. R. (1980). The place of nondiscursive symbolism, formal characterizations, and hermeneutics in argument analysis and criticism. *Journal of the American Forensic Association, 16,* 222–231.

Byrne, D. (1971). *The attraction paradigm.* New York: Academic Press.

Byrne, D., Ervin, C. R., & Lamberth, J. (1970). Continuity between the experimental study of attraction and real-life computer dating. *Journal of Personality and Social Psychology, 16,* 157–165.

Campbell, D. T., & Stanley, J. C. (1966). *Experimental and quasi-experimental designs for research.* Chicago: Rand McNally.

Cappella, J. N. (1990). The method of proof by example in interaction analysis. *Communication Monographs, 57,* 236–240.

Cappella, J. N., & Palmer, M. T. (1990). Attitude similarity, relational history, and attraction: The mediating effects of kinesic and vocal behaviors. *Communication Monographs, 57,* 161–183.

Cathcart, R. (1981). *Post communication: Rhetorical analysis and evaluation* (2nd ed.). Indianapolis, IN: Bobbs-Merrill.

Cegala, D. J., Wall, V. D., & Rippey, G. (1987). An investigation of interaction involvement and the dimensions of SYMLOG: Perceived communication behaviors of persons in task-oriented groups. *Central States Speech Journal, 38,* 81–93.

Chaffee, S., Nass, C. I., & Yang, S-M. (1990). The bridging role of television in immigrant political socialization. *Human Communication Research, 17,* 266–288.

Champion, D. J. (1970). *Basic statistics for social research.* Scranton, PA: Chandler.

Chase, S. (1954). *The power of words.* New York: Harcourt Brace.

Christenson, P. (1992). The effects of parental advisory labels on adolescent music preferences. *Journal of Communication, 42,* 106–113.

Chung, K. L. (1975). *Probability theory with stochastic processes.* New York: Springer-Verlag.

Coelho, C. A. (1990). Acquisition and generalization of simple manual sign grammars by aphasic subjects. *Journal of Communication Disorders, 23,* 383–400.

Cohen, J. (1960). A coefficient of agreement for nominal scales. *Educational and Psychological Measurements, 20,* 37–46.

Coke-Pepsi slugfest. (1976, July 26) *Time,* pp. 64–65.

Copi, I. M. (1968). *Introduction to logic* (3rd ed.). New York: Macmillan.

Copi, I. M. (1986). *Introduction to logic* (7th ed.). New York: Macmillan.

Cozby, P. (1973). Self-disclosure: A literature review. *Psychological Bulletin, 79,* 73–91.

Cozby, P. C. (1989). *Methods in behavioral research* (4th ed.). Mountain View, CA: Mayfield.

Cragan, J. F., & Shields, D. C. (1981). *Applied communication research: A dramatistic approach.* Prospect Heights, IL: Waveland Press.

Craig, H. (1952). Woodrow Wilson as an orator. *Quarterly Journal of Speech, 38,* 145–148.

Crawford, J. E. (1980). *Taxonomy of questions in communication research.* Unpublished manuscript, Dept. of Communication, Arizona State University.

Cronbach, L. J. (1970). *Essentials of psychological testing* (3rd ed.). New York: Harper & Row.

Crowne, D. P., & Marlowe, D. (1960). A new scale of social desirability independent of psychopathology. *Journal of Consulting Psychology, 24,* 349–354.

Dahlstrom, W. G., Welsh, G. S., & Dahlstrom, L. E. (Eds.). (1972). *An MMPI handbook* (Vol. 1). Minneapolis: University of Minnesota Press.

Delia, J. G., & Grossberg, L. (1977). Interpretation and evidence. *Western Journal of Speech Communication, 41,* 32–42.

Denzin, N. K. (1983). Interpretive interactionism. In G. Morgan (Ed.), *Beyond method: Strategies for social research.* Newbury Park, CA: Sage.

DeStephen, R. S. (1983). Group interaction differences between high and low consensus groups. *Western Journal of Speech Communication, 47,* 340–363.

Deutsch, M., & Krauss, R. (1965). *Theories in social psychology.* New York: Basic Books.

Devito, J. A. (1986). *The communication handbook: A dictionary.* New York: Harper & Row.

Dewey, J. (1910). Science as subject-matter as a method. *Science, 31,* 121–127.

Dickson, P., & Goulden, J. C. (1983). *There are alligators in our sewers and other American credos.* New York: Delacorte Press.

Dominick, J. R., & Rauch, G. (1972). The image of women in network TV commercials. *Journal of Broadcasting, 16,* 259–265.

Ellis, D. G. (1979). Relational control in two group systems. *Communication Monographs, 46,* 153–166.

Emerson, R. (Ed.). (1983). *Contemporary field research.* Boston: Little, Brown.

Emerson, S., & Furman, J. (1991, November 18). The conspiracy that wasn't. *The New Republic,* pp. 12–15.

Emmert, P. (1989). Philosophy of measurement. In P. Emmert & L. L. Barker (Eds.), *Measurement of communication behavior,* (pp. 87–116). New York: Longman.

Emmert, P., & Barker, L. L. (Eds.). (1989). *Measurement of communication behavior.* New York: Longman.

English, H. B., & English, A. C. (1958). *A comprehensive dictionary of psychological and psychoanalytical terms.* New York: McKay.

Erickson, B. H., & Nosanchuck, T. A. (1977). *Understanding data.* Toronto: McGraw-Hill Ryerson.

Feigl, H. (1945). Operationism and scientific method. *Psychological Review, 52,* 250–259.

Feller, W. (1968). *An introduction to probability theory and its applications* (2nd ed., Vol. 1). New York: Wiley.

Feller, W. (1971). *An introduction to probability theory and its applications* (3rd ed., Vol. 2). New York: Wiley.

Ferguson, M. (1983). *Forever feminine: Women's magazines and the cult of femininity.* London, UK: Heinemann.

Festinger, L., Rieken, H. W., & Schachter, S. (1956). *When prophecy fails.* New York: Harper & Row.

Fisher, B. A., & Drexel, G. L. (1983). A cyclical model of developing relationships: A study of relational control interaction. *Communication Monographs, 50,* 66–78.

Fisher, B. A., Glover, T. W., & Ellis, D. G. (1977). The nature of complex communication systems. *Communication Monographs, 44,* 231–240.

Fisher, B. A., & Hawes, L. C. (1971). An interact system model: Generating a grounded theory of small groups. *Quarterly Journal of Speech, 57,* 444–453.

Fisher, W. R. (1987). *Human communication as narration: Toward a philosophy of reason, value, and action.* Columbia: University of South Carolina Press.

Fleiss, J. L. (1971). Measuring nominal scale agreement among many raters. *Psychological Bulletin, 76,* 378–382.

Fleiss, J. L. (1981). *Statistical methods for rates and proportions.* New York: Wiley.

Folger, J. P., & Poole, M. S. (1982). Relational coding schemes: The question of validity. In M. Burgoon (Ed.), *Communication yearbook 5.* New Brunswick, NJ: Transaction.

Fox, D. J. (1969). *The research process in education.* New York: Holt, Rinehart & Winston.

Friedman, H. (1968). Magnitude of experimental effect and a table for its rapid estimation. *Psychological Bulletin, 70,* 245–251.

Gallup, G., & Rae, S. F. (1940). *The pulse of democracy.* New York: Simon & Schuster.

Gardner, R. J., & Zelevansky, L. (1975). The ten commandments for library customers. *Special Libraries, 66,* 326.

Gerbner, G. (1971). Violence in television drama: Trends and symbolic functions. In G. A. Comstock and E. A. Rubinstein (Eds.), *Television and social behavior: Vol. I. Media content and control.* Washington, DC: G.P.O.

Gibaldi, J., & Achtert, W. S. (1988). *MLA handbook for writers of research papers* (3rd ed.). New York: Modern Language Association of America.

Giere, R. N. (1979). *Understanding scientific reasoning.* New York: Holt, Rinehart & Winston.

Glass, G. V., & Hopkins, K. D. (1984). *Statistical methods in education and psychology* (2nd ed.). Englewood Cliffs, NJ: Prentice-Hall.

Glass, G. V., Peckham, P. D., & Sanders, J. R. (1972). Consequence of failure to meet assumption underlying the fixed effects analysis of variance and covariance. *Review of Educational Research, 42,* 237–288.

Gordon, W. I., & Infante, D. A. (1991). Test of a communication model of organizational commitment. *Communication Quarterly, 39,* 144–155.

Graham, W. K., & Dillon, P. C. (1974). Creative supergroups: Group performance as a function of individual performance on brainstorming tasks. *Journal of Social Psychology, 93,* 101–105.

Gravlee, G. J. (1981). Reporting proceedings and debates in the British Commons. *Central States Speech Journal, 32,* 85–99.

Guttman, L. (1944). A basis for scaling quantitative data. *American Sociological Review, 9,* 139–150.

Haiman, F. (1949). An experimental study of the effects of ethos in public speaking. *Speech Monographs, 16,* 190–202.

Hale, J. L., Boster, F. J., & Mongeau, P. A. (1991). The validity of choice dilemma response scales. *Communication Reports, 4,* 30–34.

Hall, S., & Jefferson, T. (1975). *Resistance through rituals: Youth subcultures in post-war Berlin.* London, U.K.: Hutchinson.

Hammer, M. R. (1984). The effects of an intercultural communication workshop on participants' intercultural communication competence: An exploratory study. *Communication Quarterly, 32,* 252–262.

Hansen, C. H., & Hansen, R. D. (1990). The influence of sex and violence on the appeal of rock music videos. *Communication Research, 17,* 212–234.

Hawes, L. (1972). Development and application of an interview coding system. *Central States Speech Journal, 23,* 92–99.

Hensley, C. W. (1975). Rhetorical vision and the persuasion of a historical movement: The Disciples of Christ in nineteenth century American culture. *Quarterly Journal of Speech, 61,* 250–264.

Herson, M., & Barlow, D. H. (1976). *Single case experimental designs: Strategies for studying behavior change.* New York: Pergamon Press.

Hill, F. I. (1972). Conventional wisdom—traditional form: The President's message of November 3, 1969. *Quarterly Journal of Speech, 58,* 373–386.

Homans, G. C. (1961). *Social behavior: Its elementary forms.* New York: Harcourt, Brace & World.

Hoogestraat, W. E. (1960). Memory: The lost canon? *Quarterly Journal of Speech, 46,* 141–147.

Hoover, K. (1979). *The elements of social scientific thinking* (2nd ed.). New York: St. Martin's Press.

Hopkins, K. D., & Glass, G. V. (1978). *Basic statistics for the behavioral sciences.* Englewood Cliffs, NJ: Prentice-Hall.

Hsu, T. C., & Feldt, L. S. (1969). The effect of limitations on the number of criterion score values on the significance of the F test. *American Educational Research Journal, 6,* 515–527.

Hubbard, R. C. (1985). Relationship styles in popular romance novels, 1950–1983. *Communication Quarterly, 33,* 113–125.

Huesmann, L. (1982). Violence and aggression. In D. Pearl, L. Bouthilet, & J. Lazar (Eds.), *Television and behavior: Ten years of scientific progress and implications for the eighties.* Washington, DC: G.P.O.

Huff, D. (1954). *How to lie with statistics.* New York: Norton.

Humphreys, L. (1970). *Tearoom trade: Impersonal sex in public places* (Enl. ed.). Chicago: Aldine.

Isaac, S., & Michael, W. B. (Eds.). (1981). *Handbook in research and evaluation: For education and the behavioral sciences* (2nd ed.). San Diego, CA: EdITS.

Jablin, F. M., Seibold, D. R., & Sorenson, R. (1977). Potential inhibitory effects of group participation on brainstorming performance. *Central States Speech Journal, 28,* 113–121.

Jackson, D. N. (1973). *The IPA.* San Francisco: Psychological Research Organization.

Jacobs, S., & Jackson, S. (1979a, November). *Collaborative aspects of natural argument.* Paper presented at the Speech Communication Association Convention, San Antonio, TX.

Jacobs, S., & Jackson, S. (1979b, November). *Routes for the expansion of influence attempts in conversation.* Paper presented at the Speech Communication Association Convention, San Antonio, TX.

Jones, R. (1973). The nature of research. In R. H. Jones (Ed.), *Methods and techniques of educational research.* Danville, IL: Interstate.

Judd, C. M., Smith, E. R., & Kidder, L. H. (1991). *Research methods in social relations* (6th ed.). Fort Worth, TX: Holt, Rinehart & Winston.

Kaplan, A. (1964). *The conduct of inquiry: Methodology for behavioral science.* Scranton, PA: Chandler Publishing.

Katz, W. A. (1982). *Introduction to reference work* (Vol. 1). New York: McGraw-Hill.

Kazmier, L. J. (1988). *Business statistics* (2nd ed.). New York: McGraw-Hill.

Kerlinger, F. N. (1986). *Foundations of behavioral research* (3rd ed.). New York: Holt, Rinehart & Winston.

Kibler, R. J., & Barker, L. L. (Eds.). (1969). *Conceptual frontiers in speech-communication.* New York: Speech Association of America.

Kiefer, M. (1992, June 17–23). A question of class: What we have here is a failure to communicate. *New Times,* pp. 8, 10.

Kirk, R. E. (1982). *Experimental design: Procedures for the behavioral sciences* (2nd ed.). Belmont, CA: Brooks/Cole.

Kline, S. L., & Floyd, C. H. (1990). On the art of saying no: The influence of social cognitive development on messages of refusal. *Western Journal of Speech Communication, 54,* 454–472.

Klofas, J. M., & Cutshall, C. R. (1985). The social archeology of a juvenile facility: Unobtrusive methods in the study of institutional culture. *Qualitative Sociology, 8,* 368–382.

Knutson, J. F., & Lansing, C. R. (1990). The relationship between communication problems and psychological difficulties in persons with profound acquired hearing loss. *Journal of Speech and Hearing Disorders, 55,* 656–664.

Koenker, R. (1961). *Simplified statistics.* Bloomington, IL: McKnight & McKnight.

Krantz, D. C. (1979). Naturalistic study of social influence on meal size among moderately obese and nonobese subjects. *Psychosomatic Medicine, 41,* 19–27.

Kratochwill, T. R. (Ed.). (1978). *Single subject research: Strategies for evaluative change.* New York: Academic Press.

Kraut, R. E., & Johnston, R. E. (1979). Social and emotional messages of smiling: An ethological approach. *Journal of Personality and Social Psychology, 37,* 1539–1553.

Krejcie, R. V., & Morgan, D. W. (1970). Determining sample size for research activities. *Educational and Psychological Measurement, 30,* 607–610.

Krippendorff, K. (1980). *Content analysis: An introduction to its methodology.* Beverly Hills: Sage.

Kruglanski, A. W. (1973). Much ado about the 'volunteer artifacts.' *Journal of Personality and Social Psychology, 28,* 350.

Lamm, H., & Trommsdorf, G. (1973). Group versus individual performance on tasks requiring ideational proficiency (brainstorming): A review. *European Journal of Social Psychology, 3,* 361–388.

Lannon, J. M. (1986). *The writing process: A concise rhetoric* (2nd ed.). Boston: Little, Brown.

Larson, S. G. (1991). Television's mixed messages: Sexual content on "All My Children." *Communication Quarterly, 39,* 156–163.

Leedy, P. D. (1989). *Practical research: Planning and design* (4th ed.). New York: Macmillan.

Leno, J. (1991). *Headlines III: Not the movie, still the book.* New York: Warner Books.

Levinson, S. C. (1983). *Pragmatics.* Cambridge, U.K.: Cambridge University Press.

Li, C. (1975). *Path analysis: A primer.* Pacific Grove, CA: Boxwood Press.

Lofland, J., & Lofland, L. H. (1984). *Analyzing social settings.* Belmont, CA: Wadsworth.

Longman dictionary of psychology and psychiatry: A Walter D. Glanze Book. (1984). New York: Longman.

Lutz, W. (1989). *Doublespeak.* New York: HarperPerennial, HarperCollins.

Manusov, V. (1992). Mimicry of synchrony: The effects of intentionality attributions for nonverbal mirroring behavior. *Communication Quarterly, 40,* 69–83.

Marks, D., & Kammann, R. (1981). The nonpsychic powers of Uri Geller. In K. Frazier (Ed.), *Paranormal borderlands of science* (pp. 113–121). Buffalo, NY: Prometheus Books.

Marwell, G., & Schmitt, D. R. (1967). Dimensions of compliance gaining behavior: An empirical analysis. *Sociometry, 30,* 350–364.

Mason, E. J., & Bramble, W. J. (1989). *Understanding and conducting research: Application in education and the behavioral sciences* (2nd ed.). New York: McGraw-Hill.

Matlon, R. J., & Ortiz, S. P. (Eds.). (1992). *Index to journals in communication studies through 1990.* Annandale, VA: Speech Communication Association.

Matsumoto, D. (1991). Cultural influences on facial expression of emotion. *Southern Communication Journal, 56,* 128–137.

McBath, J. H. & Jeffrey, R. C. (1978). Defining speech communication. *Communication Education, 27,* 181–188.

McCroskey, J. C. (1966). Scales for the measurement of ethos. *Speech Monographs, 33,* 65–72.

McCroskey, J. C. (1967). *Studies of the effects of evidence in persuasive communication.* East Lansing, MI: Michigan State University, Speech Communication Research Laboratory, SCRL 4-67.V10.

McCroskey, J. C. (1972). *An introduction to rhetorical communication* (2nd ed.). Englewood Cliffs, NJ: Prentice-Hall.

McCroskey, J. C. (1977). Oral communication apprehension: A summary of recent theory and research. *Human Communication Research, 4,* 78–96.

McCroskey, J. C. (1978). Validity of the PRCA as an index of oral communication apprehension. *Communication Monographs, 45,* 192–203.

McCroskey, J. C. (1982). *An introduction to rhetorical communication* (4th ed.). Englewood Cliffs, NJ: Prentice-Hall.

McCroskey, J. C. (1992). Reliability and validity of the willingness to communicate scale. *Communication Quarterly, 40,* 16–25.

McCroskey, J. C., & Young, T. J. (1981). Ethos and credibility: The construct and its measurement after three decades. *Central States Speech Journal, 32,* 24–34.

McDonald, D. (1980). *The language of argument* (3rd ed.). New York: Harper & Row.

McGervey, J. D. (1981). A statistical test of sun-sign astrology. In K. Frazier (Ed.), *Paranormal borderlands of science* (pp. 235–240). Buffalo, NY: Prometheus Books.

McGuire, M. (1977). Mythic rhetoric in Mein Kampf: A structuralist critique. *Quarterly Journal of Speech, 63,* 1–13.

McNeill, P. (1990). *Research methods* (2nd ed.). London, UK: Routledge.

McQuail, D. (1984). With the benefit of hindsight: Reflections on uses and gratifications research. *Critical Studies in Mass Communication, 1,* 177–193.

McQuail, D., Blumler, J., & Brown, R. (1972). The television audience: A revised perspective. In D. McQuail, (Ed.), *Sociology of mass communications.* Harmondsworth: Penguin.

Mechling, E. W. (1979). Patricia Hearst: MYTH AMERICA 1974, 1975, 1976. *Western Journal of Speech Communication, 43,* 168–179.

Meehl, P. E., & Hathaway, S. R. (1946). The K factor as a suppressor variable in the Minnesota Multiphasic Personality Inventory. *Journal of Applied Psychology, 30,* 525–564.

Milavsky, J. R., Kessler, R. C., Stipp, H. H., & Rubens, W. S. (1982). *Television and aggression: A panel study.* New York: Academic Press.

Miller, G. R., & Berger, C. R. (1978). On keeping the faith in matters scientific. *Western Journal of Speech Communication, 42,* 44–57.

Millham, J., & Jacobson, L. I. (1978). The need for approval. In H. London & J. E. Exner (Eds.), *Dimensions of personality* (pp. 365–390). New York: Wiley.

A million random digits with 100,000 normal deviates. (1955). New York: Free Press.

Mohrmann, G. P., & Leff, M. C. (1974). Lincoln at Cooper Union: A rationale for neo-classical criticism. *Quarterly Journal of Speech, 60,* 459–467.

Monge, P. R. (1987). The network level of analysis. In C. R. Berger & S. H. Chaffee (Eds.), *Handbook of communication science* (pp. 239–270). Newbury Park, CA: Sage.

Monge, P. R., & Miller, G. R. (1985). Communication networks. In A. Kuper & J. Kuper (Eds.), *The social science encyclopedia* (pp. 130–131). London, UK: Routledge & Kegan Paul.

Mongeau, P. (1993, February). *The brainstorming myth.* Paper presented at the Western States Communication Association Convention, Albuquerque, NM.

Morris, W., & Morris, M. (Eds.). (1985). *Harper dictionary of contemporary usage* (2nd ed.). New York: Harper & Row.

Mortensen, C. D. (1972). *Communication.* New York: McGraw-Hill.

Myers, M. T., & Myers, G. E. (1982). *Managing communication: An organizational approach.* New York: McGraw-Hill.

Nachmias, D., & Nachmias, C. (1987). *Research methods in the social sciences* (3rd ed.). New York: St. Martin's Press.

Naisbitt, J., & Aburdene, P. (1982). *Megatrends.* New York: William Morrow.

Nisbett, R. E., & Wilson, T. D. (1977a). The halo effect: Evidence for unconscious alteration of judgments. *Journal of Personality and Social Psychology, 35,* 250–256.

Nisbett, R. E., & Wilson, T. D. (1977b). Telling more than we can know. Verbal reports on mental processes. *Psychological Review, 84,* 231–259.

Nunnally, J. (1978). *Psychometric theory* (2nd ed.). New York: McGraw-Hill.

Orne, M. T. (1970). Hypnosis, motivation, and the ecological validity of the psychological experiment. *Nebraska Symposium on Motivation, 18,* 187–265.

Osgood, C. E., Suci, G. J., & Tannenbaum, P. H. (1957). *The measurement of meaning.* Urbana: University of Illinois Press.

Ott, L., & Hildebrand, D. K. (1983). *Statistical thinking for managers.* Boston: PWS Publishers.

Paradis, A. A. (1966). *The research handbook: A guide to reference sources.* New York: Funk & Wagnalls.

Parrella, G. C. (1971). Projection and adoption: Toward a clarification of the concept of empathy. *Quarterly Journal of Speech, 57,* 204–213.

Pavitt, C. (1990). The ideal communicator as the basis for competence judgments of self and friend. *Communication Reports, 3,* 9–14.

Pearson, K. (1924). Historical note on the origin of the normal curve of errors. *Biometrika, 16,* 402–404.

Peirce, C. (1955). *Philosophical writings of Peirce,* J. Buchler (Ed.). New York: Dover.

Pfau, M., & Burgoon, M. (1988). Inoculation in political campaign communication. *Human Communication Research, 15,* 91–111.

Pomerantz, A. (1990). Conversation analytic claims. *Communication Monographs 57,* 231–235.

Popper, K. R. (1968a). *Conjectures and refutations: The growth of scientific knowledge* (2nd ed.). New York: Harper Torchbooks.

Popper, K. R. (1968b). *The logic of scientific discovery* (2nd ed.). New York: Harper Torchbooks.

Popper, K. R. (1972). *Objective knowledge.* Oxford, U.K.: Oxford University Press.

Publication manual of the American Psychological Association (3rd ed.). (1983). Washington, DC: American Psychological Association.

Quine, W. (1946). Truth by convention. In O. H. Lee (Ed.), *Philosophical essays for Alfred North Whitehead.* New York: Longmans Green.

Randi, J. (1981). New evidence in the Uri Geller matter. In K. Frazier (Ed.), *Paranormal borderlands of science* (pp. 122–127). Buffalo, NY: Prometheus Books.

Ransford, H. E. (1968). Isolation, powerlessness, and violence: A study of attitudes and participants in the Watts riots. *American Journal of Sociology, 73,* 581–591.

Ray, J., & Zavos, H. (1966). Reasoning and argument: Some special problems and types. In G. R. Miller & T. R. Nilson (Eds.), *Perspectives on argumentation.* Chicago: Scott, Foresman.

Ray, W. J., & Ravizza, R. R. (1988). *Methods: Toward a science of behavior and experience* (3rd ed.). Belmont, CA: Wadsworth.

Reinard, J. C. (1991). *Foundations of argument: Effective communication for critical thinking.* Dubuque, IA: Brown & Benchmark.

Reinard, J. C., & Boster, F. J. (1978, May). *Information processing under stress: Developments on a theory of stress coping to communication.* Paper presented at the Speech Communication Association Convention, Minneapolis, MN.

Rescourla, L. (1989). The language development survey: A scoring tool for delayed language in toddlers. *Journal of Speech and Hearing Disorders, 54,* 587–599.

Reynolds, P. D. (1971). *A primer in theory construction.* Indianapolis: Bobbs-Merrill.

Reynolds, R. A., & Burgoon, M. (1983). Belief processing, reasoning, and evidence. In R. Bostrom (Ed.), *Communication yearbook 7* (pp. 83–104). Beverly Hills, CA: Sage.

Richardson, L. S. (1970). Stokely Carmichael: Jazz artist. *Western Speech, 34,* 212–218.

Robinson, J. P., Shaver, P. R., & Wrightsman, L. S. (Eds.). (1991). *Measures of personality and social psychological attitudes* (Vol. 1). San Diego: Academic Press.

Rogers, L. E., & Farace, R. V. (1975). Analysis of relational communication in dyads: New measurement procedures. *Human Communication Research, 1,* 222–239.

Rosenfeld, L. B., & Bowen, G. L. (1991). Marital disclosure and marital satisfaction: Direct-effect versus interaction-effect models. *Western Journal of Speech Communication, 55,* 69–84.

Rosenthal, R., & Rosnow, R. L. (1969). The volunteer subject. In R. Rosenthal & R. L. Rosnow (Eds.), *Artifact in behavioral research* (pp. 59–118). New York: McGraw-Hill.

Rowland, R. C. (1987). Narrative: Mode of discourse or paradigm? *Communication Monographs, 54,* 264–275.

Rubin, R. B., Rubin, A. M., & Piele, L. J. (1990). *Communication research: Strategies and sources* (2nd ed.). Belmont, CA: Wadsworth.

Rubin, Z. & Shenker, S. S. (1978). Friendship, proximity, and self-disclosure. *Journal of Personality, 46,* 1–22.

Rushing, J. H. (1986). Mythic evolution of "the new frontier" in mass mediated rhetoric. *Critical Studies in Mass Communication, 3,* 265–296.

Sanbonmatsu, A. (1971). Darrow and Rorke's use of Burkeian identification strategies in *New York vs. Gitlow* (1920). *Speech Monographs, 37,* 36–48.

Sapolsky, B. S., & Tabarlet, J. (1991). Sex in primetime television: 1979 versus 1989. *Journal of Broadcasting and Electronic Media, 35,* 505–516.

Scheidel, T. M., & Crowell, L. (1964). Idea development in small group communication. *Quarterly Journal of Speech, 50,* 140–145.

Scott, W. (1955). Reliability of content analysis: The case of nominal scale coding. *Public Opinion Quarterly, 17,* 321–325.

Sick, G. G. (1991). *October surprise: American's hostages in Iran and the election of Ronald Reagan.* New York: Random House.

Siler, T. (1975, April 18). Best of the best. *Knoxville News-Sentinel,* p. 18.

Smith, H. W. (1991). *Strategies of social research* (3rd ed.). Orlando, FL: Holt, Rinehart & Winston.

Smith, M. J. (1988). *Contemporary communication research methods.* Belmont, CA: Wadsworth.

Snow, M. (1985). Martin Luther King's "letter from Birmingham jail" as Pauline epistle. *Quarterly Journal of Speech, 71,* 318–334.

Spitzberg, B. H. (1988). Communication competence: Measures of perceived effectiveness. In C. H. Tardy (Ed.), *A handbook for the study of human communication* (pp. 67–106). Norwood, NJ: Ablex.

Stanovich, K. E. (1986). *How to think straight about psychology.* Glenview, IL: Scott, Foresman.

Stevens, J. (1986). *Applied multivariate statistics for the social sciences.* Hillsdale, NJ: Lawrence Erlbaum Associates.

Stevens, S. S. (1951). Scales of measurement. In S. S. Stevens (Ed.), *Handbook of experimental psychology* (pp. 23–30). New York: Wiley.

Stewart, C. J., & Cash, W. B. (1988). *Interviewing: Principles and practices* (5th ed.). Dubuque, IA: Brown & Benchmark.

Stinchcombe, A. L. (1968). *Constructing social theories.* New York: Harcourt, Brace & World.

Strickland, B. R. (1977). Approval motivation. In T. Blass (Ed.), *Personality variables in social behavior* (pp. 315–356). Hillsdale, NJ: Erlbaum.

Strunk, W., Jr., & White, E. B. (1979). *The elements of style* (3rd ed.). New York: Macmillan.

Stubbs, M. (1981). Motivating analyses of exchange structure. In M. Coulthard & M. Montgomery (Eds.), *Studies in discourse analysis.* London, U.K.: Routledge and Kegan Paul.

Student. (1908). On the probable error of the mean. *Biometrika, 6,* 1–25.

Swenson, W. M., Pearson, J. S., & Osbourne, D. (1973). *An MMPI sourcebook: Basic item, scale, and pattern data on 50,000 medical patients.* Minneapolis: University of Minnesota Press.

Sykes, A. J. M. (1970). Myth in communication. *Journal of Communication, 20,* 17–31.

Tanaka-Matsumi, J., & Kameoka, V. A. (1986). Reliabilities and concurrent validities of popular self-report measures of depression, anxiety, and social desirability. *Journal of Consulting and Clinical Psychology, 54,* 328–333.

Tardy, Charles H. (Ed.). (1988a). *A handbook for the study of human communication: Methods and instruments for observing, measuring and assessing communication processes.* Norwood, NJ: Ablex.

Tardy, Charles H. (1988b). Interpersonal interaction coding systems. In C. H. Tardy (Ed.), *A handbook for the study of human communication: Methods and instruments for observing, measuring and assessing communication processes.* Norwood, NJ: Ablex.

Tatsuoka, M. (1969). *Validation studies: The use of multiple regression equations.* Champaign, IL: Institute for Personality and Ability Testing.

Thergerge, L. J. (Ed.). (1981). *Crooks, conmen and clowns: Businessmen in TV entertainment.* Washington, DC: The Media Institute.

Thomas, S., & LeShay, S. V. (1992). Bad business? A reexamination of television's portrayal of businesspersons. *Journal of Communication, 42,* 95–105.

Troester, R., & Meister, C. S. (1990). Peace communication: A survey of current attitudes, curricular practice, and research priorities. *Western Journal of Speech Communication, 54,* 420–428.

Trujillo, N., & Dionisopoulos, G. (1987). Cop talk, police stories, and the social construction of organizational drama. *Central States Speech Journal 38,* 196–209.

Tucker, R. K., Weaver, R. L., II, & Berryman-Fink, C. (1981). *Research in speech communication.* Englewood Cliffs, NJ: Prentice-Hall.

Tuckman, B. W. (1978). *Conducting educational research* (2nd ed.). New York: Harcourt Brace Jovanovich.

Vancil, D. L., & Pendell, S. D. (1987). The myth of viewer-listener disagreement in the first Kennedy-Nixon debate. *Central States Speech Journal, 38,* 16–27.

Vanlear, C. A., Jr., & Zeitlow, P. H. (1990). Toward a contingency approach to marital interaction: An empirical integration of three approaches. *Communication Monographs, 57,* 202–218.

Varenne, H. (1988). Jocks and freaks: The symbolic structure of the expression of social interaction among American senior high school students. In G. Spindler (Ed.), *Doing the ethnography of schooling.* Prospect Heights, IL: Waveland Press.

Veloso, K., Hall, J. W., III, & Grose, J. H. (1990). Frequency selectivity and comodulation masking release in adults and in 6-year-old children. *Journal of Speech and Hearing Research, 33,* 96–102.

Wagner, S. F. (1992). *Introduction to statistics.* New York: HarperCollins.

Wallas, G. (1926). *The art of thought.* New York: Harcourt Brace Jovanovich.

Wax, R. H. (1968). *Participant observation. International encyclopedia of social sciences* (p. 238). New York: Macmillan.

Webb, E., Campbell, D. T., Schwartz, R. D., Sechrest, L., & Grove, J. B. (1981). *Nonreactive measures in the social sciences* (2nd ed.). Boston: Houghton Mifflin.

Weick, K. E. (1969). *The social psychology of organizing.* Reading, MA: Addison-Wesley.

Weinberg, M. S. (1965). Sexual modesty, social meanings, and the nudist camp. *Social Problems, 12,* 311–318.

Whately, R. A. (1844). *Elements of logic.* London, U.K.: B. Fellows.

Wheeler, M. (1977). *Lies, damn lies, and statistics: The manipulation of public opinion in America.* New York: Laurel Edition, Dell.

White, P. (1980). Limitations on verbal reports of internal events: A refutation of Nisbett and Wilson and of Bem. *Psychological Review, 87,* 105–112.

Whitney, F. L. (1950). *The elements of research* (3rd ed.). New York: Prentice-Hall.

Wiemann, J. M. (1977). Explication and test of a model of communicative competence. *Human Communication Research, 3,* 195–213.

Willard, C. A. (1981). The status of the non-discursiveness thesis. *Journal of the American Forensic Association, 17,* 190–214.

Williams, F. (1991). *Reasoning with statistics: How to read quantitative research* (4th ed.). Fort Worth, TX: Harcourt Brace Jovanovich.

Wilson, T. D., & Nisbett, R. E. (1978). The accuracy of verbal reports about the effects of stimuli on evaluation and behavior. *Social Psychology, 41,* 118–131.

Wimmer, R. D., & Dominick, J. R. (1983). *Mass media research: An introduction.* Belmont, CA: Wadsworth.

Woal, M. (1987). Listening to monotony: All-news radio. *Central States Speech Journal, 38,* 28–34.

Yamane, T. (1967). *Elementary sampling theory.* Englewood Cliffs, NJ: Prentice-Hall.

NAME INDEX

Achtert, W. S., 49
Aczel, A. D., 257, 268, 298
Adair, J. G., 184
Agar, M. H., 160
Alcock, J. E., 104
Allen, M. J., 200
Alpha Epsilon Rho, 18
American Assoiciation for Public
        Opinion Research, 13
American Forensic Association, 18
American Newspaper Publishers
        Association, 18
American Psychological
        Association, 12
American Speech-Language-Hearing
        Association, 16–17
Amidon, E. J., 148
Anastasi, A., 268
Anderson, J., 106
Anthony, S. B., 74
Aquinas, St. T., 295
Aristotle, 14, 109, 120, 135, 295
Association for Education in
        Journalism and
        Mass
        Communication, 17
Association of Communication
        Administrators, 18
Aburdene, P., 141
Auer, J. J., 26, 123, 128, 168, 169
Austin, B. A., 23, 126

Babbie, E. R., 173, 175, 178
Bachrach, A. J., 112, 119, 122, 124,
        131
Baker, B. O., 233
Bales, R. F., 145–46, 149

Barker, L. L., 3, 170
Barlow, D. H., 201
Barnett, G. A., 168
Bastedo, R. W., 93
Beasley, D., 53
Berg, B. L., 152, 161, 162, 163, 166
Berger, C. R., 101, 118
Berlo, David K., 3
Berryman-Fink, C., 111
Berscheid, E., 117
Best, J. W., 53
Blum, E., 54
Blumler, J., 118
Bogardus, E. S., 243, 244
Bokeno, R. M., 91
Boneau, C. A., 286
Booth, W. C., 42
Borg, W. R., 88–89
Bormann, E. H., 137
Bostdorff, D. M., 102
Boster, F. J., 242, 247
Bowers, K. S., 184
Bramble, W. J., 37, 111
Broadcast Education Association, 17
Brown, L. M., 142
Brown, R., 118
Bryan, P., 227
Budd, R. W., 142
Burgoon, M., 169, 208
Burke, K., 136–39
Burkholder, T. R., 139
Burleson, B. R., 101
Byrne, D., 166, 241

Calabrese, R. J., 118
Campbell, D. T., 156, 157, 198, 206
Cappella, J. N., 148

Cash, W. B., 181
Cegala, D. J., 145
Chaffee, S., 105
Champion, D. J., 298
Chase, S., 111
Christenson, P., 195
Chung, K. L., 277
Cicero, 135
Cohen, J., 236
Cohen, S. P., 145
Commission on American
        Parliamentary
        Practice, 18
Copi, I. M., 106
Corax, 14
Cozby, P., 124, 232
Craig, H., 136
Cragan, J. F., 137
Crawford, J. E., 6–7
Croesus, 104
Cronbach, L. J., 236, 238, 249
Cross Examination Debate
        Association, 18
Crowell, L., 149
Crowne, D. P., 178
Cutshall, C. R., 156

Dahlstrom, L. E., 178
Dahlstrom, W. G., 178
deLaplace, M. 260
Delia, J. G., 101
Delta Sigma Rho-Tau Kappa Alpha, 18
Demosthenes, 15
Denzin, N. K., 164
Deutsch, M., 115, 116
Dewey, M., 53
Dewey, J., 131

SUBJECT INDEX